The Left Opposition in the U.S. 1928-31

James P. Cannon

WRITINGS AND SPEECHES, 1928–31

The Left Opposition in the U.S. 1928–31

PATHFINDER
New York London Montreal Sydney

Edited by Fred Stanton

ISBN 978-0-87348-916-4
Library of Congress Catalog Card Number 81-83236
Manufactured in the United States of America

First edition, 1981
Fifth printing, 2026

PATHFINDER
pathfinderpress.com
Email: pathfinder@pathfinderpress.com

Contents

About the author

James Patrick Cannon was born in Rosedale, Kansas, on February 11, 1890, into a working class Irish family. Won to socialist ideas by his father, he joined the Socialist Party in 1908 and the Industrial Workers of the World in 1911 when he was twenty-one. In the IWW Cannon worked with Vincent St. John, "Big Bill" Haywood, and Frank Little as a strike organizer and journalist. As a leader of the Socialist Party left wing after the Russian revolution, he joined the Communist Party in September 1919 and was elected to its Central Committee in 1920. One of the key leaders of the CP in its first decade, he served on the Presidium of the Communist International in Moscow (1922–23) and headed the International Labor Defense (1925–28). Won over to Trotsky's Left Opposition at the Sixth World Congress of the Comintern in Moscow in 1928, he was expelled from the CP later that year for Trotskyism. With Max Shachtman and Martin Abern he was a founding leader of the Communist League of America, the first American Trotskyist organization, and served as editor of its newspaper, *The Militant.*

Cannon was a founder of the Socialist Workers Party in January 1938 and a participant in the founding conference of the Fourth International held in France later that year, where he was elected to the International Executive Committee. Convicted with seventeen other leaders of the SWP and of the Minneapolis Teamsters union in 1941 for opposing the war policy of the American government, Cannon served thirteen months of a sixteen-month sentence at Sandstone penitentiary in 1944–45. Cannon was

the national secretary of the SWP until 1953. Thereafter he was the party's national chairman, and later national chairman emeritus until his death on August 21, 1974.

James P. Cannon's more than sixty years of active struggle in the cause of socialism are recorded in his many books. Published in his lifetime were *Socialism on Trial* (1942), *The Struggle for a Proletarian Party* (1943), *The History of American Trotskyism* (1944), *America's Road to Socialism* (1953), *Notebook of an Agitator* (1958), *The First Ten Years of American Communism* (1962), *Letters from Prison* (1968), *Speeches for Socialism* (1971), and *Speeches to the Party* (1973). This volume is one of a posthumous series of his writings and speeches.

Introduction

At the end of the economic boom of the 1920s, just before the Great Depression of the 1930s, there was a political crisis in the Communist Party of such depth that it threatened the continuity of American Marxism. A cynical, right-wing bureaucracy had consolidated its hold over the party and was standing in the way of implementing a Leninist policy. The thousands of revolutionary workers in the party—who had come to it inspired by the example of the Russian workers and the Bolshevik leaders—had no say in the direction of the CP.

The writings and speeches in this volume were part of a five-year struggle to reform that party and rebuild the revolutionary leadership in the United States.

To understand the degeneration of the Communist Party and the issues in the fight to reform it, it is necessary to know what happened to the world Communist movement and the American working class in the preceding decade.

The political degeneration of the Communist movement was the result of powerful pressures exerted by world imperialism upon the first workers' state and the parties of the Communist International. The Russian revolution came under direct military attack from 1918 to 1920 by tsarist White armies and invading troops from Germany, France, Britain, Japan, the United States, and other capitalist powers. The Russian people suffered famine, destruction of industry, and the loss of many of their best revolutionary fighters in this civil war. Afterward, they were forced to rebuild the economy from an extremely primitive level, with no aid from abroad and in the face of an economic blockade.

The civil war weakened the Russian working class. Many left the cities to fight in the Red Army or to return to the land, where more food was available. A layer became demoralized by so many years of hardship and became politically passive.

The Soviet leadership faced enormous political and economic difficulties in the early 1920s. How could production be increased in the factories and in agriculture? How could the revolution maintain the support of the peasantry and feed the workers in the cities? Without the ability to get modern machinery and tractors that could increase productivity and make it possible to build up large-scale enterprises and collectivized agriculture, they were forced to make concessions to the better-off peasants (kulaks) and the capitalists. They allowed peasants to sell produce on the open market within Russia, and encouraged investment in small industry and the leasing of nationalized factories. The New Economic Policy (NEP) was to be a temporary retreat that would help the revolution hang on until the workers of the West could make their own revolutions and come to the aid of the Soviets.

Under these conditions, aided by the pressure of world capitalism, the weight of the peasantry (the majority of the country), and the openings for petty trading under the NEP, the layer of petty-bourgeois bureaucrats in Soviet society began to grow. There had been a bureaucracy from the foundation of the workers' state. Many of the officials in charge of administering the government and the economy had carried out similar functions or been managers under the old regime. The low level of literacy in the country made it necessary to utilize these bureaucrats, despite their political backwardness; few workers were prepared to carry out those tasks. The bureaucrats were given some limited benefits for doing this work as an incentive to stay on the revolutionary side, and they worked under the political direction of the Bolsheviks.

With the end of the civil war, thousands of these officials, many of them former counterrevolutionaries, began to apply to join the Communist Party, not as a matter of political conviction but as a way of advancing their careers. They were now in a position to skim more benefits for themselves and their families as they presided over the distribution of scarce goods. A layer of Old Bolsheviks in the government and party apparatuses began to adapt their political views to their new conditions of life.

A right wing began to view the NEP as a permanent policy of the government, a path to socialism instead of a holding action. They put forward such slogans as "Kulak, enrich yourself!" and "Build socialism at a snail's pace."

The Left Opposition, formed in 1923 and led by Leon Trotsky, sought to continue the Bolshevik policy based on revolutionary internationalism. They called for a planned industrialization and the gradual, voluntary collectivization of agriculture. They also sought to restore democracy within the party and assure the control of the rank-and-file workers over the party apparatus. Lenin had begun a fight against the bureaucracy before his final illness, and the Left Opposition carried on his struggle.

Joseph Stalin, the general secretary of the party, presided over and epitomized the bureaucratization of the CP. He opened the doors to the petty-bourgeois place-seekers, led a campaign against Trotsky and the proposals of the Left Opposition, and after Lenin's death introduced the first major revision of Marxism into the party's policies: the theory of "socialism in one country." He made an alliance with the right wing against the Left Opposition but did not adopt their perspective. He proceeded pragmatically, zigzagging from right to left with the aim of preserving the privileges and power of the officeholders. Trotsky considered this bureaucratic layer a "centrist" tendency.

The outcome of the struggle in the Russian party was decided in the last analysis on the international arena, by the defeat of revolutions in Western Europe due to the betrayals of the Socialist parties and the inexperience of the young Communist parties. By 1923, with the defeat of the German revolution, the Russian workers could see no prospect of help from abroad in the near future. The backwardness of Russia and the isolation of the revolution weighed heavily upon them. World capitalism was restabilized and the workers' state would have to find a way to survive until the next international upsurge.

This situation favored the tendencies toward conservatism and nationalism within the Soviet Union. The bureaucracy was able to repress the Left Opposition within the party, and the left wing was unable to mobilize the workers to resist the further bureaucratization of the CP and the alteration of its program.

With the replacement of revolutionary internationalism with the schema of "socialism in one country," the role of the Comintern changed fundamentally. In its early days, under the leadership of Lenin and Trotsky, the Comintern had a collaborative relationship with its national sections. Although the Bolsheviks had earned tremendous respect as leaders of the first victorious workers' revolution, they never gave orders to the new CP leaders in other countries. They chose to teach them by political argument rather than wielding centralized authority to decide policies for the national sections. Their aim was to build strong parties with members educated through democratic discussion, and leaders with authority of their own, based on the class struggles in each country. The Bolsheviks relied on the same process that had built their own party and won the confidence of the Russian working people.

But the Stalinists operated differently. They manipulated the national sections, changing their policies and leaderships according to the shifting needs of the Russian bureaucracy in its attempts to maintain the status quo with imperialism. Their kind of Comintern preferred appointed leaderships in the national sections, and docile, even demoralized, memberships who would go along with whatever policies were handed down—even if it meant betrayal of the workers' struggles. World socialism was seen as something to be achieved only in the distant future, after the USSR became the most advanced society on earth and the capitalists just gave up. In the meantime, the role of the CPs outside Russia was to use their influence with the workers to build pressure on the capitalists to have more friendly relations with the USSR.

The Stalinized Comintern also forced CPs to subordinate themselves to such forces as Chiang Kai-shek's Kuomintang (Nationalist Party) in China and the right-wing union leaders of the British Trades Union Congress. These counterrevolutionary leaders were able to use Soviet support and CP cooperation as left cover in their betrayals of the Chinese revolution of 1925–27 and the British general strike of 1926. But the Soviet Union clung to these "progressive" leaders because they gave lip-service to diplomatic recognition of the USSR.

The change from proletarian internationalism to class collaboration did not proceed in an honest, straightforward way, but under the cover of revolutionary rhetoric and with several zigzags to the left. The predominant course of Soviet diplomacy shifted in the mid-1920s when the USSR began to participate in the bourgeois charade of disarmament proposals which disarmed nobody and were part of the buildup for the next world war. But when the capitalists were unresponsive to a diplomatic approach, Stalin put on more pressure by turning to the left.

The first left swing of the Comintern, launched in the Russian CP in 1928, was called the "third period" because of its place in the historical schema then in vogue among Stalinist theoreticians. They divided Soviet history into three periods: the first (1917–23), from the seizure of power to the end of the postwar revolutionary wave; the second (1924–27), the interlude of world capitalist stabilization and working-class quiescence; and the third, a new upsurge of revolutions and the final victory of socialism.

The proclamation of the "third period" anticipated the coming world economic crisis but was not based on any workers' upsurge. In fact it was a bureaucratic reaction to the threat of an imminent counterrevolution in the Soviet Union and a coverup for the disastrous defeat of the Communist-led workers and peasants in China.

The kulaks began to withhold grain from the Soviet government in early 1928. After years of amassing wealth but being unable to use it as they desired because of the limited availability of consumer goods and the restrictions on foreign trade and investment imposed by the workers' state, the better-off peasants used the threat of starvation as a weapon to wring more concessions for themselves. Faced with the threat of famine, the bureaucracy turned from its former right-wing policy to an ultraleft one: at first, they requisitioned the grain, and by 1929 they began to forcibly collectivize Soviet agriculture. They also announced a five-year industrialization plan that was supposed to result in "socialism."

In China, the Comintern called for the formation of "soviets" and the immediate seizure of power, a policy that had already led to the massacre of the workers of

Canton in December 1927.

In 1929 the Comintern officially adopted the "third period" line and CPers were mobilized against Nikolai Bukharin and the right wing, who became scapegoats for the policies the Stalinists had previously supported.

The fight against the kulaks was not carried out by convincing the poor peasants to join with the workers to collectivize the land. It was a military operation imposed upon rural Russia with such bloodiness and mismanagement that Soviet agriculture has not yet recovered. The Five Year Plan was no model of workers' democracy either. It resulted in speedup, waste, more privileges for the bureaucrats, and continued shortages for the Russian workers. This was the time when Stalin was elevated to the status of a demigod, the "master."

Internationally, despite its rhetoric, the "third period" was not a move to mobilize the masses in a fight for socialism. Objectively it weakened the left wing of the labor movement by splitting away the Communist workers to form "red" unions. The old unions, led by the Socialists or more right-wing types like William Green of the American Federation of Labor, were called "company unions," and their leaders "social fascists." The Leninist policy of calling for unity in action with these forces—the tactic of the united front, designed to mobilize the workers and break down the reformists' domination of the labor movement—was dropped. Instead the Communists called on the workers to leave their old unions and leaders and join the new CP-led unions—the policy of the "united front from below," which was no united front at all. The workers in the old unions were not attracted by the ultraleft antics and radical rhetoric; they were in those unions for good, practical reasons (many worked in union shops, and leaving the AFL union meant losing their jobs; in countries with mass Socialist parties, workers had traditional ties to the SP and its unions, and needed to see the CP in action, not just words, to be won over to it). Instead of participating in united actions with their class, Communist workers were isolated by this policy.

The worst effect of the "third period" was the failure of the German CP to campaign for a united front with the SP against the Nazis. Both parties were supported by millions of workers—together they represented the majority. Both had armed defense groups. But by its sectarianism the CP cut off the possibility of building an effective opposition to the rise of Hitler.

Superficially the "third period" policies looked like the ultraleftism of the young Communist parties. In 1919–20 many Communists thought that revolution was on the order of the day and that united action with reformist forces was "unprincipled." The ultralefts of the infancy of Communism were just learning their political ABCs. Lenin taught them in those days the lesson of the united-front policy, and most were able to overcome their ultraleft misconceptions. They were young revolutionaries with good intentions and incomplete knowledge, making a blunder that was corrected through experience and education.

The "third period" was not an infantile error. It was a conscious turn by seasoned bureaucrats. They adopted ultraleft policies that they had argued against for years, with no attempt to show either how the situation had changed or why the previous tactic had been wrong. This was ultraleftism of a senile variety, led by cynical individuals who put their bureaucratic careers ahead of the interests of the workers, including the rank-and-file workers of the CPs themselves.

❖

The Communist Party in the United States faced some big political problems from its foundation in 1919. Forced underground by the postwar witch-hunt and further separated from the U.S.-born workers by its predominantly foreign-born composition, the new party had to find a way to participate in the struggles of its class or face stagnation and decay. A layer of American-born workers and youth led the fight to reorient the CP, with the help of the leaders of the Comintern. One of the central figures in this fight was James P. Cannon.

Cannon had joined the Socialist Party of Eugene Debs in 1908, at the age of eighteen, and became an organizer of the Industrial Workers of the World when he was twenty-one. In the IWW he helped lead strikes of rubber workers in Akron, metal workers in Peoria, ore dock workers on Lake Superior, and others; he was arrested several times for this activity.

It was the Russian revolution that brought him back into activity in the left wing of the Socialist Party in Kansas City, where he became a founder of the Communist Party in 1919. As CP district organizer there in 1919–20 he organized the first underground Communist groups in the coal fields of Kansas and southern Illinois. He was elected to the Central Executive Committee of the party in 1920. In that year he became founding editor of the CP's first legal newspaper, the *Toiler,* which later became the *Worker.* He was the first national chairman of the Workers Party, the legal arm of the CP established in 1921.

Cannon was part of the CP delegation to the Fourth Congress of the Comintern in 1922, where he led the faction that favored legal propaganda work and "Americanization" of the party—an orientation toward the American labor movement with its native-born majority. This minority faction was able to convince Trotsky and other Comintern leaders to favor this course, and they in turn helped the party overcome its isolated, underground, sectarian existence. It began to participate in the unions and to advocate a labor party.

The most effective contribution Cannon made to the mass work of the party was in the field of defense of democratic rights. He initiated and was the first national secretary of the International Labor Defense, a united-front formation that defended all class-war prisoners, regardless of their political affiliations. While CPers were its main leaders, the ILD national executive body had a majority of non-Communist radicals. The ILD had thousands of members (dues were ten cents per month) with full-time organizers in major cities. It concentrated on propaganda and agitation work, helping to organize massive conferences and demonstrations around the Sacco-Vanzetti case. It published an illustrated monthly, the *Labor Defender,* which was the most popular magazine in the radical movement. It also raised money to help the prisoners and their families, and helped out when necessary with their legal defense.

The Comintern's influence on the American party took a turn for the worse after the arrival of John Pepper as Comintern representative in 1922. Instead of relaying information and offering advice, Pepper used the authority of the Russian revolution and his own flair for agitation and intrigue to become a central leader of the party as part of a faction led by Charles Ruthenberg and Jay Lovestone.

Pepper pulled off his first adventure in 1923, when he led the CP in the capture of a labor political convention to form a Federated Farmer-Labor Party that had no substantial support in the unions. The FFLP then gave its support to the Progressive Party candidate for president in 1924, Robert La Follette, until the CP pulled back from this reformist course and ran its own candidates.

Cannon collaborated with William Z. Foster, the CP

trade union secretary, to fight against Pepper's farmer-labor adventure; by 1925 they won a majority of the delegates to the party convention. However, the Comintern intervened and gave the minority led by Pepper and Lovestone the majority on the new CEC, because they were more trusted to hew to the Comintern line.

This kind of bureaucratic intervention contributed to the corruption of many of the CP leaders. Cannon wrote about this in *The First Ten Years of American Communism* (New York: Pathfinder Press, 1973) and commented on it in an unpublished interview with Harry Ring, a staff writer for *The Militant,* in 1974:

"People who commit themselves to the cause of socialism in their youth and then later turn against it, don't do it all in one step. In my observation the corruption has been a process. In most cases. With some, it's a deliberate decision, it's 'There's nothing in this business for me. I'm going to get the hell out of here, and I'll find one excuse or another and make a new life for myself, get a little of the material rewards possible.'

"But when you begin by giving away a little principle here and there for the sake of expediency you start a process that confronts you just a little later with a demand for a little more. This was particularly true in the early Communist Party when the sophisticated people began to realize the power was in Moscow and that you couldn't function in a small national party like ours if you were in conflict with Moscow.

"So people began to adapt themselves a little here and there, a step at a time, until they found themselves so compromised that there was nowhere to turn and they went the whole way. As I say, they didn't do it all at once."

Such bureaucrats as Lovestone and Pepper were a new breed in the world radical movement. The bureaucrats in the mass Socialist parties of Europe and those in the trade unions had a base in their own organizations. But the misleaders of the national sections of the Comintern were based on the approval of the bureaucracy in Moscow. They relied on Russian authority for their support in their own parties. And if that support from Moscow was withdrawn, their national support crumbled.

The new, corrupting role of the Comintern made it impossible for the CP to build a real leadership of its own and correct its own errors; most often the Comintern imposed new errors. But the Comintern's intervention was only part of the story of the degeneration of the CP. The big, objective weight that crushed the revolutionary perspective of most CP leaders was the pressure of American capitalist prosperity. They were unable to resist the bureaucratic sickness because they lost their revolutionary morale in the boom of the 1920s.

The party and the labor movement as a whole declined in membership throughout the decade. First came the blows of the postwar witch-hunt, which drove the CP underground, decimated the IWW, and defeated big labor struggles such as the 1919 steel strike. And then came the "normalcy" of capitalism in the Coolidge era.

American industry prospered in the 1920s through big increases in labor productivity brought about by improved technology and speedup. While the number of factory workers decreased 7 percent from 1919 to 1925, the output per worker increased 40 percent. Some industries boomed. Auto grew to the point where the jobs of over 4 million people were directly or indirectly dependent on it. Other industries declined. The work force in manufacturing remained steady through the decade, while white-collar and service jobs increased from 11.5 million to 16.7 million.

Over a million Blacks migrated from farms in the South

to northern cities between 1915 and 1928. Some had gotten industrial jobs during the war; there were 5,000 at Ford by 1923 cranking out the first alphabet cars, Model Ts, at nonunion wages. The former sharecroppers were part of a more general flow of people from the farms to the cities. The number of working women also rose in the twenties, from 8.3 million to 10.6 million—a quarter of the work force.

This was a period of prosperity for the capitalists but not for most workers. There was high technological and seasonal unemployment. Wages were low except for the most skilled. Over half the workers earned less than $1,300 a year when the cost of maintaining a family of five at a minimum level of decency was over $2,000. Farm workers made less than $50 per month.

The 40-hour week was rare. Unionized workers averaged 45 hours per week; most in the textile and garment industries worked 48 or 54 hours, with some working as many as 60.

The labor movement declined drastically as the ossified, craft-oriented AFL leadership was unable to find a strategy to counteract the legal and illegal union-busting attacks, a barrage of antiunion propaganda, runaway plants, and high unemployment, in a period of relatively stable cost of living. From its peak of 4–5 million members in 1920 (over 19 percent of the work force), the AFL dropped to 3.6 million by 1923, and by 1930 only 10 percent of the nonagricultural workers were unionized.

Hardest hit were the industrial-type unions in mining, textile, and garment. The International Ladies Garment Workers Union went from 105,400 to 32,300 in the decade. The Mine, Mill and Smelter Workers, successor to the powerful and militant Western Federation of Miners of Bill Haywood and Vincent St. John, went from 21,100 to 4,000. The United Mine Workers, the most powerful union in the country in 1920 with almost 400,000 members, had only 150,000 by 1929.

Unemployed workers in the roaring twenties had to beg for charity. Where state relief programs existed, they treated the poor as if they were responsible for their own poverty, and punished them accordingly; in some cities workers on relief lost their right to vote. There were no state relief programs until 1929. Unemployment insurance did not exist. The reserve army of unemployed was used to threaten those with jobs and keep wages low. There was no effective minimum wage law. Older workers were especially vulnerable; pensions were extremely rare—only 1,221 workers were retired on pensions in the whole country in 1928.

These conditions made going on strike a risky proposition. More strikes lost than won their demands. During the 1919–22 labor upsurge millions had become involved in large numbers of strikes—over three thousand per year. But the frequency of and participation in strikes fell off to only a third of that level later in the decade.

Some of the political errors of the CP in the 1920s can be traced to this lull, as inexperienced and impatient leaders tried to find ways to relate to the workers politically and were tempted into Pepperite adventures. Eventually a layer became demoralized and began to adapt to the situation politically.

Jay Lovestone developed the theory of "American exceptionalism" in 1927, projecting the capitalist prosperity and labor quiescence into the indefinite future. He thought the U.S. economy was so strong that it was immune to the coming world economic crisis and to socialist revolution for the foreseeable future.

James P. Cannon and others fought against this right-wing

theory but were unable to oust Lovestone, who still had the support of the Comintern, now headed by Bukharin of the right wing of the Russian party. The CP was bogged down in permanent factional warfare that poisoned its internal life and prevented its growth. It was impossible for even the best of the leaders of the national sections of the Comintern to understand what was going on, as the Comintern muddied the political waters and kept the factions swirling in them.

The Comintern's biggest contribution to the political confusion was its suppression of the ideas of the Russian Left Opposition, which were the key to understanding the situation and finding a way to end it. Not only were Communists around the world kept ignorant of these ideas, but from 1924 on they were enlisted in a campaign against "Trotskyism" that reached into every local unit of every Communist Party, where condemnatory motions were passed unanimously and anyone who raised questions was expelled.

❖

James P. Cannon became the first central leader of the American CP to join the Left Opposition when he was able to read Trotsky's criticism of the draft program of the Comintern at the Sixth World Congress, which he attended as a delegate in 1928. He saw that this document provided the overview he needed in order to understand the problems he had been grappling with in the U.S.

However, launching a fight for the new program in the American CP would mean the biggest political and personal upheaval of his life. Cannon described his dilemma in the 1974 interview mentioned above:

"I was settled down. I had an insured place in the party as the head of a faction, I had an office and a staff and a swivel chair. And I knew that it was going to cost me my head and also my swivel chair. That made a lot of people hesitate and back away. At first it was a lone decision. I'd made up my mind before I told anybody what I was going to do because I knew it wasn't safe to talk to people about such things as that. It might be reported, you might be crucified for just talking about it. That was the atmosphere in the party. You had to proceed cautiously. I talked to Rose [Karsner] first about it and had her read the document, and I think that it played a big role in my decision. [Her reaction was,] It's right. It serves the interest of the movement. Go ahead and do it and don't maneuver. Don't go half way. Lay your cards on the table. That was her position. Before I even talked to Shachtman or Abern.

"And the fact that I had made up my mind to do it at any cost, for the time being, helped me to convince others. I didn't present it to them as a subject, let's discuss it. I always told them, this is what I am going to do. You see, people's whole lives were in the party—their work, their personal associations, their social life, everything was in the party. And it was no small penalty to pay, severance from all that. That's what it meant. Cut off everywhere! People afraid to speak to me on the street, they could be seen. They wouldn't even go near us for fear they would be suspected of collaboration of some kind."

Thanks to his past work as a leader of mass defense campaigns and of opposition to the Lovestone group, Cannon had a group of supporters and was able to win a layer of them to the platform of the Left Opposition before his expulsion in October 1928, when this collection of his writings and speeches begins.

The Left Opposition in the U.S. took the name Communist League of America (Opposition) and operated as an expelled faction of the party.

The CLA saw the CP as the revolutionary party in this country, and the Comintern as the revolutionary International, despite their bureaucratic leaderships. The league was oriented toward the revolutionary workers in the party, the only large group of organized revolutionaries there was. To abandon them to the bureaucrats, to turn away from the CP before exhausting all possibilities of reforming it, would have been a light-minded and sectarian act. The CLA set out to become the vanguard of the vanguard workers in the CP.

The expelled CPers immediately launched a newspaper. Cannon proposed calling it *The Militant* after the term used in the old IWW for a "real active fighter in the movement." Cannon was listed as editor of the paper, since he was the best known of the CLA leaders. Max Shachtman was the actual managing editor; he had formerly edited the *Labor Defender.*

The Militant was the main tool of the CLA in its work among CPers. It reprinted Trotsky's criticism of the Comintern program and other documents, polemicized against the errors of the CP leadership, and set forth the CLA's views on the class-struggle issues of the day. Until 1932, when an internal bulletin was begun, the paper also served as the vehicle for the internal written discussions of the CLA, carrying discussion articles before national conferences.

In its first months, the CLA recruited over a hundred members and expected to continue growing rapidly as Lovestone's right-wing policies continued to alienate militants in the CP. Despite this growth it was not an easy time. The CLA had to fight off Stalinist goons to establish its right to sell the paper and hold public forums. But with these sales and meetings they were able to reach many CPers and find some who were willing to risk joining the CLA.

However, with the ouster of Lovestone and the "third

period" turn in mid-1929, the CLA faced new problems. Many Communists took the ultraleft rhetoric for good coin. They figured that the "right danger" had been removed, "American exceptionalism" had been defeated, and a campaign to organize the unorganized into "new unions" was about to revolutionize the labor movement. These had been some of the main proposals of the old Cannon faction and were key elements of the CLA platform. So what was the CLA shouting about now?

To many people, the CLA's criticisms of the CP's ultraleftism seemed like nit-picking. The CP-led unions organized some militant struggles. They were defeated largely due to the sectarianism and ultraleftism of the CP, and the inadequacy of the bureaucratically appointed leaders. But these defeats came during a period of defeats for the labor movement as a whole, and the CLA's astute criticisms of them did not inspire the victims of the "third period" to join the CLA in large numbers. Most were lost to radical politics.

The Great Depression that began with the stock market crash in October 1929 had been predicted by most radicals, but its depth was a shock to even the most conscious revolutionaries. Unemployment jumped by over 2 million in two weeks. Layoffs swept one industry after another. While wage rates remained at pre-depression levels at first, millions worked only part time, making under ten dollars per week; the employers began to cut wage rates by late 1930, pleading poverty. With local relief programs swamped, the unemployed were destitute. In New York City, 85,000 survived only by the charity breadlines that were set up; ninety-five people starved to death in the city in 1931. Thousands were on the streets selling apples—the Hoover administration, in its effort to paint as rosy a picture of the economy as possible, counted apple sellers as employed. By spring 1933 a third of the work force, 15–16 million, were totally unemployed. It was worse in the biggest industries: 64 percent of coal miners and 58 percent of factory workers were unemployed.

The workers were stunned. Not until the slight recovery of 1933–34 did workers mobilize to join the AFL unions and strike to force the employers to recognize them.

Nevertheless, the CP had a good deal of attractive power in this period. It was identified with the Russian revolution, and in those days of high unemployment American workers were impressed with the job security and other benefits Russian workers had won. The CP also carried out work in the Black communities against evictions and around the Scottsboro defense case, which won them a number of Black supporters. The party was large enough to build a sizeable movement of the unemployed in the early thirties too.

The CLA was excluded by the Stalinists from the new unions, the defense movements, and the Unemployed Councils. This made it necessary to work underground to reach activists in these movements—a slow process involving very few cadres. The CLA's focus was propaganda, explaining the revolutionary program and attacking the Stalinist misleaders in the pages of *The Militant.* The Left Opposition found itself isolated from the main body of revolutionary workers in the United States.

This affected people in and around the CLA in various ways. A few simply capitulated to the Stalinists, sacrificing political principles because they thought it more important to do "mass work."

Others, notably the followers of Albert Weisbord, a self-proclaimed sympathizer of the Left Opposition, looked toward an alliance with the Lovestoneites to gather enough forces to be able to intervene in the AFL unions. This get-rich-quick scheme ignored the principled differences between the two groups.

Within the CLA membership there developed cliques that were susceptible to the influence of petty-bourgeois politics. A group around Joseph Carter in New York became notorious for picking up the slanders raised by the Stalinists, the sectarian IWW leaders, and other opponents of Leninism, and parroting them inside the league as "criticisms" of its National Committee, and especially of Cannon.

Among the CLA leaders the impact of isolation was more complex. They generally agreed on the tasks of the group as an expelled faction of the CP, with minor differences over the tempo and scale of the propaganda activities of the league. There were bigger disagreements between Shachtman and the other NCers about his relations with the European sections of the Left Opposition in his capacity of international representative of the league. Shachtman tended to support petty-bourgeois currents that disoriented the groups politically and soon found their way out of the International Left Opposition.

But what aroused the most heated controversy were organizational questions. Shachtman accused Cannon of organizational inefficiency and conservatism, and viewed Cannon's search for contacts in the labor movement as nonpolitical and opportunist. Cannon never claimed to be a great administrator; he tended to be slow in answering correspondence, and the national office functioned more efficiently when it was in the hands of Arne Swabeck and Rose Karsner, or Martin Abern. Cannon's attention toward revolutionary syndicalists and former collaborators in the CP like Bill Dunne was not based on nostalgia, as Shachtman thought, but was an example of Cannon's concern that these forces be drawn together into the revolutionary movement, not letting them be written off for their previous errors.

Cannon opposed some of Shachtman's organizational proposals as unrealistic or premature for a small group. His early reservations about launching the weekly *Militant* turned out to be right when the paper had to be cut back to a semimonthly in July 1930 because of poverty; but he erred in arguing against accepting help from Trotsky to reestablish the weekly a year later, when prospects were a little better for sustaining it.

Cannon commented on the breakdown in collaboration and in personal relations among the founding leaders of the league in his 1974 interview:

"I think, you see, as we began to get the writings of Trotsky, it opened up a whole new world for us. And they discovered, this is my assumption, that while they had always taken what I had said for gospel, they discovered that there was a lot of things I didn't know. That I was just beginning to learn from Trotsky. What they didn't know was that I was learning as well as they were. Shachtman, at least, I think, had the idea that he had outgrown me. He studied the writings very seriously and assiduously and was very prolific in expounding in his speeches. . . . And there were other incidents, friction, and so on. I ran into some great personal difficulties. My children's mother died suddenly and unexpectedly and there was some terrible complicated personal problems that arose out of it. And I couldn't work for a while. I had to work at an outside job trying to get by, and I had the double problem of the children.

"They took that to be the sign that I was quitting the movement, I guess. And this stirred up a bitter anti-Cannon attitude with the new young people in the league, so that every branch meeting was a big hassle and argument about something or other of no great consequence. That's what happens when a movement is in decline and hard pressed. Squabbles develop and people begin to look around for somebody to blame for the troubles of the movement."

Cannon's personal "dog days" after the death of his wife, Lista, in late April 1929, lasted into 1930. His political work declined to the point where he did not come to the National Office or to branch meetings regularly for months. While he did write several articles and letters for the movement, he was not part of the functioning national leadership on a day-to-day basis. Not only his factional opponents but his old friends and supporters worried about his political future.

While he was immersed in personal matters, Cannon's life still centered on politics. The poetry and fiction he wrote in that period, never completed or published, had political themes—characters from labor history, and from Cannon's days as a young Wobbly.

The frictions that arose between Cannon and Shachtman in 1929–31 disrupted the functioning of the National Committee but did not reach the ranks or produce any open factional battles. Then in the following two years a full-fledged faction fight erupted which almost split the CLA in early 1933, just when the league's prospects were becoming brighter. The issues and outcome of that fight are covered in the next volume in this series.

❖

The speeches and writings in this volume reflect the main work and the most important accomplishment of the CLA—the struggle to maintain the Marxist program and rebuild the revolutionary leadership in the United States. Cannon's role in this was key to the success of the venture. Of all the cadres of the CLA he had the broadest class-struggle experience to draw on, from the free-speech fights and strike battles of the IWW to the best days of the young Communist Party, where he had led important political fights to orient the party toward the masses of American workers and arm it with a Leninist trade union program. This experience equipped him to learn the party-building lessons of the Russian revolution from Trotsky and apply them on American soil.

While Cannon was limited to a small-group existence and bogged down in factional struggles that put a premium on patience and propaganda, the spark of the agitator enlivens his writings and speeches, and the young IWW rebel shines through.

In 1928, at the age of thirty-eight, Cannon began his apprenticeship in Bolshevism in the school of the Left Opposition. Today's revolutionaries can learn a lot from his experiences and mistakes, and take inspiration from the moral courage of those who kept alive the authentic ideas of Marxism in the "dog days" of the Left Opposition.

Only one of the items in this volume is currently in print in another collection. The rest are either published here for the first time or are long out of print. The introductory note preceding each item indicates its nature and origin. The articles or speeches that were originally published in *The Militant* are identified by publication date; unpublished letters and speeches appear under the date when they were written or given. Much of the material in this book was taken from Cannon's private papers, which are at the Library of Social History in New York. We are grateful to Albert Glotzer for contributing many letters by Cannon to this collection.

This volume does not include all of Cannon's writings

and speeches that have been preserved from 1928 to 1931. Left out are letters of a routine or repetitive character, some articles of less general interest than those reprinted here, poetry and fiction, and speeches preserved only in the form of sketchy notes rather than transcripts. A few items have been abridged, and this is indicated by ellipses (. . .) in the text. Where major portions have been cut, this is indicated in the source note.

There were two considerations in deciding what to excerpt and what to print in full: keeping this book to a reasonable length and eliminating unnecessary repetition. In his correspondence Cannon often wrote to several people at the same time, covering many of the same points in each letter while adding some new ones. Since these items appear together in this book, such repetitions have been removed, but all new material has been left intact.

As aids to the reader there are extensive editorial notes (indicated by superscript numbers in the text) and a glossary of names, organizations, and political terms, at the back of the book.

Fred Stanton
MAY 1, 1981

For the Russian Opposition

Against opportunism and bureaucracy in the Workers (Communist) Party
October 27, 1928

This statement by James P. Cannon, Martin Abern, and Max Shachtman was presented to the meeting of the Political Committee of the Communist Party that expelled the three authors. It was published in the first issue of *The Militant,* November 15, 1928. Paragraph 15 was omitted to avoid problems for the party in the International Labor Defense; however, the party included that paragraph when it published the statement in the *Daily Worker* on November 16, 1928.

1. In view of the necessity of concentrating the full attention of the party on the election campaign, we have refrained up till now from any statement or step calculated to open a party discussion on disputed questions until the election campaign has been ended and the preconvention discussion opened.

2. We have definite views on a series of fundamental questions vitally affecting the whole future of the party and the Comintern which it was our intention to bring

before the party in the preconvention discussion period.

3. The "discussion" of these questions conducted up till now has not been a real discussion since many of the documents—in our opinion some of the most important political documents of our time—have been suppressed and concealed from the parties of the Comintern or presented to them in garbled form. The opportunity which has come to us in the recent period to read a number of these documents dealing with some of the most disputed problems of the Comintern in the past five years, together with the rapid confirmation of their correctness by the whole course of events, has shaped our views and convictions. We consider it our revolutionary duty to defend these views before the party.

4. We had intended to undertake this task at the opening of the party discussion after the election campaign. However, the arbitrary actions already taken against us (our removal from all positions on October 16) and the plain indications shown in the present hearing of the intention to take further organizational measures and to begin a public campaign against us in the party press make it necessary to state our position without further delay. It must be made clear to the party that the measures are being taken against us solely because of our political views. These views must be presented to the party as they really are.

5. We present them here in outline form and will elaborate on them more fully in our appeal to the Central Executive Committee against the actions taken by the Polcom.

6. We stand on the main line of the document entitled "The Right Danger in the American Party" (excepting certain erroneous formulations dealing with the world position and role of American imperialism), presented to the

Sixth World Congress of the Comintern by the delegation of the Opposition, in the drafting of which we actively participated.[1] As set forth in this document, we believe that the present leadership of the party, mechanically imposed upon the party by the ECCI against the will of the membership, is a consciously developing right wing whose course and actions are all in the direction of undermining the position of the party in the class struggle. Its activities since the presentation of the document "The Right Danger in the American Party" to the world congress, have confirmed and not refuted this estimate. The irresponsible adventurism, factional degeneration, and bureaucratic corruption of the Lovestone group leadership are an organic part of its fundamental opportunist character.

7. The latest decision of the secretariat of the ECCI, which undertakes to dismiss a whole series of principled questions raised in our indictment of the party leadership with a formal motion, giving no answer whatsoever to the burning questions of the party in all fields of the class struggle, serves only to strengthen the mechanical stranglehold of the right-wing leadership upon our party.[2] This bureaucratic secretarial method of dealing with disputed principled questions must be emphatically rejected by the party both in form and content, since it has nothing in common with Lenin's teaching regarding the ideological leadership of all Communist parties by the Comintern and the unremitting struggle against opportunism on all fronts.

8. The present attempt of some of the leaders of the Foster-Bittelman group who signed the document on the right danger to abandon that platform, to moderate the struggle against the Lovestone-Pepper right wing, and to

effect a political coalescence with them in order to direct their attack against those who remain true to that platform and develop its logical and inevitable international implications, in no way alters the fundamental correctness of the document. It merely demonstrates the political instability of these leaders, which hampers the process of developing an opposition to the present right-wing leadership and line of the party on a principled basis. We have no doubt that the supporters of the Opposition who have regarded the struggle against the right-wing leadership as a principled question will continue to adhere to this position despite the vacillations and maneuvers of a section of the leaders.

9. The problems of the American party are organically bound up with the fundamental questions confronting the Communist Party of the Soviet Union and the Comintern, and cannot be solved separately from them. The left wing of the American party, taking shape in the principled struggle against the right-wing leadership of the party (Lovestone-Pepper group), will go forward only insofar as it recognizes the necessity of a struggle against the right danger on an international scale and links up its fight in the American party with the Bolshevik fight for the fundamental tenets of Leninism in the Communist Party of the Soviet Union and in the Comintern.

10. The Opposition in the Communist Party of the Soviet Union led by L.D. Trotsky has been fighting for the unity of the Comintern and all its sections on the basis of the victory of Leninism. The correctness of the position taken by the Russian Opposition over a period of five years of struggle has been fully confirmed by events.

a. The struggle led by Trotsky since 1923 for party democracy and against bureaucratism as the pressure of another class upon the party of the proletariat, was absolutely correct then and is even more so now. The adoption of this position by Zinoviev, Kamenev, and others in 1926, and the attempt by Stalin to adopt it now, demonstrates the tremendous pressure of class forces which impel the Communist Party of the Soviet Union to this platform.[3] The struggle for party democracy, against bureaucratism, and for a regime of genuine Leninist self-criticism are burning questions now for every party and for the Comintern as a whole.

b. The necessity for a more relentless struggle against the kulak and the nepman—for an orientation exclusively toward the workers and hired hands, united with the village poor and lower peasantry and in alliance with the middle peasantry—proclaimed by the Opposition, becomes clearer every day. The trend of events and the irresistible pressure of class forces is already driving a deep cleavage in the leadership of the Communist Party of the Soviet Union, and is forcing the Stalin group to struggle against the right wing (Rykov, etc.), with other elements (Bukharin) vacillating between the two.

The platform of the Russian Opposition, prepared for the Fifteenth Congress of the CPSU, indicates the revolutionary policy for the present situation in the Soviet Union. The prediction and warning contained in this platform against the inevitable growth and aggressiveness of a genuine right wing in the party (Rykov, Tomsky, etc.) has been precisely confirmed in the intervening period, particularly in recent months. The activities of this right wing have already necessitated organizational measures in the Moscow and other organizations of the party—a proof of the awakening of the proletarian masses of the party to this danger. The "left" course of the Stalin group in the direction of a struggle against the right dangers, for party democracy and self-criticism, against the bureaucrats, the nepmen, and the kulaks, can become a real left course only insofar as it abandons zigzag movements, adopts the whole platform of the Opposition, and reinstates the tested Bolshevik fighters who have been expelled to their rightful places in the party.

c. The attempts to revise the basic Marxist-Leninist doctrine with the spurious theory of socialism in one country have been rightly resisted by the Opposition led by Trotsky. A number of revisionist and opportunist errors in various fields of Comintern activity and its ideological life in general have proceeded from this false theory. To this, in part at least, can be traced the false line in the Chinese revolution, the debacle of the Anglo-Russian Committee, the alarming and unprecedented growth of bureaucratism in the Comintern, an incorrect attitude and policy in the Soviet Union, etc., etc. This new "theory" is bound up with an overemphasis on the power and duration of the temporary stabilization of capitalism. Herein lies the true source of pessimism regarding the development of the proletarian world revolution. One of the principal duties of every Communist in every party of the Comintern is to fight along with the Opposition for the teachings of Marx, Engels, and Lenin on this basic question.

d. The Opposition was absolutely correct when it demanded the immediate rupture of the Anglo-Russian Committee and the concentration of all the fire of the Comintern and the British party upon the leaders of the British Trades Union General Council (Purcell, Hicks, and Company) immediately after the betrayal of the general strike.[4] The maintenance of the Anglo-Russian Committee after this event did not serve as a bridge to the British masses but as a partial shield of the traitorous leaders from the fire of the Communists.

e. Rarely before in history has a Marxist-Leninist appraisal and forecast been so completely and swiftly confirmed as in the case of the Opposition theses and proposals (Trotsky, Zinoviev) on the problems and tasks of the Chinese revolution.[5] The line of the ECCI, formulated by Stalin, Bukharin, Martynov, etc., and the rejection of the proposals of the Opposition, which were suppressed and concealed from the parties of the Comintern, have brought catastrophic results and hampered the genuine development of the Communist Party of China and the revolutionary-democratic dictatorship of the workers and peasants. In view of its world-historical importance, a real discussion of the problems of the Chinese revolution, with all the documents being made available, is imperative for all parties of the Comintern. The prohibition of this discussion must be broken down, the truth must be told and the enormous errors exposed down to their roots. Only in this way can the great lessons of the Chinese revolution be learned by the parties of the Comintern.

11. We demand the publication of all the documents of the Russian Opposition, without which the party members do not and cannot know the essential issues of the struggle and cannot form intelligent opinions in regard to them. The discussion of these issues heretofore has been conducted in an atmosphere of prejudice, misrepresentation, terrorism, outlawing of all thought and inquiry, the substitution of official say-so for the study of documents and facts on disputed questions. All this has been part of a campaign of unparalleled slander against Trotsky—who, after Lenin, was the outstanding leader of the Russian revolution and the Comintern—and was accompanied by the falsification of the history of the revolution itself.

12. We intend, at the coming plenum of the Central Executive Committee, to propose that our party shall take the initiative in demanding the return from exile and

the reinstatement into the Communist Party of the Soviet Union with full rights, of Trotsky and the other imprisoned and exiled members of the Russian Opposition. Violence and persecution against counterrevolutionaries is a revolutionary duty; violence and persecution against tried and loyal Bolsheviks is a crime.

13. The consolidation of the Opposition in the American party, which logically and inevitably merges with the path of the Opposition in the Communist Party of the Soviet Union led by Trotsky, has developed in the struggle against the right danger. The pitiful attempt to characterize this Opposition as a "right" tendency, related to the noncommunist elements such as Lore who have been fighting the party from the right, and anticommunist elements like Salutsky, who have gone completely over to the side of the labor lieutenants of capitalism, does not in the least correspond with political reality and is designed to cover the progressive drift of the party leadership to the right.

On the contrary, the attempts to exclude us from responsible party work, and even from the party itself, along with the proletarian communists who support us, while at the same time the control of the party apparatus and the party leadership in such unions as the needle trades consolidates more firmly in the hands of the opportunists, who fight their communist worker critics with expulsion and physical violence—all this can only accelerate the rapprochement between the right wing and petty-bourgeois elements now outside the party.

14. The Lovestone group leadership, by its opportunist political outlook, its petty-bourgeois origin, its corrupt factionalism, its careerism and adventurism in the class struggle, is the greatest menace to the party. Its mechanical grip on the apparatus of the party grows steadily tighter

and chokes out its inner life. Capable, experienced, and trustworthy comrades are one by one removed from responsible posts and replaced by faction agents, incompetents, and upstarts, unknown and inexperienced in any serious work in the class struggle. The party itself, the mass work, and the mass organizations under the influence and direction of the party are thereby undermined.

15. The action of the Polcom in arbitrarily removing us from our positions in the ILD, where we have worked loyally and effectively for the building of this mass organization, for our political views alone, is a most ill-considered and dangerous step, fraught with the gravest consequences to the future of the ILD. There has never been any criticism of our work in the ILD by the Political Committee of the party, the executive committee of the ILD, or by any of the three conferences of the ILD. All of these bodies have uniformly endorsed and commended our activity in this capacity. The disruption of the work which will be caused by our unjustified removal and the certainty that we will be replaced by incompetent faction agents in no way interested in this work or qualified to perform it, cannot but bring the most harmful results. Such actions demonstrate again the reckless irresponsibility of the present party leadership in relation to all mass organizations and mass work.

16. By its whole character the Lovestone leadership is the logical American banner-bearer of the demagogic and unscrupulous international campaign against the leaders of the Russian Opposition. The aspirations of certain former leaders of the opposition in the American party to grasp this banner for themselves are pathetically futile. The hopes of the Foster group to escape thereby the factional persecution of the Lovestone group and to secure their organizational positions can succeed only insofar as

they surrender their former opposition standpoint. The whole course of the Lovestone group, which has no roots in the labor movement, is toward a monopoly of the party apparatus, and cannot be otherwise.

17. We declare our intention to appeal to the plenum of the Central Executive Committee to reverse the action of the Polcom against us, which is motivated by neither principled foundation nor party interest, and is the result purely of factional considerations and bureaucratic fear of discussion and criticism.

18. The arbitrary decisions made against us cannot in the slightest degree change our position as Communists, since the party we helped to found and build is our party. Reserving the right to express our viewpoint and opinion on these disputed questions, we will continue to adhere to the discipline and decisions of the party as heretofore. Under all circumstances we will continue to live with the party and work for its future.

19. We demand that simultaneously with the announcement of the decision of the Polcom on the outcome of this hearing, our statement shall be given to the party in the same manner.

James P. Cannon
(MEMBER OF THE POLITICAL COMMITTEE AND CEC)

Martin Abern
(MEMBER OF THE CEC)

Max Shachtman
(ALTERNATE TO THE CEC)

To the party members

October 28, 1928

The following letter was sent to the members of the Communist Party with the text of the previous statement.

Dear Comrades:

Yesterday the undersigned presented the attached statement to the Political Committee, which had been called into special session for the purpose of conducting our trial. In this statement, as will be seen, we clearly and openly declare our agreement with the platform of the Russian Opposition and demand that the party publish their platform and other important political documents which up till now have been suppressed and concealed from the party members.

The Political Committee refused to publish the suppressed documents and immediately declared all three of us expelled from the party because of our views.

Such methods, which substitute bureaucratic control for ideological and political leadership, have permeated our party to an alarming degree, adversely affecting its policies, choking its inner life, weakening its influence, blocking its growth. These methods tend to transform the party from a living body of revolutionaries into an institution which makes thought unlawful. When loyal communists are expelled for their views, when inquiry and discussion on principled questions are prohibited, when the party members fear to think, when they vote for decisions without in the least understanding them, the party is in danger. That is the meaning of the atmosphere created in the unscrupulous and demagogic struggle against Trotsky and the Russian Opposition during the past five years. That is the real meaning of our expulsion for stating our views. The proletarian masses of the party must awaken to this danger and take up the fight against it. They must break through the bureaucratic crust which has formed itself on top of the party. They must demand full information on all sides of the question so that they can decide for themselves intelligently and not merely from wrong and non-Leninist conceptions of formal discipline. To help bring about this awakening we have addressed our statement of views to the Political Committee and now address it to the party ranks.

As is known to all active communists, we are not people who only yesterday began to work for revolutionary ideas. The step we have taken is a seriously considered and deliberate one, based on a firm conviction of revolutionary duty.

Since we are communists, bound to the party by our whole conception and by our lifetime of revolutionary activity, it goes without saying that our struggle, like the struggle of the Russian Opposition, will be conducted solely on a party basis. Our expulsion, like the expulsion of the Russian Opposition, can only be temporary. The permanent victory of a machine over a correct political line never yet happened and never can happen to the Communist Party. We will appeal for reinstatement to the plenum of the Central Executive Committee and from it, if necessary, to the party convention and to the Communist International. All those who share our views and stand with us will react to measures taken against them in the same way.

It is our aim to bring the documents of the Russian Opposition, a treasure of revolutionary work, to the party members as rapidly as possible. All comrades who are willing to help in this revolutionary task or who wish to receive the material are invited to correspond with us at the above address.

With Communist greetings,

James P. Cannon
(MEMBER OF THE POLITICAL COMMITTEE AND CEC)

Martin Abern
(MEMBER OF THE CEC)

Max Shachtman
(ALTERNATE TO THE CEC)

Study the documents

November 2, 1928

The following letter was written to Albert Glotzer in Chicago.

Dear Al—

I just received your letter. I wrote a long letter to Arne [Swabeck] today which is for you also. Ask him to show it to you. Will aim to answer your letter in detail tomorrow, or perhaps tonight yet. The enclosed material, which is about one-sixth of the criticism of the program, will give you something to read.[6] Will send complete proofs in a few days. Study it. You will not hear these questions discussed either in the so-called group or in the DEC [District Executive Committee] because both are equally strangers to them. They want you to condemn Trotsky because the CI has condemned him, not because they can give any coherent or intelligent explanation of the error of his position. Lenin said, "Anyone who takes things on a say-so is an idiot."

Why is every line that Trotsky writes contraband? What are they afraid of? We can read the *New York Leader* weekly and you, being, as I understand it, a reformed Jew, can read the *New York Forward* daily, without being in the least influenced in the direction of Social Democracy. But Trotsky, it appears, is such a Social Democrat and counter-revolutionist that grown-up communists must be forbidden to read what he writes for fear of being convinced, as almost invariably happens.

I am greatly crowded for time at the moment and only meant to say two words with this enclosure. But, you see, I have the zeal of the disciple and my pen runs away with me. More soon. Meantime don't let extraneous or secondary questions disturb you. The only thing that is really important is to be right, to be sure of oneself, to know the *reasons* for a position from all sides. Everything else follows from this.

I would greatly appreciate it, Al, if you would send us a copy of the caucus letter of the Young Statesmen of the YWL who have set out with a great clatter to ride two horses going in opposite directions at the same time. Also similar material from the leaders who claim the distinction of having been the first to inform on us to Lovestone and Pepper. We all send love and we don't mean maybe.

Jim

P.S.—The Philadelphia group of the YWL will be with us—at least the most decisive ones. You remember "Morgie" there. It was funny to see the New York group of "National Leaders" trying to bulldoze him. He has more stamina than the whole bunch of them put together.

The question of the Russian Opposition should be studied by the various issues involved. The program criticism deals primarily with "socialism in one country" and the Chinese revolution. We have more material on the latter subject which you will receive in due time.

C.

Concerning our expulsion

Published November 15, 1928

This letter to Albert Glotzer was published in the first issue of *The Militant.*

Dear Comrade:

We were very glad to receive your letter and to hear of your reaction against our expulsion and your wish to receive more information and advice as to procedure. Enough of such letters have already been received to make it clear that the attempt to dispose of the principled questions we have raised by the simple mechanical expedient of our expulsion from the party will meet with resistance from the worker communists in the ranks.

Your statement that our expulsion took you by surprise and that the comrades there want to know more than they can learn from the official communications is echoed in other letters also, and quite naturally. Another letter, which came today from a communist coal miner, says, "At the beginning I was tremendously surprised. The entire matter hit me so hard that I don't know whether I have come back to earth or not."[7] The people who gamble with the proletarian movement regard the expulsion of loyal fighters for the party as a clever trick, a quick and easy solution of troublesome questions. The rank-and-file militants and the serious revolutionaries who have built the movement and stood loyally by it in its hardest days will take another view in exact proportion as they learn the facts and understand the disruptive consequences of this criminal act. Our foremost task is to make these facts known to the party, and we will endeavor to do this at all cost.

The suddenness with which the whole issue has burst upon the party was unavoidable on our part. The Polcom majority declared us expelled from the party for our views without even waiting for the plenum of the Central Executive Committee, before the party members had the slightest inkling of the situation and before we had the opportunity to inform them. Their object was to confront the party members with our expulsion as an accomplished fact and then to terrorize them into an endorsement of it before the slightest information is in their hands.

They expelled us, as they have expelled many good communists before, in order to deprive us of the possibility of speaking to the party as party members. Then they tell the party it has no right to listen to us because we are not members of the party. Such shallow trickery can be based only on the most profound contempt for the intelligence of the rank and file of the party. To allow such methods to succeed would be to give the power of self-perpetuation to any clique which might gain control of the apparatus and to reduce the principle of democratic centralism to a fiction.

According to such procedure the fact of expulsion settles

the question. But in the absence of any preliminary discussion, the party can decide the question wisely and responsibly only if it knows why the expulsion took place and what the expelled members have to say. A party member who does not demand that right, who keeps quiet, or who votes to endorse this act of bureaucratic disruption for fear of expulsion, is not acting like an upstanding communist whose vote means understanding and conviction.

"How does it happen that you became a supporter of the Russian Opposition and insist so categorically on the right to defend it—even up to the point of temporary expulsion from the party?" This is the question asked by many comrades as well as by you. "The question is five years old, Trotsky is expelled, and the questions are settled—why bring it up again?" Well, it is true that the question is old, but it is by no means settled and cannot be settled on the present basis. This is the answer. We are late in learning the truth, late with the performance of our international duty, but that is by no means entirely, or even mainly, our fault. It was possible for us to secure adequate information and judge for ourselves only recently.

We do not demand or expect anyone to accept our views on our say-so. All we ask of those who have stood closest to us in the past, and of the broad circles of the party which are being stirred to a new interest in the question by our stand and our expulsion, is that they study the question honestly and objectively on the basis of the material which we will provide. From honest study of the material will come conviction, as was the case with us. We have no doubt, either, that they will defend these convictions as we do, regardless of personal consequences, because the very essence of the matter is the overshadowing importance of the issues involved.

The wisdom of our action in presenting a clear and direct

statement of our position was questioned; but it seems quite clear that its correctness has already been established. The party needed an alarm bell; it needed an awakening from the stupor of factional intrigue over small questions. The party needs plain speech now above everything. Strategy, of course, is not to be excluded in such a fight, but it must be strictly subordinated to the major task of telling the truth and stimulating the party members to demand the truth. This is the real duty of leaders now. It is from this standpoint, in our opinion, that you and the other leading comrades must decide your course—from the standpoint of your responsibility as leaders to the party and to the rank-and-file comrades who have confidence in you and look to you for guidance.

It is true that the raising of the fundamental questions of Bolshevism which have arisen on an international scale over a period of five years plays havoc with second-rate and tenth-rate questions of controversy and the group which concerns itself exclusively with them. The fate of the "loyal" opposition to Lovestone and Pepper is indeed a sad one. But the fate of all groups which base themselves on purely local or national issues cannot be otherwise when the larger questions are brought up.

At the Chicago DEC meeting the majority has already demanded "united support" of the CEC in the fight against "Trotskyism." This only confirms what we predicted from the first. The group which wants to fight "Trotskyism" and, at the same time, wants to fight the Lovestone-Pepper group, which has a copyright on that fight and makes its political living that way; the group which does not know from one day to another where the greatest danger lies and where to direct its blows—will naturally and very quickly demonstrate its complete bankruptcy. There is no place for it. Its elimination from the scene proceeds inevitably from the whole situation.

We wish to say a few words regarding the attitude of those comrades who seriously and from their own knowledge and conviction count Trotsky's position prior to 1917 against him. Such an attitude is in no way contrary to ours. We know that Trotsky and Lenin had differences in the prerevolutionary struggle, and we know that Bolshevism took shape and the Comintern was founded on the basis of Lenin's doctrine, to which Trotsky came over. Do we not know also that Trotsky from 1917 fought side by side with Lenin; and that even when Trotsky differed with him afterward, Lenin never allowed a campaign against him, but on the contrary placed the greatest confidence in him and helped to elevate him to the highest positions? To our own knowledge he spoke at the Fourth Congress of the Comintern as the outstanding leader (next to Lenin) and he made the main report. We know that he had fewer differences with Lenin after 1917 than any one of the leaders, although they do not tell us that in the official information.

We have not the slightest doubt, from a study of all the material dealing with the period 1917–28 that we have been able to secure, that "Trotskyism" as a political tendency in conflict with Leninism was liquidated prior to the October revolution. The disputes of twenty years ago are made the center of the fight against Trotsky in recent years only because his opponents and defamers are not able to stand up against him on the actual merits of the present controversies. What is the great historic significance of the action of Zinoviev and Kamenev in uniting with Trotsky in 1926 but an acknowledgment that the campaign against "Trotskyism" in 1923–25 had been a false one? Zinoviev, who above all others "educated" us in this campaign, said so in so many words.

The struggle of the past five years has revolved around the living issues of the present period. It is our absolute conviction, based on the most objective study of all material we could secure—and carried on in the face of previous prejudice—that on all of these basic questions of the period, the questions around which the whole life and future of the international Communist movement revolve—Trotsky has been in the main correct and the true defender of Leninism.

Regarding our expulsion and the expulsion of others which is already being prepared, a few words should be said. The great significance and unbounded consequences of such criminal acts by the Political Committee cannot be overestimated, and no kind of diplomacy or expediency will be able to subordinate such an issue. It will inevitably rise up and confront the party at every turn. The expulsion, for their views alone, of loyal communists, founders of the party, with honorable records of fifteen to twenty years of activity—in contradistinction to the shady records of many of those who expelled us—cannot be covered up or minimized by any kind of slander. For we are revolutionaries who will fight for our right to belong to the party and will not let anything tear us away from it. The Polcom "settled" the question by summarily expelling us, but it will arise again immediately after the election campaign when others will demand our reinstatement and are also expelled.

Expulsion is a dangerous fire to play with in a party which has all too few forces of the kind that are being expelled, forces loyal to the party and working for its future, who have contributed not a little in building the party and establishing its prestige among the workers. As the struggle continues and our material is made available to more and more party members, the issue will grow more acute.

The wholesale expulsion of proletarian fighters while the petty-bourgeois careerists and adventurers are attracted and drawn to the center—this is the only possible logic of the expulsion course initiated by the Polcom.

We do not believe it is in principle possible for any comrade who disagrees with such a course and understands its unavoidable consequences to give any kind of support to our expulsion. To say that a protest against our expulsion can be made only if one agrees with the position of the Russian Opposition on all points seems to us to be putting the question upside down. It would be more correct to say that the expulsion can be endorsed only if one is convinced that the position is wrong on all important points and that we have become enemies of the party, which no communist adult believes.

We surely intend to advise a certain tactical line to some of the rank-and-file comrades to avoid expulsion without repudiating their principles. But leaders to whom the party is looking are duty-bound to speak clearly and tell the party just what they think, even if it is not a complete support of one position or the other. What is wrong about voting against expulsion when one does not know the facts and has not had sufficient opportunity to adopt a definite position one way or the other? What kind of an atmosphere is it in the party, what form of party democratic rights exists, when members feel compelled to vote one way or the other on the spot without any real knowledge of their own? A party uprising against this whole system will be one of the most fruitful results of our fight.

It is to be expected that those who deprived us of all rights to defend our views in the normal party way will now raise a great hue and cry because we take other means of bringing our position to the party membership. They pervert the great Leninist principle of discipline based on a correct revolutionary policy, into an instrument for shutting the mouth of the loyal party member and protecting their own opportunist policies and disloyal acts from any real criticism and exposure. Such bureaucratic machinations have nothing in common with Leninist organization principles. We would be unworthy of the name of revolutionists if we allowed our views to be suppressed by such sophistical methods.

It is only miserable bureaucrats and philistines who can keep silent about their views on principled questions. Revolutionaries advocate them. The issues of the Russian Opposition and their indissoluble connection with our own specific problems will be discussed by the party in spite of all. And it is our task to see to it that this is not a one-sided discussion, or rather distortion, of the questions, but a presentation of them to the party as they really are. The regeneration of the party and the reconstitution of its leadership on a proletarian communist basis will proceed from this.

Yours fraternally,

J.P. Cannon

Fortress of the world revolution

Published November 15, 1928

The following article was published in *The Militant.*

Eleven years have gone by since the Russian workers took the hammer of revolution in their hands and broke the chain of world imperialism at its weakest link. The history of the whole intervening period represents on the one hand the efforts of the imperialists to forge that chain together again and bind it tighter around the enslaved masses and, on the other hand, the struggle of the proletariat to tear it apart from the whole of humanity.

The Russian revolution was not merely a national event—it was the beginning of and signal for the international proletarian revolution. Herein lies its true meaning, its great historic significance. From this standpoint the revolutionary workers of the world hail the cause of Soviet Russia as their cause on the eleventh anniversary of her October.

The Russian revolution broke forever the unity of the

world and divided it into two hostile camps—the camp of imperialist exploitation and the camp of social revolution. At one polar extreme stands America, the strongest imperialist world power. At the other stands the USSR, the land of the workers' rule. The antagonism between them, and the systems they represent, is irreconcilable. They cannot live together permanently side by side. The victory of the Soviet system on a world scale means the liberation of enslaved humanity and its ascent to heights of culture and achievement beyond our dreams—to socialism and beyond that to communism. The victory of imperialism would hurl civilization into the abyss. Such is the issue of the epoch of wars and revolutions in which we live and fight.

The Russian revolution revivified the revolutionary movement of the world and inspired the proletarian masses with new confidence and hope. It lifted up the banner of socialism, trampled in the mud of social patriotism by the traitor leaders of the Socialist parties, and made it again synonymous with internationalism. Lenin, the leader of the Russian revolution, was also the leader of the Communist International, which arose out of the ruins brought about by social treason in the war. Eleven years of the dictatorship of the proletariat has confirmed everything that Lenin taught about the international significance of the revolution and the indissoluble bonds between it and the world proletariat.

Soviet Russia is the fortress of the world revolution. While it stands, the imperialist system shakes on its foundations. Every attempt at stabilization brings greater insecurity and deeper contradictions. The example and the brotherly help of Soviet Russia inspires and strengthens the movement of the workers and oppressed peoples throughout the world. The flag of our socialist fatherland is the flag of our hope. On this eleventh anniversary we again hail it as our own.

Between the Soviet republics united in the USSR and the international revolutionary proletariat there is an organic connection. They are bound together spiritually and politically. They are united by ties of mutual solidarity which no power on earth can break. Just as the Soviet republics constitute an impregnable fortress of the world revolution, so is the international proletariat the protector of the Soviet republics. The revolutionary workers see in every blow aimed at Soviet Russia a blow aimed at their own cause, and react against it as such. The defense of the Soviet Union is our own fight. It is and will be a central rallying slogan of the labor militants of the entire world. "Defend the Soviet Union!" is a slogan leading the workers to follow the example of the Russian revolution. So they must conceive it. So will the victory of socialism in Russia and throughout the world be finally secured.

The victory of the Russian proletariat grew out of the World War. The establishment of the dictatorship of the proletariat in Russia and the organization of the Communist International—two vast achievements historically linked together—are the plus signs against the slaughter of the millions and the collapse of the Second International. The imperialist warmakers and their "Socialist" lackeys unleashed forces which they could not control.

The imperialist masters of the world want to take back these gains of the workers wrested out of the bloody pit of war and revolution. Armaments are being multiplied on an unprecedented scale. War clouds darken the skies. War plans grow apace. They are aimed primarily at Soviet Russia and through it at the entire international labor movement.

The celebrations of the workers throughout the world on

this eleventh anniversary of the Russian revolution must therefore be dominated above all by the solemn realization of the war danger and the steel resolve to meet it by revolutionary means; by the resolve to put all our weight and all our sacrifice in the scale for the cause of Soviet Russia, which is the cause of the oppressed and exploited.

Tactics in the Chicago CP

November 16, 1928

The following was a handwritten letter to Albert Glotzer.

Dear Al—

We got your letter finally and are now impatiently awaiting news of the YWL meeting where the question was scheduled to come up. I hope it will be a complete report when it comes. We have written a long letter to Arne today. He will show it to you and save us the trouble of repeating here. We made the error of failing to convert a comrade stenographer to our cause, so we, who once had only to put our feet on the desk and say, with an air of importance, "Take some letters, please," must now type our own with the two educated fingers we have. But it's our own fault. We were warned about the penalties of "Trotskyism." We are still trying, however, and if you get a flood of neatly typewritten letters and documents from us soon, you will know that the "Thin Red Line of Heroes" has gained a female recruit.

We were very glad to get the report of Hathaway's

maiden appearance in Chicago as a political leader with a diploma from the Lenin School in his pocket, if not in his hand, and the solemn observation that our troubles began when we left the jungles of Fosterism and began to live in the political trees. If this is the net result of three years in the Lenin School, don't you think we should propose to Trotsky that he celebrate his return to the leadership of the Red Army by making a bonfire of this whole institution as a menace to the education of the youth? We once had the ambition to send you there, but I think now we should reconsider it. Could we not achieve the same result in shorter time and with much less expense by locking you up in a small room for a month with the Foster caucus until you get that way yourself?

Here is another question to ponder over: If it took Hathaway, Gomez, etc., only about six weeks to discover that our three-year fight with Foster was all wrong, how long will it take them to make the same discovery about our five-year fight with Lovestone and Pepper? Frankfeld, who is younger and quicker than they, has already made the second discovery, we hear. The youth leads—in foolishness if not in wisdom.

As our letter to Arne indicates, we do not understand the tactics you and he have been following. Did you have any idea of being able to remain and work effectively in one caucus with people who take such a stand as Gomez and Chilofsky? It seems absolutely clear, in view of the irreconcilably different positions between you and them, that you should have been consciously working from the first for a split and the formation of a separate group, however small, which you could develop along your own lines. You will pay dearly for every day this is delayed; and every opportunity passed by for a frontal attack on their line and a concealment of your own will be a factor in discrediting and compromising you. It is simply incomprehensible that you and Arne allowed Hathaway to escape with questions, without a direct and frontal attack against his whole line. Better late than never: begin a militant fight for your own position and organize a group to support it.

❖

I do not think Hathaway's political arguments require any answer. But I know that he is an inveterate liar, and he follows the practice of telling the comrades "confidentially" a lot of things which are not so. These I am willing to answer in detail if you will catalog them.

❖

We are trying to hurry the printer with the rest of the proofs on the program criticism, and expect to get them this week. A still more timely document—Trotsky's analysis of the crisis in the Russian party, his statement to the Sixth Congress—was sent to Arne last night in German. We have not got the English translation yet. Much other valuable material is also on hand in German. The trouble is to get it translated and get the money to print it. We sunk everything we could raise or borrow, personally and politically, to pay for the printing and postage on 10,000 copies of the first issue of *The Militant.* About 9,000 are mailed out to individual readers of the party papers! However, the next issue is already secured and our support is growing. The response to the paper in the next two weeks will be an indication of what we can expect.

The fight is already in the open in New York, Kansas City, Minneapolis, and Philadelphia. We realize Chicago is a sleepy city, but we hope for news soon that it is waking up.

Hastily,

Jim

The party 'discussion' opens

Published December 1, 1928

The following article was published in *The Militant.*

After not a little delay, occasioned by the customary cabling back and forth, by cabled appeals of protest by the Foster group which were rejected over the same cables, the statement of the Lovestone-Pepper CEC on our declaration and expulsion was published in the *Daily Worker* on November 16.

The statement of the party majority covers much paper, but it had no space to answer the criticisms of the Opposition on a single point. Our declaration raised principled questions. They answered with an administrative instruction to the party to expel all those who share our views. We said what everybody knows, that the questions have never been discussed, and we demanded a discussion. They replied, "The discussion is closed." We said the position of the Russian Opposition has been correct on all important questions; we gave reasons for our statement and demanded the right to defend these views in the preconvention [discussion]. They disposed of this political proposal with legalistic references to the decisions of the Communist International.

Such, in brief, is the political content of the long-delayed and much labored-over statement of the Lovestone-Pepper faction, which, by grace of Bukharin, constitutes the majority of our Central Executive Committee. We might add that, as an extraordinary concession on their part (and considering the fact that the party members had already read it in *The Militant*), they printed our statement to the Polcom, including even a paragraph which we, for party reasons, had thought best to eliminate from publication.

They merely recite that the CI has decided against the Trotsky platform—a fact which everybody knew before—and pass that off for an answer to the principled arguments of the Opposition. The merits of the decision of the CI, which all communists have a right and duty to discuss and which is the real point of dispute, are not defended by one word of the statement. Thus the pedagogical overseers show their contemptuous estimate of the party members. They do not consider it necessary for the party comrades to know for themselves the issues involved. The party comrades are merely informed of the decisions—discussion is not allowed.

The bureaucrats who rule by decree set up a conception of the Comintern which Lenin never knew. Instead of a living body of revolutionaries generalizing from world experience, as Lenin conceived the Comintern, they want to palm it off as an institution which decides, while the party members need only to be informed of the decisions. The teachings of Marx and Lenin on the centralized international organization of the communist workers are completely lost in such a conception.

In this caricature of Leninism, the communist who knows for himself and defends his position because he knows, is thrown aside in favor of the one who does not know and asks no questions. In such a scheme there is no recognition of the possibilities of errors and no provision for a correction of them. Tomorrow they will go a step further—indeed they have already started on this path—and attempt to establish the same relationship between the party members and the CEC of the party. Then the Foster group, which is now helping to establish this principle which denies our right to criticize the decisions of the Comintern, will be repaid for "faithful service" in the form of an instruction to cease criticism of the decisions of the CEC regardless of the errors contained in them—the greater the error, the less the right to criticize. As for the ordinary worker in the party ranks who has no faction behind him, his right to open his mouth ceased long ago.

"The Communist Party is not a debating society." Behind this statement, true enough in itself, all the bureaucrats who fear discussion seek to hide their incompetence. We communists are not a group of interminable debaters. Neither are we an army of voting robots. The automatic hand raiser is no communist any more than the undisciplined, endless talker. The one of these conceptions is just as far away from Leninism as the other. We hold to the principle of democratic centralism just as firmly as we reject the suppression of discussion and the substitution of official commands for ideological and political leadership.

The great principled questions raised by the Russian Opposition—questions of decisive importance for the whole future of the world proletarian revolution—have never been fairly and fully discussed in any party of the Comintern, including our own party, and consequently, have been decided wrongly. This is the essence of the matter, which the statement of the Lovestone majority ignores entirely because it is fatal for their whole case.

The party comrades do not know the issues from all sides, and cannot know them, for the reason that the material of the Opposition was not published—it was suppressed. There has been no real and serious discussion in the party—it was prohibited. The communist militants who have had the opportunity to read the documents and learn the truth are not allowed to speak within the party—they are expelled.

The Foster group, which had the honor of carrying the "information" against us to Lovestone and Pepper, received their reward in the statement: a condescending pat on the back, which was no doubt appreciated, even if it was accompanied by a rough box on the ear, to say nothing of a number of boots to the bottom.

The difficulties of the Foster group arise out of the contradictions in its position. It is claimed that Christ wrought miracles, but we do not believe that even he ever succeeded in riding two horses going in opposite directions at the same time. The Foster group took a forward step when it united with us in the fight against the right wing (joint fight against the Panken maneuver,[8] common platform at the February and May plenary meetings of the Central Executive Committee, common platform on "The Right Danger in the American Party," etc.).

Its failure to develop the international implications of our common opposition stand, its failure to see that the problems of our party and the fight against its right-wing leadership are indissolubly bound up with the Bolshevik fight of the Russian Opposition, arrested the forward development of the Foster group and prepared the ground for its disintegration. Its pitiful, if short-lived, attempt to out-do the opportunist leadership in demagogy against the Russian Opposition and against us, only sharpened its contradictions and made its whole position politically impossible. Those who do not stand clearly on principles, foresee their implications, and understand their logic are bound to play a sorry role when principled questions are placed on the agenda.

The resolution of the District Executive Committee of New York, under the direct inspiration of the Central Executive Committee majority, demands that the Foster opposition repudiate the statement "The Right Danger in the American Party" if it really wants to fight "Trotskyism," and logically so. The Lovestone-Pepper group of opportunists represents on an American scale what the opportunist opponents and calumniators of the Russian Opposition represent on a Russian and international scale. The Lovestone faction leaders are merely the American representatives of the anti-Trotsky faction in the Communist International, and have been imposed upon the party by it. They are not and never can be leaders of our party in their own right. On the other hand, the course of the American Opposition, insofar as it develops consistently, merges with the path of the Russian Opposition. This is the logic of the whole situation. Between these two stools there is no place to sit.

The Foster group, by its present policy, weakens itself, strengthens the right-wing leadership, and confuses the party. They take part, shame-faced and utterly contemptible, in the obscene lynching campaign against us, saying we have no right to oppose the decision of the Communist International on the Russian questions. The right-wing leaders retort: "Very good. We appreciate your help in lynching and expelling communists by wholesale, but the same rule you are supporting applies to you also. You have no right to oppose the decision of the Communist International on the American question. Your own expulsion is next on the agenda."

And why should they not speak this way? Is there some secret paragraph of the statutes of the Communist International which says that the decision on the Russian question is sacred and may not even be discussed under penalty of expulsion, while the decision on the American question may be opposed with impunity? These decisions are to a large extent bound together. For our part we are against both and openly say so.

We have no doubt that the overwhelming majority of the supporters of the Foster group—above all its proletarian and nonbureaucratized section—will soon find the right way out of the present dilemma. In the interest of the party, the sooner the better. The first step on this path will be to break with the tactic of trailing after the expulsion policy of the right-wing splitters and to take up the struggle against it.

The statement of the CEC majority says: "We feel confident—on the basis of our experiences during the attack of the government in 1919–20, when the party was driven underground—that the core of the party and its leadership are sound."

This can be said only with certain qualifications, which, in the interest of historical truth, must be mentioned. It is true that the core of the party membership, the expelled communists among them, held their ground in those days of trial. We, with them, stood at our posts and faced the raids, arrests, and indictments, as the record shows. This is true also of a section of the present leadership. But others of the present leadership—and not the least prominent ones—played the part of cowards, for whom the record of that time of trial by fire is a record not of glory but of shame. Those for whom history holds no honor should not write it.

The statement of Lovestone and Pepper entirely evades discussion of the principled issues raised by our stand for the Russian Opposition. It sets up the false theory of the Comintern as a bureaucratic machine. It makes unfortunate reference to party history where silence would have been wise. But it is the section of the statement dealing with the question of the "right danger" which most clearly and obviously stamps the whole document as the work of cynical charlatans—of people who imagine that facts may be turned upside down, that black may be made to appear white, and that any kind of fraud may be perpetrated if only one has a monopolistic control of the party press and if nobody's memory reaches back further than a month or two. With an ironical grin the opportunists declare war on opportunism; the bureaucrats demand the extermination of bureaucratism.

Our document "The Right Danger in the American Party," which sums up a long struggle against the opportunist policies of the present leadership of our party, deals quite fully and adequately with this question, as will be seen by a study of it. It explains the economic and political basis of the right danger in the present period and proves the opportunist line of the Lovestone group in its general conceptions and concretely in every field of party work.

Our document does not rest on general assertions. Facts and documents from the party records are cited in each case—minutes, resolutions, articles, speeches, etc. One need only refer to the support of the Socialist faker Panken in the election last fall; the motion to send comrades into the Socialist Party to "bore from within"; the refusal to support a national left-wing conference in the miners' union until the strike was a year old and had spent its force;[9] the opposition to the policy of organizing the unorganized into new unions—to mention only a few examples of the systematic opportunism of the party leadership, cited in our document, to show that the struggle within the party, which now takes on a sharper form, has not been waged over trifles.

Our "factionalism" has consisted of a stubborn daily fight against the opportunist course of the majority in the above-mentioned and in all other cases. In the Political Committee, at the February plenum, at the May plenum, and at the Sixth World Congress, the opposition fought on this line and proved its indictment of the right-wing leaders to the hilt.

The present declaration of the CEC majority on the question of the right danger must be taken together with its previous attitude. Before the Sixth Congress and at the Sixth Congress, they denied the existence of such a danger. They formed a close unity with all the extreme right elements in the party and defended all their own opportunist mistakes. They claimed that America was "exempted" from the international situation in this respect.

Under pressure of our hammering, our analysis, our elucidation of the problems, the fact of the right danger was indisputably established and was formally recognized by the Sixth Congress. It might be supposed that such an outcome would create an impossible situation for the "leaders" whose calculations had all been directly opposite, who had been following a right-wing line and firing only against the left. But our adepts in the art of political legerdemain were not even embarrassed. They solved the whole problem for themselves by turning around and immediately starting to pull their own right-wing rabbits out of our hat.

They forgot, and they expect the party to forget, everything they have done and said and written for more than a year. All the opportunist blunders (and worse than blunders) which they have committed or condoned, which we criticized and which they defended or denied, are now admitted and attributed to us as—"Trotskyism," as "outright opportunism."

Let the party member who claims the right to read and think for himself turn to our document "The Right Danger in the American Party," submitted to the Sixth Congress of the Communist International at a time when the opportunist leaders were still denying the existence of such a problem. He will find there a catalog of all the features of opportunism in our party which are cited in the CEC statement (and many more which it still tries to conceal), with documentary proof in each case of the responsibility of the authors of the CEC statement for these systematic opportunist crimes and mistakes.

The Lovestone-Pepper group of leaders, like their counterparts in other parties of the Comintern, like all opportunists and bureaucrats, rely on suppression of discussion and expulsion to maintain themselves in power. They want a party without any democratic rights of the members. They want a party with a sterile inner life. They want a party where the voice of the proletarian communist will be silenced. They want a party of passive hand raisers at the bottom and a petty-bourgeois clique of insolent bureaucrats at the top.

This is the real meaning of our expulsion, of the mass expulsion of rank-and-file communists, of the vile calumny heaped upon all those who dare to stand up and challenge them.

The fight against such a regime in the party and in the Communist International is an urgent revolutionary task. The proletarian masses in the party must awaken and take up this fight. They must break through the bureaucratic crust which has formed on top of the party and restore a normal party life in accord with Lenin's teaching. To help bring about this awakening we addressed our statement to the Political Committee with a full realization of the consequences. With the help of the communist workers in the ranks of the party we will continue to fight along this line until our aims are achieved.

'The Real Situation in Russia'

Published December 1, 1928

This review of Trotsky's book *The Real Situation in Russia* was published in *The Militant.*

In this book, written by Trotsky at the height of his powers as a revolutionary fighter and thinker, is to be found, for the first time in English, the authentic platform of the Russian Opposition led by him, and his annihilating reply to the five-year campaign of calumny and falsification which has run unchecked and unanswered in the official Communist press of the world.

This reply, after a silence of five years, consists mostly of documentary proofs which completely shatter the edifice of lies and which cannot but make the communist who has been fed exclusively on official misrepresentation rub his eyes in wonderment. The last letters of Lenin, which show that he foresaw the coming struggles and relied on Trotsky to defend his views, contain information hitherto unknown by our party. This information is directly opposite to all we have been told.

The other principal section of the book is the platform of the Russian Opposition, prepared for the Fifteenth Party Congress. Contrary to all party procedure established under Lenin's leadership, the platform was outlawed and refused official publication. Oppositionists who attempted to print it illegally were thrown into prison. It has never been published to this day by the Communist International or by any of its affiliated parties.

It is true that our party, which had never seen it, voted against it "unanimously," as did the other parties, but its validity remains unchanged by those machine-made votes. It is a document of Leninism from the first word to the last. It is the platform on the basis of which alone the Communist Party of the Soviet Union can solve its problems on the revolutionary path. The events themselves, which have been transpiring since the outlawing of the platform and the expulsion and exile of its authors, testify to this in louder and more insistent tones every day.

We have been told many times that the platform of the Russian Opposition is counterrevolutionary, Menshevik, Social Democratic, etc. But, strange to relate, none of these classes and elements, from the big bourgeoisie to its petty-bourgeois and philistine retainers, appreciate it as such. Of course, all enemies of our movement seek to exploit the controversies in our ranks, and the jailing and exiling of the Opposition supporters was no exception. Those who jailed and exiled them—and those whose occupation it is to defend this infamous crime—seek to prove thereby that Trotsky is identified with the imperialist enemies of Soviet Russia and their lackeys. But if we turn to the columns of the bourgeois press to read their sober estimate of Trotsky's platform, we find a different and a highly instructive story.

The authentic organs of big capital put their thumbs down on this platform. And that is not all. The little hangers-on—from the pale, sanitary *New Republic* to the scavenging *Jewish Daily Forward,* from the bourgeois-liberal *Nation* to the sexless liberal *Modern Quarterly*—all do the same.

The *New York Times,* the most authoritative spokesman of American imperialism, reiterating what it has already said in a score of editorials, says in an unsigned review of *The Real Situation in Russia* by Trotsky and *Leninism* by Stalin, on July 29, 1928:

> Back of Trotsky's political grievance against Stalin is his personal grievance. . . .
>
> When we turn from Trotsky to Stalin we find instead of the feverish indignation of a disappointed man the calm and confident arguments of a practical executive who has had no difficulty in adjusting his theories to the daily emergencies of power. . . .
>
> The publication of Trotsky's book will doubtless turn some American Communists from Stalinists into Trotskians. But let us repeat, though it will not make Stalin a hero in the eyes of the sinful bourgeoisie it will probably cause them to rejoice that he and not Trotsky is exercising power in Moscow.

So bays the big dog of American imperialism. Let us now turn to the *New Republic,* which contains a review of Trotsky's book in its issue of November 7 from the pen of the well-known J.B.S. Hardman (Salutsky), the literary henchman of the labor fakers who rule the Amalgamated Clothing Workers by blackjack and revolver—and expulsion of communists. We were assured only the other day in the statement of the CEC that we would be able to rely on the full support of Salutsky in our fight for the platform of the Russian Opposition. But Salutsky seems to have different ideas. In fact, if you make allowances for the differences of style and manner of expression common to literary people, you will see that his ideas are essentially the *same* as those of the *New York Times*. He says:

"Trotsky's criticism, obviously overemphasized, will not convince those who are outside the struggle. His repeated claims that he and not the Stalinites are true to the tenets of Leninism will seem queer to the non-orthodox. Indeed, why may not revolutionists occasionally run out of the footsteps of canonized authority? Nor will Stalin be destroyed by pointing to the fact that Lenin had little use for him."

Salutsky goes a step further and deals a blow at this sentimental nonsense about the imprisonment and exiling of the Oppositionists. He has made editorial defense of the blackjacking of communists in the Amalgamated Clothing Workers union too many times to have any squeamishness on this point. He writes:

"Trotsky resents the violence which the Stalin regime employs against the Opposition, but Stalin did not father the idea of a one-minded, strait-jacketed party, intolerant of even friendly criticism, Lenin did. Trotsky knows it, and he advanced the argument that 'Violence can play an enormous role, but only under one condition—that it is subordinated to true class policy.' But is not Stalin ready to say that his is a true class policy?"

Let the apostles of violence against communists study the writings of Salutsky. They can get some clever arguments from him. They will also find that this "ally" of Trotsky has a most unique way of "supporting" him:

"Trotsky wishes the party preserved in its revolutionary virginity. He wishes it to remain a party of no compromise, of no trading with capitalism, the enemy. Not so Stalin. He has his ear to the ground. He senses that the early revolutionary zeal is over. Not only the country is tired, the revolutionists themselves are. One may arouse their patriotism for self-defense, but it would be difficult to move them to a crusading march. Hence his theory of 'Socialism in one country.' The Soviet State is a reality. Stalin seeks to preserve it. . . ."

Finally there is the review of Trotsky's book in the "liberal" *Nation* of November 14, 1928, by Albert Rhys Williams, which does nothing but expose Williams as a petty-bourgeois philistine of the grossest sort. For this mere journalist, the world-shaking problems raised by the Opposition are resolved into four simple "truths": That the peasant is the real "hero" of the Russian revolution; that the struggle is one between individual leaders; that the documents presented in Trotsky's book have been printed before in the party press and not suppressed; and that the exiling, imprisonment, and disemployment of Opposition workers and leaders is a jocular business which even the Opposition takes in the spirit of good, healthy fun.

Williams declares that the documents printed in Trotsky's book were published and not outlawed or suppressed. This is a conscious, deliberate, and typically American journalistic falsehood. The platform of the Opposition was *never,* to this day, printed in the Russian or international party press. For proof of this, turn to *Inprecor,* vol. 7, no. 64, published November 17, 1927. There, in a report of Stalin's speech at the meeting which expelled Trotsky, is a whole section which begins "Why did we not print the well-known 'Platform of the Opposition,'" and ends "These were the reasons which compelled us to refuse the publication of the 'platform' of the Opposition."

The section of Trotsky's book dealing with the falsification of history by the official apparatus has not been, and is not now, printed anywhere in the official party press. The testament of Lenin, first denied as a forgery but now admitted to be genuine, was not printed anywhere in the party press. In short, 99 percent of the material contained in this book of Trotsky's has been either suppressed or outlawed by the machinery and press of the CPSU, the Comintern, and its national sections.

So much for Williams's attempt to convince the American communists that they have already had adequate opportunity to study this material which has never been printed before. But it is in his treatment of the persecution and violence against the Opposition that he reaches the lowest depths of philistinism. According to this shallow "feature writer," the whole thing was a comradely joke, accompanied by merriment on all sides. He recites that the comrades of one victimized Oppositionist gave him a party on the eve of his departure. For Williams this is proof that exile is a happy event. "A real old time Russian *vecherinka* [evening party]," says this trifling dilettante.

According to him, the revolutionist who does not whine under punishment does not feel it. If he had utilized his literary connections with our own American revolutionary movement, in the days when scores and even hundreds were being sent to prison, he could easily have learned that the last nights of freedom for many of them going off to serve long sentences was made the occasion for parties in their honor, at which there was no wailing by the victims; and with equal intelligence he could have passed off the whole affair as a good-natured jest.

We might ask this complacent word-juggler, however, to explain the humor in the imprisonment of George Audreytchine and of scores of others who attempted to print the platform of the Opposition, which he says was printed legally. We might ask him for proof that the hundreds and even thousands of communist workers who were expelled from the party and *simultaneously deprived of employment* for supporting the Opposition, had absolutely no hard feelings about the matter.

The philistine article of Williams is reprinted from the bourgeois-liberal *Nation* by the *Daily Worker* with a eulogistic introduction, in which the editor, Robert Minor, refers to Trotsky's book as counterrevolutionary. This, however, does not of itself make Trotsky's case hopeless. It will be remembered that Minor once wrote against Lenin, using for his medium of expression the capitalist press. Minor changed his mind a little about Lenin.[10] Why should we not be optimists and trust that he will also learn better in the case of Trotsky?

Gangsterism!

Published December 15, 1928

The following article was published in *The Militant.*

On Monday evening, December 10, two women comrades, Maria Reinl and Pauline Gutringer, who were selling *The Militant* on the sidewalk in front of the Workers Center on Union Square, New York City, were set upon by an organized squad which had been detailed to execute the slogan given out by party officials—to "prevent the sale of *The Militant* at all costs and beat up the Oppositionists."

"Get out of here, you counterrevolutionary prostitutes!" This and similar commands, mixed with unprintable obscenities, were hurled at the two working-class women before a crowd of several hundred which quickly gathered.

Screaming epithets and calling the women comrades every name in the vocabulary of the underworld, they seized the two comrades by the arms and began to push them away. The communist women resisted and stood their ground. The papers were torn from their hands.

Comrade Reinl attempted to recover some of the papers and received a fist blow in the face.

The police appeared and *immediately seized the two women,* leaving their attackers unmolested. The two communist women who had attempted to sell *The Militant* on the sidewalk were then forcibly driven away by the police.

These events are the direct result of a planned campaign of incitement by party officials who themselves never yet took part in a fight and who lacked even the courage to participate in the attack on the women comrades. Wolfe, who ran away from the party like a craven during the Palmer raids and also after the Bridgeman raid,[11] directly incited to physical violence against the Opposition in his speech at the Workers Forum on November 25. Dr. Markoff, in his speech to the Italian party membership meeting on November 28, said, "The Oppositionists are worse than Mussolini and his Fascists. We must beat them politically and physically." Party comrades have been directly instructed by such functionaries as Miller and Benjamin that they must not speak to the members of the Opposition but should spit upon them. More than that, physical assaults against comrades attempting to sell *The Militant* on the streets have been directly discussed and planned in committee meetings of the party in the New York district, where every kind of bourgeois and anticommunist literature is freely sold in the party's bookstore.

The methods of violence which the bureaucrats are copying from the labor fakers are necessary only for a false policy. Their methods condemn their policy and will defeat it, for communist ideas are stronger than the gangster's fist.

None of the Foster comrades participated in the shameful gangster attack. It is primarily the proletarian revolutionists in the party ranks who must defeat this course.

They must burn the incipient fascist tactics out of the party with a white-hot iron. They must compel a free discussion of the disputed questions in a normal communist way.

For our part, we will take up the challenge of gangsterism incited and organized by poltroons who never yet took a blow on the picket line or in a raid. Our task and duty is to reach the Communist workers with our views. Since we are deprived of our party rights by expulsion and suppression, we must do this through *The Militant.* We will sell *The Militant* before every workers' institution and meeting. The rights of the revolutionary workers are higher than the rights of landlordism. We will maintain these rights by struggle. In this struggle our strength will be multiplied by steadfast belief in our views and by our courage to defend them.

Our appeal to the party members

December 17, 1928

This speech was given at the plenary session of the Central Executive Committee of the Workers (Communist) Party. It was published in *The Militant* of January 1, 1929.

Comrades:

Many of the most important events and turning points in our party life have been summed up in party gatherings which stand out in party history as the expression of these events. The present meeting of the Central Executive Committee, called to confirm the control of the party by an opportunistic and bureaucratic leadership and to endorse the expulsion of its opponents, is such a gathering. It will represent in party history a downward curve.

In most of the significant party meetings of the past, certain features, certain details stood out and gave in themselves an indication of the whole character of the gatherings. This is true also of this one. Let me mention a couple of these characteristic features of the present meeting of the Central Executive Committee.

We were impressed as we entered the hall to see Comrade Devine occupying the post of chairman—a new distinction for him; and you have all heard him tell us with a brusque authority—which is also new for him—that we will be given one hour and no more to answer the three-hour report against us. The chairmanship of Comrade Devine will not be forgotten, for it is a symbol of the meeting.

He is the district organizer in that district (Minnesota) where the expulsion of proletarian communists for their views has attained the widest proportions. Twenty-one comrades there have already been expelled, and they are precisely the comrades whose names have stood out in the labor movement of Minnesota for years as the very banner of communism. The prestige our party enjoys in the labor movement there is due mainly to them. And it is to their loyal, untiring, and sacrificial work that we owe the 5,000 votes—more than 10 percent of the total votes for our presidential candidates—which we received in the elections in Minnesota.

The election of Comrade Devine, who is responsible for the expulsion of these communists, as chairman of the plenum has a meaning in the light of those facts. It signifies the conferring of exceptional honors upon the district organizers who bring about the greatest disruption. It puts the seal of approval upon the policy of mass expulsions of proletarian communists. Thus the chairmanship of Devine is a symbol of the plenum.

The second significant detail I wish to mention is the selection of Pepper as the reporter against us. This fact epitomizes the plenum, and the whole issue around which it centers, better than anything we could say. It demonstrates in deed that the fight against us, because it lacks all principle, must be placed from the beginning on the lowest basis and must use the vilest instruments. The selection of Pepper, the bearer in the Communist movement of all that is most corrupt and most detestable to revolutionaries, as the reporter against us, to bring here the demand for our expulsion, in itself discredits that demand.

The very fact that the sewage of slander against us and our comrades is poured out officially here through the mouth of Pepper puts an evaluation on this slander, it answers and refutes it. I will not insult a single communist by defending him against the accusations of this characterless adventurer, whose unspeakable record shames the Communist movement of the world. The communist militants who constitute the forces of the Opposition, with the honorable record of the years behind them, are in no need of such a defense. For revolutionaries, the calumny of a Pepper is only a mark of distinction and a badge of honor. It is those who elected Pepper as the reporter against us who will have need of this defense before the party and before the proletariat, which judges the party by its spokesmen.

In the period that has intervened since our expulsion on October 25, we have continued to regard ourselves as party members and have conducted ourselves as communists, as we have done since the foundation of the party and even for years before that. Every step we have taken has been guided by this conception. Those acts which went beyond the bounds of ordinary party procedure in bringing our views before the party, were imposed upon us by the action of the party leadership in denying us the right and opportunity to defend our views within the party by normal means. Our views relate to principled questions, and therefore it is our duty openly to defend them in spite of all attempts to suppress them.

We are bound to do this also in the future under all

circumstances. However, we said on October 25 and we repeat now that we are unconditionally willing to confine our activity to regular party channels and to discontinue all extraordinary methods the moment our party rights are restored and we are permitted to defend our views in the party press and at party meetings. The decision and the responsibility rest wholly with the majority of the Central Executive Committee.

Events since our expulsion have only served to confirm more surely the correctness of the views of the Russian Opposition, which we support. The momentous developments in the Communist Party of the Soviet Union and throughout the Comintern have that meaning and no other. Life itself is proving the validity of their platform. Even those who fought that platform, who misrepresented it and hid it from the party and the Comintern, are today compelled, under the pressure of events and forces which overwhelm them, to give lip-service to it, to pretend to adopt it. Many of the statements and proposals of the Opposition which were branded as counterrevolutionary a year ago are today solemnly repeated, almost word for word, as the quintessence of Bolshevism.

Meanwhile their sponsors—the true leaders and defenders of the Russian revolution—remain in exile, and there is no guarantee whatever that the present advertised "left course" will mean anything more than a cover for further concessions to the right wing, whose policy directly undermines the dictatorship. The victorious fight of the party masses in Russia and throughout the Comintern against this disgraceful and dangerous course cannot be much longer postponed.

[Note: Here followed an exposition of various parts of the platform of the Russian Opposition which are connected with the present developments, such as the internal questions of the Soviet Union, the crisis in the Communist Party of Germany, etc., etc. Since these questions are being elaborated in separate articles in *The Militant* this part of the speech is deleted to avoid repetition.]

Our views on the problems of the American party and its leadership outlined in our statement to the Political Committee on October 25 hold good today and have been underscored by the whole conduct of the Pepper-Lovestone faction since that time. We spoke then of "its opportunist political outlook, its petty-bourgeois origin, its corrupt factionalism, its careerism and adventurism in the class struggle" as "the greatest menace to the party." To speak now about the present party leadership with objectivity and precision, we could not use different language to characterize it. This estimate is written in unmistakable words in the election campaign, the trade union work, the inner-party regime, and in all phases of party life and activity.

Since October 25, the Pepper-Lovestone leadership has taken further steps on the course of bureaucratic disruption which confronts the party today as a deadly menace—a course which began with the expulsion of communists, copied from the labor fakers, and which has already taken another weapon from the same arsenal: the weapon of gangsterism. Everyone sitting here knows the facts about this. You know that inspired and organized gangster attacks have been made against us on the public streets, not once but several times.

Woe to the party of the workers if its proletarian kernel does not arise and stamp out these incipient fascist tactics at the very beginning! The blows from the blackjacks of gangsters which have descended on the heads of the Opposition communists are blows at the very foundation of the party. This abominable gangsterism, for which the leaders of the two factions collaborating against us, the

Lovestone faction and the Foster faction, are directly responsible, is hated by every honest worker. It discredits the party before the working class and threatens to deprive the party of its moral and political position in the struggle against these methods of the trade union reactionaries.

Only the blindest bureaucrat, or the most irresponsible dilettante adventuring in the movement, can fail to see the unbounded consequences of the bureaucratic expulsion policy of the Lovestone-Pepper leadership and react with alarm against it. It directly threatens the existence of the party. The first step was the expulsion of three members of the Central Executive Committee in the futile hope that the issues could thereby be disposed of. But the very next day these issues arose again in a wider circle as a result of the action against us, and called forth new expulsions. In the six weeks which have elapsed since that time more than sixty proletarians have been expelled from the party for their views and glibly denounced as renegades and counterrevolutionaries by people who are scarcely worthy to criticize them in any respect.

Bureaucratic suppression has its own logic. It begins with the expulsion of individuals and ends with the disruption of the movement. Yesterday we saw the attempt to suppress the views of the Oppositionists, who fight the party regime on principled grounds. Today already inspired resolutions from the party units are making the same demand against the limited criticisms of the Foster group, with the threat of organizational measures after the packed and gerrymandered convention has "endorsed" the regime. Bureaucratism is alien to the proletarian communist movement. Bureaucratism cannot stand criticism. It cannot stand discussion. Bureaucratism, which is an expression of bourgeois influence, and Lenin's proletarian doctrine cannot live together.

The regime of bureaucratic strangulation which expels its outspoken opponents and bludgeons the party into silence has become an international phenomenon of the period. This is the only key to an understanding of its absolutely unprecedented excesses. A real struggle against it cannot be made without an understanding of its international scope. On this, as well as on the other principled questions, the fight of the proletarian communist elements in all parties unites with the Bolshevik fight of the Russian Opposition under the leadership of Trotsky.

At the Fourteenth Congress of the Communist Party of the Soviet Union, Stalin issued a warning against the course he later adopted, and predicted its disruptive consequences. He defended there the refusal to expel Trotsky from the Political Bureau and said: "We are against the policy of lopping off, of blood-letting (it was blood they wanted). It is a dangerous thing. One day you lop off this limb. Tomorrow another and the next day a third. And after a while what becomes of the party?"

Stalin forgot these words, so full of prophetic significance. He formed a factional combination with the right wing to suppress and expel the left, the Opposition. He gave the signal for the same line in all the parties of the Comintern. As a result, in the recent years we have seen everywhere a strengthening of the opportunist elements, an enormous development and entrenchment of bureaucratism, and wholesale expulsions of the proletarian left—the core of the workers' vanguard. All the little Stalins in all the parties are bolstering themselves up by these means.

This meeting of the Central Executive Committee has an unusually large attendance, which has been gathered together to applaud our expulsion. The composition of the audience is also symptomatic. Of the two hundred or more in the hall, almost every one is a functionary or employee of the party, or of an organization or institution closely related to the party. There are not half a dozen workers from the shops present. The opportunist leaders of the needle trades are here, but the rank-and-file communists, who fight for communist policies against them, are barred. The fiction of "proletarian representation" was never more clearly exposed than it is by these simple facts. All this is in correlation to the shifting class composition of the upper circles of the party.

The wholesale expulsion of proletarian fighters goes hand in hand with the steady recruitment of all kinds of dubious petty-bourgeois careerist and half-baked intellectual elements. The class composition of the party, particularly in the New York district, has been seriously affected by this process in recent years and has had a direct expression in the opportunistic policies of the party and the strengthening of the opportunist elements generally.

In the upper circles of the party, in the party apparatus, this increased proportion of nonproletarians is enormously expanded. Under the Lovestone regime these elements are appearing more and more on all sides as party representatives, officials, managers, directors, teachers, supervisors. Coming to these positions without sufficient prerequisites, they bring with them the detestable careerist attributes of insolence, arrogance, and pride of office, antagonizing and alienating the worker elements and thrusting them aside.

The "education" dispensed in the party school under such auspices is becoming a distorted caricature of revolutionary training. It is led almost exclusively by schoolteachers, dentists, professors, journalists—everything except proletarian leaders tested by the class struggle.

The party must examine this question in direct connection with the struggle against the right danger and the opportunist leaders who are its bearers. It is necessary at once to take a complete registration of the party membership with the object of precisely determining its class composition. A reorganization of the party apparatus from top to bottom, up to and including the Central Executive Committee, placing the overwhelming majority of the positions in the hands of experienced and tested party workers of proletarian origin, must be effected at once. For the next period, until a proletarian stabilization has been achieved in the party and its apparatus, the party membership must be closed entirely to nonproletarian elements. Even then their admittance to the party must be carefully restricted and supervised.

The failure of the party to grow in the favorable objective circumstances, the defeats it has suffered where victories were possible, its poor showing in the election with the field to itself as the party of the class struggle, the collapse of its trade union work, etc., are due primarily to the false leadership. Official bombast and factional trickery can no longer obscure or hide these condemning facts. The fight for the party is a fight against the systematic opportunist policy of the leadership and the bureaucratic regime with which it fortifies itself against control and correction from below.

This internal regime is tied up with the external opportunistic line and is an expression of it. A serious struggle for a correction of the opportunist external policy, which weakens the party and consequently the class before their enemies, is impossible without the most determined, stubborn, and relentless fight for party democracy. Party democracy is the means whereby the policy of the party can be corrected and its leadership reorganized on a proletarian, communist basis.

The raising of the issue of party democracy, and the education of the party membership on its meaning and significance, are made all the more necessary by the confusion that prevails on the whole question of party government, of forms of working-class organization, of centralization and discipline, which prevails. This confusion is fostered by the monstrous distortions of Lenin's teachings disseminated by the party leadership and is the direct result of them.

The Tenth Congress of the Communist Party of Russia, held under Lenin's leadership at the end of the civil war, said: "The form of organization and the methods of work are entirely determined by the specific character of the given historic situation and the problems which arise out of that situation."

The resolution of the Tenth Congress said further: "The needs of the current movement demand a new organization form. That form is workers' democracy." We do not advocate the mechanical adoption of the forms and methods prescribed by Lenin for the Russian party, which works under vastly different conditions from ours. But if workers' democracy could be proclaimed by Lenin for the Russian party, with the responsibility of the proletarian dictatorship on its shoulders, then it is a hundred times more applicable to our party under the given historic circumstances in America.

The present leaders and teachers of the party distort and misapply all these conceptions. They substitute the idea of discipline in the formal, mechanical sense for the Leninist doctrine of democratic centralism. Our party, which ought to be the champion of workers' democracy throughout the entire labor movement, is making the very word taboo. All democracy is indiscriminately labeled bourgeois democracy. This false and thoroughly reactionary idea is heard on all sides, and Comrade Weinstone, who has become the full-blown type of party martinet, has made an interjection here to the same effect. Party democracy, of course, does not exclude, but presupposes centralization and discipline. It is just the bureaucratic distortions and mechanical conceptions of discipline which give rise to syndicalist prejudices in this respect.

The party must make an end of this by struggle against the leadership that fosters and expresses it. The first step is the breaking down of the disruptive expulsion policy and the reinstatement of the expelled communists with the right to express their views in the party by normal means. The policy of administrative gagging, suppression, and terrorism must be overthrown. The worker communist must be able to feel at home in his own party. He must have the right and feel the freedom to open his mouth and say what he thinks without being called into the office of some party official or other, like a recalcitrant workingman in a factory, and threatened with discipline. All talk of party democracy in the face of suppression on all sides and the wholesale expulsion of comrades for their views is a swindle.

The party needs a real and free discussion. The suppressed documents of the Russian Opposition, dealing with the vital world problems of the period, must be printed and made available for the party members. The party must have the right to discuss the questions upon which there are differences, and not merely those upon which there is general agreement. The party must discuss the international questions and not merely the national and local ones. The party must have the right to discuss the questions confronting the Communist Party of the Soviet Union in order to participate intelligently in their solution. The party members must have the right to discuss *all* the questions of the Comintern, since they are part of the Comintern and should not regard it as an institution standing apart from them and making decisions without their participation.

There is one feature of the proceedings against us which gives them a tragicomic aspect. We see sitting here, ready to raise their hands to expel us, not a few comrades who exercised this privilege once before. Olgin, Trachtenberg, Kruse, and others raised their hands just as high to expel us communists, us defenders of the Russian revolution, us followers of Lenin and Trotsky, from the Socialist Party in 1919. Then as now they did not spare slander and vituperation in the process. We were also in those days called renegades, agents of the capitalists, and even spies and provocateurs. It was not we but they who had to repent the actions and swallow the words. We survived all that—the expulsions and the slander—because we were communists, and we will survive it now for the same reason.

We live and struggle in the epoch of wars and revolutions, when the events of days and weeks transcend in their magnitude and importance the events of years and decades of other times. We communists, who are the standard-bearers of the interests of the proletariat and the fighters for the future of humanity, cannot for a moment forget the immensity of our historic responsibilities, which are only magnified by the fewness of our numbers here in the reactionary citadel of world imperialism.

The sharpening international complications which push us every day nearer to the verge of imperialist war, the great and unavoidable difficulties of the Soviet Union in its capitalist encirclement, the colossal problems and tasks confronting our party in the class struggle—these facts are raising the question of party unity, of the full utilization of all the tested forces, in all its insistence. The burning issue of party unity demands a solution, not on the basis of bureaucratic machinations but on the basis of Lenin's teachings.

We speak here for this unity. We declare ourselves ready to do all in our power to bring it about and make it secure, disregarding all the slander against us. We make one demand only: that we have the right to maintain our views and to defend them within the party by party means.

We pioneers of Communism in America, standing here at the plenum of the Central Executive Committee, fully conscious of the great solemnity of the occasion, and with a full sense of responsibility for our words, say openly to the plenum and to the entire party: The views for which we have been expelled are Leninist views. We stand by them. As revolutionists we can do nothing else, and we will continue to stand by them and work for their victory in the future. On this basis we present our appeal for the reinstatement into the party of ourselves and the other expelled comrades who share our views.

Pepper ended his report against us with the prophecy that this will be the last time we will ever address a party gathering. But this statement will be refuted by the facts of the future just as his other statements are refuted by the facts of the past. In the past during our entire lives we have always fought on the side of the working class when some of those who expel us, including Pepper, stood on the other side of the barricades. We will be at our posts also in the future. Let the Peppers make predictions to the contrary if they wish. It is not we revolutionists with unsullied records who will be discredited thereby. For such talk of the future only invites a recollection of their own dishonorable past which discredits them.

The party needs the scores of loyal and tested communists who are being expelled today, and cannot spare them. The party will make its voice heard and assert its will. The party will call us back to our rightful places in the ranks, and will do this sooner than you dream. We say this because the platform of the Opposition represents the class interests of the proletariat on an international scale, and the Communist Party will adopt that platform. We say this because we have confidence in the proletarian ranks of the party, in their revolutionary spirit and will. Therefore our final words at this meeting are a revolutionary salutation to the party which we have helped to found and build and from which no power on earth can tear us away.

For an open policy

December 20, 1928

This was a letter to Albert Glotzer in Chicago.

Dear Al:

This is a reply to several of your letters addressed to the three of us. With me doing the dictating and Shachtman, who has become proletarianized since his expulsion, acting (unwillingly!—M.S.) as stenographer.

We note what you say about Mike [Zalisko]. Waverings of this kind of course are to be expected, and even some desertions under the heavy pressure in which we have to carry on our struggle. Nevertheless, I hope you have succeeded in overcoming that in this case.

We printed a list of expulsions in no. 3 of *The Militant,* which you have probably seen by this time. There is a group of eight Italian comrades in New York, several Finnish comrades, and other individual expulsions to be added to it next week. The total now runs up to about seventy in the U.S. and over a dozen in Canada.

Your letter of December 11, even though it was a short one (I mean the one addressed to Max), has the same strain which we have spoken about before. You say it is your policy "not to expose our elements too much." We are firmly convinced that this attitude is wrong and is mainly responsible for the failure to have greater success in Chicago. It gives the offensive entirely to the other side. What the Opposition needs is comrades who support its platform and spread its propaganda broadcast. Silent sympathizers motivated mainly by the fear of expulsion do not help in such a fight. I have written about this before and have referred to it at length in the letter to Arne with particular reference to the miners. I wish you comrades would take this question up at your next meeting and change the policy. I recall one of the reports we received stating that only the five expelled attend the meetings. What about the comrades still in the party who agree with us? If they don't attend meetings and don't participate in the work, what help are they to us? There are and always will be enough comrades in the party who will complain against the expulsions because they do not see the further implications of the fight. It is a big waste to have our comrades who really agree with our platform in whole or in large part confine their activities to this.

In your letter you enclosed a copy of the letter from Angelo with a note that it is not to be made public at this period; as we wrote to Arne, this tactic is beyond our comprehension. Also, why did Angelo allow the meeting to end without a vote being taken, and why do we allow the bureaucrats to get away with this kind of a game in Gary and other places? All this means that they are *out-maneuvering* us in the Chicago district and making it appear that the five expelled comrades are isolated. We fear that this will be so in reality if the tactics are not changed.

We were very much obliged to get the detailed information about the individual comrades in the letter of December 11 to Marty. We are very glad to note that Edwards did not fall for their maneuvers to compromise him, and hope the others will take the same stand, not merely declaring their position in the committees but telling the whole party membership about it.

You should see Comrade Kolarik. His letter appeared to be very sympathetic, and he could get supporters for us among the Czecho-Slovaks if he agrees with our position, as he is quite an able comrade.

I note what you say about Caddie Hill and wish to warn you against the attitude of rejecting the support of any comrades who want to come with us. I think we told you that she sent a five-dollar contribution, and that is a practical demonstration of sympathy. Why don't you try to get her to apply for readmission into the party and take part in the Opposition group? The same applies to Jurich. You know it was the opinion of all that his expulsion from the party was a frame-up, and we should not make the slightest concession to these disreputable methods by blacklisting any comrade whom they select without good communist reasons. If he supports the line of the Opposition and has been refused admission into the Party without good reason, he should be eligible in our opinion to participate in the Opposition group, on condition of course that he again reapplies for admission into the party. If they refuse to accept him it is their responsibility, not ours. In general they are following the policy of framing up and expelling a number of comrades for secondary or fake reasons in order to conceal and minimize the number who have been expelled on political grounds. We must not let them succeed with such a tactic. They expelled eight or ten good comrades in Cleveland this way. But we are going to try to organize every one of them, as we consider them good communists.

We agree with your theory that there will be further shifting after the convention. This will be hastened also by international developments. In the meantime it is quite possible that some of those who have already taken the step with us will weaken under pressure. We must anticipate this possibility and not allow it to bring demoralization into the ranks. Our special task in the next period is to organize and educate all our supporters and to build a firm foundation under *The Militant*. . . .

We had two letters from Allard, the first of which was printed in no. 3 of *The Militant*. Have not heard from him since. Paul Simonson hasn't seen the light yet. We made the first break in the YWL in New York and now have a group of three there definitely with us and many more are on the way. Only one of them has been expelled so far.

I am speaking in New Haven at a mass meeting tomorrow night, and we are having a big public meeting at the Labor Temple here on January 8. Immediately after that, I start on a tour which will include Minneapolis and Kansas City. I will land in Chicago on the sixteenth and be there three days, and will also be in Chicago again on the twenty-second during the day on the way to Kansas City from Minneapolis and on the twenty-sixth also during the day on the way from Kansas City to New York. A comrade here has promised to donate fifty dollars toward the expenses of the trip. I will come there loaded down with arguments (against you mainly, Al—M.S.), information, and militancy. If you can get Kruse or Simons to agree to a debate, you are authorized to offer them a bonus of one-half of the wages due to Shachtman from the ILD.

You ask how our supporters are standing up. So far the

only one who has weakened is Watkins in Minnesota, and he was not really with us but merely reacted against the expulsions in one meeting. Rose [Karsner] is with us but is ill, and you will hear about her a little later.

Fraternally yours,

Jim

A burglary—its political meaning

Published January 1, 1929

The following article was published in *The Militant.*

On Sunday evening, December 23, the residence of Rose Karsner and Jim Cannon, where the editorial work of *The Militant* is also conducted, was entered by burglars during the absence of the occupants.

The burglary was a professional job. Deep, defacing marks on the door-jamb indicate that entry was effected by forcing the lock, which was a strong one, with a jimmy. It was also quite obviously timed for the occasion, as Comrade Karsner had been confined to the house by illness and Sunday evening was the first time in several weeks when there was no one home.

The following material was taken: our letter file, account book, receipt book, editorial material, some manuscripts, bank book, partial list of subscribers to *The Militant,* and some other material of this kind. Nothing else was taken.

The robbery subjects us to some temporary inconveniences

but will not seriously disrupt our work, as we had taken the precaution to keep copies of the most important manuscripts and addresses in another place in anticipation of such an event. Its perpetrators can learn from the stolen material our meager financial situation and lack of resources, and the names of some comrades who had been in correspondence with us but who have not yet taken a definite position on the questions at issue.

That is all. There is not a line in our correspondence relating to any activities or "connections" of ours which conflict in the slightest degree with our public declarations in *The Militant,* and no such "evidence" can be produced by the organizers of the burglary unless it is forged. On the contrary, definite and complete proof is contained in our stolen correspondence to refute every one of such accusations.[12]

A question for communists of far more importance than any "exposures" in the *Forward* style of stolen or forged material *is the political significance of underworld methods in party disputes.* Four years ago when the proposal first came before the Political Committee that our party should sanction such methods in a trade union fight, we took a determined stand against it in principle. We said then that the toleration of such a procedure would prove to be a Frankenstein, that it would inevitably lead to the corruption of the left wing and even of the party itself; that it would lead to giving up the ideological and political struggle for the mobilization of the masses—which is the weapon of communism—and submitting disputes to the arbitrament of the gangster's blackjack and the burglar's jimmy—the weapons of reaction. We exaggerated the danger then, as we thought, in order to stamp out such tendencies at the very beginning. Many things have happened in the meantime.

Let the proletarian communists in the party ranks ponder over this question and ask themselves: Who brings these absolutely unprecedented methods into factional disputes in the party? What class influence is behind them, and *where do they lead?*

They will search in vain for the necessary key to these questions unless they see them in their political connection. Bureaucratism, expulsions, gangsterism, and burglary are not isolated phenomena. They are all bound together and they are the expression and instruments of an adventurist leadership and its opportunist political line. This leadership, lacking a proletarian class basis and outlook, lacking any experience or contact with mass movements, regarding the inner-party struggle for control of the apparatus as an adventure and an end in itself, is an absolutely artificial, unhealthy, and impossible leadership for a proletarian party. It resorts to these methods alien to communism because its regime is collapsing and it cannot maintain itself in any other way. It resorts to bureaucratic administration and to expulsion of communists because it fears control from below. It incites and organizes gangsterism and robbery because it has no principled ground. It cannot stand up in the ideological and political fight.

This leadership—corrupt, bureaucratic, and opportunist through and through—is driving the party with all means and all speed to a split. The expulsion of almost a hundred communists of the Opposition is only a beginning. There are an equal number under charges. They are laying the ground for the beginning of the expulsion of the Foster group after the convention. Clear indications of this are already to be seen in their entire preconvention campaign and by the removals and suspensions now taking place on various pretexts.

The Pepper-Lovestone faction, leading the party to defeats

in the class struggle and faced with an ever-growing revolt from below, must and will expel the entire articulate proletarian opposition. The bureaucratism, the expulsions, the gangsterism and burglary are all parts of this process.

It is impossible to wage an effective fight against these methods without attacking the false political line which they express and with which they are bound up. And it is likewise futile to quarrel with them merely over the formulation of theses and resolutions (as the Foster group leaders do) without exposing their lack of principle, without fighting for party democracy, against bureaucratism, corruption, and underworld methods. These people have no definite principles. They can change their slogans from "Fire Against the Left" at the May plenum to a hue and cry about the "Right Danger" at the December plenum; they can change from opposition to the building of new unions in April to the policy of organizing new unions overnight—and on paper—in August, without changing their fundamental position and their completely cynical attitude in either case.

It is the task of the Opposition, in the light of the recent events, to wage its fight against the Lovestone leadership more stubbornly and relentlessly than before, to expose its incompetence and corruption from all sides, sparing nobody who in one way or another is a party to it.

About eighteen months ago, Comrade Weinstone came to us in alarm with the declaration that the corruption, opportunism, and cynicism of the Lovestone group leaders was such that they would destroy the party if they secured control. He supplemented all that he knew of them by what he had learned as a member of their faction. He proposed a bloc with us and with the Foster group to secure the party against this. In our opinion, this proposal corresponded with the best interests of the party.

The bloc was formed and a majority of the Central Executive Committee was secured in support of it. This majority was set aside by the Executive Committee of the Communist International on the initiative of Bukharin, and the Lovestone faction was mechanically entrenched in control of the party. The fears expressed then by Weinstone were nonetheless valid, and they have been confirmed a thousand times in the intervening period. Weinstone has capitulated to the "corrupt faction machine of Lovestone and Pepper," as he characterized it then, and has become a henchman of it. The issue remains, however, and is clearer now, in all its international implications, than ever before. Those who see that issue and fight on that line as a part of the Russian and International Opposition are the true defenders of the party and its future.

Platform of the Communist Opposition

Published February 15 and 22, 1929

The following platform, addressed to the Sixth National Convention of the Workers (Communist) Party by James P. Cannon, Arne Swabeck, Martin Abern, and Max Shachtman, was published in *The Militant.*

The position of the Russian revolution

The present position of the Russian revolution and its Marxist-Leninist foundation is the dominating factor in the world movement that must determine the course of every communist and revolutionary worker. It overshadows all other questions. An examination of its present status and an analysis of the conditions of its development are prerequisites to the solution of all other main problems of the strategy and tactics of the revolutionary movement. Just as the revolutionary communist movement all over the world was molded and hardened in estimating the significance of the events of 1914–17, marked by the collapse of the Second International and the rise of the Bolshevik revolution, so world Bolshevism, its maintenance and growth, is conditioned upon the estimation of the course of events in the Soviet Union and the Communist International in the period of the last four to five years. All other questions are subordinated to this and flow from it.

The collapse of the Russian revolution as the dictatorship of the proletariat would signify the retardation for decades of the revolutionary movement in Europe and America and the uprisings of the colonial peoples, whose main point of support today is the victory of the Russian October. A collapse would be followed by an unequaled reign of reaction throughout the world and would entail a restoration of world imperialist rule without precedent in the last two or three decades. Our primary concern is therefore with the fate of the Russian revolution, which directly affects the fate of all the Communist parties. The defense of the Russian revolution against external attacks and internal dangers is therefore the first and foremost task of all communists and every conscious worker. We are defenders of the Russian revolution since 1917. There is no break in the continuity of our position, for our present fight is directly connected with and follows from our whole previous line.

The attitude of official optimism and light-minded equanimity which finds that all is as it should be, without inquiry as to the actual facts and the basic trends of development—and seeks to prohibit such inquiry—is the worst kind of "support" that can be given the revolution. This attitude is actually one of criminal neglect, and results in disarming the proletariat before its enemies and deluding it before difficulties. To base oneself only on faith and precedent is to drug oneself into impotence. Communists must give conscious and understanding help.

The origin of the present crisis in the Soviet Union lies in the contradiction between the existence of a Soviet regime in a country with a predominantly peasant economy, and the pressure of the capitalist encirclement. This crisis has been sharpened and aggravated by the false policies of the leadership. These policies are rooted, further, in the overestimation by the present leadership of the duration and depth of the temporary stabilization of capitalism, which began after the defeat of the German and Bulgarian proletariat in 1923.[13]

Our entire epoch is one of capitalism in dissolution, of imperialist wars, and of the socialist revolution of the proletariat. Imperialism is the final stage of capitalism, of the domination of finance capital, monopolies, and international trusts, of the division and redivision of the world among the imperialist powers, wherein the only method of "remedying" the disproportion between productive development and capital accumulation on the one hand and the division of markets, colonies, and spheres of influence on the other, is the resort to imperialist war. In sharpening the contradictions between the productive forces of world economy and national state barriers, imperialism evoked the last war and is preparing the next. This does not exclude, within the period of decline of capitalism, the possibility of a partial economic revival or even the development of productive forces. Lenin, at the Second Congress of the Communist International, rightly pointed out that there was "no absolutely hopeless situation." The state of preparedness of the proletariat to wage a revolutionary struggle for power is a determining factor in the destruction of capitalism. Thanks to the treachery of the reformist Social Democracy, to the strategic though temporary postwar concessions of the bourgeoisie, and to the weakness or bad leadership of the Communist parties, the bourgeoisie has been able to achieve the present relative stabilization of capitalism.

But this estimate of the current stabilization differs radically from that implied in the Stalinist, revisionist "theory" of socialism in one country, that is, a stabilization for decades, for a whole epoch. This conception, which is an approach to the Social Democratic view of capitalism as organically stabilized, found expression in the resolution of the Fourteenth Congress of the Communist Party of the Soviet Union on Stalin's political report, which declared that "in the domain of international relations, it is quite clear the period of 'respite' is transforming itself into a veritable epoch." Later, the resolution of the Enlarged Executive of the CI of July 1927 spoke without restrictions of the technical, economic, and political stabilization of capitalism. History's answer to this estimate was the Chinese revolution, the British general strike, the Indonesian uprising, and the Vienna events,[14] not to mention the millions of unemployed. The estimate of stabilization given at the Sixth World Congress is so eclectic that it permits of varying interpretations.

Revision of Leninism and the crisis in the Comintern

Upon this essentially erroneous estimate was based the theory of the possibility of the complete construction of a socialist society in one country (Russia), a theory entirely alien to the teachings of Marx, Engels, and Lenin, and directly contrary to every principle of revolutionary internationalism. Integrally combined with this reactionary "theory" is the idea that a self-sufficing national economy can be maintained if only the danger of imperialist military intervention is warded off. That this inevitably leads to opportunism before the world bourgeoisie (particularly before the United States, which is the basic counterrevolutionary force in the world today) is shown in the signing of the Kellogg Pact by the Soviet Union and the notorious Litvinov proposals.[15] That it leads to the abandonment of all that Lenin taught on the revolutionary struggle against war and the role of the labor bureaucracy is shown in the capitulation of the Russian trade unions in the Anglo-Russian Committee. That it leads to the subordination of the Communist Party to the national bourgeoisie and the abandonment of Leninism on the national and colonial questions is shown by the catastrophic course followed by the Comintern in the Chinese revolution. That it leads to the conversion of the Communist parties into pacifist instruments of defense instead of instruments for organizing the armed insurrection in their own country primarily, is shown by the petty-bourgeois anticruiser petition campaign of the German party.[16]

All these lines of policy are consciously or unconsciously based on the need of preventing military intervention against the Soviet Union so that an isolated socialist construction can be completed there. The net result of this opportunist conception and course is the increasing danger of imperialist war against the Soviet Union, for revisionism here as everywhere brings neither revolution nor reform.

The growing war danger comes at a time when the crisis in Russia is reaching a sharp point. The departure from the proletarian revolutionary path, coincident with the beginning of the fight to cut the Leninist Opposition led by L.D. Trotsky from the party, has reached a stage where the enemy classes have grown to an alarming extent and exert a tremendous pressure upon the party and state apparatus. From Bukharin's "Peasants, enrich yourselves" and the theory that the kulak would grow into socialism, it has been a short step to the present situation where the exploiting elements in the village (the kulaks) have stepped forth into the arena with confidence, boldness, and arrogance to demand increased concessions and political rights. From the brutal campaign to suppress party democracy in the fight against the Leninist Opposition it has been a short step to the consolidation of a bureaucratic apparatus through which the new bourgeoisie exerts its ever-increasing pressure. Never before have the kulaks, the nepmen, the bureaucrats been so strong, so imperious in their demands, so threatening in their progress. The policy of the Stalin regime, which is based less and less on a class foundation, and more and more on a bureaucratic agglomeration, is undermining the positions of the proletarian dictatorship and permitting the rapid advancement of the classes alien to the proletariat whose program is the breakdown of the foreign-trade monopoly; the recognition of the tsarist debts; entrance into the League of Nations; unlimited concessions to international capital—particularly a rapprochement with American imperialism; the moderation of the pace of industrialization; penetration of the cooperatives and the Soviets; and the attainment of the suffrage hitherto reserved to the toiling masses. This is the program and the danger of Thermidor. It is the restoration of capitalism, in the beginning, probably, still under the present social forms.

The line of the present Stalin regime in this situation is a zigzag between capitulation in deeds to the right and temporary jumps to the left—that is, one step forward and two steps backward.

The Leninist Opposition, on the contrary, has been fighting tooth and nail against this imminent danger to the revolution. It has unfurled the banner of Leninism and stood by it in the face of an unprecedented campaign of slander and persecution. In the struggle against the Opposition and away from the line of Bolshevism, the present regime has by its very nature been compelled to resort to the bureaucratization of the Communist International, for under normal conditions of party democracy and free discussion, such caricatures as are now offered the revolutionary workers in the name of Leninism would be categorically rejected by the members of the International. To maintain its unprincipled domination, the present regime has therefore resorted to the suppression of discussion, the expulsion of communists, violence, arrests, imprisonment, exile, and deportation. In the name of Bolshevization, a campaign has been carried on particularly since the Fifth Congress of the Comintern which has as its net result the elimination of all elements who questioned the opportunist course of the Comintern. It has abolished party democracy and replaced it by control from above by irresponsible, appointed functionaries. Bureaucratic command and decree have been substituted for ideological discussion and leadership. The mechanical reorganization of party leaderships solely on the basis of their unhesitating readiness to endorse whatever is done by the Stalinist regime and to condemn whatever is done by the Leninist Opposition, is a daily occurrence. The influence and strength of the most important Communist parties have been reduced to an alarming extent (Germany, Czechoslovakia, France, England, United States, etc., etc.). It has brought about the development in the leading parties of the Comintern of right-wing or centrist leadership and line and the rending of these parties by violent factional struggles that are reflections of the internal struggle in the CPSU. The expulsion of the Leninist Opposition in all countries was achieved. The revisionist theories behind the opportunist line of Stalinism (socialism in one country, etc., etc.) flowered to full bloom.

The smoke screen of 'Trotskyism'

To conceal the essence of its right-wing deviations and bureaucratic misdeeds, the Stalin regime invented the myth of "Trotskyism," which it represents as the real danger to Leninism. Trotsky's differences of political line with Lenin were liquidated in 1917, on L.D. Trotsky's acceptance of the April Theses of Lenin and his entrance into the Central Committee of the Bolshevik Party on the basis of his agreement with the tenets of Bolshevism. But even those prerevolutionary differences were never as great as the differences of the Stalin-Bukharin regime now with the principles of Leninism. Differences between Lenin and Trotsky after 1917 rose out of the efforts of the two leaders of the revolution to solve concrete problems on the basis of the same theoretical program, and were never so great as the differences between the present ruling faction and Lenin. The Opposition will fight against the falsification of the history of the party and the revolution for factional ends, which has assumed such monstrous proportions in the demagogic campaign against L.D. Trotsky, in whom we recognize Lenin's chief collaborator in the leadership of the Russian revolution and today the foremost representative of Leninism in the world.

The Opposition is not conducting a war for "Trotskyism"; such a political tendency does not exist. It is fighting for the principles of Leninism. In the Soviet Union, under the rain of calumny and repression, the Leninist Opposition, led by its inspiring leader Comrade Trotsky, has fought persistently against all forms of revisionism and opportunism and for Bolshevism. The Opposition has sounded the alarm against the Thermidorian danger and proposed a correct policy to combat it in favor of the further socialist development of the country—in the period of retarded world revolution—through a correct policy of the distribution of the national income, through taxation of the nepman and the kulak to accelerate the process of industrialization and to improve the conditions of the workers, through credits and other cooperative assistance to the poor peasantry, through a correct price policy, and so forth. The Leninist Opposition is organizing the workers for the defense of the Russian revolution on two fronts of essentially the same enemy: against imperialist intervention from without and against the danger of Thermidor from within. Such a real defense, based on a correct class policy, can be accomplished only if the deepgoing reforms proposed by the Opposition are adopted and an end is made to the splitting of the Communist Party and the imprisonment and exile of thousands of the best Bolsheviks. The leadership which organized the defense of the Soviet Union under the direction of Lenin is still best able to carry it out today.

War danger and the defense of the USSR

The problem of the defense of the Soviet Union and the victory of October is inseparably bound up with the struggle against the danger of war. The inevitability of imperialist war inherent in the basic contradictions of capitalist society is not removed by the temporary and partial current stabilization. Indeed, the war danger proceeds from the innate contradictions of the stabilization process—that is, contradictions and antagonisms of capitalist imperialism which have again grown acute by reason of the world struggle for markets. What we are witnessing in the present period is an intensified, feverish armaments and militarization race preparatory to the actual outbreak of war. Combined with this is the customary accompaniment of imperialist jockeying for positions, formation of alliances and breaking of others, and diplomatic jugglery. In this prewar period, the imperialists in their respective countries have the open or semiconcealed support of the Social Democrats and the labor bureaucracy (armaments program of the German SDP; Boncour's militarization plan in France;[17] Henderson, MacDonald, and Company in England; the American Federation of Labor's open proimperialist, promilitarist position, and the endorsement by the Socialist Party of the Kellogg Pact, etc., etc.). To complete the picture are the innumerable conferences that help delude the workers and develop pacifist illusions among them: Locarno and Kellogg pacts, "disarmament" proposals, and the like.

The existence of the Soviet Union, with a proletarian dictatorship supported by the foreign-trade monopoly, bars the way to a "free market" for capitalism of one-sixth of the globe. This intensifies the antagonisms of the whole of the imperialist powers against the USSR and the tendencies toward the formation of an anti-Soviet bloc for intervention, which has so far been retarded by the mutual rivalries of the imperialist powers and their desire for a more "favorable" moment of internal difficulties of the Soviet Union, and through fear of the revolutionary action of the masses at home. The opportunist policies of the Stalin regime have weakened the international position of the Soviet Union. The by no means unavoidable defeats of the Chinese revolution and the great British strikes have enhanced the confidence of the bourgeoisie and weakened the power of resistance of the workers. The best defense of the Soviet Union is the building of the revolutionary capacities of the Communist parties. The fear of an insurrection at home, led by the Communist Party, is the greatest restraining influence upon the bourgeoisie against intervention.

The events of the past two years have made it necessary to restate the Leninist viewpoint on the revolutionary struggle against imperialist war. The policy of the Stalin regime has, in theory and practice, forsaken this line. It has set up a conception of some superhistorical recipe to be used in fighting the war danger. The fight against the war danger and intervention in the USSR has been abstracted from the general revolutionary struggle of the proletariat. Considerations of a "diplomatic nature," for "Soviet State reasons," "for special circumstances" have been advanced to replace the basic and permanent considerations of general revolutionary policy, instead of the one being an indivisible part of the other. This was true in the Stalin-Bukharin policy in the Anglo-Russian Committee, where they capitulated before Purcell-Hicks-Citrine and Company, because the latter would allegedly prevent Chamberlain and Baldwin from conducting their imperialist intervention policy. Reformist methods here also produced catastrophic results. It was true in the policy followed in the Chinese revolution, where the revolutionary movement was sacrificed by the Stalin-Bukharin line for the sake of maintaining alliances with the "anti-imperialist" generals of the Chiang Kai-shek–Feng Yu-hsiang stripe. It remains true today in the non-Leninist policy pursued in the so-called League Against Imperialism, where uncritical combinations are made from above with petty-bourgeois, reformist, and nationalist elements who are in many instances neither more nor less than the bellwethers of imperialism. It is true in the case of the Soviet Union's signing of the Kellogg Pact without denouncing it as a cover behind which the imperialists are preparing the imperialist war and the anti-Soviet intervention. This opportunist line only adds to the illusions of the masses, and disarms them before their enemies.

The only road for the revolutionary struggle against war is that indicated by the teachings of Lenin on the question, in his writings during the last war, so admirably summarized in his "Theses of Instructions to Our Delegation to the Hague Conference." The communists must relentlessly combat all pacifist illusions among the workers, point out to them the inevitability of imperialist war, teach and train them that it can be overcome only by the socialist revolution of the proletariat. We must show that there are no "exceptional circumstances" to justify an opportunist or capitulationist policy in which the interests of one section of the proletariat result in sacrificing those of the proletariat as a whole.

The impending war situation makes the American communists particularly responsible and their tasks especially great and difficult. This is especially so since the present situation is characterized by a world struggle essentially between American and British imperialism. The antagonisms between these two powers become sharper and more intense every day, and may lead to the actual outbreak of military operations at a least expected moment.

The role of American imperialism

Every estimate of the present situation must proceed from the fact that the world center of economic gravity has shifted to the United States. American imperialism now levies tribute from practically all the capitalist countries of the world. This development, which has risen to its height in the period after the world war, has bound up the fate of American imperialism with the economy of the whole world in an inextricable form. No analysis of its future economic course, internally as well as externally, can be made without a consideration of its international position.

The effect of America's direct intervention in European affairs after the war was the temporary, partial stabilization of European capitalism. This stabilization occurred in direct connection with the defeat of the German proletariat in 1923 and resulted in the consolidation of Social Democracy for the time. In turn it enabled the United States to avoid the convulsions that would have affected it inevitably in the event of the development of the revolutionary wave in Europe.

The United States has expanded its productive capacity, which has brought about a further contraction of markets for European capitalism and consequently a contraction of the European market itself. The postwar chaos of Europe has made it impossible for the debtors of that continent to present a sufficiently consolidated united front, to which they are inclined. The very strength and expansion of American imperialism has laid the foundation for the most violent struggles in Europe and in the colonial countries. The European powers must fight among themselves for a larger ration in world economy, and against the United States for the same reason. The pacifist effect which American intervention had upon the European situation in the beginning is now being transformed by the processes of development into a revolutionizing effect. American imperialism is now beginning to look for a solution of its own approaching internal convulsions at the expense of Europe, and primarily of Germany, and increased exploitation and imperialist raids on Latin America and China.

The present Experts' Conference on the Dawes Plan is becoming a focal point of this contradiction. The report of the Reparations Agent in Germany of 1928, which, contrary to the 1927 report, gave an optimistic analysis of the situation, was made with an eye to "solving" the conflict between reparations payments and the Allied debt to the United States by increased pressure on Germany.[18] The proposal to issue bonds protected by lien on the German railways, to cover the Dawes payments—and by payments of reparations to the Allies to enable the latter to pay their debts to America—will only lead to the multiplication of difficulties. For the United States to carry even one-half of such a bond issue, involving something like two billion dollars for its share, would mean that the important banks of this country would add almost 20 percent to their present holdings in investments and in government and other securities. An absorption of such an amount by the American banks, which, according to the *Magazine of Wall Street,* are "today water-logged with securities which they never ought to have bought at all," would result "at this critical moment of our financial history" in bank inflation.

The inability of the "experts" to solve the reparations and debts problems in a satisfactory manner is an earnest of the developing position of the United States with regard to Europe.

At the same time, in the desperate struggle of the European powers to maintain their heads above the wave of American world domination they have even succeeded to a partial extent in regaining their position in world production. As between the periods of 1920–24 and 1927, the share of Europe in world production of anthracite, iron, steel, and the consumption of cotton has increased an average of 9.22 percent, while the share of the United States has decreased an average of 7.55 percent. A most bitter competition for markets is becoming sharper in every corner of the world, primarily between the United States and Britain. There has even developed the movement to raise the already tremendously high tariff walls of the United

States in the coming session of Congress.

It is not necessary nor is it correct to view the United States as "about to reach the apex of its growth" in order to see and understand the maturing crisis in the country. American imperialism, by the very fact that it is developing in a different period from that of the rise of Great Britain—the period of war and revolution, and national and colonial uprisings—is therefore doomed to a much more rapid tempo of the development of its internal and international contradictions than was England. And this is true precisely because of the phenomenally rapid expansion it has experienced in the past decade.

The present economic situation and the working class

The present economic situation in the United States is characterized by the following features:

The contraction of the world market by the stabilization of European capitalism and the decrease in the rate of the rise of American exports. The sharpening of the competition in the East and in Latin America between the United States and the European powers (England, Germany, etc.).

The tremendous concentration of industry and the intensification of rationalization, whereby technical progress has outstripped the expansion of the home market. There is a growing disproportion between the rate of expansion of productive capacity and the rate of growth of production and consumption. The opening up of the South to industrialization on a higher technical level, instead of creating a "New Ruhr" (Lovestone) only brings with it new contradictions. The newly proletarianized population of the South will not develop an addition to the home market to absorb sufficiently the growth of production, and the hopes placed in the "new South" will further be partially offset by the intensification of the coal and textile crises in the North.

The home market has been further contracted by the creation of a standing army of unemployed workers numbering several millions. Although the index figure for production of big industry has risen from 146 in 1919 to 171 in 1927 (1914 equals 100), the index for workers employed in big industry has fallen from 129 in 1919 to 114 in 1927 (1914 equals 100), although population growth for the same years was from 106 to 120 respectively. In addition, there has been an influx into the ranks of the unemployed of declassed farmers. The agricultural production index figure for 1918–19 was 132 (1900 equals 100) and rose to 148 in 1924. Active participants in agriculture fell in the same period from 106 to 100, although the agricultural population grew—also in the same period—from 112 to 115. These figures further indicate that although in certain specific and by no means general cases real wages have increased, the wages of the American working class, and therefore their purchasing power, have on the whole decreased. This tendency is being accelerated by the growing series of wage cuts.

American capitalism has been unable to overcome the serious depressions in agriculture and in the coal, oil, textile, lumber, shipping, and other industries, nor will it be able to prevent the coming decline in the iron and steel and automobile industries.

The rapid increase in brokerage loans, in face of an average trading volume of more than five million shares a day, presages the beginning of the end of the "bull" market, far more profound than the price fall of June 1928. The fact that rates for stock market loans had to be doubled and quadrupled has caused the more realistic of the bourgeois economists to be very cautious in their predictions for the coming year.

The fate of American imperialism, we repeat, is now bound up with its dependence on world economy. Conversely, the situation in Europe is directly linked with the development of American national economy. The United States will seek to use Europe as a shield to take the blows of its own difficulties. This will in turn create such situations in Europe, above all in Germany, where, with proper revolutionary leadership, a new wave of proletarian revolt will be initiated, or the relations between England and America will come to the breaking point. This rapidly materializing process will change the correlation of forces in the United States in favor of the revolutionary proletariat, by undermining the base of the American labor aristocracy.

Meanwhile, the internal contradictions of American imperialism, bound up with its world economic interdependence, are maturing a severe crisis which is foreshadowed by the current partial industrial depression. The present situation, which is only the harbinger of this coming crisis, has already brought to a high level the process of rationalization and attack upon the standards of the working class that is causing it to move progressively away from its previous inertia into a period of struggles. The realization of the crisis, which will intensify the process of rationalization, increase unemployment, and lead to more severe attacks on the living standards of the workers, will result in an even broader basis for the radicalization of the American workers and their entry into struggle. This process of radicalization is taking place now. It is a process which must be analyzed not only in comparison with the leftward movement of the European workers, but chiefly in comparison with the historical backwardness of the American working class. Upon this development is conditioned the coming period of struggles of the American workers and the necessity for the revolutionary party to understand it and prepare itself properly for it.

Results of the elections

The results of the recent presidential elections were nothing but a barometer—and a weak, inaccurate, distorted barometer—of the developments and perspectives outlined above. The victory of the Republican Party and its candidate, Hoover, signified the still growing power—accompanied though it is by sharpening contradictions—of American capitalism, and the grip of the main party of the bourgeoisie on the masses. This power was sufficient for the Republicans to break through the "solid South" for the first time since the Civil War, aided by those irresistible economic forces which have been undermining the social-political basis of the traditional Democratic Party for the past decades.

The election as a whole, however, makes it impossible for anyone to speak unconditionally of a "conservative landslide" or a "victory for reaction" or a "defeat for Smith." The vote for Smith by no means represented entirely a vote of satisfaction with the present state of affairs. The nature of the Smith vote disputes this. In the first place he received such a tremendous vote as has rarely before been received even by a winning candidate, which does not contribute at all to the theory of the "destruction" of the Democratic Party. His vote, furthermore, was composed largely of workers in the big industrial centers, where he made tremendous gains, and of the hard-pressed petty bourgeoisie and farmers.

Millions of workers saw in Smith, his record, and his program, a possibility of change from the rule of finance capital, the eight-year orgy of corruption, reaction, and imperialist policy of the Republican wing of capitalism.

Votes which would otherwise have been cast for the Socialist and even the Communist parties went this time to Smith on the basis of the popular American belief that "he has a good chance to get in." It is entirely true that the workers who cast their votes for Smith were deluded and betrayed, that Smith in actuality is as much the instrument of imperialism as Hoover. But hundreds of thousands if not millions of workers did not vote for him as an instrument of reaction and an opponent of change. Smith, with his hypocritical "friendship" for labor, his "prolabor" record and program, succeeded in deceiving his working-class support into voting for him as an "opponent" of the current reaction.

The vote against Hoover expressed to a certain extent the growing radicalization of the masses on an American scale, and with parliamentary limitations. Political developments have lagged historically behind economic developments. Proceeding from the fundamental viewpoint of the historical backwardness of the American workers it is apparent that the anti-Hoover vote was a political—that is, an insufficient, a distorted, an even reactionary—expression of the radicalizing processes taking place in the economic life of the American working class. In the present period, a leftward drift of the workers in Europe will express itself, for example, in a desertion from the Social Democracy and a growth of the power and influence of the Communists. In the United States, such a drift assumes much more moderate and backward forms.

Neither does our analysis signify that the elections were the best available barometer of the radicalization of the workers. On the contrary, it was one of the poorest. The indications of the radicalization process, which is bound to be accelerated in tempo in the coming period, are to be found chiefly in the daily economic life and struggles of the workers of this country. They are to be found in the movement for the formation of the new industrial unions, in the growing discontent of the workers even in the old AFL unions, and the growing mood for struggle that is partly exemplified by the increasing participation in strikes.

Relative to the possibilities, the Communist Party made a poor showing in the elections, which cannot be explained away solely on the basis of the disfranchisement of foreign-born workers and Negroes. In the 1924 elections the party was on the ballot in fourteen states and received 33,361 votes. The vote for the party in the same fourteen states in the 1928 elections was only 31,128—that is, a decline of 2,233 votes. For the same fourteen states we received .001146 of the total vote cast in 1924; in 1928, we received only .000846 of the total vote cast in the country. Thus we lost in those states (the most important ones, too, like New York, Pennsylvania, New Jersey, Illinois, Indiana, Massachusetts, Minnesota, Wisconsin, etc.) absolutely, in number of votes received, and relative to the total vote cast. Our total vote in 1928 in all the thirty-four states where we were on the ballot was 45,710, an increase over 1924 not at all commensurate with the fact that in this election we were on the ballot in twenty additional states, that is, more than twice as many as in 1924.

This alarming showing cannot be explained, either, by the "Smith sweep," for there was a "La Follette sweep" in 1924. It cannot be explained by the terrorism of the bourgeoisie or vote-stealing; that condition also existed in 1924. In addition, it must be remembered that in the period between the two presidential elections, the party had more opportunities for growth, popularity, and influence than ever before. It led a number of the most significant strikes and mass movements: Passaic, the miners, New Bedford, the Sacco-Vanzetti agitation, and so forth and so on.[19] The real explanation for our failure is in the fact that the Stalinization of the party, here as elsewhere, has had terrific results. The party has been corrupted and weakened by factionalism and opportunism, finding its chief source in the Lovestone-Pepper leadership supported by the Comintern. It has brought about a steady decrease in party membership, factional distrust, irresponsibility and dilettantism, and has weakened the party in the class struggle in every instance. It is the greatest obstacle in the crystallization and growth of the Communist movement in this country. There is no other basic explanation for our parliamentary decline and can be no other.

We deal here only with main lines, and omit the repetition of such points as the opportunist and corrupt parliamentary methods of the Lovestone-Pepper clique, the buying of signatures and electors, the false conception of the labor party and its role in the election, the failure to act with sureness and speed in selecting our candidates and putting our ticket into the field, the factionalism rampant throughout the campaign, and so forth. We have dealt extensively with these features of the election in other documents, notably "The Right Danger in the American Party" and articles in the press.

Struggle for a class movement of the American workers

Due to the strong position of American capitalism, which has enabled it to bribe large sections of the workers and to provide a higher general standard of living than that of the other capitalist countries, the American workers, from a class standpoint, are in a primitive stage of development. The American workers are not class conscious, they have not yet developed even the concepts of social reformism or independent political action, and, on the whole, are permeated through and through with the ideology of capitalism. These incontestable facts are the starting point of the communist approach and indicate our fundamental task: to struggle for the creation of a class movement of the American workers, for the development of class consciousness, and to lead them toward revolutionary concepts in struggle.

The fight for a class movement of the American workers is in the first place a fight against the capitalist ideology which dominates them. The labor bureaucrats of the AFL and the unaffiliated unions of the same type are the direct bearers of this ideology in the working class and must be fought as such. The labor bureaucracy is a part of the capitalist rationalization and war machine—its "labor" wing. De Leon's classic definition of the reactionary labor leaders as "labor lieutenants of the capitalist class" holds doubly good today. The distinctive features of these labor leaders in comparison to the social-reformist leaders of Europe consists in the fact that they are outspoken defenders of the whole capitalist regime and all of its institutions, without "socialistic" pretense or class-struggle phraseology. Their program is a program of stark reaction. They repudiate the class struggle in words as well as deeds. They oppose any kind of independent political action. They support the whole military program of American imperialism and will indubitably be a powerful ally of the capitalists in lining up the workers for the coming war and demoralizing the struggle against it. They decline affiliation with the reformist Amsterdam International. They oppose even the mildest proposal for social legislation and reform, and sharply differentiate themselves from all of its advocates. The condemnation of the Brookwood Labor College at the last convention illustrates this attitude.

This bureaucracy is the chief influence against the class movement within the workers' ranks—the strongest, the best organized, and the representative of the most reactionary program. The specific nature of the American labor bureaucracy—its present source of strength—also makes it the more vulnerable in the period of growing radicalization. The very first steps of the workers towards a class movement can be taken only in direct struggle against them. The relentless and irreconcilable fight against the AFL leadership, based on a correct analysis of its specific role as the outspoken bearer of capitalist ideology, is a prerequisite for effective work in developing the struggle of the workers, increasing their class understanding, and leading them to the fight for broader political aims.

The indiscriminate lumping together of all the various forms and methods of deluding the workers and holding back their class development, and the elements that represent them (capitalist welfare schemes, AFL program, La Folletteism, liberal churchmen, liberals and progressives, Republican and Democratic parties, bourgeois economists and efficiency experts, etc.), under one head, as is the current policy enunciated in the theses of the two factions, is profoundly erroneous. It glosses over the distinctive features and specific role of each and consequently makes impossible an estimate of their relative importance at the moment and the formulation of the most effective tactics of struggle against them.

The Socialist Party has progressively degenerated since the expulsion of the communist left wing in 1919, and in great labor struggles of recent years, particularly in the needle trades, became the open ally of the employers and the AFL bureaucracy. It appealed for votes in the last election campaign on the basis of petty-bourgeois liberalism. The union struggles as well as the election campaign showed its influence to be in decline. In view of its tradition and its phraseology, however, its potentialities as an influence against the class movement of the workers are very great. The Communists must fight the Socialist Party on all fronts in the most direct and irreconcilable manner. A correct estimate of its position and function is necessary for this. The Socialist Party is not dead, and its possibilities for a new growth in a period of growing radicalization of the workers will be greatly strengthened by false tactics of the Communists. The Socialist Party fights on the side of imperialism against the workers in its own way, but it is wrong to describe it as an organic and indistinguishable part of the AFL machine. It is true it will always form a united front with the latter against any serious movement of the workers, but there is an important difference in function and division of labor between them.

The function of the AFL bureaucrats is to stifle all progressive tendencies in the working class and to defend capitalist institutions as they are. The function of the Socialist Party and of the related social reformists is to exploit these progressive tendencies under more or less "radical" phraseology and to divert them into harmless reformist channels which avoid a real collision either with capitalism as such or the AFL bureaucrats. The new "campaign" of the Socialist *New Leader* against the Civic Federation policies of Woll and the "Progressive Manifesto" of the *Labor Age* group, are highly significant expressions of this specific role of these social reformists. The influence of these groups at present is weak, but the growth of discontent of the workers and their mood for struggle will give them the possibility of expanding it on a wide scale. The Communists must unmask them and make their deception clear to the workers. Otherwise there is great danger of them gaining the leadership of workers' movements and strangling them.

The main reservoir of labor militancy is the masses of

unskilled and semiskilled workers in the unorganized, basic industries. The full horror of the capitalist rationalization falls directly upon them, and the attacks of the capitalists in the present depression and coming crises strike them first and hardest. The party must turn its face to these unorganized masses, put itself at the head of their struggles, and lead in the work of organizing them into new industrial unions. This historic task must be accomplished in the fire of struggle against the capitalists and their state power as well as against their agents in the labor movement—the reactionary bureaucracy of the AFL, the Socialist Party, and allied groups of social-reformist elements. In this protracted struggle on all fronts extending over a period of years, the decisive break of the workers with the ideology of capitalism will be effected and the genuine class movement of the workers will be built.

Trade union policy

A correct policy on the trade union question and its consistent execution by a sound Communist leadership are decisive for the expansion of the party as the leader of the struggling masses. Moreover, the tactics of the left wing led by the party—a dynamic force of gigantic importance—will be one of the most vital determining factors in the future course and development of the trade union movement.

The narrowing base of the AFL and the increasingly reactionary conduct and policy of its leadership raise before the party and the left wing the problem of organizing the unorganized workers in the basic industries, primarily the unskilled and half-skilled, who are becoming radicalized and ready for struggle. It is the task of the party and the left wing to lead in the work of organizing these masses into new industrial unions. The center of gravity in our trade union work belongs in this sphere. This has been indicated by the whole situation for some time, and the long delay of the party in shaping its course in this direction, due to the resistance of the leadership, has already had extremely harmful consequences.

The history of the party has been also the history of continuous struggles for the correct line on the trade union question. Isolation from the masses in their struggles was the price paid by the party for its false trade union policy in its earlier years. The trade union program adopted in 1920, which called for a boycott of the AFL and support of the IWW, was corrected only after a stubborn and protracted struggle conducted by the main nucleus of the present Opposition. It was not until the Unity Convention of June 1921 that a realistic program steering the party into the trade unions and outlining the plan for the formation of a broad left wing was finally adopted. The entrance into the party of a number of experienced trade unionists was facilitated by this decision and this in turn gave a great impetus to its practical execution. Isolation gave way to a speedy penetration of the party into the trade union struggle, to the wide expansion of the Trade Union Educational League as a bona fide movement of the left wing, and to the appearance of the party as an important factor in the labor party movement.

The rich results of this policy adopted at the 1921 convention were in themselves an irrefutable proof of its correctness. It was not executed, however, without one-sidedness and distortions. In reacting against the basically false policy of the 1920 convention, which called for the "destruction" of the AFL, the party went to another extreme and developed an AFL fetishism. "Dual unionism" became a bogey, and practically all independent unions and movements were labeled as such. This very terminology graphically illustrates the great concessions to the labor reactionaries implicit in the one-sided policy, for it is their language. "Dual unionism" is their time-worn epithet for all revolting groups of militants. This fetishism blinded the party to its tasks and duties in the unorganized fields and narrowed its base of operations too much to the organized, more-or-less skilled workers. It was a factor in the delay of the party shaping its course toward the unorganized and shifting its center of gravity there—a course made imperative by the changing circumstances.

This shift of emphasis to the formation of new unions of the unorganized has been accepted in words after a long and stubborn struggle of the opposition for this line. But the work has not yet begun in earnest. The practice of the party leadership in this field is marked more by sporadic spurts and spectacular stunts than by planful, systematic, and deliberate work. Moreover, the turn of the emphasis to new unions of the unorganized, which ought to be indissolubly bound up in one comprehensive policy with the intensified work in the old unions, is already being interpreted and applied one-sidedly.

The work in the old unions has been virtually abandoned. This fact is clearly revealed in the almost complete disappearance of party representatives from trade union gatherings. Still worse, the leaders of the factions are competing with each other in the elaboration of "theories" which preclude the idea of serious work in the old unions in the future.

The factions are outdoing each other in irresponsible striving to be "left" in this burning question. These theories and practices are a menace to the party and threaten to put it off the track again. It is time to sound a warning and begin a determined struggle against them. The building of the new unions and the work in the old unions must be carried on together and not the one set up against the other.

The role of the AFL leadership as the outspoken agents of American imperialism in peace, in war preparations, and in war, does not at all obliterate the fact of three million members in its affiliated unions. The new "theories" are attempting to rationalize the AFL out of existence as a federation of unions and to arbitrarily preclude the possibility of its future expansion and growth in an organizational sense. The unrelenting struggle against the labor agents of imperialism in general and an unceasing exposure of their role as a bulwark against the working-class resistance to war is an obvious necessity. The struggle against them for the organization and leadership of the unorganized workers is the main aspect of the fight. But the matter does not end there.

The workers organized in the AFL unions have an enormous strategic importance. We must fight the bureaucrats for influence over them from within, no matter how arduous the task, no matter how severe the persecution and discrimination against us. The abandonment of this struggle now taking place under cover of high-sounding "radicalism" will only prevent the crystallization of an insurgent movement within the old unions and free the hands of the bureaucrats for more effective sabotage of the organization of new unions, for these two processes are bound together. The net result will be to strengthen the effectiveness of the AFL bureaucracy as a part of the capitalist war machine.

The decline of the AFL in membership and influence during recent years is an incontestable fact. But it still represents a powerful force, both in an organizational and ideological sense, on the side of reaction. And its further expansion in a period of growing mass struggles and serious work by the left wing in the building of new unions, particularly in the event of war, is by no means excluded. The assertions to the contrary, conjured up to support the new "theories," are purely arbitrary.

The obvious fact that the big employers under "normal" conditions prefer their own company unions to the most conservative trade unions and fight militantly to destroy the latter is not of itself sufficient ground for such a contention. The whole rationalization process, with its unbearable and increasing exploitation, drives the workers to revolt and to the endeavor to form class organizations. The coming period will see such struggles on a large scale. Under such conditions it is not only possible but even probable that employers, who reject the conservative trade unions now, would accept them as an alternative to new unions under militant leadership and would even collaborate with the bureaucrats in their formation.

Such a possible perspective in no way "removes the base" for the building of new industrial unions of the unorganized workers as the main task of the party. On the contrary it makes the energetic execution of this task all the more imperative. The greater the progress the party makes with this work, combining it with increased activity in the old unions, the stronger will be the barriers against the betrayals of the coming revolts by the AFL machine.

The attempt to classify the entire membership of the AFL unions as aristocrats of labor, immune from class-struggle agitation, which is implied and even partly stated in the new "theories," is likewise false. Deep currents of discontent, full of potentialities for future struggles, already exist in the old unions, and they will increase in the coming period. The recent manifesto of the pseudoprogressive group of *Labor Age* is primarily a reflection of this discontent in the ranks of the unions, which the reformists seek to divert into harmless channels. The appearance of the new movement, even in a nebulous form, with pseudoprogressives at its head, is a sign of the abdication of the Communists and the left wing, who in recent years have led these movements. It is a warning that continued neglect of the struggle in the old unions clears the road for the reformist stultification of potentially revolutionary movements within them.

The party must clarify its tactics on the trade union question without delay. The organization of the unorganized into new unions, the foremost and basic task, must go hand in hand with intensified work in the old unions, including those which exist alongside of new unions, and a revival of the discarded united-front tactics. The party must penetrate every movement of opposition and revolt against the bureaucracy, forming united fronts with all honest progressive workers, exposing the particularly deceptive and dangerous role of pseudoleft and pseudoprogressive leaders, and struggling against them for the leadership of the opposition movements.

In 1925 the present Opposition conducted a struggle against the narrowing of the TUEL into a purely Communist body with a Communist program, and for broadening it into a united-front organization. This was one of the most progressive struggles in the history of the party. The revival of the left wing in the miners' union and the subsequent leadership of the party in a great miners' mass movement were the result of the change in course brought about by this struggle. That basically correct line must be restated and insisted on in view of the departures that have been made from it recently.

The TUEL, which, thanks to false policies, has degenerated into a mere shadow of the party existing on paper, with little or no organization or life of its own, must be revived as a bona fide united-front organization of the party and nonparty militants in the unions, the organizing center of the new unions and the left wing in the old. The actual participation of influential nonparty workers in the activities of the TUEL and in its leading committees is one of the absolute prerequisites for this proper functioning of the TUEL on a genuine basis of broad organization. And this holds good with a hundredfold emphasis in regard to the new unions which are being formed. The leading role of the party in the new unions and in the left wing of the old unions is necessary for their development into higher forms of struggle. But the construction of the leading staff of these movements on a narrow party basis with mechanical forms of party control—above all mechanical faction control, which is the growing practice under the present party regime—is fatal to the growth and development of these movements.

In the work of forming new unions of the unorganized workers, no less than in its work in the AFL, the party must revive and apply the united-front tactic. Maintaining always its independence and freedom of criticism, the party must form alliances with groups and organizations willing to cooperate with us on a minimum class-struggle program, and win the nonparty militants over to the platform of communism by degrees in the course of joint struggle. An approach to revolutionary syndicalist workers in the spirit of Lenin is especially necessary.

The party must strive to establish its decisive influence and leadership in these united-front struggles by its initiative, superior tactics, and conscientious, persevering work. These methods must replace the growing tendency toward exclusiveness and mechanical, monopolistic party control, which result only in the narrowing down of the base of the new movements and organizations, in their degeneration into impotent cliques, in their isolation and defeat. Under the present conditions and relation of forces, the party cannot put forth the demand for arbitrary and mechanical control without endangering the developing movements and blocking its own approach to the awakening nonparty masses. The leadership of the Communists, which is alone able to steer the new movements on a correct course, must be won in struggle.

The chief danger to the progress of the party in its trade union work is the opportunist leadership of the party. Constantly oscillating between conservative passivity before the AFL and adventurist plunges in the formation of new unions without adequate preparations in advance, regarding the workers as objects for maneuvering rather than as class brothers in arms, dabbling with mass movements in dilettante fashion, and permeating all the trade union work with corrupt and poisonous factionalism, the Lovestone-Pepper leadership has already proved itself ten times over to be a positive barrier in the path of the party and the left wing, and a weight in the scale against the proletariat. Its potentialities for harm in the impending struggles, with all their vast difficulties and possibilities, are enormous.

The Lovestone-Pepper leadership rejected the proposal of the opposition in May 1927 to begin preparations for the mobilization of the left wing in the United Mine Workers through a national conference, and followed a do-nothing policy month after month while the strike was being cut to pieces by the operators and the Lewis machine. It was not until April 1928, after the strike was a year old and had already spent its force, that a national conference was finally held. It resisted the course toward a new miners' union and did nothing to begin organizational work in the unorganized fields. (Conservative passivity, fear of the labor fakers, lack of faith in the masses.) Then it plunged into the calling of the strike in the unorganized fields in April 1928 without the slightest preliminary organization. (Adventurism and irresponsibility.) It sabotaged and delayed the proper organization of relief work for months out of internal party factional considerations. It excluded and discriminated against the most qualified and authoritative leaders of the miners' movement in the formation of the leading bodies of the new union.[20] It pushed aside real organizers of the workers and flooded the coal fields with incompetent faction agents. It reduced the party fraction at the convention of the new union to a fiction and decided all questions in advance through a small steering committee of the CEC selected on a faction basis and comprising a majority without experience or authority in trade union work. (Criminal factionalism, callous disregard of the basic interests of the movement.) The Lovestone-Pepper leadership lost interest in and virtually withdrew from the new union at the most critical time, immediately after the convention. It made no serious attempt to provide the necessary financial help for the necessary organizational work. Even funds which properly belonged to this work were diverted. The Lewis machine was thus given the opportunity to entrench itself again through lack of real competition from organizers of the new union. (Dilettantism and irresponsibility.)

The same methods have marked the course of the party leadership in other trade union fields. The formation of the new union in the needle trades was unduly delayed while opportunities were lost and the right wing advanced. Here a bloc of crass opportunists is maintained in leadership while the left wing of genuine communists is suppressed. In the textile industry a policy of passivity before the old unions was followed by the sudden formation of a national textile union prematurely, without sufficient preparation and without an adequate base in local organizations.[21]

These evil methods, repeated systematically, are accumulating into a crushing weight upon the party and the left wing, and leading to failure and collapse at the time when the possibilities are greatest and the demands heaviest. They directly threaten to discredit the idea of new unions, to demoralize the workers and destroy the prestige of the party for years to come. The Bolshevik struggle to organize the workers cannot be separated from the struggle to reorganize the leadership of the party on a proletarian communist basis.

The perspective of a labor party

The perspective of coming mass struggles involves the question of developing these struggles in a political direction and unifying them in a centralized form. The movement for a labor party is today at low ebb as a result primarily of the passivity of the workers and the decline in movements of struggle in the past period. The coming period of developing economic struggles will very probably be reflected in tendencies toward the revival of the labor party movement.

It is not reasonable to expect that the masses of the American workers, who are still tied ideologically and politically to the bourgeois parties, will come over to the Communist Party politically at one step in a period not immediately revolutionary. All past experience, and particularly the recent experiences in the mining, textile, and needle trades industries, where the workers who supported Communist leadership in strikes did not vote for the Communist ticket, do not sustain such expectations. The perspective of a labor party as a primary step in the political development of the American workers, adopted by the party in 1922 after a sharp struggle in the party and at the Fourth Congress of the Communist International, holds good today, although the forms and methods of its realization will be somewhat different than those indicated at that time.

It is therefore necessary to keep this perspective of a labor party before the eyes of the party and the working class. We speak here not for the immediate formation of such a party, and surely not for the adventurism and opportunism that has characterized this work in the past, particularly in the organization of fake labor parties that had no genuine mass basis. The labor party must have a mass basis and must arise out of struggle and be formed in the process of struggle. To this end, the propaganda slogan must be really revived, and as soon as it has found roots in the masses and their experiences in the struggle, it must become an agitational and finally an action slogan.

The labor party must not be an enlarged shadow of the Communist Party. It must have a mass basis, else it will be a caricature. It must permit the freedom of action, independence, and criticism, of the revolutionary elements within it. It must not have an exaggerated importance attributed to it as the "leader" of the working class to liberation, and so on, for no illusions about its role can be permitted except at the expense of the revolutionary interests of the working class. It must not be based on individual membership.

The organization of two classes in one party—a farmer-labor party—must be rejected in principle in favor of the separate organization of the workers, and the formation of a political alliance with the poor farmers under the leadership of the former. The opportunist errors of party comrades in the Farmer-Labor Party of Minnesota and other states flowed inevitably from, and were secondary to, the basically false policy of a two-class party, pursued by the party leadership, in which farmer and worker are ostensibly on an "equal basis," but where in reality the petty-bourgeois ideology of the former actually dominates.

The struggle for a labor party, as part of the struggle for the development of a class movement of the American workers, requires an intransigeant fight against the AFL leadership and the Socialist Party, who represent obstacles to this development. The main base of the future labor party will be the new industrial unions formed in the coming struggles against the employers, the government, and the labor fakers and reformists. The left wing, organized in the old unions, will also play a very important part. The radicalizing effect of these struggles and the circumstances which give rise to them will create the conditions for the formation of the labor party and for the effective participation of the Communists and their independent struggle for leadership of the masses.

Work among Negroes

The party as a whole has always greatly underestimated the tremendous importance of revolutionary work among the Negro masses. The American Negroes are destined to play a great role in the coming revolution. The Negro proletariat of the North and the great mass of Negro peasantry in the South form a tremendous reservoir of revolutionary force which has hitherto remained untapped. What is needed is a recognition of the importance of this work, a correct policy in it, and serious attention to it.

It must be the main task of the party in this field to mobilize the white workers to fight for the rights of the Negro masses to full social, economic, and political equality and to unite with them in their struggles. Not an attitude of liberal paternalism but an attitude of comradely support in a common battle, will give an impetus to the movement of struggle and resistance among the Negroes and will pave the way for the expansion of party influence among them. The organization of the Negro masses for struggle goes hand in hand with the mobilization of the white workers for the defense of the Negroes against persecution and discrimination.

A prerequisite for this is the persistent struggle against race prejudice (white chauvinism), which is sedulously cultivated by the ruling class and dominates large sections of the white workers. It is even reflected in certain sections of the party. This can be rooted out only by a broad ideological campaign explaining the reactionary, anti-working-class origin, nature, and result of the bourgeois "theories" of "white supremacy," and utilizing every concrete instance in this sense. Such a campaign has not yet even been begun in our party press. The attempt to deal with the question by purely mechanical methods is false.

The Negro question is also a national question, and the party must raise the slogan of the right of self-determination for the Negroes. The effectiveness of this slogan is enhanced by the fact that there are scores of contiguous counties in the South where the Negro population is in the majority, and it is there that they suffer the most violent persecution and discrimination. This slogan will be the means especially of penetrating these Negro masses in the South and of mobilizing them for revolutionary struggle. The party must at the same time decisively reject the false slogan of a "Negro Soviet Republic in the South" at this time, raised by Pepper. This theory is still being propagated in the party press and in official party literature despite its rejection even at the Sixth Congress of the Comintern.[22]

The work among the Negro masses must from the very beginning be based on leadership by the Negro proletariat and not by the Negro petty bourgeoisie. The party's orientation in the past has been based more on the latter than the former. Only through the domination by the Negro proletariat in the movement will the party be able to advance the work of organizing the Negro peasants, tenant farmers, sharecroppers, etc., in the South in an effective and revolutionary sense.

The Stalinization of the American party

The departure of the Communist Party of the Soviet Union from the line of Lenin has been reflected in the Communist International and all of its sections. The Stalinization of the Comintern, which is the evil fruit of the demagogic and unscrupulous struggle of the Stalin-Bukharin revisionists against the Bolshevik Opposition led by Trotsky, is represented by opportunist politics and a bureaucratic internal regime in the Comintern and in the parties. Stalinization has brought about an enormous and absolutely unprecedented bureaucratization in the apparatus.

The weaknesses of the Communist International and its national sections, and the faction struggles which undermine them, flow directly from the faction struggle in the Russian Communist Party. Stalinization carries schism and disintegration into all the parties. This is the main source of the evils in our party. A recognition of this fact is the only key to the understanding of our party problems and the organization of a communist fight to solve them. The struggle for the regeneration of our party, for the correction of its policies and the formation of a proletarian communist leadership, is an international fight. All attempts to wage this fight on purely national grounds, within the framework of Stalinist "legality," are unprincipled and futile.

The direct responsibility of the Stalinist faction for the

Lovestone-Pepper regime in our party and all its corrupting consequences, is clearly demonstrated by the facts of party history in recent years.

This leadership was established in the party in 1925 by cable of the ECCI plus the jesuitical machinations of Gusev, the representative of the ECCI, after it had twice been decisively rejected by the party membership. Again in 1927 a cable from the ECCI prohibited a majority in the Central Committee (the bloc of Cannon-Weinstone-Foster groups) from exercising their right to reorganize the Polcom and elect party officers—thus safeguarding the Lovestone control. The "Supplementary Decision" cabled to the party later in 1927 called upon the party to support the Lovestone group after the ECCI had been compelled to reject its main line.

Further help in mobilizing the party for the Lovestone faction was given a little later by cables hypocritically protesting against the "factionalism" of the opposition while ignoring and condoning the most criminal and corrupt factional practices of the Lovestone group. Ewert, present leader of the "conciliators" group in the German party, in his capacity as representative of the CI to our party in 1927, helped the Lovestone faction to gerrymander and steal the party convention in Tammany fashion. The secretarial decision of the ECCI after the Sixth World Congress in 1928 ignored all the big political questions and simply declared the contentions that the Lovestone leadership follows a right-wing line (which were proven to the hilt in the Opposition document "The Right Danger in the American Party") to be unfounded and thus again indicated its political support of this faction.

By all these means—by political pressure, by direct organizational interference, by abusing the confidence of the party members in the Communist International, by tricks and machinations—the centrist leadership of the CPSU and the Comintern has strengthened and supported its American counterpart and entrenched its control in the American party.

This Stalinization of the party has reduced the dues-paying membership from 16,325 in 1925 (convention report January–June) to 7,277 in 1928 (financial reports January–August), in a three-year period which offered abundant possibilities for the party to grow. It has brought about a particularly heavy loss of native American and trade union elements, reducing the proportion of such elements in the party, always far too small, to insignificance. Party democracy does not exist. There is far less freedom of expression in the party today, working under legal conditions and during a preconvention discussion period, than there was normally in the underground, illegal party. Bureaucratization has become a cancer eating out the party life. The class composition of the party has deteriorated and the main sections of the party leadership, its decisive upper strata, are predominantly petty bourgeois. Permanent factionalism rages in the party year in and year out, and absorbs its main energies. The whole course of disruption and disintegration is being crowned now by the wholesale expulsion of the Opposition—proletarian communists, founders of the party, and its most loyal, reliable, and tested militants.

Self-criticism

The "self-criticism" of the ruling faction consists in making tardy admissions of the least significant of the errors they committed, without indicating any connection between them, or the basis upon which they arose. The important and more dangerous mistakes committed by them are "admitted" only under the most severe pressure, and even then, in most cases, they are falsely ascribed to the opponents of the very errors. The nature of the errors, the reasons and responsibility for them, are never established. The result is that they are either repeated in the same form, or else they are repeated in an inverted form caused by irresponsible swings to the opposite extreme.

A genuine Leninist self-criticism is a primary prerequisite for the establishment of clarity, the raising of the ideological level of the party, and the elimination of the distrust and cynicism caused by its absence. Instead of self-criticism, the party leadership has instituted a regime of diplomacy, concealment, distortion, and self-praise. Its own "achievements" are paraded and exaggerated in the most revolting shopkeeper's manner. A blank check of immunity from any error or crime is an automatic premium to any of its faction supporters.

In this poisonous atmosphere the disparity between words and deeds grows greater every day. Resolutions, theses, and motions are made primarily for the record and not to be carried out. They remain on paper in the party archives, to be pointed to only to justify this or that action, after the fact. They are carried out only insofar as they are in harmony with the temporary, opportunist interests of the leadership. The absolute impossibility of making the deed conform with the word in the present situation lies in the fact that any correction of party line or improvement of its condition can be made only in the sharpest struggle against the present party leadership. Since the present leadership is exclusively interested in its self-preservation at all costs, the word remains a hollow, farcical gesture.

Party democracy

The absence of any genuine self-criticism in the party goes hand in hand with the growing bureaucratization of the leadership and functionary staff of the party, its deproletarianization, and the increasing lack of workers' democracy in the ranks.

The wholesale expulsion of proletarian fighters goes hand in hand with the steady recruitment of all kinds of dubious petty-bourgeois careerist and half-baked intellectual elements. The class composition of the party, particularly in the New York district, where almost half of the party membership is concentrated, has been seriously affected by this process in recent years and has had a direct expression in the opportunist policies of the party and the strengthening of the opportunist elements generally.

In the upper circles of the party, in the party apparatus, this increased proportion of nonproletarians is enormously expanded. Under the Lovestone regime these elements are appearing more and more on all sides as party representatives, officials, managers, directors, teachers, supervisors. Coming to these positions without sufficient prerequisites, they bring with them the detestable careerist attributes of insolence, arrogance, and pride of office, antagonizing and alienating the worker elements and thrusting them aside.

Accompanying this is the alarming growth of the tendency to replace in various positions those comrades who have built and worked in the party since its formation with those who have only recently joined the movement from the Socialist Party, the Zionist movement, liberals, etc., etc.

The party must examine these questions in direct connection with the struggle against the right danger and the opportunist leaders who are its bearer. It is necessary at once to take a complete registration of the party membership, with the object of precisely determining its class composition. A reorganization of the party apparatus from top to bottom, up to and including the Central Executive Committee, placing the overwhelming majority of the positions in the hands of experienced and tested party workers of proletarian origin, must be effected at once. In this connection, the party must reject categorically the gross mockery of proletarianization which the Lovestone-Pepper group is carrying out. It consists of the formal addition to certain party committees of unknown comrades who are never intended to function in the committees except to serve as proletarian window dressing behind which the opportunists and petty-bourgeois careerists can work with greater security. For the next period, until a proletarian stabilization has been achieved in the party and its apparatus, the party membership must be closed entirely to nonproletarian elements. Even then their admittance into the party must be strictly supervised.

An analysis of the number of comrades employed in the apparatus (in the party national and district offices, in the party press and their administration, in the large number of auxiliary organizations, in the numerous cooperative institutions, etc., etc.) will reveal the striking fact that the party has a staff of paid functionaries and technical workers equal to more than 10 percent of the party membership, who are not employed in industry or in agriculture. This bureaucratic crust is smothering the party.

The fight for the party is a fight against the systematic opportunist policy of the leadership and the bureaucratic regime with which it fortifies itself against control and correction from below. This internal regime is tied up with the external opportunistic line and is an expression of it. A serious struggle for a correction of the opportunist external policy which weakens the party and consequently the class before their enemies is impossible without the most determined, stubborn, and relentless fight for party democracy. Party democracy is the means whereby the policy of the party can be corrected and its leadership reorganized on a proletarian communist basis.

The raising of the issue of party democracy and the education of the party membership on its meaning and significance are made all the more necessary by the confusion that prevails on the whole question of party government, of forms of working-class organization, of centralization and discipline. This confusion is fostered by the monstrous distortions of Lenin's teachings disseminated by the party leadership and is the direct result of them.

The present leaders and "teachers" of the party distort and misapply these conceptions. They totally neglect to take up this burning problem at all in their respective faction theses. They substitute the idea of discipline in the formal, mechanical sense for the Leninist doctrine of democratic centralism. Our party, which ought to be the champion of workers' democracy throughout the entire labor movement, is making the very word taboo. All democracy is indiscriminately labeled bourgeois democracy. Party democracy, of course, does not exclude but presupposes centralization and discipline. It is just the bureaucratic distortions and mechanical conceptions of discipline which give rise to syndicalist prejudices in this respect.

The party must make an end of this situation by struggle against the leadership that fosters and expresses it. The first step is to break down the disruptive expulsion policy and to reinstate the expelled communists with the right to express their views in the party by normal means. The policy of administrative gagging, suppression, and terrorism must be overthrown. The worker communist must be able to feel at home in his own party. He must have the right and feel the freedom to open his mouth and say what he thinks without being called into the office of some petty official or other, like a recalcitrant workingman in a factory, and threatened with discipline. All talk of party democracy in the face of suppression on all sides and the wholesale expulsion of comrades for their views is a swindle.

Americanization in the Bolshevist sense

As a result primarily of historical conditions, the American Communist movement was from the beginning predominantly a movement of foreign-born workers, whose revolutionary and socialist traditions had a European background. Their passage to communism was fundamentally a reaction to events in Europe, above all the Russian proletarian revolution, and this reaction was not closely connected with the class struggle in the United States. In its formative years the party stood aloof to a very large extent from the great mass struggles of that time—the steel strike, the general strike of the miners, and so on—and did not recruit its forces from them. The left wing in the Socialist Party and the Communist Party into which it evolved were dominated by foreign-language federations. The "American" leaders, for the most part, were the "English expression" of this movement.

This anomalous situation imparted to the early movement an unrealistic and extremely sectarian character and caused deep internal contradictions and struggles. The long struggle against federation domination and the federation form of organization, although formally an organizational question, was fundamentally a political struggle for the Americanization of the movement. It was closely bound up with the struggle against sectarianism: for a realistic trade union policy, for "legal" activities and a legal party, for the labor party, and for the predominance of American workers in the leadership.

This character of the party and its leadership in the formative years militated against its effective participation in the class struggle and greatly weakened its recruiting power among the American revolutionary workers. The IWW movement of that time, which was a great reservoir for communism and a large part of the natural base for an American Communist movement was not attracted, and the anticommunist strategy of the reactionary anarcho-syndicalist leaders was greatly facilitated. The party failed likewise, for these reasons, to recruit thousands of revolutionary-minded American workers in the Socialist Party and in the left wing of the trade unions.

The violent internal struggles were called forth by the contradictions between the composition, tactics, and leadership of the party, and the conditions for its existence and effective functioning in the class struggle. The struggle of a minority to overcome these contradictions, in which the present Opposition was in the forefront from the very beginning, received powerful support from the Communist International, particularly in 1921 and 1922. The new course of the party—its emergence from the underground, its adoption of a realistic trade union policy, and its participation in the labor party movement—was the result of this struggle. The recruitment of native workers and active trade unionists began and, particularly under the leadership established at the 1923 convention, developed progressively.

The disruption of the leadership and the alteration of the course of the party in 1925 halted this development; and the past three years have seen a retrogression. The proportion of native workers in the party and its decisive leadership today is insignificant, and the recruiting power of the party among these elements has greatly declined. Even in great mass struggles like that of the miners, the party is unable to gain, and still less likely to keep, any considerable number of new members of this type. It remains primarily a party of foreign-born workers with its decisive working-class membership narrowing more and more to the needle trades. This state of affairs, bound up with the problem of party policy and leadership, is fatal for the growth of the party as a factor in the class struggle in America.

It is necessary to state these facts openly and fearlessly, and to insist on a change of course in the most resolute manner. The new course for the Americanization of the party in the communist sense must be adopted. Conscious, deliberate, and systematic efforts must be made in all class-struggle activities by every member of the party to attract native workers into the party and into its leadership in all of its spheres. The selection of party representatives, the methods of approach, and so on, must be decisively influenced by this aim. There must be a simplification and popularization of propaganda and agitational work. Far greater attention to simple, modest tasks of a movement in its elementary stage of development. Greater responsibility and concentration on main struggles and activities, and less sensation-mongering, less pretentiousness, bombast, exaggeration, fake campaigns, and "high politics." Use of language comprehensible to the American workers and more related to their traditions.

The problem is to unite the inspiration of the Russian revolution, which is and has been the strongest influence on the revolutionary wing of the American labor movement, with a realistic approach to the specific tasks of the American communists. This now applies especially to the defenders of the Russian Opposition, which is the representative of the victory of the Russian October. This unity will be the means of permeating the American workers with the spirit of internationalism while strengthening and developing the communist influence in the class struggle in America.

The efforts made in the past to pervert the revolutionary essence of this program to adapt the party to its specific tasks, have served only to justify the present composition of the party and the laxness in improving it, but have in no sense invalidated the correctness of our proposals, which are as vital today as ever, if not more so.

The party, the groups, and our perspectives

The party today is in the throes of a factional crisis which has raged continuously since 1923. This factional struggle, which the ECCI frequently declared "has no basis in principle," is the product of the Stalinization of the party and the imposition upon it from above of an artificial and incompetent leadership. At bottom this struggle, which numerous "unanimous" resolutions could not stop and which broke out afresh after each proclamation of "unity," has been a conflict between the proletarian and the petty-bourgeois tendencies.

As a result of the failure to understand the struggle in the Communist Party of the Soviet Union, which is the main source of the factional situation in our party, the proletarian tendency has made numerous mistakes and has not always been able to formulate the issues clearly, since this could be done only with an international orientation and perspective.

The ruling faction in the party, on the other hand, was strengthened by its international connection with the Stalin-Bukharin regime and received direct and continuous support from it. The Lovestone-Pepper faction is an American replica of the international faction which is undermining the Comintern and weakening the position of the Soviet Union. This faction of Lovestone-Pepper is a combination of the old ultraleft and "Goose Caucus" elements of the underground party (who fought the formation of the legal party) and the centrist leaders of the "Workers' Council" group (who fought the underground Communist Party). The Lovestone-Pepper group of intellectuals balanced between them, "reconciled" their differences, and shifted the leadership of the combination to the petty-bourgeois, intellectual, and careerist elements. This faction was patched together for the purpose of securing and holding "power" in the party at all costs and under all circumstances. It has no roots or traditions in the working class and no firm or definite line of policy. Its course is an opportunist-adventurist shifting from day to day according to factional and inner-party exigency, to which its external policies are always subordinated. In the struggle against the Opposition Communists the party leadership has already resorted to methods of a pronounced fascist character (gangsterism, burglary).

The personal records of the leaders of this faction are so malodorous as to render them absolutely ineligible for leading positions in a communist party, which must gain and hold the confidence of the workers to such a large extent through its leaders. Pepper, the Moscow representative of the faction, was a social patriot during the war, a war correspondent of the Austro-Hungarian Empire. Prior to the Hungarian Soviet Republic he was a minister in the bourgeois government who arrested communists, denounced them as "left counterrevolutionaries," and advocated mass terror against them. Lovestone, while a member of the Central Executive Committee of the party in 1920, testified for the state of New York in the trial of Harry Winitsky, securing thereby the dismissal of two indictments against himself while Comrade Winitsky went to prison. Wolfe ran away from the party during the Palmer raids in 1919 and disappeared for two years. After the Bridgeman raid in 1922 he again deserted the party and went to Mexico against party instructions, returning in 1925. Wicks made a renegade speech before a body of businessmen in Gary, Indiana, in the winter of 1920, during the height of the terror against the Communists, as a "reformed red" and "exposer" of the Communist movement and the steel strike. Olgin fought the Russian revolution and the communists in the columns of the yellow *Jewish Daily Forward.* Minor attacked Lenin and the Bolshevik revolution in the capitalist press. Trachtenberg, Engdahl, and Kruse fought on the side of Berger and Hillquit against the communists during the split of 1919 and for two years afterward. At the Socialist Party convention in 1921 Kruse protested against and branded as a lie the accusation that he wanted to join the Communist International without reservations. Kruse expelled communists from the Socialist Party and the Young People's Socialist League—and is expelling some of the same comrades from the party in the Chicago district today.

Almost the entire editorial staff of the *Freiheit* was trained in the school of the *Forward* and the reactionary Zionist press, and conducted there the same kind of a campaign against the Communist Party that they now conduct against the Opposition. An examination of the records of many of the lower and district functionaries of the present regime will reveal similar facts. The Lovestone-Pepper faction leaders are a distinct type of adventurers in the movement. These are the people who expel and calumniate us.

The Foster-Bittelman group represents a section of the forces organized in the beginning of the struggle in 1923 which signalized the crystallization of the proletarian tendency. It is now dividing itself into two parts—the Foster wing and the Bittelman wing—and this process will go deeper as a result of the contradictions in its position. Its attempt to struggle against the ruling faction on purely "national" questions while supporting the regime in the International which this faction represents, renders its whole position untenable.

Lack of principle, characterlessness, intellectual and political cowardice on the part of the Foster-Bittelman group of "leaders," so clearly and so disgustingly revealed in the whole preconvention and "anti-Trotsky" campaign, are the manifestations and the result of their contradictory and impossible position.

The support these leaders have received in the preconvention struggle represents in the main the effort of the proletarian tendency within the party to find a "legal" expression for its opposition to the Lovestone-Pepper regime. These proletarian elements who have not yet developed the full implications of the struggle and do not yet understand its international character have mobilized around the Foster-Bittelman faction. The leaders of this faction exploit these proletarian tendencies for picayune factional aims and the struggle for organizational positions. They thus play the part of a shield for the opportunist adventurers who control the party. Their role is to restrain and confuse the proletarian tendency; to muddle up the issues and hold back the struggle into channels prescribed by the international Stalin regime; to prevent an understanding of the great world questions which are bound up with the conflict between the proletarian and the petty-bourgeois tendencies in our party.

This faction of inner-party opportunists, lacking firm principle, has a deep internal conflict between the impulse for struggle against the party regime, which comes from below, and the mood for capitulation in the top circles, and is constantly staggering back and forth between them. Their frequent and contradictory "statements" and "declarations" reflect this antagonism, from which the faction cannot escape and which it cannot reconcile. Their difficulties grow from day to day, and a collapse of the faction, foreshadowed by the Foster-Bittelman split, is by no means improbable at the party convention.

An attempt to continue the faction struggle after the convention will bring new blows from the Communist International and organizational persecution. The leading circles of the faction, strongly bureaucratized, stand in deadly fear of this, and they are preparing to capitulate and withdraw their thesis that the Lovestone-Pepper leadership constitutes the right wing and the main danger to the party. On the other hand the proletarian supporters of the faction demand a continuation of the struggle and will revolt against a capitulation, and move closer to the Opposition, which fights on a principled line.

The "politics" of the faction leaders consists of the search for an expedient formula to reconcile this conflict. But the whole situation excludes and prohibits such a reconciliation. In any case, further splits and disintegration of the faction which has based itself on temporary expediency are inevitable.

The Opposition is a nucleus of communists who have participated in the founding of the party and who have played a decisive and progressive part in all the work and struggles of the party since its inception. Most of them were active in the revolutionary movement for years before the party was organized. They constitute a group of comrades who have worked together on a common line for a longer time than any group that ever existed in the party.

The present Opposition was in the forefront of the party struggles against underground sectarianism. It formulated and fought in the front ranks for the correct trade union policy, for the legal party, and for the labor party. Four of the expelled communists—Cannon, Swabeck, Abern, and Edwards—were delegates to the Fourth Congress of the Communist International and led the successful fight there on these questions after a protracted struggle in the party. They were the first to take up the fight against the Federated Farmer-Labor Party and the adventurist politics connected with it in 1923. They were the organizers of the revolt against the Pepper regime and the movement which began then to form the proletarian tendency into a group. The present Opposition led the fight in 1925 against the narrow base of our trade union work and thereby helped the party to again break its isolation and get the miners' mass movement under way. The Opposition as at present constituted has worked together as a unit for a consistent line of policy which has been in the main correct, and works today along the same line.

The decisive role of the present Opposition in the historic struggle against underground sectarianism and trade union "leftism" is in no way contradictory to our present stand. We see no more virtue in "left" radicalism now than we saw then, and we offer no ultraleft panaceas to the party. Our main fight now is on another front because the circumstances have placed the danger of centrism and opportunism in the foreground (although sectarianism, particularly on the trade union and labor party questions, is by no means liquidated).

The present struggle in our party and in the entire International is before all a struggle against opportunism and bureaucratic corruption, which are undermining them. The struggle against these deadly perils takes precedence over all others. The struggle facing the communist vanguard in all parties today is the struggle to preserve the Communist movement. This is the historic mission of the Opposition on an international scale. The task of the Opposition is to fight with all its power against the opportunist and bureaucratic degeneration of the party, without slipping onto the side track of sectarian isolation. This requires first of all firmness of principle and a realistic line of tactics based on fundamental principles.

This, the actual line of the Opposition, is perfectly clear to the Social Democrats as well as to those elements within the party who stand furthest to the right. The whole centrist group of the Workers' Council, which joined the party as late as 1922, the opportunist trade union leaders in the needle trades, the entire bureaucracy of the Finnish section—all these have unanimously and enthusiastically denounced the Opposition. Those elements of the Finnish section in New York and Massachusetts who have come into conflict with the party regime on questions of the Finnish movement, have likewise rejected the platform of the Opposition. All these facts are known.

The attempt of the party leadership in its statement in the *Daily Worker* of February 15 to make the Opposition responsible for alleged combinations with reactionary and antiparty elements against the party ("The American Trotskyists, the renegade Cannon group, have now formed openly an alliance in the Finnish co-operatives with the fascists, with the white guardist followers of Mannerheim, the bloodhound of the Finnish proletariat, with the fakers of the Salvation Army and with the Social Democrats gathered around the *Raavaij* against the Workers (Communist) Party of America") is a deliberate slander worthy only of the school which invented the infamous tale about the "Wrangel officer" and the Russian Opposition.[23]

All tendencies to break away from the party to the right, to moderate the struggle against the Socialist Party, or to form an indiscriminate combination of opportunist and antiparty elements against the party have nothing in common with our views or aims. Our line is a principled line. We fight as a detachment of the International Leninist Opposition for the regeneration of the Communist movement in the struggle against opportunism from without as well as from within the party. While excluded from the party we carry on our revolutionary work in the class struggle on the basis of our platform.

The Stalin-Bukharin regime converts the faction struggle into a game of befuddling the party membership and pulling wires from Moscow. The Opposition in the American party, uniting with the line of the Russian Opposition, breaks through this disgraceful and corrupting game. It brings clarity into the party struggle and gives the proletarian tendency a firm guiding line. It elevates the struggle to an international principled basis, gives it a revolutionary content, and begins the education of the party in struggle for Leninist fundamentals on the great world questions of the period.

Our fight as a part of the International Opposition for the Leninist line on a world scale is at the same time a fight to preserve the Communist movement in America and to build it into a working-class power able to fulfill its great historic mission.

The present Opposition fought for the Russian revolution since 1917 and for the Communist International since the first day its banner was raised. Our fight today is a continuation on the same line and for the same basic principles.

We raise before the party convention the question of restoring the party membership of the expelled comrades of the Opposition on the basis of the foregoing statement of aims and views. We also propose to the convention that it take a stand for the reestablishment of the unity of the Communist International by calling for the reinstatement of the Russian and International Opposition, and for the immediate cessation of those measures which especially undermine the party and the proletarian dictatorship and strengthen the enemies of the working class—the arrests, exile, and banishment of the Russian Opposition.

The party organization

The organization of the party, in the party units and in the trade union and language fractions, represents today a state of chaos and demoralization. The execution of the reorganization and the functioning of the party from top to bottom since that period have brought confusion, inaction, and indifference into the party ranks.[24]

The basis of party organization today is the shop nucleus and the street nucleus (international branch). This is correct. The organization of street nuclei (international branches) where shop nuclei cannot be organized had as its purpose an accelerated political development and general activity on the part of all members. The former language branches formally were liquidated in order that the foreign-speaking member might be brought into the sphere of general American labor and political activity and party life, and get away from the narrow existence of his national grouping.

But what do we find actually? The street nuclei or international branches are for the most part nonfunctioning bodies in a political sense. Organizationally, there is the anomaly that three, four, or five street nuclei, with twenty or more members each on the record book, will meet in the same room or hall at the same hour, often mixing or combining their work (New York district). Presumably the street nucleus is organized on the territorial (living area) basis of the members. Generally throughout the party the street nuclei are formally organized in that manner.

Actually the street nucleus (international branch) loosens this practice and membership becomes general regardless of residence. This, however, is not the main defect. The defects are so outstanding, and known to any member who wants to see, that it is but necessary to mention them in general outline form. The functions conducted by the street nuclei are mockeries of working-class activity and political life. It is common practice that the party members at their unit meetings find themselves confronted with an orgy of ticket-selling, money-collecting, and similar technical activities, till they feel that they are petty salesmen and agents instead of active communists concerning themselves with the vital issues of the working class. Bureaucratism is rampant; the functions of political activity, discussion, and decision are usurped by the committees and officials.

It is necessary that the party organization be overhauled. Shop nuclei must be formed in such places where there are sufficient members working to make it possible for the nucleus to function actively (issuance of a shop paper, organization of the unorganized, etc.).

The street nuclei (international branches) must be constituted on a genuine territorial basis and have a membership of not less than twenty-five or more than fifty. The party shall emphasize the character of work of the nucleus. Namely, that the units shall concern themselves with political and labor problems (discussion and action on shop problems, trade union questions, parliamentary activity, strikes, etc.). All technical work, such as payment of dues, other financial collections, etc., shall be placed as a subsidiary part of the agenda and conducted at specific periods only, and in such a manner as in no way to interfere with the main tasks.

The general vitalization of party life for each member is

essential. Each member must feel himself as a factor and contributor to the life and needs of the party. The practice of thinking and administering from above, without real consultation and participation by the membership, must give way to the opportunity for each member to contribute his ideas. Mere orders are not sufficient to produce healthy party life and participation in the class struggle. Thought from the membership is a prerequisite. The membership must have the opportunity through more frequent membership meetings (on a city or section scale,[25] depending on the size of the membership) to take up the major issues and campaigns of the party in order that they may thoroughly understand the party's objective and better be able to carry out its aims. The practice which has made the meetings of functionaries (officials) almost the main and the only medium of discussion must be liquidated. Such practices are breeding grounds for bureaucracy, for separation of the rank-and-file members from the officialdom, both high and low. More frequent membership meetings will make it possible for the rank-and-file worker to contribute his views and to check the functionary; at the same time the officials thereby can obtain a clearer picture of the actual views of the membership and the resources and capacities of the party, and the party work can thus be better carried out. All organizations, and the party organization too, tend to develop always a certain inertness and tradition that conservatize. These tendencies must be guarded against by a continuous reinvigoration from below.

Trade union fractions

The trade union fractions of the party, where they are not utterly liquidated, are lifeless, functioning usually only in time of union elections. In a large measure this is due to the virtual liquidation of the work in the existing trade unions and the wrong line being developed in the party in this respect. Functioning trade union fractions in every trade and industry, in each local union, district council, etc., are absolutely essential for the extension of party influence in the trade unions. Lifeless or nonfunctioning trade union fractions foster the development of a noncritical attitude toward the so-called progressives and left-wingers in the labor movement, of an easy-going opportunism and adaptability on the one hand and a completely "leftist" or sectarian attitude on the other. The latter tends to confine activity in the trade unions and among the unorganized to the Communists alone.

The trade union fractions must be organized and brought to life in the unions. The TUEL must become a genuine organization and not remain just a Communist body. The party center must put this work in the foreground, and work out also for each industry a concrete program around which and through which the fractions may be vitalized and become the real instruments of the trade union work.

Agrarian work

The severe crisis in agriculture, with all its sharp consequences for the masses of poor farmers and farm wage workers, has not been entirely overcome by American capitalism. It has remained one of the chief sources of weakness in the armor of the American bourgeoisie, and a broad field for agitation and organization for the Communist movement which has not been taken advantage of except to an insignificant extent.

The party has indeed followed a consistently opportunist line in this field of work, having gone so far as to give virtual endorsement to the hypocritical McNary-Haugen

Bill and other bourgeois "remedies." It has further failed to separate the various strata of the agricultural population from each other, and has therefore not succeeded in approaching any of them properly. The farmers have been looked on "as a mass" solely as objects for maneuvering in farmer-labor party movements. It is necessary to change the course of the party in this respect.

The first step the party must take is to obtain contact with the agricultural wage workers, the proletarians on the farm. It is the primary duty of the party to carry on this work, and especially to have a correct approach to the syndicalist workers (the IWW), who have been the only organized force in this field up till now.

The ranks of the party must be open to only those farmers who accept the proletarian viewpoint on property. It must concentrate its chief efforts among the farmers upon organizing the tenant and heavily mortgaged farmers, who feel the heavy oppression of the bankers, railroads, mill owners, and big farmers. A guarantee for the proper functioning of the movement of the poor farmers, that they will remain on the correct path of struggle instead of succumbing to the pressure of the big farmers, is that the proletarians and semiproletarians on the land shall have the preponderance of leadership in the movement.

The Negro tenant farmers, sharecroppers, and those who are slaving under a system of virtual peonage in the South, must receive the special attention of the party. It is possible to organize them: this has been demonstrated in the past by the fact that organizations of the Negro poor farmers have arisen spontaneously in the South. It is possible to unite them with the poor white farmers: this has also been demonstrated by past experiences even in the reactionary South, where, in Texas for example, strong organizations of Negro and white poor and tenant farmers existed and functioned for some time.

Young Workers League

The situation in the Young Workers (Communist) League merits the deepest attention of the entire movement. The leadership and line of the league have merely been a miniature replica of the factional and corrupt party regime. The evils of the Lovestone-Pepper leadership in the party have appeared in an even more grotesque form in the Zam-Herberg (Lovestone) leadership in the league. Rampant factionalism, petty-bourgeois cynicism and super-sophistication, occupation with "high politics" are corrupting the league like so many diseases. The league has become nothing more nor less than a faction agency for the Lovestone regime. Instead of the league being in the forefront of the struggle against opportunism in the party, it is always ready to endorse it unconditionally.

In every struggle where splendid opportunities for growth were presented, the league failed signally to take advantage of them. In the face of the growing exploitation of the working youth and the possibilities for the development of struggle, the league has either lost membership or stood still. There is an increase in the mood of passivity among the league members, and the inner life of the league becomes constantly more barren and withered. The leadership of the league has been a dead hand on the organization.

A symbol of the situation is the fact that the founders of the Communist youth movement in this country, and its leadership at the period of its swiftest and healthiest development (Abern, Carlson, Edwards, Shachtman, etc.) have now been expelled. In their stead has been placed a leadership which cannot have the confidence of the mass of the membership or the young workers, which has brought only disintegration, factionalism, and degeneration into the league. Instead of helping to turn out this leadership and replace it with a sound proletarian core which alone is able to solve the difficulties with which the league is pressingly confronted, the Executive Committee of the Young Communist International has followed a course which has in actuality resulted in the entrenchment of the Zam-Lovestone leadership in the league. The same course has been followed by the party leadership in its relationship to the youth.

The league (and even the Pioneers!) is at present being mobilized against so-called Trotskyism, that is, against the fundamental tenets of Leninism. Instead of the Communist youth being permitted to develop freely their natural inclinations against opportunism and revisionism, they are herded into blind support for the liquidation of the basic teachings of Bolshevism. The main task of the league members is to fight relentlessly for the line of revolutionary principles now being defended by the Leninist Opposition. An additional prerequisite is the eradication of all corrupt, petty-bourgeois tendencies in the league, of opportunist following in the path of the party faction regime, of "smart-Aleckism," cynicism, and playing with the working-class movement.

Financial worries

February 20, 1929

The following letter was written to Albert Glotzer in Chicago.

Dear Al,

Our thesis is all finished and it is a great relief to get it off our hands. The trouble now begins with the printer, who refuses to print the paper till he gets some money, which we haven't got. The failure to get out the issue will, of course, have a bad effect, but it can't be helped. There is no chance to get out the February 15 issue this week on that account. Our hope now is to get it out early next week.

It is bad to have all these financial worries on top of the other problems and tasks. The main cause of our difficulties in this respect is the *too casual* attitude of the comrades supporting us and their apparent illusion that we have all the money we need. We must make the comrades understand that the smallness of our numbers, the odds against us, and the immensity of the issues involved in the struggle (the preservation of the Communist movement) require real sacrifices from the pioneer fighters. Only this understanding and spirit will enable us to do the work laid out for us.

The comrades do not begin to realize the handicaps we work under. For example, several of the local groups have their own mimeographs, but we haven't been able to get one. We have no office or other minimum facilities for efficient work—to say nothing of a stenographer. We now have the manuscripts translated on the Chinese and Anglo-Russian questions, and several new articles of Trotsky's (untranslated), but can't get them printed. On top of all this our personal economic situation is becoming altogether impossible. Our main problem now is the financial problem.

❖

We are working today on a campaign to raise money, and the Chicago group will receive a letter and other material in a few days. Our cause is growing steadily, and the prospects are for a new shift in our direction after the convention. But if we can't succeed in making *The Militant* a weekly and publishing the material in pamphlets, there is danger of stagnation and the beginning of retrogression in our movement. For those who understand what is at stake there can be no limit to what we do or give to prevent this.

❖

I had a great success at the Boston meeting last Friday night. Nearly three hundred were present, and the sympathetic attention of the audience at the beginning became enthusiastic support at the end. The party sent a squad of hecklers to the meeting, but they got so much the worst of the exchanges that they only helped the meeting and discredited themselves. Some comrades still in the party came to see me the next day and promised to organize a new group for a demonstration immediately after the convention. An old Wobbly friend of mine since 1914, one of the Leavenworth prisoners, was at the meeting to help protect free speech. He promised to bring a bunch from the waterfront next time. The game of breaking up meetings hasn't been much of a success so far, although there are possibilities of its sporadic revival. Our protest meeting here next Tuesday may see such an attempt.

❖

In regard to your letter of February 17, I think you should read again Trotsky's letter in the last *Militant,* "The Situation in Russia," to get a clearer estimate of the center—and the possibilities of it, or part of it, changing its position radically in the event of a serious movement of the workers.[26]

Your third point, on basing ourselves on the fundamental interests of the masses and decisively rejecting party fetishism and theories of its infallibility, is the same standpoint we have. It is one of the most important ideas to impress on the comrades who have become stultified with an absolutely non-Marxist conception of the party and of separate and superior interests of the party. Marx disposed of this *theology* in the *Communist Manifesto.* It needs to be restated and hammered into the consciousness of the comrades.

❖

Your fourth point, on our perspectives in regard to the International as well as the party, requires the most careful and objective thought now. The chasm has surely been deepened and widened by the last events, and they must steel our comrades for the struggle no matter what form it takes. We must be prepared unconditionally to carry the fight for the Russian revolution and for the preservation of the Lenin movement under all circumstances and at all costs. Any sign of capitulation moods under the impact of this new campaign against the Opposition must be hit with a hammer—they would signify nothing but cowardice and treachery and would undermine and destroy the communist nucleus we are forming in struggle for fundamentals. We have not seen or heard of any such tendencies anywhere in our ranks. The criminal playing with the life of Trotsky seems to have had the opposite effect.[27]

However, we must guard against impatience and too-hurried conclusions. The present trend is clearly and surely in the direction of an irremediable split. But we must remember that the Russian Communist proletariat has not spoken decisively yet. A determined movement on their part would change the whole situation and the relation of forces. They may yet do this before it is too late. We must prepare the comrades organizationally and spiritually for the event of a final and complete break without losing sight of the other possibility. In these times when the Russian revolution and the world movement it called forth are hanging in the balance, we must work night and day—and we must strive to see all things clearly, as they really are, and fear no consequences.

I don't think it is quite correct to say we can return to the International only on the condition that our line is accepted. I can conceive of a situation where the action of the Russian workers would compel a shifting of forces sufficient to bring about the reinstatement of the Opposition and create the conditions for a continuation of the struggle within the party. I hardly think it is too late for this, and it surely is the best hope for the salvation of the revolution. Everything we and the Opposition groups in the other parties do, helps. The *international* support of the Russian Opposition has a vast importance, and in the last analysis it may have a *decisive* importance.

Our section in the theses on the trade union question collides very sharply with the new "theories" of all the factions—Lovestone, Bittelman, and Foster—especially with the rigamarole which excludes the possibility of an organizational growth of the TUEL and rationalizes the withdrawal from the AFL. The article of Bittelman and his new acolytes is nothing but charlatanism of the most transparent sort from start to finish—typical Talmudistic fakery which passes for "theoretical" genius in that pitiful faction of tenth-rate functionaries.

I see where Browder, in his article in the *Daily Worker* (Browder and Zack), demands from Dunne, Hathaway, and Gomez a repudiation of our 1925 fight on the trade union question. In our thesis we recount the whole history of the struggle in the party on the trade union question and emphatically reaffirm the 1925 position.

Our thesis makes the attempt to restate some fundamental tactical lines which are being thrown overboard in the present orgy of fake leftism. I am very sorry we can't send you a copy. We expected to get it off the press tomorrow, but the printer couldn't see it that way. It is not quite as long as the other theses, but will take the whole eight pages of the next issue. Too much to type without a steno.

In the fight,

Jim

The Communists and the 'progressives'

Published March 1, 1929

The following article was published in *The Militant.*

On the heels of the recent convention of the American Federation of Labor, which outdid all others in reaction, there have appeared a number of manifestations of a new "progressive" movement which call for the most serious consideration of the communist and left-wing workers.

The most important of these manifestations is the manifesto printed in the February number of *Labor Age.* This manifesto outlines a platform of sixteen points which is only a slightly modified restatement of the practical platform of the left-wing militants in the labor movement. It includes the organization of the workers in the basic industries into industrial unions, trade union democracy, the five-day week, independent political action, social insurance, and most of the other standard demands of the left wing. Action of a certain sort has accompanied this attempt to formulate the platform of the new progressives.

The conflict between the Brookwood Labor College and the AFL Executive Council, which has opened fire on it, is one phase. On March 2, these apostles of trade union reform unfurled their banner at a polite luncheon in New York City under the auspices of the League for Industrial Democracy, an auxiliary of the Socialist Party headed by Norman Thomas. Also should be mentioned the crusade which the Socialist *New Leader* has been conducting against the [National] Civic Federation policies of Matthew Woll. In all these developments the trend toward a crystallization of a respectable body of progressive opinion within the labor movement can be plainly seen.

The sponsors of the movement are the group around *Labor Age* and the Brookwood Labor College—Muste, Budenz, and others, including quite a few, such as Brophy and Hapgood, who have had relations with the Communists in united-front movements in the past; a considerable number of trade union officials around the country; and the Socialists, who have fought side by side with the AFL bureaucrats against us. Hillquit, Thomas, Oneal, and Company are devoting much attention to the movement and are aiming for the hegemony of it. It would be erroneous, however, to regard the movement as simply the creation of the Socialist Party. Its basis appears to be much broader and, if it continues to develop, will very probably include a much wider circle.

These events are not accidental. They reflect in the first place the unmistakable growth of discontent of wide sections of the workers and their impulse to struggle against the present state of affairs. They are a reaction to the position of the ruling officialdom, which grows ever more brazenly reactionary, smothering these sentiments of the workers and giving them no expression. The virtual abandonment of the old unions by the Communists, who have stood at the head of most of the opposition movements in the past five years, facilitates the emergence of the reformist group and affords the Socialists an opportunity to regain some of their lost positions. The new movement is a challenge to the Communists for the leadership of the coming fights.

These progressives are weathercocks, who reflect certain winds blowing in the labor movement. Their emergence now, with demands which connote militancy, is an indicator of the radicalization of the workers growing within the old unions as well as in the ranks of the unorganized masses. Their role, objectively speaking, is to express this radicalization in words, to harness it in action, and to head it off from any real collision with the capitalists and the AFL machine. And their field for this function is by no means confined to the old unions. A strongly organized bloc of these elements in the AFL can also exercise a great influence on the struggles of the unorganized.

The question whether they will succeed in stultifying the promising movements of the proximate future or whether the very movements of the workers they express and, to a certain extent, help to create are developed in the direction of real class battles, depends very much upon the activities and tactics of the Communists. Communist tactics will have a tremendous bearing on the outcome of the impending struggles of the workers. And one of the most decisive aspects of these tactics is the question of our attitude toward the progressives and the movement which they indubitably express.

International experience will be useful to us in this question, but it cannot provide us with a ready-made formula. Nothing approximating an analogy to the situation and stage of development of the American labor movement exists in any of the European countries. The fight there is between the Communists and the Social Democrats for the leadership of the masses. This is so in America only in the needle trades, a small sector not representative of the whole labor movement. The struggle here is for the creation of a class movement of the workers and the expansion of Communist influence within it. And this, of course, is also a struggle against reformism of all kinds.

The events of the past few years have not altered this basic perspective. Our fundamental tactical line, modified in the light of experience, with the errors and distortions corrected, still holds good. Contrary opinions only substitute wishes for realities. We are not done with the progressives. On the contrary, the question of our attitude towards them and relations with them will take on a tenfold greater significance in the coming period of mass struggles than in the period behind us.

Let us look back at our established tactics on this question. Numerous resolutions, unanimously adopted by the party, as well as resolutions of the CI on the American question, could be quoted. All of these resolutions emphasized the tactic of the united front with progressive elements, and in practice we followed this line.

Such tactics, fundamentally correct, were the key to much of our progress in the trade unions. There were attempts to liquidate them, but these attempts were defeated by a sharp party struggle in 1925 and by the intervention of the Comintern.

In applying this tactic of the united front, the party made many errors. The bloc with Brennan in anthracite, for example, was formed under conditions which actually rehabilitated this discredited faker and failed to build the Communist influence. The noncritical attitude toward Brophy, Hapgood, etc., worked against the militancy of the fight in the miners' union and the firmness and cohesion of the left wing. Some of the maneuvers in the needle trades were more disgraceful back-room bargains with fakers than communist actions to mobilize the masses. But to react against such distortions with the abandonment of the united-front tactic, is like cutting off one's head to cure a toothache. This, it seems, is what is now being proposed, if we are to judge by the party comment on the new progressive manifestations.

The old tactic of united front with criticism and an independent policy is to be replaced by the tactic of straight-out denunciation and completely independent struggle, according to the comment on the new progressives which has appeared in *Labor Unity* and the *Daily Worker.* This looks simpler and easier, but how will it work out? It is not without significance that the same comrades who wanted to pull the party onto this track in 1925 come forward now as the spokesmen of the new revelation. Now, as then, they see the progressive leaders only as individuals and roundly denounce them as fakers. They fail now, as before, to see the movement of workers they express and, to a certain extent, represent. And that is the most important and decisive thing for the Communists.

Earl Browder, back from the Far East in a very revolutionary mood, makes short shrift of these new progressives in the *Daily Worker* of February 25, 26, and 27, 1929. He recites their past treacheries, vacillations, and cowardice with such indignation as to make one wonder what he expected of them. Such conduct is the inevitable result of reformist policy. That is why the revolutionary Marxists formed the Communist Party. The question is not what the reformists will do when the fight grows hot—that should be known in advance—but how can the Communists best develop the struggles of the workers and expand their influence. It is from this standpoint that we must evaluate our past experience with the progressives and draw conclusions for the future.

Proceeding in this way, we have to take issue with Browder's deductions. He says:

"We will no longer waste our energies and time in disastrous attempts to work with these fake progressives. . . . We will never again put forward such a 'progressive' as Brophy as leader for the *tens of thousands of revolutionary miners who have nothing but contempt for such spineless quitters*" (our emphasis).

What pompous nonsense! What disregard of the facts of the protracted struggle to build the left wing among the miners! What a ridiculous attempt to punish the party for his own illusions and disappointments about the progressives.

Did we get our influence among the miners and eventually gain the leadership of a great mass movement in 1928 by having nothing to do with progressives? Quite the contrary. At the beginning of 1926 the left wing in the miners' union was demoralized and the party was isolated. It was the bloc with Brophy and other progressives which gave us access to the masses of miners, who at that time were not "revolutionary miners who have nothing but contempt for such spineless quitters," but admirers of these same Brophys. It was the prestige of Brophy and others, and the confidence the miners had in them primarily, that gave the movement its wide basis at the start.

It was only later, as the struggle grew sharper, that our direct influence grew and the true character of the Brophys was revealed to the miners and they became alienated from them. Our mistakes, particularly our failure to criticize Brophy and others, hampered this process, but in spite of that, the united front yielded rich results and proved its validity by them. And that is precisely the value of the united-front tactic: it mobilizes the workers for struggle and strengthens the Communists as against the reformists. However, to say that the "tens of thousands of miners" even now are "revolutionary" is somewhat of an exaggeration.

The Communists must learn from the experiences in the miners' struggle and draw the conclusions, not to reject the tactic of the united front, but to correct the errors in its application and employ it widely in the future in all fields.

Another stronghold of the new sectarianism remains. It is the theory that the shifting of the center of gravity in our trade union work to the formation of new unions—an absolutely necessary shift—does away with the troublesome problems of the progressives.

"We are entering upon a new course . . .," says Browder, "the course of independent struggle, independent leadership, independent organization, inside and outside the existing trade unions." But are all the influential leaders we encounter in this new field to be pure Communists and left-wingers, who will not disappoint us? Anybody who thinks so is working to build another Socialist Trades and Labor Alliance and not a mass labor movement of the progressive sections of the workers.

And it is just this theory that is beginning to confront the new union movement as a real menace. The current practice of monopolizing the control of the new unions in a mechanical way, of arbitrarily excluding relations and compromises with influential leaders who reflect the hazy development of masses of workers—this practice will be fatal for the movement. It disregards the stage of development, the relation of forces, and all the realities of the situation.

Results of the party convention

Published March 15, 1929

The following article was published in *The Militant.*

The party convention which was to "end the faction struggle and unify the party" ended with a free-for-all fist fight, the sharpening of the internal strife, the wide distribution of new caucus documents, and a race to Moscow by representatives of both factions.[28] It could not be otherwise. This bankruptcy is only the reflection of the political and ideological collapse of the Stalinist regime in the Communist International, a regime which stultifies revolutionary thought, suppresses discussion, and undertakes to solve all difficulties which arise from its barren policy with organizational manipulations. The unanimous endorsement of the Stalin leadership by the convention was an appropriate act.

The convention sessions themselves were an empty formality. The real activity consisted of a long series of caucuses by the two factions and was confined almost exclusively to the paltry struggle over the office of party secretary. The mechanical exclusion of the Opposition prevented a discussion of the great principled questions which confront the Communist International and which lie at the bottom of the fierce factional struggles in all the parties. The convention delegates, carefully selected from the standpoint of their indifference to these questions, naturally could not touch them—they do not even understand them—and this failure doomed the convention to ignominious futility from the start. Without facing these issues, which are the determining factor in the whole Comintern, and taking part in the effort to solve them on the right basis of principle, there can be no "liquidation of the factional struggle" no matter how often the "unprincipledness" of this struggle is proclaimed.

Almost the entire activity of the two caucuses—which met in joint session occasionally as the Sixth Convention of the party—was devoted to the maneuver of Stalin which was represented by the two representatives of the Executive Committee of the Communist International: the proposal that Foster should be appointed secretary of the party.[29] The fact that a secondary organizational question of this kind should become the central problem of the convention is in itself a significant characterization of the gathering. The motive behind this Stalin strategy is quite obvious. In the first place it was a form of pressure on the Lovestone faction to make a complete break with Bukharin. It was also designed to graft Foster onto the Lovestone faction as its "American" expression and decoy for the proletarian communists who are fighting it under the banner of the Communist Opposition. It was easy to accomplish the first aim, for here it was a question of dealing with people without definite principles or loyalties. The second aim had no chance to succeed. It failed to consider the principled motives that animate the proletarian supporters of the Opposition and it underestimated their political intelligence.

The reactions of the two groups in the convention to this proposal regarding the secretaryship throw an interesting light on their actual character. The Bittelman group went into convulsions of enthusiasm over it and regarded it as, almost, the "final victory." For it they completely forgot their "political line," they scrapped their convention theses, they declared a still more "merciless" struggle against the Communist Opposition and howled for "unity" with the "Right Wing"—with Lovestone, Pepper, Wicks, Stachel, Wolfe, Minor, Olgin, or anyone else of a similar stripe who would accept it. How can such an attitude be explained? It is only a few weeks ago that Bittelman issued a statement, signed also by a number of lieutenants and new recruits, repudiating Foster's position on very important questions from a principled standpoint. Foster himself stated in his article that Bittelman had denounced his position as "liquidating everything connected with Communism." Foster's articles reaffirmed his stand as against that of Bittelman and all the rest of the group. How then can the appointment of Foster be regarded as such a great "concession" to the Bittelman faction that everything else can be cheerfully sacrificed? The incident demonstrates quite clearly that organization positions play the main role in this case and that the theses (cast aside so soon and so lightly) and the big talk about political line (forgotten already) were merely trimmings. What kind of a group is this which divides over political questions and reunites over organization questions?

The attitude of the Lovestone group to the Stalin maneuver was more businesslike, practical, and "political" in the Stalinist sense. They took away its main motive by introducing a resolution for Stalin and against Bukharin—thus refuting at the same time the accusation that they are purely and simply a right wing. They can also be center or left if occasion demands. Their next step was to discredit the proposal to make Foster secretary of the party. For this they put forward their "proletarian" delegations to attack Foster's war record openly in the convention. The article signed by W.J. White in the *Daily Worker* of March 4 was part of this campaign, and poor White of course did not write the article. It is quite obvious that Bedacht and Lovestone wrote it. "Where was the 'leader' of the Opposition during the past war?" asks the article. "Does his record in the past war assure reliability in the coming war? It does not." With words like these and others even more blunt and outspoken on the convention floor, the carefully coached "proletarians" hammered at the candidacy of Foster for the secretaryship. Thus the Lovestone caucus was solidified against the "war danger" and Foster. They finished by electing three secretaries with equal rights, one of whom is Foster in the same position he held before the convention and with even less prestige.[30]

The Bittelman-Foster caucus document accuses the Lovestone faction, because of its rejection of Foster as secretary, of placing the convention "in the position of open hostility to the C.I."—that is, to the Stalin faction. But that doesn't follow at all—the wish probably influences the thought that thereby they would receive the favors that come only to the "loyal" ones. They didn't understand Lovestone's maneuver any more than they understood Stalin's. It is absurd to think the Lovestoneites will split on this question. Their aim was to discredit the idea of Foster as the actual leader of the party so completely that Stalin will either withdraw his demand that Foster be appointed secretary; or, if Stalin insists, on the ground of the exigencies of the fight against "Trotskyism," they can finally accept it without in any way endangering their real control.

Eight delegates of the Lovestone caucus, including Weinstone, split from the faction over this issue on the platform of the literal acceptance of all decisions of the Stalinist leadership of the Comintern regardless of their contents and no matter how much one contradicts another. The nimbleness which such a platform requires in these days makes Weinstone its natural leader. Two years ago he broke with Lovestone because he thought the CI really meant to unify the party. A year later he returned to the faction because he thought the CI was against Foster. Now he makes another switch because he read the latest cablegram literally, without thinking of what it really means. He hasn't got things straight yet.

The convention session of Friday evening, March 8, was broken up by a free-for-all fight which began with the refusal to grant the floor to a minority delegate and was soon followed by a general melee which spread throughout the hall and among the visitors in the balcony, until the singing of the "Internationale" brought a lull during which the meeting was adjourned. Such a thing never happened before in all the history of our party—not even in gatherings which ended in splits. This unheard-of scandal is the first interest payment received by the party on its investment in the methods of gangsterism against the Opposition. It is a warning. The methods of the labor fakers cannot be played with "just a little"—they will permeate the whole movement and undermine its ideological foundations. And to what base uses is the noble song of the international proletariat being put? Nowadays they sing it at meetings of the Opposition to compel the audience to arise and prevent the speaker from being heard;

and at party meetings, it seems, they are beginning to sing it when a physical fight breaks out—if possible, before the cops arrive. Such desecration is a sign of the times. Hooliganism is a symptom of degeneration.

According to the *Daily Worker* of March 11 the convention unanimously accepted the open letter of the Comintern (printed in the *Daily Worker* of March 4) without reservations and declared complete agreement with it. All the previous theses, countertheses, statements, and declarations of the two factions were scrapped in favor of this document which, on the most important questions, is much nearer to the platform of the Opposition than to the theses of the other groups. It would be a grave mistake, however, to conclude that this action signifies a change of course on the part of either of them or a removal of the basis of the quarrels. It is merely a gesture of internal diplomacy and an easy bureaucratic way of saying the CI is always right. The light-heartedness with which the open letter was accepted as a substitute for their various theses and other documents demonstrates how little importance they themselves attached to them. Such practices reduce the authority of leadership to nothing.

The open letter represents a great departure from the line of the Sixth Congress on the position of American imperialism and the perspectives of revolutionary development in Europe. Bukharin's report to the Sixth Congress was almost as one-sided in its awe before the power of American imperialism, in its failure to estimate its involvement in the general crisis of capitalism and the revolutionary implications of its world aggressions, as was the conception of Pepper and Lovestone. The open letter represents a partial attempt to "correct" this line under pressure of the criticisms of the International Opposition, in a typical Stalinist manner, without saying so or explaining the reasons. Trotsky's criticism of the Draft Program makes a Leninist appraisal of the world situation and particularly the role of American imperialism. This is the real source of the belated half-corrections of the mistakes of the Sixth Congress partly revealed in the open letter. In accepting this new line they accept a part of that which they glibly pronounced a Menshevist and counterrevolutionary program. Such turns are easy for people whose words signify nothing but factional speculation. In practice it means nothing. Tomorrow they can reverse the position and it will mean just as little.

A section of the open letter of considerable interest to us is that which stresses the necessity of a course toward the Americanization of the party in the communist sense. This runs like a single thread throughout the document and is listed in the summary as one of the four conditions for the development of the party on the path toward transformation into a mass party. We also emphasized this point in our platform; and it is not a new opinion of ours. "The Party can become a mass proletarian Party only on condition that it widens its base by creating its main strongholds in the ranks of the American workers." "The course on the American workers and the decisive branches of industry must run through all the activities of the Party." Such expressions in the open letter are almost literally the same as those in our platform.

The need for such a course was not even mentioned in the theses of the Lovestone and Foster-Bittelman factions. They considered this idea, which we have brought forward repeatedly and insistently in the past, as a "deviation" peculiar to us, a part of our "pessimism," etc. Now they blandly accept it—and forget it. The "ideological campaign" to permeate the party with this consciousness and the thoroughgoing organizational readjustments which such a course necessitates will not be thought of. It is impossible to educate a party in this way.

Having withdrawn their own theses and adopted the open letter, both factions have once again found a "common platform" as a basis for "unity." According to tradition this should be the signal for the intensification of the factional struggle, and the Foster caucus document proceeds along that line. It accuses the other side of giving only "the customary lip service to the line of the C.I." Platforms have no real meaning in this degenerated struggle for power in the party. Stalinization has produced the type of bureaucrats in all the parties who have no definite standpoint, no stability of principle, and for whom the prevailing winds in the Russian party are decisive.

It was the elder Liebknecht who said that a revolutionary must be able to change his mind within twenty-four hours if the interest of the revolution demands it. The Stalinist regime has modernized and "improved" this excellent formula to read: A bureaucrat must be able to change his position in twenty-four minutes if ordered to do so, without inquiry into the merits of the change or the reason for it.

"The peculiar characteristic" of the Lovestoneites, says the caucus document of Bittelman and Foster, "is their unprincipledness, which reflects within our Party the methods and practices of the bourgeois Parties." This is quite true. But it does not prevent the authors from declaring in the same document "our readiness . . . to join with all comrades in the Convention . . . for the merciless struggle against and liquidation of the counter-revolutionary Cannon-Trotsky Opposition." "Unprincipledness" and the "methods and practices of the bourgeois Parties" are the necessary basis of such a combination against communists.

The "political differences" between the leaders of the

two factions are eliminated. We are told this in so many words by the unanimous resolution of the convention, which says: "The political questions at issue between the Majority and the Minority of the Party no longer exist after the acceptance of the political platform of the Open Letter." This is true, however, only of the leaders. Their political coalescence at the top is accompanied by deeper and wider divisions below. The development of international events, the pressure of the class struggle, and the criticisms of the Opposition strengthen and clarify the proletarian tendency in the ranks. These factors create the conditions for its consolidation on a principled basis and make the growth of the Opposition certain.

The new line decreed by the convention and echoed in the caucus document of the Bittelman group, for a stronger attack against the Opposition, will react in our favor. It clears the air and draws the line of struggle between the petty-bourgeois and proletarian tendencies more sharply. It leaves less room for "intermediaries" who catch the half-formed opposition sentiments of the workers in the ranks and divert them into futile factional wrangles over small questions. It is bound to bring about a further cleavage in the ranks of the minority which will draw the proletarian elements closer to us and push the bureaucratic functionaries at the top into one camp with Lovestone. More energetic and deliberate work on our part to accelerate this cleavage will be work for the reestablishment of the unity of the communist forces on a principled line.

It is our task, above everything, to make the issues clear to the workers in the ranks and to base our activity upon them. What has been done up to now is only a beginning. The Opposition on an international scale has only completed the first stage of its development, the stage of formulating the platform and organizing the vanguard. The struggle for the winning over of the Communist masses is before us.

The establishment of *The Militant* as a weekly and the holding of a national conference of the Opposition are the next steps on the path to this goal.

The coming national conference of the CLA

Published April 1, 1929

The following discussion article was published in *The Militant* under the title "Next Steps in the Struggle."

It is now more than five months since our declaration in support of the Russian Opposition, made on the occasion of our return from the Sixth Congress of the Communist International, was answered by expulsion from the party. The period which has intervened since that time has seen a steady development of the work of popularizing the main ideas of the Opposition, a task which has been carried on in the face of a campaign of falsification and incitement reminiscent of Palmer's days and having not a little of the same essential content.

There could be no better testimony to the revolutionary impulses in the party ranks than the fact that the revolutionary platform of the Opposition was able in so short a time to make its way through the cordon sanitaire of corrupted bureaucracy and to find supporters in every section of the party, in all parts of the country, who stood up in defense of that platform even to the point of expulsion from the party. These are the vanguard fighters for the communist ideal, and the living proof of its vitality. Their firmer union on a national scale and their collective preparation for the next stages of the struggle now stand on the order of the day. The national conference of the Opposition, which will convene in Chicago on May 17, will be devoted to these tasks. The thoughts of the most reliable and tested militants of American communism are turning to the forthcoming conference, which is fraught with such a great significance for the future.

The conference will sharpen the line of our struggle and work out the organizational forms for the next stage of its development. The action of the convention in rejecting our appeal and denying us the right to be heard, will naturally have no influence in halting this determination. The convention, which was packed and prearranged by the mechanical exclusion of the Opposition, accomplished nothing whatever except to demonstrate again the bankruptcy of the regime. Formal decisions arrived at in this way cannot be taken as a substitute for conclusions based on free collective work of revolutionaries.

The question has been asked by timid people in the party ranks whether the action of the convention, which was inspired and is fully supported by the Stalin leadership in the Comintern, will prompt the Opposition to give up the struggle and return to the party on the terms implied in the present policy toward the Opposition on an international scale. It is a significant feature of the Opposition movement that not a single voice in favor of this has been heard in its ranks. Despite the difficult circumstances under which we conduct our work, or perhaps because of them, the determination to carry on the fight to a victorious conclusion, no matter how long it takes or how hard the road, has been voiced on every side. We are confident that the national conference will confirm this attitude unanimously.

There has been much speculation in the circles of the party bureaucracy on the appearance of a "Zinoviev" tendency, that is, a tendency toward capitulation, toward treason to principle, in the ranks of the Opposition. Such things are, of course, possible on the part of individuals, but we do not believe they will be seen. The nature of the campaign against us was not without its positive side in our favor. The fact that expulsion and unprecedented calumny had to be faced by every party member coming out for our platform restrained those afflicted with weak knees and faint hearts from joining our struggle. Those who passed to our side through this selective process only grew firmer in their convictions and stronger in their confidence under the pressure on us.

The experience of the International Opposition has not been in vain. The nature of the struggle is so clear now that Zinovievs, Fischers, and Maslows can no longer be attracted to it. It will be the duty of the conference to sum up this international experience and to say that capitulationist tendencies are a foreign substance in the movement of the Communist Opposition, which must be cast aside in the most ruthless fashion at their first appearance.

Capitulation on the terms of the bureaucratic destroyers of the Communist International means to give up participation in intellectual and political life at a time when the movement stands most in need of this participation by all the creative forces. It means to become a silent partner in the criminal destruction of the Russian revolution and the Communist International. It means treason to communism and to the cause of the working class.

We have no doubt that the conference will estimate the question in this way and give a revolutionary answer to it. In doing so it will have to go beneath the surface and attack the germs of this disease which present themselves in the form of "ultralegalism" in the struggle for our views. This is the advice frequently given to us by "sympathizers" of our cause who think it sufficient to hold views in secret and do nothing to advance them because it is prohibited by the bureaucrats. This advice must be specifically and categorically rejected by the conference, as it has been in all of our activities since the expulsions began. The movement of the International Communist Opposition is a fighting movement, and it will triumph by struggle. We can agree to give up extraordinary methods and organization in this struggle only when our party rights and the party rights of all our comrades throughout the International are restored.

While confirming the fighting methods we have employed in the communist struggle for our views, and working out the organizational forms for their intensification and further development, the conference will also have to answer the question of a new party. This tendency, the antipode of capitulationism, has a superficial attractiveness. It could be seriously entertained by the Opposition, however, only if it had become clear that the Communist International, of which our party is a part, had definitely left the proletarian path. This is by no means the case. The bureaucratization and opportunist politics of its upper stratum are the objects of our attack.

The Comintern possesses enormous revolutionary resources in its proletarian ranks which are beginning to assemble and take shape. The Opposition must continue to base itself on them. Our policy will become the policy of the proletarian forces of the Comintern if the correct tactics in furtherance of it are employed. A split in the Comintern is the aim of the Stalinist bureaucrats. The unification of the Comintern on the basis of Leninism, against the bureaucrats and opportunists, is the slogan of the Opposition. With this slogan we will defeat all attempts to isolate us from the party membership. The tactics proceeding from this slogan will be the means of helping the proletarian tendency in the party to find the right line and march on the same path with us.

Alongside the task of penetrating ever deeper into the party ranks with our agitation, we have the task of recruiting and organizing the revolutionary workers outside the party, who are becoming attracted to our banner in large numbers. This is a revolutionary duty of the greatest importance which the Opposition must perform. The present leadership has failed miserably in this. Among these nonparty communists are thousands and tens of thousands who have been alienated and estranged from the party but who remain true to the cause of communism. The problem of organizing them is not separate from the work within the party ranks but is bound up with it. The national conference of the Opposition must work out the organizational form for this double task.

Financing our publications

April 1, 1929

The following letter was written to V.R. Dunne in Minneapolis.

Dear Vincent:

Your telegram woke me up in the middle of the night, and I haven't been able to sleep soundly since, waiting for more information which you said was coming by mail. If it really pans out, it is just what we need to put us on our feet.

We have heard from Trotsky. He wrote to Eastman about the publication of some new books. He sent greetings to all the American Oppositionists and said he would write to us directly very soon. His health, he says, is good. He has recovered from the malaria and is busy writing. He finished a big theoretical-polemical work at Alma-Ata on the relations between Marx and Lenin, the distortion of Leninism by the epigones Stalin, Bukharin, Zinoviev, etc., on the prerevolutionary questions, permanent revolution, etc. He is writing now his autobiography and will have it finished in thirty days.[31]

If the proposition you mentioned in your telegram could contemplate the publication of such books it would be a great undertaking indeed. We are keenly anxious for more details.

In addition to this we have already sufficient material for half a dozen pamphlets on questions of the five-year struggle which have never been published in English; much of it is not yet translated. As soon as we get more information from you as to the nature and extent of the proposition you mentioned, we will get definite information and estimates on the cost of publishing the material.[32]

We have done quite a little figuring lately on the whole question of publishing material, including of course *The Militant.* If we could get together at one time as much as a thousand dollars, we can buy a secondhand linotype and a few fonts of type and do our own printing at about half the cost we pay now. If the proposition you have in mind would be for an amount of this size or larger and could be loaned for a long enough time, it might be possible and advisable for us to get a linotype and do the work ourselves, saving the printers' profit. This would also practically assure the weekly *Militant* and would put us in shape for a real development of our work.

❖

The Fosterites, who formerly opposed gangster tactics against us, have now capitulated to them and are making up for past derelictions by leading the attacks on us at meetings and on the boys who sell *The Militant.* What a corrupt and characterless crew they are! The CI commission which was here for the convention supported these methods, and that was all the Fosterites needed, because they want to make good with Stalin at all costs. The interests of the movement and its reputation before the workers are small considerations for these degenerated fakers.

There is a positive side to this development, however. It will help to alienate the honest workers in the Foster camp and break down its paralyzing influence as an intermediary between us and the Lovestone faction. It will help the process of crystallizing a new group of the Opposition on our platform within the party. All that is lacking for this even now is a leader with a little intelligence and guts.

Our opinions are leaning more and more toward the idea of forming a Communist League at the conference which, while maintaining itself as an opposition, will also begin to recruit new workers with a uniform system of dues payments, cards, etc. We think now that this single type of organization will replace our original idea of workers' clubs existing alongside Opposition groups. The swifter development of events here as well as internationally seems to us to create the conditions for the quicker passing over the double form of organization which we first projected.

We have just put the tenth number of *The Militant* to the press. Things have surely happened in the past five months! Let us hope for as much in the next five. The way things have begun to move in the International, that is not too much to expect.

Grus [Regards],
[James P. Cannon]

Greetings to Leon Trotsky in Turkey

April 1, 1929

The following letter was written to Leon Trotsky in Prinkipo, Turkey.

Dear Comrade Trotsky:

We have received your address from Comrade Eastman and take this first opportunity to send direct to you the fraternal greetings of the Oppositionists in America. We are hoping to receive soon a letter which will be suitable for publication in our paper. The news about your improved health was especially reassuring, as this had been a matter of great concern to all of us.

We are arranging a national conference of the Opposition, which will convene on May 17 together with a delegation from the Opposition in Canada. It is our plan to consolidate our forces there into a definite organization somewhat along the lines of the Leninbund of Germany, which, while maintaining its position as a part of the Opposition in the Comintern, will also conduct its own general activity in the class struggle, publish its own organ, and begin to recruit new workers into its ranks as well as attempting to maintain a faction within the party.

There is a general agreement in our ranks, but we do not wish to make any public announcement of our intentions until we have heard from you and learned your opinion regarding the plans and perspectives of the Opposition on an international scale. It seems to us that international collaboration and coordination of work is now one of the most pressing needs of the Oppositionists in all countries.

We assume the French or German comrades have informed you of the development of the Opposition movement in the American and Canadian parties since the Sixth Congress, if you have not seen the references to it in *Pravda* or *International Press Correspondence*. However, we will give a brief account of it here, since we think it not without significance as a sign of a *new wave* of the Opposition movement after it had been "finally liquidated" at the Sixth Congress.

Comrade Spector, the chairman of the Canadian party and editor of its central organ, and myself were among the delegates to the Sixth Congress. Prior to that we had not supported the Opposition. We had been greatly dissatisfied with the administrative measures taken against you and the demagogy of the whole campaign, but the suppression of all the documents of the Opposition had kept the main issues in such obscurity that we were not able to take a clearly defined stand in regard to them.

At the congress we succeeded in securing copies of your criticism of the Draft Program and your declaration. These made a deep impression on us and we decided to secure additional material in German and to organize a struggle for the Opposition on our return home. We refrained from any statements at the congress in order to prevent our expulsion and isolation before we would have had the opportunity to lay the foundation for the fight at home. In the meantime Comrade Eastman had translated the platform and "The Falsification of History" and published them in book form, but we did not learn of this till our return from the congress.

Two other members of the Central Committee of our party, Comrades Abern and Shachtman, joined me in a declaration to the party in support of the Russian Opposition and another member of the Central Committee, Comrade Swabeck, joined later. We were immediately expelled from the party, and we responded with the publication of our paper, *The Militant,* on November 15. It has been published every two weeks since, and the tenth issue has just come from the press. We also published the "Criticism of the Draft Program of the Comintern" in pamphlet form. We have since learned that the copy of this document which we brought back from the congress is not complete, and we plan to bring out the missing sections in another pamphlet.

Despite the campaign against us, we succeeded in gaining support in the party and have established Opposition groups throughout the country. The same thing occurred in Canada. About 150 comrades have already been expelled. We have held a number of public meetings, many of which were the scenes of fights as a result of the attempts to break them up. Only a few of these attempts were successful.

We are now working to establish our paper as a weekly; it is not certain yet whether we will succeed in the near future. In the next period we plan to publish all the documents bearing on the struggle since 1925 in pamphlet form: the Chinese revolution, Anglo-Russian Committee, etc.

We are sending you under separate cover a file of our paper and a copy of the pamphlet we issued.

With communist greetings,

J.P. Cannon

Building the Leninist leadership

April 1, 1929

The following letter was written to Maurice Spector in Toronto.

Dear Maurice:

Here it is six months since we returned from the Sixth Congress, and the tenth number of *The Militant* is on the press. Everything has developed as we planned over there, and much more successfully, with the exception of the close collaboration in literary and other activities which we marked out. As time goes by I am beginning to think about this more seriously and to wonder if the situation cannot be remedied.

Like all poor people, our greatest curse is poverty. We and the paper live from day to day, but hope shines brightly and promises to fix us up after a while. How are things developing there with regard to the preparation of the group to keep going in your absence? The failure to identify your name and contributions with the development of *The Militant* is a big shortcoming in the execution of our plans. I think you ought to take hold of this question seriously and arrange to have an article in every issue of the paper from now till the conference. We can make further plans there.

This is really a very important question from all angles. We are laying the foundations for the new movement. We do not know what is going to happen, but we do know that many things, even big shifts in the party, are quite possible within a reasonable time. One serious shake-up in the Comintern—a shake-up is preordained by the whole unstable situation—might produce remarkable changes in the party. It will be a great failure on our part if we have failed in the meantime to establish the most solid and authoritative center possible for shaping and directing the new situation. I look forward to the possibility of a centrist grouping swamping the movement if we have not done the utmost to establish the authority of *The Militant* and to consolidate a working group able to lead the whole development inside and outside the party. The next period is the time for your position as one of the leading forces in the movement on this side of the line to be firmly fixed.

How this residential participation can be financed is something I cannot tell at the present writing, but a way can be found if it is put forward as a necessity and if you are spiritually prepared for the seven lean years. Nothing we have done so far was possible; it was done only because it had to be done. What plans could we have made in Moscow last summer to ensure ten numbers of a paper and a big pamphlet in the first five months of struggle?

We must discuss this very seriously at the conference. The most depends on your own fixed resolution in the matter. . . .

The new material we announced last issue is Trotsky's reply to the demand that he stop political activity before the deportation. It is printed in the current issue, translated from the *Volkswille.* I think the material of most value for your report on the crisis in the CI is the part of the program criticism which we failed to get, which is now running in the *Volkswille.* I wish we could get it translated.

There will probably be a flood of new material now since L.D. [Trotsky] is more free and is in better health. We have written a letter to him, and you might do the same. His address is Leon Sedoff, Poste Restante, Pera, Constantinople, Turkey. We gave him a little summary of our development as an Opposition group beginning with our attendance at the Sixth Congress.

We have asked his advice about the steps to be taken at our conference. Our own opinions are becoming quite firmly fixed along the lines of forming a Communist League on the order of the Leninbund, as a single type of organization, recruiting new workers as well as party members and having fixed and uniform dues, etc.

We think it a bit premature to undertake the writing of a complete communist program. This savors too much of a complete and irrevocable split. Will it not be sufficient to say that we base ourselves on the decisions of the first four congresses of the CI and add to that our own tactical program for America and Canada? Will it be feasible to form a separate league for Canada, or cannot the Canadian groups belong to the one body at the start, as in the early days of the Communist movement, it being specifically stated that this is a provisional organization step?

I personally lean more and more to the idea that the league we form will become the main nucleus and rallying point of the future movement. This does not mean to say that possibilities in the party are by any means exhausted. I am convinced that big movements from the party in our direction are possible, but the question is: around what center will these movements crystallize? If we in the meantime have set up a stable and more or less authoritative center, in which a number of qualified comrades collaborate and new forces, young comrades free from the Stalin school of fakirism and corruption, are developed, the new movement will inevitably concentrate around that center, especially if it has a strong press. On the other hand, if we merely drift along as an isolated and uninfluential handful, a group of centrist fakers might swamp everything. The experiences of the Spartacus Bund and the French Committee for the Third International, with the Independents on the one hand and the Frossardists on the other, should be remembered.[33]

Our faith in the vitality of Leninist ideas must lead us to the confidence in the development of such a movement. And the obvious cracking of the Stalinist regime internationally should lead us to count on it absolutely within a reasonable time—perhaps much sooner than can be anticipated. Look at the transformations which have taken place in the German party in recent years, and in our own party.

We must lay more emphasis on the direct recruiting of new workers. For this a definite organizational form is absolutely necessary. They will not join a more or less formless and exclusively "Opposition" group.

I do not know the situation in Canada, but here there are tens of thousands of radical-minded workers who are out of the party. There are actually fewer members in the party today than there were in the underground days at the worst, by at least one-third. We seem to have much sympathy among these workers and ought to begin to organize them by all means. If we could organize even a thousand or two of them and develop a weekly in the next period we will be in the best strategical position to shape the whole future course of the movement. We must accomplish this task. . . .

I wish we had a printer in our group. If we could get a secondhand linotype we could get out our paper for approximately half the cost. We are trying to raise funds for this and have some prospects, but nothing very definite so far. Where are the numerous bourgeois--petty and not so petty—who support the counterrevolutionary program of Trotsky?

I hope you will comply with Max's request to send along an article on the British elections, and follow it up with others.

Grus,
[James P. Cannon]

The labor revolt in the South

Published April 15, 1929

The following unsigned article was published in *The Militant*.

The revolt of the southern textile workers, embracing mills in three states, lifts the lid on a seething caldron of working-class discontent generated by the intensification of the labor process and the multiplied exploitation which has been taking place under the formula of "rationalization." The capitalist dreams of a strikeless America are being shattered by the hammer blows of the class struggle in Tennessee and the Carolinas. These strikes are symptoms of the coming wave of struggles which will arise inevitably out of the whole condition of labor in the trustified industries. Besides that, they have a number of features which give them a special significance in themselves. The new unionism will go through its fiery test in these battles, and, if the correct tactics are employed, its foundations will be consolidated.

The strikes in the Carolinas are the answer of the cotton

mill workers to the "stretch-over" system of speedup introduced recently under the direction of efficiency experts and which was calculated to increase and in some cases to double the number of looms operated by a worker for approximately the same pay. The miserable wage standards and long hours imposed on these unorganized workers had already provided the fuel for this fire. The report of the U.S. Department of Commerce showing the average annual wage of all workers in North Carolina manufacturing plants to be $774.20—about one-half the average wage in the North—tells its own story. The full-time weekly wage of women mill workers is $12.32 in South Carolina and $14.62 in North Carolina. For men it is $15.46 in the former and $17.41 in the latter. A fifty-five-hour week is the rule in South Carolina, and a fifty-six-hour week in North Carolina. Such conditions are the soil for a radical development of which these strikes represent only the beginning.

The present strike wave helps to demolish a popular capitalist myth, proclaimed in a million dollars' worth of advertisements—a myth not without influence even in the ranks of the left wing of the labor movement—about the docility of the 100 percent American workers of the South and their immunity from strikes and labor unionism.

The workers involved in the strikes for the most part are natives, without previous experience in labor organization, who have been lately recruited from the countryside by the rapid industrialization of the South. A special writer in the *New York Times* says: "The boast of the manufacturers of the Carolinas is the large supply of both actual and potential laborers of Anglo-Saxon stock who are not, and never have been, successfully organized into unions. . . . Coming without warning, the strikes have been a distinct shock." More of these shocks are in store.

The native workers in the industrialized South (and not

only in the South) will prove to be valiant fighters in the coming labor battles which will bring with them the establishment of the new unionism. Indeed, as the movement gains strength and scope and becomes firmly fixed in the conditions of American life, they will be the leaders of it. The ability to see and understand this fact, in all its implications, is a *sine qua non* for a correct approach to the developing new situation by the Communists and left wing. In this period, which offers the prospect of the Communists playing an influential part in the American labor movement, it is necessary that we take nothing for granted, that we put aside all preconceived prejudices and closely examine and reexamine our tactics at every stage of the struggles.

Communists have appeared in this hitherto "undiscovered country" as the organizers of the strikes—or of some of them—and in some cases have got the jump on the moribund AFL unions. And this is testimony to the vitality of the new union movement and of the Communists who are its driving force. The strikes are by no means a revolution or even a conscious political demonstration, but the activity of revolutionaries in them is a perfectly natural phenomenon. The complaint of the *New Leader* that "a great opportunity" has been "missed" because "A.F. of L. representatives have not acted promptly" is on the one hand a sour expression of wonderment and regret that Communists do not die when they are expelled, and on the other hand it is a confession that revolutionaries are the only clear and resolute fighters for reforms—for the immediate and pressing needs of the workers.

Communists are a small part of the labor movement; from a numerical standpoint a very small part. Nevertheless, they can play an influential and to a certain extent a leading part in many of the strike battles of the proximate future, and in the shaping of a new union movement, if they succeed in correlating revolutionary aims and consciousness with the realities of the situation and the workers' actual needs of the moment. It is a question of tactics. Slogans must correspond to the situation. It is worthwhile to repeat this truism because it is not always remembered, and situations are lost because of slogans and demands which appear too remote and consequently fail to rally the workers in a given situation. What applies to slogans and demands holds good for all practical activities and conduct in connection with a concrete action or struggle.

These workers who are now entering the path of class struggle—many of them for the first time—will not pass over from political backwardness and passivity, from capitalist-mindedness, to communism at one bound. Neither will their natural leaders, who spring out of the mass and express the mass, be full-fledged Leninists. Far from it. It is more likely that the typical man of influence will be a church member, a Moose, or a consistent voter for the Democratic ticket. It is with such phenomena as this, which will arise in a thousand instances, that the Communists will have to learn how to deal as the slogan of organizing the unorganized is translated into deeds. It is only by degrees, through patient and systematic work and through further development of the class struggle, that these workers and their natural leaders will develop their class consciousness and political understanding, and that individual exceptions will be found. But we cannot go by them if we are thinking in terms of mass organizations.

Just in proportion as success crowns the work for the new unions, as substantial organizations take shape, so will the question of the united front, of party relations with nonparty elements, of relations with "progressives," etc., become more insistent. The current theories about the monopolistic control of the party over these unions will break on these rocks; or else the new unions will break.

Every honest militant will support the strikers and the new unions of the southern textile workers with all his power. At the same time he will watch their development from the standpoint of the questions mentioned above. They are decisive for the future. Upon the answer to them hinges the question whether we are driving ahead toward mass organizations of the workers or futile, sectarian, paper unions.

Another question of great importance in connection with the new strike wave, under the auspices of different organizations in different sections of the same industry, is that of the program for the unification of the struggles. The Communists must give a clear and correct answer to this question. It is the subject for a separate article.

Organize the unorganized Communists

Published April 15, 1929

The following article was published in *The Militant.*

One of the most outstanding weaknesses of the American Communist movement has been the failure to organize into the party ranks the great numbers of revolutionary workers who are sympathetic to communism and to retain those who have joined in the past. The great disparity between the sentiment for communism among the advanced workers and the organized strength of the movement is a striking feature of the situation which reflects the bankruptcy of the party leadership. The growth of the influence of communist ideas on the one side and the decline in the number of organized Communists on the other presents a crying contradiction, a great evil in itself and the soil for the growth of other evils, among them a strengthening of bureaucratic and clique tendencies which are already developed to an enormous extent.

We do not speak here of the failure to produce a "Mass

Communist Party," which is promised every six months in theses and proclamations. The conditions for a mass party in the true sense of the word have not existed in America. Our reference is to the failure to utilize the actually existing possibilities and to recruit into the organized Communist ranks the workers who belong there. A consideration of only a few of the most indisputable facts will suffice to show how really great has been this dereliction, and to confront the Communist militants with a number of serious questions as to what the future holds.

Let us first take some available figures which show the trend of organizational retrogression. The National Office financial reports for the first eight months of 1928 show an average dues-paying membership of 7,277. Compare this figure with the 1925 convention report, which showed an average dues-paying membership for the first six months of that year of 16,325. Here is a loss of 9,048 members—more than 55 percent. This is the first shocking reminder, in terms of membership figures, of what the present leadership of the party signifies. And the figures do not tell the whole story. Since 1925 we have had the experience of a number of important strikes, the great Sacco-Vanzetti movement, and other opportunities to popularize our movement among the workers. Why did not the party double its membership in the past three years instead of decreasing it by more than half?

Go back further. In 1919 there were more than 100,000 members in the Socialist Party, and the left wing claimed a majority. Even James Oneal in his book *American Communism* conceded 35,000 members to the Communist Party and the Communist Labor Party at the time of the two conventions in September 1919.[34] This figure is almost five times the number of the present party membership.

It may be that all these thousands of members of the

left wing were not real material for the Communist movement and that the Palmer raids swept them away like chaff. Such a view brings us to a still more striking phenomenon. The report of the unity convention of the United Communist Party and the Communist Party, printed in the *Communist* for July 1921, shows a dues-paying membership of 12,028 represented in the convention.[35] The underground movement, nearly two years after the Palmer raids, conducting all of its work illegally, had 4,751 more members than the present party in the seventh year of its existence as a legal organization!

To the failure to retain more than a small fraction of the original members of the left wing in the Socialist Party, and the failure to make as good a membership showing as the underground movement, which worked under such great handicaps, must be added the inability to make any serious headway in recruiting from the tens of thousands of revolutionary syndicalists who should have found a place in the Communist ranks. Sympathy for the Russian revolution, which was and is the main spring of revolutionary tendencies in the labor movement, was very strong among these workers and remains so today.

The Communist International regarded them as a necessary constituent part of the American Communist movement and included them in its invitation to the Second Congress. The theses of the Second Congress declared that the measure of success attained by the Communist parties in gaining the support of the revolutionary syndicalist workers would be a criterion of their revolutionary effectiveness. The showing of the American party in this respect is a dismal one indeed, and this has been a great loss to the movement. The repulsion of such genuinely proletarian elements has gone together with the facile attraction of petty-bourgeois, intellectual, and careerist elements. This two-sided process is reflected by the present leadership of the party.

These questions should have a prominent place on the agenda of the forthcoming national conference of the Opposition. We are not merely waging a factional struggle; our responsibilities are deeper and broader. We must not only attempt to point out the right road for the future of the party, but we must ourselves take some positive steps on this road and undertake to carry out in practice the line which serves the interests of the movement. In the period that a corrupted bureaucracy forces a division within the communist ranks—and in all our work we must acknowledge the actual existence of such a division—it is our duty to take upon ourselves directly all those tasks which we have the capacity to carry out.

One of these tasks is to organize the unorganized communistic workers, to help to strengthen their grasp on basic communist principles, and to facilitate their training in the habits of disciplined organization. We have exceptional opportunities to make real headway with such an undertaking even now; and these opportunities will be multiplied as it becomes clearer to the revolutionary workers that we are not held back from revolutionary duties by any organizational fetishism or formalities.

One of the most significant aspects of the struggle which broke out into the open with our expulsion six months ago are the almost universal manifestations of sympathy for our cause which have been shown especially by the former members of the IWW—true militants of the class war—who are sympathetic to the Russian revolution and to the main ideas of communism, but who have been alienated and repelled by the party regime. There are good reasons for this. The proletarian and revolutionary essence of the Opposition platform, on an American as well as on an international scale, is obvious to these workers, and they feel an instinctive solidarity with our fight. The same is true in general also of the rank and file of the nonparty communistic workers, who are the most free from bureaucratic influences and who have no axes to grind.

We ought to welcome this development and unhesitatingly facilitate their union with us. This is a many-sided task upon the accomplishment of which much of the future of the American Communist movement depends. It involves a program of practical activities in the class struggle which we must carry on without asking the permission of the party bureaucrats. It requires a widespread application of the tactics of the united front with these proletarian elements in joint activities and struggles of various kinds. It demands an approach to them as class brothers who have a rightful place in the movement of communism.

For this a definite organizational form is an absolute necessity. The direct recruitment of these workers into the ranks of the Opposition must begin and must be pushed forward with the greatest energy. It will be one of the most important duties of the national conference of the Opposition to lay out the lines of this project and to decide on its organizational form.

Such a decision will turn a new page in the American Communist struggle. The program of the bureaucrats is to split the movement. The program of the Opposition is the unification of the movement on the line of Leninism, against the corrupted bureaucrats and opportunists. The more militantly we wage our fight on all fronts, the more firmly we organize our forces and recruit new ones, the sooner we will win the victory and accomplish our aims.

Differences on the labor party and self-determination

April 20, 1929

The following letter was written to Albert Glotzer in Chicago.

Dear Al:

. . . I notice in your note to Marty today that you disagree with the position on the Negro question and the labor party. You do not mention the trade union question except to intimate that you agree with our criticisms of the party line. In the next period this breach on trade union tactics will be the basis upon which most of the new recruits are gained. This applies particularly to the nonparty communistic workers and the former syndicalists who are coming our way.

I do not understand your difference with us over the labor party. There are a few comrades here also who take somewhat of a "left" position on this question, but the great majority of the comrades all over the country seem to agree with the line of our platform on this point. To what extent it is fully comprehended will probably become clearer at the conference. The most important thing is to see its connection with the platform as a whole. The unity of our document, the way our tactical conclusions follow from the general premises, particularly from the section which estimates the stage of development of the American working class and sets forth the struggle for a class movement as the basic elementary task, are the features which *distinguish* our platform from the worthless faction theses of the other groups—theses which are thrown into the waste basket by their authors before the ink is hardly dry. Our platform represents a unified conception which has guided our tactics for a long time already, and, in my opinion, it will continue to guide them in the future. This accounts for the *consistency* of our position in contradistinction to the continuous acrobatic flip-flops of our faction opponents.

I think it is most important that all our comrades have clear and firm views on all tactical questions, connect them systematically with our general estimate and perspective, and defend them with real conviction. Therefore it is most important that every difference or disagreement be brought out fully in more or less thesis form and discussed from top to bottom. In this way we will educate our group and equip it for the stubborn fight ahead.

If you disagree with our position on the labor party question, you ought to develop your view systematically, show how it springs from our general premise or where the general premise is wrong. Then we will have a basis to begin the discussion. The Minneapolis group has proposed that the labor party question be discussed as a special point on the agenda of the conference.

I am going to write an article on the Negro question. The discussion of this point can be postponed until then to save the time of writing it now. I participated in the commission at the Sixth Congress from which the slogan of self-determination came. This gives me an advantage which you will have when you see my article summarizing the reasons for the slogan.[36]

I would like to know the opinion of the Chicago comrades on the two trade union articles, "The Communists and the Progressives" and "The Labor Revolt in the South." Others will follow, still more sharply attacking the present policy of the party and setting forth more clearly and concretely our attitude toward the progressives. This movement is growing and the party attitude toward it is quite wrong.

There has been a very significant development here lately. We are negotiating with a good-sized group of influential former IWW members who are on the point of uniting with us. Some of them have given up their antipolitical conceptions and will join our organization directly. Others will cooperate with us in trade union work. It is our position on trade union questions which influences them mostly in our direction. The next year will see a big development along this line if we firmly insist on a correct trade union line and carry it out in actual work regardless of the party stand. The next period very likely will see us forming our own fractions everywhere with our own sympathizers grouped around us.

Other ideas for the conference are incorporated in the article in the current issue of *The Militant*.

The big problem for us now is how we are going to get to the conference. So far we haven't got money in sight to pay for the gasoline and food for the journey. But we live in hopes.

Fraternally,

Jim

Stalin will bless the Fosterites

April 20, 1929

The following are excerpts from a letter to Arne Swabeck in Chicago.

There are decided indications that Stalin is preparing to bless the Fosterites as the official representatives of Stalinism in America. Their late turn toward increased hostility toward us is the price they are paying for this. A big delegation is over to Moscow now, including all the main leaders of both factions and Weinstone, and we must be prepared for another bombshell any time. It may take the form of unity with Foster as secretary and a general strengthening of the Fosterites in the apparatus. There is also the possibility of a split, and this is not a small one either. A Lovestone split would, of course, be a split to the right; and if they should break with the Comintern their further development to the right would be a rapid one. . . .

Assuming a change of the CI policy toward the party groups which would actually strengthen the Foster group, or a split which would leave the Fosterites the "official party," would that lessen the breach between us and the party? No, and it would be a fatal error on our part if past associations would lead us to think so in the present circumstances. As far as the great questions of principle affecting the foundations of the international movement are concerned, there is nothing today which divides the Foster leaders from Stalinism at its worst. And on American tactical questions, the Foster-Bittelman leaders are today the sponsors of the worst sectarian errors. This does not change the fact that many of the proletarian supporters of this corrupt faction are and will be closer to us. But they will come over to us only in the most merciless fight against the leaders and not through any illusions about unity with them. As for the Lovestone leaders, a break with the Comintern would only represent the beginning of a break with communism, which has been for them only a field for careerist adventures.

We are not inclined to predict a split at the present time; but such a possibility should not be excluded. In any case, a change of policy and any kind of a serious shake-up will help us eventually, if not immediately.

We have lots of rumors on the Pepper question; nothing sufficiently concrete yet. It seems that he was expelled after a cable from Moscow stating there was no objection. Then it transpired that Lovestone knew of his failure to go and in fact had visited him in his hiding place. Then to protect Lovestone, Pepper was reinstated with the Fosterites voting against, and the case is still pending. We think this is about the way it actually stands. The last we have heard is that he has gone to Moscow. This we doubt. . . .

Grus,

Jim

Defending our meetings

April 20, 1929

The following excerpts are from a Letter to Maurice Spector in Toronto.

Dear Maurice:

You will notice that you made your debut as a member of the *Militant* staff in the issue just off the press and that your article on the Bloody British Battle of the Ballots suffered the minimum mutilation. We had to cut out a bit of Lloyd George's tub-thumping to make the article fit the page. We have a new printer for reasons of economy, and the type we are obliged to use now takes more space than the other. What are you going to send for the next issue?

It ought to become now a fixed procedure for you to have an article in each issue, for many reasons. Along with this you will probably notice the trend in the current issue toward giving the paper a more general character. This must be steadily developed, with the object of making the paper an authoritative spokesman of the left wing in the labor movement. I believe we can achieve a measure of success with this aim in view of the weak competition. The new *Labor Unity* is a ghastly abortion. Take away the subsidy and compulsory machine support from such papers and they would all die in a month. . . .

Did you notice that the organ of the Belgian Opposition in its last issue called for the formation of another party—an editorial article, not a formal call. We can't make out the language clearly, but it appears that their article has reference to the entire International. It is too bad that the Old Man doesn't say something on the situation in the Comintern and the tactics of the Opposition.

Our Hungarian group held a free speech protest meeting last night with great success. The fight at the last meeting aroused a storm in the Hungarian colony against the Stalinites, and it was very effectively utilized by the protest meeting. The Wobblies were there in force and one of the editors of the party Hungarian paper who was present was forced to take the floor in the discussion period. His defense of the party tactics was very apologetic, and the meeting was a great political victory for us. A gang who tried to invade the hall in a body ran into the workers' guard at the top of the steps and got such a hot reception that they retreated with more speed than dignity. They poured out of the narrow hall like rain out of a water-spout. I think we are close to the defeat of the hoodlum tactic and that we will come out of the struggle stronger. The communist movement, however, will receive some black eyes for a long time. Even after we have defeated this semifascist gang we will be held accountable for their crimes committed in the name of communism.

We are going to hold a May Day meeting. If they don't succeed in breaking it up—and I don't think they will—they might as well quit trying.

I don't think your moving here should be delayed after the conference. I don't know how it can be managed from an economic standpoint, but we will have to take the step and then solve the problem. It is impossible to build a serious political movement without consolidating a strong central staff. We will have to take this up at the conference and make all the comrades understand it. . . .

Grus,

Jim

The lost leader

Published May 1–15, 1929

The following article was published in *The Militant.* The Comintern had ordered John Pepper to return to Moscow after the Sixth Congress of the CI; after he put off leaving, the order was repeated in February 1929 and he was forbidden to attend the CP convention. He dropped out of sight around the time of the convention, and the CP leaders circulated the story that he had left for Mexico en route to the USSR; in reality he was in New York, meeting in secret with various Lovestoneite leaders during the convention. When this became known after the convention, he was expelled but quickly reinstated, returned to Moscow, and was finally expelled by the International Control Commission.

In the normal development of a revolutionary movement, its leaders grow in the course of protracted struggles; they are tested and retested in responsibilities; they become widely known to the rank and file and acquire a great moral authority as a unifying and guiding force. This was the case throughout the Comintern in Lenin's day. He, above all others, understood the great role of leadership and explained, especially in his brochure "The Infantile Sickness of 'Left' Communism," its function, its organic connection with the masses, and the importance of its stability and continuity.

The regime of Stalinism, which revises and distorts all the precepts of Lenin, reduces the Leninist conception of leadership to a ghastly caricature. Nowadays, leaders are made to order from above, their authority is artificially conferred upon them, and they rule by decree. The moral and political authority of real leadership is replaced by the simple operation of apparatus mechanics. The party members, who play no real part in selection of leadership, never know from one day to another who their leaders will be; but experiences teach them to expect sudden changes and to be prepared to wake up any morning to confront a new set of leaders without prior consultation about the matter. They learn also to remain calm at the spectacle of a bureaucrat wielding tsarist power one day and sinking without a trace the next. Sometimes there are interludes when nobody, least of all the party members, knows whether their leaders, politically speaking, are dead or alive, and they stand like ticket holders at a raffle, waiting to see what number will turn up.

We are now witnessing one of these strange interludes, and the leader whose fate is spinning on the wheel is none other than John Pepper, the scoundrel who put Communists in jail in Hungary and who has made a political living in recent years as a mercenary in the war against "Trotskyism." Pepper is as transparent a charlatan, as characterless a demagogue, as ever strutted across the stage of the workers' movement. But so much has corruptionist politics superseded the normal relations between leaders and masses, and the natural selection of the former by the latter—these qualities were no handicap to Pepper's career in our party.

He bobbed up one day and assumed command in military fashion, putting the membership through some paces and forced marches from which they are still leg-weary and foot-sore. He marched them to the Federated Farmer-Labor Party and back again without a single bivouac along the way; and his comic-opera crusades for the "Third American Revolution" and the "unarmed Spartacist uprising" in the South will surely receive mention when the history of the movement is written and everything can be told.[37]

His most recent campaign was against American "Trotskyism." He made the report against us at the December plenum, presented the motion for our expulsion, and wrote all the theses and declarations against us. He spoke there—a brief five months ago—as the leader of the party hurling mud at people who were fighting on the side of the workers when he was toasting the war with Austrian generals. But alas! Life is full of changes and uncertainties. Already the mighty Caesar has fallen and there are none so poor as to do him reverence.

The campaign against "Trotskyism" was his undoing. So much of the varnish was scraped off the party leadership in the fight that the setting up of a new "front" became a matter of urgency to the Stalin regime. Besides that, there was the little matter of the flirtation with Bukharin in the Comintern to look into more closely. The pushing forward of Foster as candidate for party secretary in place of the discredited Lovestone was the first move to change the appearance of the party leadership. The next was the demand that Pepper be taken for a ride to Moscow.

Pepper, who knows the racket, refused at first to take the ride. Insistent cablegrams, one after another, repeated the demand. Still Pepper did not go; America was his land of golden opportunity—why should he leave it? Finally after a peremptory demand threatening drastic disciplinary action, it was decided to give Pepper his ticket of leave. He forthwith disappeared, and many naive comrades actually thought he was on the high seas.

Came the dawn. And a telegram from Moscow asking where was Pepper and why. No answer and no Pepper. It was feared that he was lost, and the funny part of it all was the fact that the American working-class movement went on in blissful unconsciousness of its misfortune. Then suddenly Pepper turned up, and in New York City of all places! It seems that a keen-eyed Fosterite, strolling around the streets of Manhattan in search of the missing Apex Theory, perceived the lost leader slinking in and out of doorways and alleys around Union Square when he should have been slinking from boot to boot in Moscow. A hue and cry was raised immediately, the tocsin was sounded, and, after securing consent by cablegrams from Moscow, Pepper was expelled from the same Communist Party out of which he had expelled us only a short few months before. In expulsion, as in death, princes and paupers meet.

But matters did not end there. It soon transpired that Pepper had been in New York all the time, living not uncomfortably at a decent hotel, and that Lovestone, prior to his own departure for Moscow, had visited him there regularly even after he was supposed to have left the country.

These complications compelled a reconsideration of the decision. It was decided to brazen the whole thing out and to whitewash Lovestone by whitewashing Pepper. The latter helped with one of the most unique and fascinating alibis that has ever been concocted to our knowledge. The story, briefly, as told by Pepper in all seriousness to explain his apparent violation of discipline, was as follows:

He attempted to get to Moscow via Mexico. Disguised as

a hot tamale he had crossed the border when the Mexican revolution broke out in full force. There he was seized by the rebels on a foraging expedition, who discovered, when they stripped the supposed tamale of its corn husk, that the inside was all Pepper and no corn meal. This made them suspicious, and they wrapped the corn husk around him again, loaded him into a big cannon, and shot him back across the border. He lit on his feet running north and kept going till he reached New York City to tell the Polcom about it. He was on his way to report when he was seen on the street.

Before the Fosterites could think up an answer to this story, Pepper's faction confederates rushed through a motion modifying the expulsion so as to allow him to proceed to Moscow and to refer the case there for final disposition. Thereupon, we are informed, Pepper left for Moscow immediately and was last sighted rolling eastward through Germany disguised as a keg of beer.

Meanwhile, the question of the party leadership hangs in the balance. How it will be settled the party membership have no way of knowing, since they are not consulted in the matter. But one thing is certain: There will be other Peppers; they grow plentifully on the tree of Stalinism. This one, who became a leader of the American party without election, who wielded authority without accountability, and who departs from leadership without even the knowledge of the party members or the left-wing workers who follow the party, is a symbol of the degeneration which has taken place in questions of policy. The situation in the Russian party is reflected in all the parties of the Comintern.

Our conference and the trade unions

Published May 1–15, 1929

The following discussion article was published in *The Militant.*

On May 17 the most active militants of the Communist Opposition from all parts of the country will meet in national conference in Chicago, the proletarian center of the real America, rich in glorious traditions of working-class struggle and aspiration. Many a noble enterprise of the labor vanguard had its inception there; many a stirring battle, many a defeat, and many a brave start again. It is not unlikely that our modest conference will find a place of honor among them in the history of the American revolutionary movement. This will surely be the case if our conference approximates the accomplishment of the tasks which crowd upon it, if it does not shrink before their magnitude and gives a clear answer to the questions now on the agenda of the American revolutionary movement. We shall endeavor to do this to the best of our ability.

The importance of our gathering for the future of the

Opposition is fully understood, we believe, by all the comrades who have stood with us in the struggle up till now. And many who have not yet identified themselves directly with us await the result of our deliberations with the greatest interest. There is wisdom in collective counsel. The fact that we are finally forcing a way, despite our great poverty, to bring our foremost comrades in the various districts together for the comparison of experiences, the exchange of views, and the collective settlement of our problems is testimony to the vitality of our movement. We must make the most of the opportunity, which has not been given to us, but which we have wrested from adversity.

In the first place we ought to give a thought to the general character of the conference. We meet to face things as they are and to deal with them soberly and confidently. Exaggeration, bombast, false claims, and self-deception will be out of place; it will be for us now to put all the questions concretely, and quietly discuss the ways and means of answering them. There should be nothing to prevent our meeting having a businesslike character from start to finish. The sterile factionalism and intrigue which corrodes the party and renders its conventions futile should not trouble us at all. We have a common principled line. That is the foundation, and the only foundation, for united and harmonious and collective work. Differences of opinion on secondary questions which may exist can be discussed honestly and openly. Those who are united on fundamental lines do not fear discussion.

The conference can bring fruitful results for the movement only on the condition that we do not deceive ourselves as to the state of affairs. What we think of the position of the labor and revolutionary movement in America and its perspectives has been clearly stated in the draft of our platform. The opinions we have written there about the class immaturity of the workers' movement in America and the elementary nature of the fundamental tasks of the revolutionary elements are not new; they arise inexorably from the facts of the situation.

The evils we fight against within the Communist movement are not a new phenomenon, and they will not be done away with in a day. Our struggle, as a detachment of the International Leninist Opposition, is a revolt against the revisionist and bureaucratic corruption which has been seeping into the Comintern since Lenin left its leadership six years ago. During that time, gradually and almost imperceptibly, great changes have been brought about in Lenin's International—and all in his name. This is true of the main ideas, of the course, and of the leadership. All this is buttressed by a bureaucratized apparatus and a monopoly of the material resources and press which has attracted a veritable horde of parasites and mercenaries into its service, thrusting out the tried and reliable revolutionary fighters.

It would be foolish to think that these monstrous perversions, which have been accumulating over a period of six years, could be changed in a day. We had no such illusions and have none now. To fight for the fundamental line of Marx and Lenin within the Communist ranks today means to swim against the stream. Only those who are able to do this can remain with us. We never promised a quick victory and do not promise it now. We hold out only the prospect of a long, stubborn struggle for principle against difficulties, persecution, and slander. It is quite true that the revisionist-bureaucratic regime has profound and irreconcilable internal contradictions and is bound to collapse under the impact of the class struggle, which cannot be regulated by apparatus manipulation. But an indispensable factor for the hastening of this collapse, and for saving the revolutionary movement from collapse with it, is the firm consolidation of the Opposition Communists for a drawn-out struggle. It will be the task of the national conference to harden our forces for a siege.

It is becoming clearer every day that plain speech is necessary on the trade union questions. Without a sound policy in this sphere it is absolutely impossible to build the Communist Party as the guiding influence among the masses. And we have to say openly that our differences with the party regarding trade union tactics are increasing. This becomes all the more serious in view of the forthcoming convention of the Trade Union Educational League, where, from all indications, the false line of the party is to be reinforced by organizational forms which will inevitably develop further implications along the wrong track.

The party is wrong in bringing out a program for a new trade union movement all along the line. It is wrong in undertaking to monopolize the control of the new unions in a narrow party sense. It is wrong in exercising party leadership mechanically and stifling democracy and self-initiative in the new unions. And it is wrong in its attitude toward the new progressive movement.

The total result of these and similar associated errors will be a program and practice of organizing Communist sects rather than mass organizations. Every new experience makes this clearer. Now the consequences of these errors are immeasurable. They spell isolation for the party and the crippling of the new union movement. The policies which are now being enunciated in preparation for the national conference of the TUEL appear to us to have no relation to reality. They sound in many respects like feeble echoes of old SLP and IWW propaganda, which substituted wishes for facts.

Moreover, the present policy bears no relation whatever to the settled practice of the party over a period of years, since the 1921 convention, and which was in the main correct. And the party leaders do not even bother to explain the reasons for this complete reversal. It is like a new revelation which has to be taken for granted. A workers' political movement can be destroyed but never built by such irresponsible methods and leadership.

Consider, for example, the attitude toward the progressives. "We will have nothing to do with them," say the modern phrasemongers who see only persons and have no Marxian understanding of movements. Compare this with what Lovestone wrote in the *Communist* last May, page 277:

"The progressives are of vital importance in the development of a left wing movement of a mass character. They serve under certain conditions as one of the levers for the development of a clear-cut, broad, left-wing movement."

All of today's pronunciamentos say the exact opposite, without the slightest explanation of the reasons for the complete change of view and without attempting to show wherein last year's estimate of the role of the progressives was wrong. This is playing with leadership in the most irresponsible manner.

The statement quoted above, which in our opinion is a correct one, was formulated in a guarded way so as to appear more "left" than the actual opinions of the writer. To learn that, it is only necessary to recall the practices of united front without criticism, under the hegemony of the progressives in so many cases; personal relations at the top instead of the utilization of relations with progressive leaders for the promotion of a common movement of the workers below. But these distortions should not lead us to react to the present policy of rejecting all relations with the new progressive movement. To do so is to turn aside from one of the most important avenues for the development of the class movement of the workers and the building of the Communist influence and organization within it.

Our conference should take a firm and definite stand on this question. In our opinion the conference of the Opposition Communists should support the idea of entering every movement of a progressive character in the trade unions; they should work loyally to advance it; they should favor combinations with all elements willing to cooperate with us in the fight for a concrete program in the interests of the workers and their economic organizations. At the same time, and in order to do this effectively, they should fight and expose the fakers in the movement, criticize all reformist tendencies, and build the independent Communist organization and influence. This policy applies with equal force in the work of organizing new unions and in the work inside the old unions of the American Federation of Labor and the independent unions of a similar character.

We must not for a minute cease our efforts to convince the party of the necessity for this line; for the party is a factor of the greatest dynamic importance, and a false policy on its part will have the gravest consequences in the whole militant workers' movement, for which such unbounded possibilities are now unfolding. But in any case, our activity cannot be confined to mere criticism. Hand in hand with it must go the development of a systematic activity of the Opposition Communists in the trade union movement along the lines of our own policy. Practical demonstrations of its correctness will exert a powerful influence on the party ranks and, simultaneously, will be the means of consolidating a revolutionary nucleus within the new progressive movements which will become the center and rallying point for all the militants in the future. The more firmly we insist on this policy and the more energetically we apply it in practice, the less will be the harm done by the present phrase hysteria.

Proceeding along this line, facing all obstacles and fearing none of them, tackling all the concrete questions in a serious and workmanlike manner and giving an answer to them, our conference will render services of historic value to the American working-class movement and will perform a duty to the International.

Founding conference of the Communist League

Published June 1, 1929

The following article was published in *The Militant.*

The national conference of the Opposition Communists was held in Chicago on May 17, 18, and 19, and culminated in the formation of the Opposition forces into a national organization. The name of the organization is the Communist League of America (Opposition). The conference adopted the platform printed in the February 15 issue of *The Militant;* proclaimed its full solidarity with the Russian and International Opposition under the leadership of Trotsky; and undertook the task of organizing American communists, inside and outside the Communist Party of the United States, on the platform of the Opposition.

A constitution for the Communist League was adopted, embodying the principle of democratic centralization as laid down in the theses of the Second Congress of the Communist International. A National Committee of seven members was elected to direct the work of the organization.

The following constitute the National Committee: James P. Cannon, Maurice Spector, Martin Abern, Max Shachtman, Arne Swabeck, Carl Skoglund, and Albert Glotzer. Membership cards are to be issued and the monthly dues rate was fixed at fifty cents with an initiation fee of the same amount. The chartering of local branches will begin at once. For the time being Canadian branches will be directly affiliated and will function as a part of the single organization.

The Communist League will carry on a program of independent activities in the class struggle and will also continue to work as a faction within the party.

The conference consisted of thirty-one delegates with voting rights and seventeen alternate delegates with voice but no vote. Twelve cities were represented, as follows:

	Delegates	Alternates
New York	5	4
Philadelphia	2	2
Cleveland	1	0
Detroit	2	0
Youngstown	1	0
Chicago	5	4
St. Louis	3	1
Kansas City	1	0
Springfield, Ill.	2	0
Minneapolis	5	5
St. Paul	2	0
Toronto, Canada	2	1
Total	31	17

Groups in a number of other cities which were unable for financial reasons to send delegates sent greetings and pledges of support. A letter from Comrade Trotsky was read to the conference amid great enthusiasm. Letters were also read from Comrade Malkin in Comstock Prison, and from the Opposition groups in France, Czechoslovakia, and other countries.

The conference was permeated through and through with the pioneer spirit of self-sacrifice and determination in the struggle for principle. The delegates were almost entirely workers who came direct from their jobs. A large percentage of them beat their way to the conference; others came crowded together in battered automobiles borrowed for the occasion; only three or four paid bus fare, and one delegate rode a train—on a railroad worker's pass. Lodgings for the out-of-town delegates were provided at the homes of Chicago comrades and sympathizers. Many of the delegates paid their own expenses for meals and incidentals. None of them received wages or per diem.

The entire conference was thus carried through with an unrivaled maximum of economy. This revolutionary capacity for hardship triumphed over the handicap of the meager financial resources of the Opposition, which works without subsidies of any kind, and made our national conference possible. For a movement less vital and less confident of its future, the circumstances would have completely prohibited such a national gathering.

The sessions of the conference were conducted throughout with a businesslike efficiency and precision, in sharp contrast to the desultory, dragged-out, and time-wasting affairs which have become the rule in recent years under the regime of petty-bourgeois politiciandom. Being firmly united on main lines of principle, and free from the factional intrigue which arises from the lack of it, there was no need for the conference sessions to be held up and delayed for the deliberations of rival caucuses. It began promptly on time the first day and conducted all the following sessions precisely according to schedule.

The conference was marked by a freedom of discussion on all questions which enabled all points of view to be brought fully and fairly before the body. Collective judgment, not caucus manipulation, was the aim sought and achieved. Conflicting opinions which arose over secondary questions were brought out into the open. Earnestness without diplomacy characterized the discussions and put upon the decisions finally arrived at, the stamp of real conviction. The final results of the discussion showed a complete unanimity and solidarity of the entire conference on all the main questions, and the Opposition Communists face the heavy tasks before them as a firmly united body.

The agenda of the conference was as follows:

1. The Situation in Russia—reporter, Comrade Shachtman.
2. The Crisis in the Communist International—reporter, Comrade Spector.
3. The American Situation and the Tasks of the Opposition Communists—reporter, Comrade Cannon.
4. Trade Union Questions—reporter, Comrade Swabeck.
5. The Organization of the Communist Opposition—reporter, Comrade Abern.
6. Youth Questions—reporter, Comrade Glotzer.
7. Press and Literature Publication Program—reporter, Comrade Shachtman.

All the reports were expositions and elaborations of the various sections of the platform which represents the settled view of the Oppositionists on all the important questions confronting the American movement. The nature of these tasks has not changed since the platform was drafted for submission to the convention of the party a few months ago, and, consequently, the conference saw no necessity for the writing of a new one. After the discussion on all the main reports had been concluded, the platform was adopted by unanimous vote. Editorial revision and reformulation of some sections were made in order to express the decision of the conference to pass over from the stage of a purely internal faction of the party to a national organization also conducting independent activities and recruiting nonparty communists, without altering the line of the document. The youth section of the platform was also rewritten to deal more comprehensively and concretely with the problems of the Communist youth.

The conference adopted resolutions on the class-war prisoners of America, on the imprisoned and exiled Bolshevik-Leninists of the Soviet Union, and messages of greetings to Comrade Trotsky and to Comrade Malkin.

The report and discussion on the trade union question were a prominent feature of the conference. A constructive line of communist policy on this question, restating fundamental conceptions derived from American and world experience and sharply opposing the present false line of the party, was unanimously demanded. The policy outlined in our platform on the trade union question, as concretely elaborated in a number of articles in *The Militant* and in the report of Comrade Swabeck, was supported by all the delegates.

The discussion on this point was enriched by the speeches of comrades from all parts of the country and from Canada who have years of experience in the trade union struggle behind them. The new line of the party, outlined in the preparation for the TUEL conference and in its recent activity, was refuted and condemned on theoretical and practical grounds.

It was clear to all that the future activity of the Opposition is indissolubly bound up with its organizational form; consequently, great interest was manifested in the report on this question, and an earnest discussion followed it. Here, great progress was reflected. The tendencies toward organizational fetishism in regard to the Stalinist apparatus, the "legalistic" attitude toward the rules of the usurping bureaucrats, which affected our ranks in the beginning, had been completely overcome. Not a single voice was raised in favor of holding back our necessary organizational development on this score. On the other hand, there were signs of a reaction to the other extreme. The unbounded provocations of the subsidized corruptionists had led some comrades, who incorrectly identified them with the party, to think of a complete break with the latter.

The discussion clarified this question and resulted in the unanimous decision to organize our forces for independent activity while maintaining our position as a faction of the party and strengthening our bonds with its proletarian elements. This latter is necessary in order to assist their inevitable development toward the path of the Opposition, which is the only possible outcome of the present factional impasse in the party. The Oppositionists must have confidence in such a development and work for it. That means to keep contact with the party ranks. We were the first to grasp the significance of the world issues shaking the Comintern and to raise the banner of the International Opposition, but we will not be the last. The struggle for the consolidation of a new grouping in the party on our platform must go hand in hand with the development of our organization and the recruitment of new revolutionary workers outside the party ranks. The conference decided unanimously for this policy.

A large percentage of the delegates were representatives of the communist youth. This was a proper reflection of the composition of the ranks of the Opposition movement as a whole. The youth are the most free from bureaucratic cynicism and corruption, and the most responsive to revolutionary ideas. A large number of the foremost young Communists of the United States and Canada have already rallied to our banner—far more, proportionally, than the adult party members—and this process is only beginning. The letter from Comrade Trotsky, which placed the greatest emphasis on the struggle for the proletarian youth, met with the warmest approval of the conference.

Conflicting opinions were revealed in the discussions mainly on the labor party and on the slogan of the right of self-determination for the Negroes. The delegates who opposed the formulation of the platform on the labor party showed a number of differences and shadings ranging from a virtual opposition in principle to the position that it would be correct for us to participate in a mass labor party if it should be formed, but wrong to work for its formation. The gross errors of the party and the Comintern on this question, which have never been properly corrected or explained, have undoubtedly produced a vast confusion and skepticism about the labor party throughout the ranks of the American Communists. There is less of it in the Opposition than in the party as a whole. Such as exists among us was brought out more clearly and fully only because the discussion was open and free at our conference and there was no reason for anyone to conceal his opinions or doubts.

It was the opinion of the majority that, although it certainly is not a pressing question of the moment, the labor party question has a great importance for the future, when the radicalization of the workers will begin to seek political expression. Therefore it is imperative to have a clear and definite stand on it. A misjudgment of the probable line of development of the American workers, or a sectarian doctrine which would prevent us from approaching and influencing new upward movements, might have the most serious consequences later on. The formulation of the platform on the perspective of a labor party was adopted by a majority after a thorough discussion.[38]

Following a discussion of the disputed section of the platform on the slogan of the right of self-determination for the Negroes, it was decided to defer final action until more exhaustive material on the subject can be assembled and made available for discussion in the groups. In view of the profound importance of this question and the manifest insufficiency of informative material and discussion pertaining to it, this decision to defer final action was undoubtedly correct.[39]

The national conference, held under such adverse conditions and with such gratifying results, made a profound impression upon all who took part in it. Quiet and matter-of-fact, in glaring contrast to the bombast and ballyhoo of so many conferences which have made a noise and left no trace, our gathering generated an enthusiasm which was real and genuine. The pledging of quotas for the support of *The Militant* from the various delegations, which preceded the singing of the "Internationale" at the close of the last session, was a sign of that kind of enthusiasm which expresses itself in deeds. Such enthusiasm and conviction are our capital for the future.

The conference was a picture of the best representatives of American communism. Side by side with the young fighters, many of them at the beginning of their revolutionary activity and attending a national gathering for the first time, were not a few veterans of the movement whose faces have been familiar at all important meetings of the party since its foundation. We saw there the forces of the communist vanguard again assembling and taking shape on a national scale, and it was a heartening sight. The Opposition and its platform are on the march in America. That which was merely an idea advocated by a few individuals in the Central Committee a brief seven months ago has become a national movement taking on organizational form and functions. It has its own momentum. It will go forward in spite of all.

The characterless bureaucrats, who cannot understand how anyone can or should swim against the stream, talked a great deal about the early collapse of the Opposition movement, and, no doubt, really expected a flood of capitulations after the first few engagements. The delegations were the answer to them. They showed our ranks unshaken and more closely united than ever. Our forces have grown, slowly but steadily, since the beginning of the fight.

A significant aspect of the conference was the appearance of a true collective leadership, capable of harmonious collaboration and division of labor and bound together by a common standpoint on all important questions. The close unity of the leadership with the Opposition movement as a whole was illustrated by the conscious and deliberate support given to all its proposals by the conference delegates and by the unanimous election of the National Committee. A nucleus of leadership evolving by these processes in the heat of struggle will have an organic character. It will have a real authority and will be able to exert a unifying influence on the movement. It needs no appointment by cablegram and cannot be removed that way.

The political and organizational tasks of the Opposition are determined basically by the situation of the Russian revolution and the Comintern. Representing the stream of genuine proletarian internationalism, the Communist Opposition equally rejects the bureaucratic caricature of internationalism by the subsidized Stalin consulates, and the reaction to Social Democratic national narrowness of the right-wing Brandler groups. The course of the Russian revolution, which has now reached a turning point, is fateful for the international class struggle. The final victory of socialism in the Soviet Union, in the economic as well as military sense, can be assured only by the international revolution. In the interval only the platform of the Russian Opposition can strengthen the socialist as against the capitalist and restorationist elements in the Soviet Union.

The regime in the Russian party decides the regime in the International, and the present crisis in the Comintern is due to the fact that opportunism and bureaucratism have entered into the leadership of the CPSU and resulted in the general demoralization of the sections and the expulsion of the left wing. The Opposition refuses to identify the International with the Stalin hierarchy. It is the Opposition which in reality represents the historic line of the Third International, for the leadership of which it will struggle both inside and outside the party. The victorious outcome of this struggle depends not only on the sharpening class struggle in the USSR, in the capitalist world, and the Orient, but on the active and organized intervention of the Left Communist Opposition.

The conference turned a corner in the struggle of the American regiment of world Bolshevism and opened up a new stage of its development. It faced its problems, its difficulties, and its prospects realistically and showed a collective will to battle onward to victory. This victory will come all the sooner if the members of the Communist Opposition promptly carry out the decisions of the national conference to organize their forces more cohesively, develop a firmer and more conscious discipline, and work with increased energy to enlist new recruits under our banner, which is the banner of international communism.

After Lovestone's expulsion

June 28, 1929

The following letter was written to Albert Glotzer.

Dear Al:

We have articles on the British elections and on the Conference for Progressive Labor Action in the July 1 issue of *The Militant* now at the printer's. It was supposed to be made up today but is not ready. He has had the copy for a week already. This is the gay life of editors who haven't enough money to demand service.

We must find a way to overcome the depression that set in after the conference, financial and otherwise, but mainly financial. The conference overstrained us and we seem to recover slowly. Besides that, it has been my observation that conventions are always followed by a lull.

But big things are happening all around us. We have become so accustomed to swift developments in the past eight months that single events do not cause the commotion they would in ordinary times. The British elections are no doubt a heavy blow to the Stalin policy in the International, which means, under the circumstances, another defeat for communism. The Social Democrats not only in Britain will be strengthened and encouraged by the results there.[40] I note what you say about the effects in the Chicago Federation of Labor.

The progressive conference should be taken together with this. The Socialists, thanks partly to the false tactics of the party, are trying, with no little success, to convert this movement into the labor wing of Social Democracy. The Socialists ran the conference with a well-oiled steering committee and a worked-out program.

Now the expulsion of Lovestone, which means the beginning of the new split to the right in the party, belongs in this whole development, which represents the strengthening of tendencies and elements toward the revival of Social Democratic and the decline of Communist influence. Stalinism facilitates this backward development in the most effective way possible, blindly and ignorantly but all the more surely.

Lovestone has much greater strength than the brainless functionaries of American Stalinism even imagine. We have reports to the effect that he has a well-organized group of functionaries solidly behind him here in New York, including influential and capable elements in the needle trades. A right policy, with its apparent "realism" in American application and its apparent better adaptation to the class immaturity in America, will have a strong appeal, especially to the trade union opportunist elements, when counterposed to the childish antics of the new leadership.

The probable trend of events is graphically shown by the big editorial in today's *Volkszeitung*. Lore says it is well known that he has no confidence in Lovestone as a person. But, he says, *personalities are not the decisive question in politics.* Lovestone is supporting *Rykov and Bukharin, who have the most realistic communistic policy for the Soviet Union.* He strongly intimates that he would favor a bloc on an American Brandler platform. This, which is very apt to happen, is something to think about. The formless mass of yes-men who call themselves the leaders of the Stalinized party do not engage in this exercise, but we must.

The development of the Lovestone faction proceeds, as we see it, to the elaboration of a right tactical platform in America, concentrating heavily on the trade union question. Their line on this will *appear* to cross ours, and our comrades must be warned about being influenced by superficial appearances. From the elaboration of their right tactical platform will follow a fierce faction struggle in the party, sabotage on a scale never before experienced in its ruthlessness, and a split. The *Daily Worker* will quite probably be the victim of this struggle and split along with other institutions of the party. The present financial crisis in the daily affects the whole movement and all the auxiliaries, as we have been reliably informed.[41]

A bloc with the Lore elements will be quickly followed by a close relation with the new progressive movement, if not at first an organic fusion. The Finns and similar institutionalized blocks of lip-service Communists are quite apt to be drawn into the movement. The appearance of a right communist, or rather left socialist, party is clearly indicated. And this in turn will only be a bridge toward the Socialist Party, toward incorporation within it as its left wing. The disruption of the Communist Party as we have known it, the decline of Communist influence, and the temporary revival of the Social Democracy as a factor in the labor movement, is now taking shape as an actual probability and not merely a speculation on future developments.

The banner of communism and the entire heritage of the American movement as a revolutionary factor will pass into the Opposition. The official party of Stalinist centrism, hammered mercilessly from the right and the left, will lose to both and depend for its existence more and more on subsidy and faith.

Our tasks are enormous. It is tragic for the movement that we are so hamstrung by poverty of means just now, when the needs of the movement and the possibilities of a greater effectiveness are unfolding. It is clearer than ever that the Communist League is the nucleus of the future communist movement and the custodian of its main principled ideas. Unless we are capable of developing an activity worthy of the great role assigned to us, the wreckage of the movement will be appalling. *There is no other progressive force now.*

The comrades should discuss these thoughts and remember the two most necessary tactics: hammer the appointed leadership of defeat and demand a discussion of the three political lines.

Fraternally,

J.P. Cannon

Lore and the Lovestoneites

July 9, 1929

The following is an excerpt from a letter written to Albert Glotzer.

Dear Al:

We have to modify somewhat what I wrote about the probable attitude of Lore to the Lovestone split in my last letter. Spector and Shachtman saw him since then. He said we misunderstood his attitude toward the Russian right wing. He admits they represent the tendency toward the restoration of capitalism in Russia. He only meant to say that they favor a more reasonable internal regime in the International. In this of course he is wrong also. His attitude, as always, is full of confusion and contradiction.

He says he has no confidence whatever in Lovestone, but thinks he has shown much more character than the Stachel-Foster group of translators of statements written by the representative of the ECCI.

We are planning to hold a formal meeting with him

as we think it advisable to try to prevent a combination between him and Lovestone and also to see to what extent, if any, it is possible for us to collaborate on a political platform. . . .

New capitulations in Russia

July 24, 1929

The following excerpt is from a letter to Albert Glotzer written after the capitulation of Karl Radek, Eugene Preobrazhensky, and Ivar Smilga.

Dear Al:

. . . Yes, the new capitulations in the Russian party represent a quite serious defection which will not help us any for the immediate future. Trotsky points out in his article in the next *Militant* that it has been developing for some time, more than a year. We have had intimations of it and were not taken so much by surprise, but we know little more than Trotsky reveals in his articles. I see nothing in Radek's letter to convince anyone who is not looking for a door to crawl through. He accuses Trotsky of departing from the platform, but what is that argument worth from one who is adopting Stalin's platform? The argument about the bourgeois press is sheer demagogy. Radek gives the impression of a man who is tired of the fight. It is hardly proper for us who have stood so little pressure as yet, comparatively, to censure him for this, but that does not change the fact. The most probable outcome of the capitulations will be a weakening of the fight against the right. It is clear as day that the pressure of the Opposition is and has been the main driving force behind this fight. We incline strongly to the opinion that the collapse of the present ultraleft line, particularly in the International, will be followed by a new swing to the right.

In one of Trotsky's latest articles, not published yet here, on Brandler and Thalheimer, in which he practically brands them as a new school of Social Democrats, he characterizes the position of the Marxists as that of an international propaganda society under the present conditions, and compares it to the period of 1907–11 in Russia and the early years of the war. He emphasizes the necessity of endurance and patience and of ideological intransigeance in preparation for the future.

You will probably agree with our editorial on the Sino-Russian conflict. It is quite at variance with the position of the *Daily Worker.* That paper seems to be deliberately edited on the theory that its readers are morons who are incapable of the most elementary reasoning, and its motto is: facts don't matter. We see no real proof that the imperialist powers have instigated the Chinese attack or that they are supporting it.[42] On the contrary, there are many signs that they do not want to sanction the precedent of seizures of foreign interests in China. The statement of Stimson to the Chinese minister, reported in yesterday's *World,* that China must hand back the railroad as a preliminary to a peace conference, doesn't fit in with the *Daily Worker* theory at all. But they dispose of that quite easily by ignoring the statement and talking about imperialism in general. Their method is the best way of disarming the revolutionary workers against a real war danger.

Foster devotes an article to our trade union criticisms in the July *Communist.* We will tear him to pieces in our next issue. Too late to answer this time. The fact that they are beginning after all this time to try to argue with us is highly significant. The discussion which is prevented in the party is beginning to develop through the organs of the various factions outside. The appearance of Lovestone's paper will give this an impetus. Now that the Tenth Plenum of the ECCI has passed and answered his appeal by confirming his expulsion, it is reasonable to assume that he will resort to open propaganda. The Communist movement will present the picture of a group of contending factions, each with its own organs. What we need is a hard group of determined and convinced comrades who do not shrink from hard times and comparative isolation in the fight for the future of the movement.

The greatest loss is the continual seepage away from the movement altogether, of comrades who grow discouraged and lose faith. The weight of America's imperialist power weighs heavily on the movement. We need to develop more earnest study of Marxism and its application to the concrete period. We must educate a group of comrades who have faith in the future resurgence of the revolutionary movement when the American economic machine really begins to crack.

Fraternally,

J.P. Cannon

The crisis in the Communist Party

Published August 1, 1929

The following article was published in *The Militant.*

The crisis in the American Communist movement is a part of the crisis in the International which has been maturing over a period of years. The Communist movement throughout the world is paying, in disintegration and defeat, for the false leadership of Stalin centrism and the mechanical extermination of the Leninist wing.

The American party was slow to manifest open reactions to the International crisis, and particularly slow to develop a conscious participation in the world struggle over basic questions which lie at the bottom of the crisis, but it is catching up now with devastating speed. And what we see now is only a beginning. Greater storms are ahead. The life of the movement is at stake. Only those who rouse themselves to think and act can play the part of communist soldiers now and in the days ahead. Theological worshippers of formulae handed down from above, automatic hand raisers, are worse than useless. The cult of "corpse obedience" serves only the bureaucratic destroyers and holds back the awakening of the movement and its regeneration.

It is necessary first of all to tear aside the curtain of falsehood, deception, and trickery behind which the pitiful subsidized agents of American Stalinism try to conceal the real state of affairs from the party. The spurious "enlightenment campaign" is such a curtain. It talks of discussion of the issues—and prohibits it by organizational measures and threats. It crusades against factionalism—under the direction of the most unprincipled and corrupted factionmongers. It cries about the unity of the party—and plunges the party headlong into a new split, the second in less than a year. The "enlightenment campaign" is a bare-faced fraud, an insult to the party, and a target for the ridicule of its enemies.

Contempt for the Communist rank and file is a characteristic of Stalinism, which rules by apparatus compulsion and corrupts by subsidy. Take the case of Lovestone. For years the Stalin ECCI supported him in his criminal factionalism; time and time again it interfered to strengthen his control of the party. Foster was his comrade-in-arms in the expulsion of the Opposition Communists. Stachel, Bedacht, and Company were his partners in every perfidious faction maneuver, assuring the party that he represented the line of the Communist International. With the help of the ECCI and with the help of Stachel, Bedacht, and Weinstone, he gained the support of 90 percent of the delegates at the party convention a few months ago. Now, out of a clear sky, without Lovestone having changed his character or his actions in the slightest detail, he is expelled from the party as an opportunist and renegade. And Stachel, Bedacht, and Weinstone conduct a campaign to "enlighten" the party about the matter—explaining, however, that they, like Saul of Tarsus, suddenly saw the light and can now be trusted safely.

Why should anyone be surprised if the enemies of communism laugh and if the party members and sympathetic workers fall away in bewilderment and disgust? When we spoke at the December plenum of the Central Executive Committee about the growth of the right wing in the Russian party and the crisis in the right-center bloc, we were accused of scandalmongering and speculation. Pepper, who made the report against us, denied the existence of any differences between Stalin and Bukharin, and Foster nodded approval of the statement. Now the party, which was left in ignorance of all the developments, is blandly informed that Lovestone is aligned with the Russian and International right wing and therefore must be expelled.

The party member who takes official pronunciamentos on faith does not understand this rigamarole—and for a good reason. The right-center bloc (Stalin-Rykov-Bukharin), which has ruled the International through the six-year war against "Trotskyism," has conspired all the time to prevent the Communist workers from knowing the truth about the conflict within it. Up to the present moment the identity of the leaders of the right wing (Rykov-Bukharin-Tomsky) has not been disclosed in the official party press, although everybody knows it except the loyal party member who is supposed to know everything. The question of the right wing in the Russian party is indeed a burning question of the international movement; the fate of the Russian revolution, of the Comintern, and, consequently, of our party, is bound up with it. But the "enlightenment campaign" only obscures and muddles the great issue, keeps the membership from understanding it, and thus strengthens the right wing and Lovestone, its outstanding American representative.

The new maneuver of Stalin centrism which brands Lovestone as an opportunist and expels him from the party—seven months after he expelled us—cannot change the position of the Communist Opposition on any of the principled questions, above all on the question of the right wing. It was the Bolshevik-Leninists in the Russian party—the "Trotskyists"—who analyzed its social basis and exposed its Thermidorian character. The Opposition alone wages a real struggle against it in defense of the proletarian dictatorship. The present sham battle of the centrists against the right wing is carried out only under the whip of the Opposition.

The newly appointed leadership of the party, in order to create confusion, spreads rumors of a combination between the Opposition Communists and the Lovestone faction. Weinstone predicts such an eventuality in his article in the *Daily Worker.* These people, who themselves change with every wind and every cablegram from Moscow, do not understand a struggle on principled lines. The Weinstones and Fosters, who only yesterday collaborated heartily with Lovestone in every infamous practice against loyal Communists, who were his accomplices in gangsterism, in burglary, and slander, make this accusation with ill grace.

There can be no combination of the Communist Opposition with the Lovestone faction. A serious discussion in which the political issues are elucidated will make this absolutely clear. When we speak of the Lovestone faction in this sense it goes without saying that we refer to the leaders only and not to the honest Communist workers who have been deceived by them with the help of the ECCI. Many of these are already finding their way to our platform and will be among its staunchest defenders.

The right wing of the Russian party, with which Lovestone is unquestionably connected, is the representative of the class forces in the Soviet Union which are driving toward the restoration of capitalism. This fact, now openly proclaimed by the Stalinists, was also the case when it was in one bloc with Stalin to exterminate the Leninist wing of the party, and its bloodthirsty campaign against the "Trotskyists" was the clearest expression of its Thermidorian character. The dissolution of the Communist International would be an inevitable corollary of its victory. For those who want to fight for the preservation of our Communist movement, any kind of support for the right faction—to say nothing of a bloc with its American agents—cannot be spoken of lightly; it cannot be spoken of at all. An absolutely irreconcilable war against the right wing is the first and foremost duty of the American Opposition Communists.

The idea that the right-wing Thermidorian elements in the Russian party can really espouse party democracy—an idea suggested in an editorial in the *New York Volkszeitung*—is the greatest and most dangerous illusion. The right wing, by its very nature, by the class forces of capitalist restoration it represents, had to demand the fiercest and most criminal repression of the Bolshevik-Leninists and to drive the Stalin centrists, who were allied with them, onto this path. The condition for the existence and growth of the right wing is the annihilation of the Leninists, who are fighting for the October revolution and the regeneration of the Comintern on the line of Lenin. "Democracy" for the right wing is only an expedient in the faction struggle with the centrist apparatus, not a principle of party organization which they would or could apply.

This is true also in America. The Lovestone who demands party democracy expelled the Opposition Communists from the party for their views alone. They went further—the Lovestones and Fosters together—and expelled communist proletarians for merely protesting against the expulsions of the others. Party democracy is an absolute prerequisite for the party. It will be the mightiest weapon in the hands of the proletarian elements for the salvation and regeneration of the movement, and for its normal development on the revolutionary path. But Lovestone is not and cannot be the champion of this slogan.

The reunification of the party and the elimination of factionalism are categorical tasks for the accomplishment of which the conscious revolutionaries must band together and fight. The "Open Address" and the measures which followed it have not and cannot solve this problem. Crisis, splits, paralysis, and disintegration are the results so far. And the coming period will only intensify the crisis, widen the splits, and increase the demoralization, until the course is changed. To bring this change about, a discussion and an education of the party, a correct line of tactics in the class struggle, and a bona fide leadership, freely chosen by the party and standing on its own feet, are necessary. They are lacking now.

The present makeshift leadership, a conglomeration of yes-men and parasitical place-hunters who confess their sins for self-advancement, patched together from the tag ends of the old factions and appointed by cablegram from above, cannot overcome the crisis and unite the party. The stop-gap leadership of today can only make matters worse. It has all the faults of the Lovestone regime without any of its strength or independence. It confuses the party by giving the outward appearance of a change from petty-bourgeois politiciandom and factional corruption which does not exist in reality.

Lovestone is out but Stachel remains. And Stachel is in

charge of the campaign against factionalism. Is this not a spectacle for gods and men? Stachel, the organizer and right-hand man of Lovestone in every evil enterprise of disruption, the most dubious character that ever floated to the top in the foul waters of party factionalism, an individual with no tradition, experience, ability, or integrity, the factionmonger who lived by factionalism—Stachel has made the sign of the cross and become the apostle of unity.

Wolfe is removed from the Political Committee and Wicks, equally characterless and with far less ability, takes his place. Gitlow is slated to go, but Bedacht, who by his own confession was steeped in moral and political corruption, is promoted. Add a few Amters and Tallentires—the number makes no difference because they weigh nothing—and Foster. This is the new leadership.

The new leadership has no real authority. Its temporary existence signifies the abolition of a genuine leading body and the establishment of a receivership over the party by the Stalin ECCI. This so-called leadership enjoys no confidence in the party ranks, and the loyal party members who want salvation by faith alone are falling back on the formula: "The CI is the leader of the party." In regard to real authority this is literally the case. The CEC is only the rubber stamp for the representative of the ECCI, who in turn relies on cabled instructions at every change in the situation. The CEC does not even venture to write its own statements; this is obvious from their language. Such expressions as "defeat all efforts of drawing the Party away from the political path of the 6th Congress" and "sending the direction to the devil" show that the CEC does not even do a decent job of translating the statements it signs.

Their method of "fighting" the right wing only strengthens it as an ideology in the party. There is no education of the party on the political issues. The victories over the right are mechanical and temporary. The Lovestone right wing was nurtured too long to be suddenly uprooted by decree.

The political line of the leadership is heading toward catastrophic defeats for the party which will weaken its position in the class struggle and sharpen the crisis in the party. The false tactics of counterfeit leftism in the preparations for the TUEL conference, in the Gastonia defense, in the needle trades, and in other questions will bring swift and devastating reactions.

The leadership which promises to unite the party will itself fall apart into factions; in fact it is already doing so. The groupings which are taking shape around Foster on the one side and Bedacht on the other are common knowledge in the circles of informed functionaries. These are not purely arbitrary and personal groupings, as they may appear. They have a political base in the impulse of Foster, whose real trend is toward labor progressivism, to find a way out of the blind alley of fake leftism on the trade union field, and the wish of Bedacht to "make good" for his confessed sins of opportunism. This base will widen as the harmful results of the present tactics accumulate. Under the impact of the class struggle, and of the blows of the right wing on the one side and the Communist Opposition on the other, the present Central Executive Committee, lacking independence of thought and action and any real principled foundation, is doomed to defeat and collapse.

Stalinism is breaking up the ranks of international Communism, and the American section is now beginning to feel the full force of the international crisis. This is the meaning of the crisis in the party. The Communist forces must reform themselves and build anew. Help will not come from above; the source of the disruption lies there. The struggle against disintegration must be organized from below. The revolutionary workers must awaken. They must give up blind obedience and begin to think and to act independently. The struggle must cease to be an affair of the bureaucratic upper crust and become the concern of the Communist workers in the mass. The development of the initiative of the party ranks and their conscious intervention in the struggle is the hope for the future of the movement. This means, as a beginning, a fight for definite aims along the following lines:

1. In place of the fraudulent "enlightenment campaign," a real discussion of the three political tendencies which are now taking definite shape in the American party. Such a discussion calls for the publication of all important documents and a free opportunity to explain and clarify the conflicting views. Only in this way can the party be educated politically and enabled to act consciously, solving its problems without inner convulsions. We stand for such a discussion because we know that in it the Leninist line will prevail and the right wing, which thrives on bureaucratic measures, will be politically annihilated.

2. Genuine party democracy in place of the regime of administrative terror and suppression. A situation must be created where nothing is taken for granted and where incompetent bureaucrats can no longer hide behind official authority. The members must assert and take the right to speak out what they think without fearing organizational measures and threats. The reinstatement of the expelled Oppositionists with full rights to defend their views is the first prerequisite. Without this, party democracy is a sham.

3. A genuine proletarianization of the leadership, in which bona fide workers, leaders in class-struggle activities who have independent opinions and the ability to defend them, play an active part in all the leading bodies. This must replace the present system of electing harmless

proletarian elements for show purposes only.

4. A reorganization and reduction of the party apparatus, which, including the functionaries and employees of auxiliaries, now exceeds 10 percent of the party membership. These paid officials, remote from the actualities of the class struggle, are a crust over the party, stifling its normal life and monopolizing party discussion and direction. The drastic reduction of this staff and the election of fresh worker elements will strengthen and invigorate party life.

5. Subsidies of all kinds must be absolutely abolished and the party adjusted to operate by its own means derived from membership dues and contributions. Opposition to subsidy is no principle. Mutual assistance of revolutionary parties has played a positive role in the past and no doubt will do so in the future. But in the present situation, subsidy has become an instrument for corruption, for bureaucratization and crushing out independent party life. Opposition to subsidy under these conditions is a fight for the integrity of the party.

6. The party must have a real convention, preceded by an honest discussion and the honest selection of delegates, to work out its problems and select its own leaders.

Vincent St. John

Published August 1, 1929

The following article was published in *The Militant.*

The death of Vincent St. John in San Francisco marks the passing of another of the great figures of the American revolutionary movement whose deeds helped to make its tradition and whose names will not be forgotten. "The Saint," as he was known by those who knew and loved him, died at the age of fifty-six after a long illness complicated by high blood pressure. He will be sincerely mourned by thousands whose lives were influenced by him, particularly by those who belonged to the old guard of the IWW in its bravest days, when he was its moving spirit and guiding intelligence.

Vincent St. John, like Haywood and Frank Little, was trained in the hard school of the Western Federation of Miners, that model labor union whose mighty struggles threw their shadow across the world in the latter years of the nineteenth century and the first years of the twentieth.

A metal miner by trade, he joined the Western Federation in 1894, and became one of the most militant fighters in its ranks and an influential voice in its councils. Despite his modesty of disposition, his freedom from personal ambition, and his lack of the arts of self-aggrandizement, his work spoke loudly and brought him widespread fame.

His stirring deeds as a pioneer organizer became legends of the movement and remain such today. Until 1907 he was a member of the Executive Board of the WFM. In that strategic position he became the leader of the left wing in the looming struggle between conservative and revolutionary unionism which centered around the question of affiliation to the IWW, which the Western Federation had played a major part in founding in 1905.

At the second convention of the IWW in 1906, St. John headed the revolutionary syndicalist group, which combined with the SLP elements to oust Sherman, a conservative, as president and establish a new administration in the organization with a revolutionary policy. He became the general organizer under the new administration, breaking with the WFM on the withdrawal of the latter body and giving his whole allegiance to the IWW.

He presided at the 1908 convention, which saw the split with the SLP and the elimination of the "political clause" from the preamble. St. John was the leader of the proletarian "direct action" forces which defeated the "political" wing of De Leon. Thereafter, he served as general secretary of the IWW until 1914, and undoubtedly did more than anyone to shape its course and prepare the ground for its later development under the active leadership of Haywood.

He withdrew from activity on leaving the office of general secretary and engaged in a mining enterprise, doubtless with the illusory hope of acquiring a fortune to help finance the organization of the workers. Despite his retirement at that period, fear of his abilities and the prospect of his return to the office vacated by the imprisonment of Haywood dictated his own arrest and subsequent conviction with the Chicago group of IWW wartime prisoners. He served two and a half years at Leavenworth before commutation brought his release.

From his earlier concepts of revolutionary socialism, St. John, in revolt against the parliamentary reformism of the Socialist Party and the sectarian, ultralegal concepts of the Socialist Labor Party, developed along the line of revolutionary syndicalism, the path taken by many of the best proletarian fighters of the period. In many respects this represented a step forward from parliamentary socialism, but the prejudices and theoretical falsity of the syndicalist or industrialist position were storing up disasters for the future.

The philosophy of the IWW, which St. John did so much to shape, was too simple for the complex situation brought about by the entry of the United States into the World War. The great sacrifices and heroic deeds of its members were unavailing against this handicap and were greatly discounted by it. To the great loss of the workers' cause, St. John, and with him the great majority of the leading militants of the IWW, failed to make the theoretical and tactical adjustments necessitated by the experience of the World War and the Russian revolution. Their limited industrialist concepts remained unchanged.

Communism, especially its American representative, impressed them unfavorably, and they could not swim with the current of the new movement. The enormous errors, presumptuousness, and tactlessness of the party leadership are partly responsible for this calamitous state of affairs. American Communism should have been a natural growth out of the soil of the prewar movement represented in part by the IWW. The early years of the party were weakened and hampered by this failure; and the IWW movement, alienated from Communism, lost its old-time vigor and passed into an inevitable degeneration and decline.

But despite the tragedy of the after-war years, the earlier work of the IWW militants—and St. John in the front rank—retains all its validity. They wrote much of the tradition of the American revolutionary movement in letters of fire that will never be extinguished. The modern movement of Communism which is the heir to their achievements, should value this tradition highly and honor the memory of the men who made it. The memory of Vincent St. John will always be a treasure to the revolutionary workers of America in their aspiring struggle for the workers' world.

For those who knew "The Saint" as a man and friend, his untimely death brings a deep and poignant grief. He was a most admirable personality—brave and resolute, loyal and honest. He was a gifted and inspiring leader and organizer who gave himself, throughout the years of youth and manhood prime, untiringly and unsparingly to the workers' cause. And with the highest executive qualities he combined the rare gift of friendship, of warmly human consideration and concern for others, of loyalty in personal relations, which bound men to him in life-long affection.

Those who were so bound to him, who knew the warmth of his handclasp, enshrine his memory in their hearts along with the best memories of the great cause for which we live and strive.

Hail and farewell, soldier, man, and friend!

Unity and the Gastonia strike

August 13, 1929

The following letter was written to Hugo Oehler, a sympathizer of the Communist League who was working in the leadership of the Communist Party in the Gastonia textile strike.

Dear Comrade Young:

We received your letters and greatly appreciate the information you sent. An article by you would be most welcome. If you wish we can rewrite it entirely so that there will be no danger of your style showing. The most important thing is to have an article based on really authentic information as a basis for our conclusions.

Outside the sectarianism in conducting the campaign for Gastonia defense, another great error in policy, from our point of view, is the failure to employ the slogan of unity in the fight to organize the textile workers.[43] The first ray of light on this—and quite probably a reaction to our criticisms—is seen in the article of Bill Dunne in the *Daily Worker.* Toward the end of this article appears the following:

"Dewey Martin, C.W. Saylor and Sophie Melvin will tell the delegates to the Convention [of the North Carolina Federation of Labor] of the struggle in Gaston County and ask them to endorse a united front movement of all textile workers, regardless of union affiliation, for the 8-hour day, the abolition of the stretch-out and the 100 per cent organization of the textile industry in a militant industrial union."

The first part of this sounds like a restatement of the tested tactics of the united front. It is negated by the last proposal, which specifies "a militant industrial union" in the sense that it must be the NTW. That is not a serious united-front proposal. In fact it caricatures the slogan. We have to see the hundreds of thousands of textile workers and not merely the few thousand under the immediate influence of the Communists. We have to recognize that a number of strikes, very probably involving more workers than we have, are under the control of the UTW. Unless we devise ways and means of expanding over a wider front and extending our influence into the ranks of the other strikes we will finally be condemned to an isolated position in a small sector of the industry. The means to this is the tactic of the united front.

In our opinion we should appear everywhere as the real champions of united struggle. That means that we must work out proposals which have a bona fide character for cooperation in an organization drive, the setting up of joint committees, etc. This does not mean to have any illusions about the acceptance of these proposals by the UTW officials. Our object should be to make our good faith apparent on the face of our proposals and through them find a way to the workers outside our influence now. This will not weaken our work to strengthen and consolidate the independent force we now have. It will help it. The slogan of unity is the strongest slogan with the workers. There is something fatally wrong when the Communists give it up.

A careful agitation along these lines within the party now will go a long way to turn the left wing aside from the debacle it is heading for in the preparations for the TUEL conference. Is it not possible for you to work out concrete proposals for inside agitation embodying this idea on the question of the organization campaign and aiming at a real united front for the defense movement? The policy in this latter field is scandalous. The IWW, the anarchists, the SLP, and the SP and the Muste group have all declared in favor of the Gastonia defendants. The present policy allows them to get away with lip service. A united-front policy, actually proposing united action, would force them into line or out of it. In any case it would result in the widening of the present movement four or five times at least. This might be the balance of the scale in favor of the prisoners. A wide movement before the trial has far more weight than after conviction. The Sacco-Vanzetti case and the Haywood case show this. There ought to be a proposal that the ILD issue a call to all organizations to unite in conferences for Gastonia as was done in the Sacco-Vanzetti case and was done in the campaign for the Passaic strike. Such a movement within the party is a burning necessity now. You ought to be able to recruit supporters for such a line, beginning with Bill Dunne.

What you say regarding Dunne interests us very much. From our point of view, he is the best of the present leading forces and one of the few not so hopelessly corrupted and bureaucratized that confidence in their future value for the revolutionary movement cannot be had. We notice that he also writes some nonsense in carrying out the new line, but less than the others. We hardly believe his heart is in it.

The news about the success of the Southern Textile Conference is most gratifying. It shows that conditions are really unfolding for a push forward of the revolutionary movement in preparation for the great resurgence which is coming in the future. This makes the question of tactics all the more important. The foremost duty of the revolutionary wing of the party is to fight with all resources for the right line.

We are gradually developing a new group of supporters inside the party who will be prepared to work within along the lines of the strategy worked out. What is needed is the gradual development of a leadership for this new inside group. If you could get one or two more prominent comrades to agree with you fully it would have a great advantage for the advancement of our cause. Try your best to do this. If it can't be done, the conditions will soon mature for you to commence it alone. Other leaders to help will be found in the course of the fight.

If it is at all possible for you to see us when you come to New York, do so. A note to our mail address making an appointment to meet you will be enough. Let us know about this and the other matters mentioned in the above letter.

Our movement is going through a process of hardening and consolidating for the siege ahead. A definite trend toward consolidation on an international scale is also to be seen despite the new defections in Russia. Do you get the paper? Is it safe to send it to your address?

Brown

We have to build anew

August 14, 1929

The following excerpt is from a letter to Albert Glotzer.

Dear Al:

. . . After the last issue of *The Militant* there should be no more question as to our stand on Lovestone. We are taking a shot at his appeal again in the coming issue. We got a copy of the whole document. It is nothing but an enlarged printed edition of the old onionskin factional circulars. Compared with the first declarations we issued, setting forth a clear political line, it is a pitiful document indeed. It ought to help the comrades to get the measure of the leadership which was supported for years by the ECCI.

I wrote a reply to Foster somewhat along the line you suggested in your letter and then went over it and toned it down a bit in keeping with our established style of dignity and restraint. It will please you anyway better than it will please Foster. You are right about him—and the same thing applies to most of the others. They have become bureaucratized and corrupted to such an extent that they are hopelessly lost to the revolutionary cause. The sooner we realize this and give up illusions, the better will we be able to deal with them. Of Dunne we have hopes. He is writing some foolish stuff on the trade union question and the "new line" but so far has steered clear of a direct collision with us. I do not think he has much heart for the business.

I agree with what you say about the necessity for some serious work of Marxian education. We will have to devote a session of the committee to it in the near future. Our great problem is to dispose of the forces we have to the best advantage. I note what you say about the young and the old-timers. The latter surely have a part to play from which they cannot be "excused," but we are building a pioneer movement, and that means that the youngsters will necessarily play an increasingly important part, both in the ranks and the leadership. Ours is a long, hard fight, and the youth will be our main reliance.

We realize more and more that we have to build anew, almost from the ground up. The bluster and froth and excessive radicalism of the official party is only another sign of its inner deterioration. The latest antics of "Red Day," the uniformed pioneers, and the slogan of "struggle for the streets" are gestures of despair where they are not indications of infantile romanticism reminiscent of the "armed insurrection" period of the party. The movement will ultimately pay heavier than we dream for this criminal irresponsibility. Wicks as editor of the *Daily Worker* is the most appropriate representative of this tendency.

What is going on with the Springfield group? Lovestone's appeal refers to the application of Voyzey for reinstatement and we can't get a word out of Angelo. Have they accepted the ousting of Lovestone as the solution of the principled questions involved in the struggle of the Opposition?

It was to be expected that the stand of the Opposition on "Red Day" would sharpen antagonism against us for the moment. But the party members will gradually get accustomed to our practice of telling the truth without any varnish on it. After they test the new policy by experience, our words will have more influence with them. The soundest basis for leadership is the proof of a correct position established by events over a period. The influence of demagogy is transient. In the long run, the revolutionaries will look for leadership to those who told them the truth in the face of all their prejudices. . . .

Grus,

Jim

Where is the left wing going?

Published August 15, 1929

The following article was published in *The Militant.* It was subtitled "An Answer to William Z. Foster with a Footnote on His Political Biography."

William Z. Foster, who has succeeded Lovestone as the chief of American Stalinism, makes his debut as an unterrified warrior against "counterrevolutionary Trotskyism," after a long and discreet silence on the subject, in the July number of the *Communist.* The publication of Foster's article ("Right Tendencies at the Trade Union Unity Conference") opens a debate on the trade union question which the Stalinists avoided as long as possible.

In his first attack on the Opposition Communists, Foster justifies his appointment to the leadership of American Stalinism by an exhibition of those talents and methods which he perfected in the school of Gompers and which have contributed not a little to the corruption of the Communist movement in America since his belated adhesion to it. The Communist movement will be the gainer by this forced discussion of specific questions at issue and by the occasion it offers to examine the personal qualities and the history of Foster which have made him the logical successor to Lovestone as the warden of the Stalin barracks.

The first task in replying to him is to clear away the fog and put the questions as they are. Foster tries to represent matters as though we are opposed to organizing the unorganized. That seems absolutely incredible to anyone familiar with the facts. But Foster, inevitably proceeding on the theory that nobody reads, or remembers what he reads, puts it down in type as the keystone of his argument against us. And to make the case "stronger" he links our position with that of Lovestone, whom yesterday he helped to expel us.

A few facts will suffice to dispose of this falsification. The *Communist* for July 1928 contained an article by me which was a digest of my speech at the May 1928 plenum of the CEC. In this article, which outlines views consistently maintained since that time, I insisted on a course "to put the main emphasis and center of gravity in its trade union work on the organization of the unorganized and the preparation for strikes." This was the main theme of my article, although the necessity of combating any tendency to leave the old unions was also underscored. Foster's attempt to represent us as opposed to this line and to connect us with Lovestone, who really opposed it, is quite amazing when it is recalled that the same issue of the *Communist* in which my article appeared also contains an article by Foster, as a sort of reply to me, written, as the introduction states, at the instruction of the Lovestone CEC and "expressing the C.E.C. position."

Our trade union position does not change from day to day, and we maintain now, as before, despite the incalculable damage being done by the adventurist and irresponsible policy of the party, that the organization of the unorganized must be the first point on the left-wing program in the present situation. This idea is brought out in our platform and it runs through a dozen or more articles in *The Militant* dealing with various phases of trade union work.

But this matter does not end with Foster's falsification and our exposure of it. The differences between us on this point are real enough, and they consist in this:

For us, the organization of the unorganized and the formation of new unions is only one phase—although at present the most important phase—of our program, and it is indissolubly connected with the work in the old unions and the slogan of trade union unity. For the Stalinists, the formation of new unions and the empty chatter about a new revolutionary trade union center have become a trade union program in themselves.

For fear of facing the whole issue, this has not yet been stated in clear and definite programmatic form. But it is the plain implication of all the talk nowadays, and it is the practice. The TUEL as a left wing in the old unions does not exist any more. The nature of the current propaganda precludes any serious work in the AFL. One could easily compile a page of quotations from the party press to show that the policy is understood to mean that we are to join the new unions and leave the AFL. One quotation from the pen of the eminent Patrick H. Toohey, secretary-treasurer of the National Miners Union, in the *Daily Worker* of May 24, illustrates the drift:

"The many thousands of honest workers who are still in the A.F. of L. will quickly learn that they are being betrayed *and will leave it* to join with the unorganized workers of the entire country" (our emphasis).

Foster, the most careful writer, expert in the use of the

qualifying clause, past master in the art of "leaving the door open" so that his words can be interpreted to mean one thing or the direct opposite—depending on the way the cat jumps—furnishes the inspiration for the conclusions of the cruder Tooheys. In the *Daily Worker* of May 13, Foster wrote as follows:

"By the same token that *it would be wrong to draw these individual workers* into the corrupt A.F. of L. unions, *so it would be incorrect to try to affiliate them collectively* through the new unions to the A.F. of L. *The A.F. of L. leadership does not want such revolutionary unions* and even if it should in any case accept them it would only be to destroy them."

These quotations are the same in essence and they are both wrong because they set up a dogma which cannot always be followed. If we are in principle opposed to drawing *individual workers* into the AFL, if we consider it incorrect to try to *affiliate them collectively,* and if this attitude is motivated, as Foster motivates it, by the fact that "the A.F. of L. leadership does not want such revolutionary unions," then Toohey is correct also about the necessity of the honest workers *leaving* the AFL. Green and Company do not want them either. With such views, how can a left wing be consolidated for a stubborn fight in the old unions? It cannot be done, and because of such views, which now dominate the party policy, it is not being done.

These tactics are false. They spell isolation and defeat for the left wing, the strengthening of the reactionary stranglehold on the unions, and the eventual defeat of the program for organizing the unorganized. And of all those responsible for the damage these false tactics are doing to the future of the party, Foster is the most culpable. He is not one of those brainless windbags who are able to talk themselves into the belief that the new "Revolutionary

Trade Union Center" is just what the workers are waiting for. He knows better, and supports a false policy out of factional expedience and personal opportunism. This is a crime against the working class.

In his article in the *Communist,* Foster gingerly touches on the question of the united front with the progressive elements in the unions against the reactionaries, which was the main strategy of the party in the trade unions since 1921, and which Foster advocated in his book *Misleaders of Labor* as the key to the conquest of the unions.

Now Foster dismisses the whole strategy with a few words, repudiates seven years of party trade union work under his direction, and dumps overboard the book which embodied his settled conclusions on the trade union movement—all in a few sentences which make no attempt to explain the error of the old policy or the reasons for the new one. Everything is covered with the soul-saving formula: we made a mistake and the RILU corrected us. It would be more merciful and humane to "educate" the left-wing workers with a club than to slug them with such methods.

The new progressive movement in the trade unions is a symptom of rank-and-file pressure which will very probably show greater vitality in the future. The Communists should regard it fundamentally from this standpoint and steer a course toward contact with it, regardless of the shady character of some of those represented in its present leadership. Since when did this become wrong, and why?

Only a year ago, in his article in the July 1928 *Communist* referred to above, Foster wrote:

"The middle group will tend to organize and cooperate with the left wing. The so-called Muste Group, while not in itself large, is an evidence of this tendency. To consolidate the real opposition forces in the old unions, is the task of the T.U.E.L."

The explanation of the error in these conceptions is Foster's task, not ours. We still maintain them. But he tries to avoid that duty by ascribing the policy of the past exclusively to us and, with characteristic generosity, by giving us "credit" for some particularly gross mistake of his own.

"Cannon . . . was one of the very worst defenders of the erroneous united front policy of the T.U.E.L. He understood it and fought for it to mean that we should make alliances with every crook and faker in the labor movement who made even a pretense of being in opposition to the ruling labor bureaucracy. This was the substance of his conception of trade union work."

Who? Where? When? This is a very strong accusation, which ought to be supported by some facts and proofs. Since Foster fails to supply them, we will make up the deficiency. The only time and place this was a serious issue dividing the Central Committee was in the needle trades, particularly in the ILGWU. In 1925, when Sigman was in a conflict with other sections of the bureaucracy over questions of patronage, after he had expelled the left wing, the Foster faction proposed to make a combination with the Sigman forces to secure a majority at the 1925 convention in Philadelphia.

We fought this utterly unprincipled combination, which threatened to undermine the moral and ideological foundations of the left wing, and combined with Ruthenberg to defeat it. The whole story is told in the minutes of the Political Committee for that period. There it appears on the agenda half a dozen times with half a dozen motions from us prohibiting it. We challenge Foster to make these minutes public. This will be far more convincing than general accusations which cannot be supported.

But, while we fought against the abominable horse-trade with Sigman, and others of the same stripe, which

Foster also proposed, we declined to join in the orgy of purity and repentance which came afterward, and which wanted to do away with all dealings with all fakers under all circumstances. We were, and are, against this theory because it condemns the left wing to sterility and destroys its maneuvering capacity. It is in reality only the reverse side of the Sigman proposal and is almost equally harmful.

One of the greatest weaknesses in the current trade union policy of the party is the withdrawal of the slogan of unity. This was a central slogan of the party and one of its mightiest weapons in the fight against the reactionaries. The slogan of unity was one of the most effective means of mobilizing the masses in the needle trades under the left-wing banner. And conversely, although there are other factors, the decline of left-wing power and influence and the revival of the right wing in this field are closely related to the dropping of this slogan.

These lighthearted reversals of basic policy are made all the more reprehensible by the failure to offer any explanations. They are carried out in a purely administrative way, by decision of committees, as though the masses did not exist. The education of the party is stifled by these methods, and the masses cannot understand what the Communists want. In these conditions the reactionaries and the Socialists grow and consolidate at the expense of the Communists, and the right wing in the party is nurtured.

This process, now clearly visible, is part of the fruit of the new line of counterfeit leftism. The national conference of the TUEL can really serve the cause of the workers if it calls a halt to this course and steers the trade union work of the left wing back onto the main line of revolutionary policy. A formal ratification of the adventurist tactics which Foster and others are now propagating will weaken the position of the left wing still more and make its recovery more painful and difficult.

❖

Stalin centrism selects the instruments which are qualified to serve its mission, which is to befoul the banner of communism and destroy the Communist International. It attracts to its service those who adapt themselves easily and swim with the current. It creates a happy hunting ground for the bureaucrat and careerist. It bestows the marshal's baton on those who can reconcile contradictions and change positions in the shortest time. The consecration of Foster as the new American chief of Stalinism is not without logic and a reason. His past has prepared him for the present, as an outline of his career will show. His record is a record of zigzags and changes from right to left according to the mutations of the working-class movement. Above all others he has shown that he knows how to adapt himself. And this is the first requirement of a Stalinist overseer.

Foster began his career as a revolutionist, first in the Socialist Party and later in the IWW. This is an important fact to remember in connection with his later activities and allegiances. He left the IWW in 1911 at a time of low ebb in the fortunes of that organization of militants and went to the AFL. There, according to his own testimony and that of Gompers and Fitzpatrick before the Senate committee investigating the steel strike, some extracts of which are printed on another page, he adapted himself to the philosophy of Gompers, so much that he found no obstacle in rising to high positions by official appointment.

During the war the tide ran strongly against the "reds" and Foster, by his own testimony, went with it—for the war. He who had been a revolutionist fought on the other side of the barricades in those fateful days. The man whom Stalin has appointed to "lead" the fight against the war danger, was for winning the last war "at all costs," "bought either $450 or $500 worth of bonds," made dozens of speeches, and "carried on a regular campaign" in the stockyards "to help make the loans a success."

These are the credentials which qualify him to denounce us as counterrevolutionaries and renegades. They are not unlike the credentials of other leaders of the Stalin slander squad throughout the International.

In 1921 the left tide in the labor movement was flowing and Foster discovered the Russian revolution—and that not without considerable persuasion and inducement. When Ralph Chaplin and the writer went to see him early in that year he was still hesitant and evasive. He replied to a direct question as to his belief in the proletarian revolution with the strange words, as I remember them: "Well, I used to have a lot of faith. I walked twenty miles once to vote the Socialist ticket."

His entry into the party in 1921, following a trip to Russia and an agreement to support and build up the TUEL, was an undoubted advantage to the movement, just emerging from the underground and seeking contact with the masses. His trade union prestige and connections were a great factor in giving life to the trade union tactics adopted at the unity convention earlier in that year, which retain their validity today. Even his conception of dual unionism as the cause of all the evils in the radical movement served a purpose in correcting the sectarian currents on this question.

As a party leader he failed to justify the hopes placed in him and was not long in demonstrating that he had learned more from Gompers than from Lenin. His methods were marked by an ingrained and incurable dishonesty.

His inability to put any question squarely, his systematic muddling and misrepresentation of issues, and his subordination of the task of educating the party to the immediate aim of securing votes in a faction struggle, had a sad effect on the workers around him. Their political development was arrested in its most elementary stages, and what became finally crystallized as the Foster faction was always a picture of political impotence. His influence as a political force in the party dwindled progressively, and the new role of leadership he now enjoys could have been conferred only by appointment.

The reaction in the Communist International represented by the dominance of apparatus centrism is flowing now, and Foster is riding with it. In political questions his chief characteristic has been adaptability, incapacity to withstand pressure and maintain a position as a minority. He has always been fighting for power but always sacrificing or adapting his position to the exigencies of that fight. A record of the various positions he has taken on disputed party questions would be a chart of shifts in pressure from one side to another in the course of the struggles.

He used to be against dual unions to a dogmatic extreme intolerable for one who tried to view the labor movement from a Marxist standpoint. Now the "left" tide in the Comintern has carried him to a directly opposite position. The same on the question of the progressives. It is really hard to believe that the man who talks so radical now was an ally—and more than an ally—of Fitzpatrick a few short years ago. A new change in Comintern policy, which under the present regime is apt to come any time on twenty-four hours' notice, will find Foster on the bandwagon ahead of everybody shouting for the new line and denouncing anyone who holds on to the slogans he is promoting today. No one would welcome a new shift in policy to the right more than Foster. He has an innate conservatism and talks radical now because he must, with tongue in cheek, like an atheist priest repeating his prayers.

Foster fits well into the world machine of Stalin, which has replaced the original staff of Lenin's International. Between his present role and his old one there is an intimate connection. Such leaders will last as long as centrism maintains itself in the International, and will go down with it.

Defense policy in Gastonia

August 19, 1929

The following letter was written to Hugo Oehler.

Dear Comrade Young:

It is clear from your letter that the question of cooperation on policy in the Gastonia struggle and in the textile struggle generally has suffered by our failure to keep in closer communication. If it is at all possible, we should have a meeting before you go to Cleveland. Can't you arrange to go there by way of New York and stop over here a day or so? I am sure such a meeting would be very fruitful.

Regarding the slogans of the Gastonia defense: I have not seen any of Lovestone's material on this and therefore don't know anything about his position except the references in the *Daily Worker*—and in such reports we take very little stock on any subject. However, statements that we "agree with Lovestone" signify nothing. There is no law to prevent Lovestone from having an intelligent opinion on such an obvious question as the Gastonia defense, and at any rate a more correct opinion than the party leadership has.

We are very sorry to see you favoring the present line on Gastonia defense, and your statement that this is in reality the policy of the "CEC Committee of Gastonia" makes things much worse because it implies that you and Bill [Dunne] are partly responsible for it.

What does the slogan "The right of self-defense against armed attack of bosses' agents" signify? Well, when it is put as the leading and in fact the only slogan, as the current material on the case indicates, it signifies that all twenty-three of the prisoners are going to take upon themselves the responsibility for the shooting of the policeman who was killed. In effect it means to plead guilty and claim justification. It throws the door wide open for any kind of manufactured evidence against the prisoners, and particularly against the Communist leaders whom the mill owners want to convict as an example. By implication, at least, it accepts the theory which the other side is always striving to establish—that the Communist leaders are responsible legally every time a policeman, scab, or thug is shot in a fight during a labor struggle. Such criminal folly put forward as Communist tactics is enough to make the mind reel.

Are the twenty-three prisoners prepared to admit that they fired the fatal shots? Is any one of them willing to do so (assuming that the party would sanction such an insane proposal)? Is the prosecution in a position to prove absolutely who killed the policeman? I understand that none of these conditions exist. What we have is a *legal theory* (an old one) of the prosecution that the strike leaders are responsible for any violence that occurs during a strike, and a *defense slogan* which fits into this theory like a man's neck fits into a noose.

I will not go so far as Weisbord, who you say calls the policy "the same as a provocateur agent," but I will say confidently that every provocateur in the party—and there are no doubt many of them—will get instructions to cheer for this policy. It is right in their mitt, like much of the other "radical" noise in the *Daily Worker* these days. The lives of the prisoners seem to be a small stake in this game. And have the probable consequences of this policy been given a second thought? It may well destroy what is left of the party, opening the door for every faker in the country to blame the Communists for a conviction and smoothing the way for all kinds of future frame-up cases, in which the Communists are disarmed beforehand.

You say this slogan "is putting it on a class-struggle basis." Since when did the fight against labor frame-ups and the defense of the right to organize and strike cease to be based on the class struggle? From our point of view, these are the proper slogans for this fight. This is the real nature of the case, and, besides that, these slogans will rally the broadest movement of support. The exposures of the Mooney case and the Sacco-Vanzetti case have saturated the working class with a conviction that the bosses frame-up charges against labor leaders and that the real crime of the accused in labor cases is organizing the workers. The new, "revolutionary" defense policy rises on stilts above this great reservoir of support for the Gastonia prisoners, and disregards it.

Of course, there will be, as there have been, cases where the defense rests on "the right of self-defense against armed attack." But this is only where the responsibility for the shooting is so clearly and directly established that it cannot be denied. The Carl Pierson case was such a one. Pierson was a leader in the railroad shopmen's strike in 1911 who killed a policeman when the latter attacked him with a gun. It was a purely individual case, the responsibility for the shooting was not denied, and no others were involved. But in all the other famous cases, from the Haymarket martyrs on, the prosecution has claimed and *the defense has denied* that others, particularly leaders, were criminally responsible for the killing of bosses' agents in a struggle. The party today is abandoning this old, established, and correct labor strategy for a new one at the expense of the prisoners and of the movement. It is fortunate for the party leadership that there are no mature and experienced people involved in the case. They would very probably tell the party to go to hell and provide other subjects for the gruesome experiment.

You have a big responsibility. It is your duty to think this matter through and begin a struggle to correct the line before it is too late. Try in every way to get Bill to help you to put the defense movement on the basis of a fight against the frame-up and a defense of the right to organize and strike.

❖

We have an editorial on Gastonia in the paper now on the press, setting forth the above views, of course in a much milder and more careful tone. We also raise again the necessity of a united-front movement in defense of the prisoners. You know that our delegates were refused admission to the Gastonia conference in Chicago called by the ILD. On top of that, *Solidarity* prints a letter sent to the ILD a month ago by the General Executive Board, offering help and cooperation in the defense, which they say *was never answered*. The defense movement so far is merely a money-raising party affair. The conferences consist only of the delegates from the party and its auxiliary and sympathizing bodies. This is no united-front movement at all. There is still time to change this. A bona fide call should be issued for a united movement. The local conferences should be organized on a broad basis. This is covered in the copy of our statement which I am enclosing. It is of the greatest importance for you to make a fight for this line. Before the trial is the time to organize the movement; it is fifty times more effective then than after conviction.

I don't think you should hesitate because of accusations that you are proposing a "Trotskyist" tactic. There are plenty of precedents to refer to—the whole past work of the party since 1921 in fact. Don't be deceived by the local atmosphere or the superficial appearance of things in the party. The new line of ultraradicalism is artificially forced on the party membership and is bound to fail in the party as well as in the class struggle. Your impulse for a harder and more sincere fight against the right wing is all for the good of the movement. But the right wing can't be defeated with "leftist" policies. On the contrary, it will grow and feed on the reaction against them.

The third point of your letter—the question of the new union—and the UTW—is dealt with in the copies of *The Militant* sent you from Chicago and in the previous letter. From this you will see that the statement that we are opposed to the building of a new union there and favor sending the workers into the AFL union is false and without the slightest foundation. The falsification of issues or of the position of another is not a Leninist or a Marxist method of political controversy. Bill Dunne never learned such methods in our group, and we were greatly surprised to hear from you that he made such statements.

The aim in the South should be to strengthen and consolidate the position of the new union in every way possible and on the widest front. United-front tactics—a systematic series of proposals designed to clearly establish the Communist policy of trade union unity—will be necessary now and in the future in order to accomplish this successfully.

The UTW remains what it was before—one of the most reactionary and corrupt of the AFL unions. It would be folly to look to it as the organizer of the workers for the struggle against the mill owners. But it will grow and expand on the rising movement and the Communist scare, with the cooperation of the bosses in many cases. We must never lose sight of these workers. In the last analysis they will be decisive. Therefore, while building up our own independent strength, we must constantly be devising ways and means of making contact with them. The means to this is the tactic of the united front.

Regarding the building of new unions in the present situation, our position has not changed since we began to fight for this idea more than a year ago in the party. My article in the *Communist* for July 1928, which was based on my speech at the May plenum of that year—to which Foster wrote an answer at the instruction of Lovestone and Pepper—is a part of the historical record showing we were pioneers of this policy. What we are against is the policy of building new unions at any price and leaving the old unions. And we are against *forgetting* the old unions once a new one has been started. The Leninist trade union policy is the fruit of twenty years of struggle and experience of the Bolsheviks on an international scale. What the party needs now is a restudy of this policy as incorporated in the documents of the Second, Third, and Fourth Congresses of the CI.

Pardon the length of this letter and please answer right away.

Fraternally,

[*James P. Cannon*]

Hopes for Minneapolis

August 24, 1929

The following letter was written to Albert Glotzer.

Dear Al:

Enclosed is a receipt for two dollars for subs. They are put on the list. We are glad to see that you keep hammering on this line of activity—it is most important and not enough comrades do it.

Too bad the picnic fizzled. We have been having a run of hard luck lately, and we have to get ourselves together and force a favorable turn some way. It is time for us to begin to think about getting our second wind after the year's tussle. It is ten months now since the fight broke into the open. A great ten months in our lives and also in the history of the movement. We stand too close to our work to fully realize its significance.

Glad to hear you are going to Minneapolis. It ought to do you and them good. In many respects the Minneapolis group is the best all-around unit we have. We expect great things to come out of that nucleus. It is, so to speak, an advance edition of what the genuine American Communist movement will look like when it gets under way.

There is nothing to suggest what you should do there, unless it would be to provide them the occasion for a few meetings. It would be worthwhile for you to speak at the group meeting on the subjects we have discussed in our letters as a basis for a good discussion in the Minneapolis group. You also ought to speak at a couple of street meetings. We are having them regularly in New York now with good success.

Don't be too quick to make a final judgment of Bill [Dunne] and don't be too harsh. We cannot know what another shake-up will bring. His long association with our group should not be discounted; he was not one of the hangers-on like Hathaway or Simons, serving his own interests. His heart was in our fight, and all his conviction was with our main ideas. I am far from holding myself blameless for the estrangement which grew up between us before the break. I would go a long way to make it possible for him to work with us again. The least we can do is to leave the door open and to hope.

We will need more experienced and capable people. Most of the forces for the future will be developed fresh out of our ranks, but some will come from the faction which now calls itself the party. . . .

We have had a lengthy discussion of the proposed slogan "Unity of all Communist forces against the right." In my reply to Foster you will see our attitude expressed. We agree with all you said in the letter of August 19. "Tenacity" is the slogan of the Opposition for the present period. The proposed slogan would lead us onto a false path of *softening* the fight against the centrists, who are the cover for the right and the carriers of corruption and degeneration, at the moment when it must be sharpened and made more merciless, more annihilating. Notice Trotsky's article "Who Is Leading the Comintern Today?" . . .[44]

Have written at length on all points to Young. He is way off the track, but in a letter yesterday he agreed to push for our line on the question of the united front in organization and in defense. On the slogan "self-defense" I wrote a long letter but have had no reply from him. It seems that he and Bill claim to be the sponsors for this adventuristic, Social-Revolutionary slogan. That makes it bad, but I hope we can change him. . . .

We have had a number of long and fundamental discussions about the situation and the perspectives lately. As a result we have decided to make another big push to speed up activities all along the line, sharpen the struggle against the rights and the centrist fakers, and make a determined drive for the linotype and the establishment of the weekly. We have set November 7 as the outside date to realize this aim. More about it later.

If you see a man running around without a head, it will probably be a man named William Zigzag Foster, who started an argument with the Trotskyites. Too bad.

Fraternally,

J.P. Cannon

The new unions and the Communists

Published November 30, 1929

The following article was published in *The Militant.*

In the correspondence from the Illinois coal fields there is room for serious thought. These informative and authoritative letters from the fields of battle—models of proletarian journalism giving a fresh meaning to the term *workers' correspondence*—cast a searching light upon a disease in the new union movement which threatens its existence.[45]

This sickness consists—to speak plainly—in the importing of the labor fakers' arts into the new unions under the fraudulent banner of "Communist leadership." To the shame of Communism this rotten business held the stage under the Communist Party auspices at the district conference of the National Miners Union at Belleville, Illinois. And the scene enacted there was only a replica, made cruder by enlargement, of the routine game being played in all the new unions and which is evoking in all of them the inevitable revolt.

This strangulation and disruption of promising movements for the organization of the workers in important industries is becoming an old story. For a long time the situation among the marine workers has been crying aloud for industrial organization. Experienced and capable militants are not lacking for the job—men who have been through the mill, who enjoy the confidence of the seamen and know how to organize them. But, thanks to the Foster wrecking crew, the marine workers' organization has its being largely in the bombastic headlines and lying news stories of the *Daily Worker.* The position of the Auto Workers Union was recorded in a letter from Detroit printed in a recent issue of *The Militant.* The party bosses have "captured" this union, captured it and locked it up in the party office where the auto slaves will never find it.

The Needle Trades Industrial Union, which had the most favorable chances of all, is today only a pale shadow of what it might have been. And the National Textile Workers Union—the football of party factionalism since its ill-starred birth—lies paralyzed while the party experts debate and golden opportunities go by. The new union movement as a whole, inoculated with the Foster medicine, is reeling like a victim of poison moonshine.

What is the matter?

Like the left-wing organizations in all spheres of labor activity, this great potential movement of new unionism is registering the ruinous effects of the internal crisis of the Communist Party. The appointed party leaders carry over into the mass organizations the same foul practices which signalize their rule in the party. They set as their first task the control of the new unions, and they effect this control by methods that insult proletarian intelligence as they offend proletarian morality.

Unearned and appointed leadership has no faith in

itself. It prefers mechanical control of half-dead organizations to the struggle for influence in living movements. Foster and Company want leadership in the new unions ensured and guaranteed in advance by mechanical measures. Ninety percent of their "mass work" and 99 percent of the funds at their disposal are devoted to this barren accomplishment. The result is an absolutely artificial selection of the leading bodies of the new unions and a stifling of their inner life.

Everything is cut and dried in these unions. There is little for the members to do at the meetings except listen to long-winded speeches. There is nothing for them to decide—everything is decided for them in advance. Intelligent nonparty workers are systematically squeezed out through the application of the asinine formula—which follows the doctrine of the "third period" as pestilence follows famine—that everybody who is not a Communist is a traitor. Every party quarrel is immediately transferred into the union, and one who gets crossways with the party regime immediately becomes a target for slander and frame-up, as is now the case with John Watt, president of the National Miners Union.

The reckless gambling with the workers' movement which marked the career of the Lovestone faction as the American representatives of Stalinism, has been elaborated in previous documents—documents which Foster signed jointly with us. The conduct of the present party bureaucracy, headed by Foster, who learned from Gompers, is distinguished from that of Lovestone only by a vaster clumsiness and a profounder ignorance.

The methods of the Foster overseers are in conflict with the needs and interests of the new unions and with the impulses in their deepest ranks toward a genuine workers' movement. The explosion at the Belleville convention of the miners—where 40 percent or more of the delegates bolted—is an alarming reminder of this conflict.[46] We see in the miners' union—and not only in the miners'—the portentous appearance of a lineup of honest rank-and-file elements against the party; or, rather, of the party against the rank-and-file militants—for the party martinets are the aggressors in the whole evil circumstance and are responsible for it.

This revolt from below against neofakerism tricked out in counterfeited communist badges, which broke out in the miners' union and which smolders in others, is a sign of internal health and strength. The question whether it will remain a negative protest or become a positive force for the regeneration of the movement is a burning one. Indeed, matters have come to such a pass that the part to be played by the new unions in the stormy days ahead hinges upon that question.

The answer lies in the first place with the politically conscious forces of the communist vanguard, who alone are capable of grasping the problem in its manifold aspects and of organizing the struggle to cope with it.

Without the intervention of the most conscious and uncorrupted elements in the Communist ranks to right the situation, the left wing will pay for the sins of the party mismanagement with a recrudescence of syndicalism. Signs of this already are not lacking.

For this struggle we have no new or magic formulas, and none are needed. The teachings of Leninism on the work of communists in the trade unions, as laid down by the fundamental documents of the Communist International, are a sufficient guide. It is time to study them again, to make them part of the consciousness of the revolutionary workers, and to set them up against the monstrous perversions practiced today in the name of communism.

The new unions are at a fork in the road. One way—the way of the party bureaucrats—leads to degeneration and collapse; the other, to a period of expansion and healthy growth, for which all conditions are favorable. In the interest of the latter it is of vital importance now for the members and supporters of the Communist League to bring into the foreground some fundamental conceptions, to make a sharper and more aggressive fight for them in the unions, and to organize the conscious militants inside and outside the party for this fight. The issue must be brought into the open before the workers. The Foster fakers will howl about our exposure of the shameful game they are playing at the expense of the movement. Let them howl. And see that stronger blows are dealt against them.

The organization of the workers for the elementary struggle is the primary revolutionary task, and the building of the new unions the most important medium for its execution. The revolutionaries will fulfill their historic task only to the extent that they understand the proper relations between the masses and the vanguard and create an internal regime in the unions which attracts and holds the masses.

This means a struggle to make the new unions democratic organizations in reality, and not merely in hypocritical declarations. They must function as self-sufficient bodies, freely determining their own course, working out their own rules and selecting their own leaders. The right of expression for various divergent political views and tendencies must be firmly established. The workers who are banded together there for a common struggle against their exploiters must be able to feel that they are in their own house, not the tolerated guests of the party. The meetings, conferences, and conventions of the new unions must have a formal and binding character.

Only so can the new unions develop into genuine mass organizations; and unless they become such they are doomed. They must aim to include in their ranks not simply Communists and a fringe of sympathizers, but the masses, without whose participation the unions have no power. Not only the politically conscious, but the politically indifferent, the backward, even the reactionary (who are the vast majority) must find a place in the unions. Formal proclamations on this score are plentiful but mean nothing. What is necessary is a deliberate course in this direction.

The leading forces in the new unions ought to represent a united front of the Communists with the progressives. The shallow-minded phrasemongers imagine that the formation of new unions disposes of the vexing problem of progressives. A greater absurdity is hardly conceivable. There is not a single organization of workers which expands beyond the paper bounds of a party auxiliary—that is to say, of a duplicate of the party membership—where a united front with the progressives is not a categorical condition for growth and development. In America there are only a few thousand scattered Communists among millions of politically indifferent and reactionary workers. The key to the unity and consolidation of the new unions, to the problem of leadership and the expansion of revolutionary influence, is combination of the revolutionary with the progress-minded workers. Without this, it is impossible under the present conditions to organize new unions on a mass basis. Pig-headed insistence on a Communist monopoly of the directing organs does not—as experience has amply demonstrated—result in Communist leadership of the masses. It simply results in the exclusion of the masses from the union.

The mechanical-control sickness must be eliminated if the new unions are to live. There is nothing revolutionary in the dogma that Communists should control the unions by arbitrary and bureaucratic means. The French Communist Party was severely condemned for this very nonsense at the Fourth Congress of the Communist International, when Lenin and Trotsky were at the helm. It is the refuge of feeble people who are afraid of the rough-and-tumble fight for influence and leadership. In its effect it is sectarian and reactionary. It has become a fetter on the development of a workers' mass movement—the primary revolutionary task—and a source of discredit to Communism.

Communist leadership of the masses is one of the prerequisites for the revolutionary victory of the proletariat. But, conversely, the organization of the "million masses"—to use De Leon's classic phrase—is likewise a preliminary necessity to the constitution of a genuine class movement on the road to a struggle for power. It is only in this process that the revolutionary leadership can expand. Tactics and methods at this stage of events ought properly to be judged by how they help or hinder this work of organizing the masses. And by this standard, the "mechanical control" idea stands condemned.

Leadership of the masses cannot be "captured" without their knowledge or consent. Communist influence, which precedes and evolves into leadership, can be based only on service to the broad workers' movement which the workers understand and approve. Serious and consistent work for the building of the new unions in preparation for the great, impending struggles will do more than anything else at the present time to promote the influence of the Communists. Clear the way for this work.

The struggle for the South

Published January 25, 1930

The following article was published in *The Militant.*

The theses of the unlucky leaders of the Communist Party nowadays seem to be written in order that events may speedily refute them. Such is the fate of the Foster revelation of a year ago regarding the "decline of the A.F. of L." The formal opening of the AFL campaign in the South brushes this theory into the discard, while, incidentally, it confirms all that we said on the subject in our platform (*The Militant,* February 15, 1929).

The conference at Charlotte, N.C., was staged on a scale designed to attract the maximum of attention; and the resources placed at the disposal of the United Textile Workers ought to remove all doubt that the reactionary McMahon organization henceforth will contest the field with the Communists far more aggressively than was the case in the year just passed, which marked the entrance of the National Textile Workers Union into the South. The

Federated Press dispatch of January 16 states that fifteen organizers have been assigned to the work of organizing the southern cotton-mill workers into the UTW and that twenty-five will be in the field in the near future. Along with this goes the announcement of imposing financial support to the campaign. Discounting much of this as typical promotion talk, the entry of the AFL as a real contender in the southern labor situation remains a clearly established fact which none but fools can deny.

In all the preparations for their campaign in the South, the reactionaries run true to form as the "labor lieutenants of the capitalist class," as De Leon called them many years ago. Peaceful partnership with the bosses and war to the knife on the workers' vanguard—the sword and shield of labor reaction—is the undisguised program, as frankly proclaimed at the Charlotte conference. "No strikes are to be called," is the promise to the exploiters of labor by Thomas F. McMahon, president of the UTW;[47] and "give us a trial" is the supplementary plea of William Green, in the name of the AFL. Coupled with this supplication to the bosses to give them a chance to "be of service" is the inevitable declaration of war on the Communists. "There will be a never ceasing conflict between the American Federation of Labor and these destructive people," is the pledge made in Green's speech at the conference, reported in the *New York Times* (January 7, 1930).

The whole strategy of the reactionaries is elucidated here: to make their appeal to the employers and offer them a safe alternative to the left-wing unions.

In all this there is nothing new, much as it may surprise the ignoramuses who explain this—and all other—phenomena by the newly baked theory of "social fascism." In offering itself as a strikebreaker and bulwark against radicalism, the United Textile Workers is repeating its own inglorious role of the past. During the Lawrence strike of 1912 it made a contract with the mill owners and attempted to stampede the strikers back to work on the bosses' terms—a maneuver exposed and defeated by the militant IWW. It did the same thing in the Paterson strike of 1913, coming in at the height of the strike and openly conspiring with the bosses and police to break it.

Such instances in the American labor movement are innumerable. They can be found in every field where labor militants have come to the front as the organizers of the workers. Even today's strike of the Amalgamated Food Workers in New York against restaurants "signed up" with the AFL union is an old story. The writer recalls an identical situation in Minneapolis in 1913, when IWW restaurant workers on strike were confronted one morning with a card in the window proclaiming the establishment to be a "union house."

The theory of "social fascism" is not necessary to explain the AFL campaign of treachery in the South to anyone who knows the ABC of American labor history and the role of the labor lieutenants of the bosses. This harebrained theory serves no purpose except to muddle and confuse the workers and thus, in its objective consequences, to weaken them in their fight.

What part are the "progressives" of the CPLA playing in this conflict in the South? They are playing a characteristic one which gives the honest progressive worker a good opportunity to compare their words with their deeds and to judge them accordingly. In a New Year's manifesto, A.J. Muste, the head of the Conference for Progressive Labor Action (CPLA), called for "militancy, determination and idealism" in the labor movement, and predicted: "The year 1930 will be a year of strikes and of renewed aggressiveness on the part of the American workers." These are the words, and they are fair ones. What of the deeds? Several CPLA leaders are assigned as organizers in the AFL campaign, with its pledge of "no strikes" and its war to the knife on the left-wing exponents of "militancy, determination and idealism" in the labor movement.

The CPLA people are playing the role of come-ons for the labor fakers. They were present at the Charlotte conference, but the reports contain no reference to any protest on their part against the reactionary program. One of the committee of three appointed by Green to direct the campaign is Paul Smith, who is not unknown to the "progressives" of the West. His sole occupation as the AFL "organizer" for several years has been to break up central labor bodies tainted with signs of "militancy, determination and idealism."

The central labor councils of Detroit, Seattle, Minneapolis, Great Falls, and other cities which supported some of the planks in the CPLA program know him for this work and for no other. The Federated Press release for January 8 says, "Smith . . . is regarded as a policy man within the A.F. of L." You bet he is. His policy is reaction, and it will govern the campaign, as everybody knows. The "progressives" will work under him and according to his policy.

The AFL chiefs want to serve the interests of the employers; but they are not the same as the employers, and their programs at the moment are not identical. If one is to understand the labor situation in the South, it is necessary to see this important differentiation, much as it conflicts with the dogma of "social fascism." The southern bosses are not yet ready to accept the AFL as an alternative to left-wing unionism. They are determined to fight it also, as they did at Marion.[48] They want no union at all. The mill owners' press greeted the Charlotte conference with full-page advertisements against all labor organizations, citing the case of "ruined Massachusetts," where unionism is alleged to exist.

From this conflict of programs, great struggles may arise, despite the wishes of the AFL leaders and their program of "no strikes." Even if the reactionaries succeed in temporarily defeating the left-wing union, the issue will be by no means settled. It is quite possible that the struggle between the right and left for the leadership of the workers will take other forms than those indicated at the moment. The clearer this is seen, the better will be the safeguards against pessimism and panic in the event of a temporary defeat of the left union.

Under the present conditions, the center of gravity lies in the head-on fight between the rival unions—the reactionary UTW and the left-wing NTW—for the support of the workers. The support of the NTW is the first duty of the class-conscious workers. This applies not only to the southern textile workers but to the proletarian vanguard throughout the country; the textile workers cannot be organized against the bosses and the AFL without the help of the entire American movement of militant labor.

Of what should this support consist? Well, first of all it should be to try to understand the whole situation and then to tell the truth about it. This is the way a communist approaches every problem of the class struggle. The robotlike support of everything said and done in the name of the left-wing union regardless of its wisdom or its folly; the craven acquiescence in false policy which throws the new union off the track; the treacherous silence of accomplices in factional disruption which plays the game of the mill owners and the labor fakers—all this is the business of soulless functionaries who have lost sight of the interests of the workers. Communist revolutionaries will scornfully reject these criteria of "support" which are designed only to shield the Foster wrecking crew from accountability to the workers.

The party leaders, by false policies and by factional jugglary of the most criminal kind, have laid heavy handicaps on the National Textile Workers Union, and are sending it into the great contest weakened and ill-prepared. They threw away the great opportunity to dramatize the southern struggle around the Gastonia case and to mobilize all the best forces of the working class for the support of the NTW. By abandoning the historic struggle of American labor against the frame-up system, they lost the chance to line up the northern workers, and they cleared the way for multiplied persecution in the future—one of the greatest obstacles to the organization of the southern textile workers.

Their failure to employ united-front tactics of approach to the Marion strikers and to link this situation up in a national agitation with the Gastonia fight was likewise a costly blunder. The striking workers of Marion who were shot down on the picket line belong to us; it is thanks only to the multiplied bungling of the party bureaucrats that McMahon and Company are enabled to wave the tradition of Marion as a banner for their reactionary campaign.

On the organizational side, the Foster leadership has no less to account for. Considering the great historical importance of the struggle in the South and the immensity of the task, the organizing force and the financial support assigned to it were ridiculously inadequate; and the constant juggling and shifting of forces, dictated as a rule by party factional exigencies, greatly hampered the campaign. These mistakes of the past might be passed by if there were signs of change and improvement; but this, unfortunately, is not the case. The latest exploits of the party bosses in the NTW are blows against its future.

The principal achievement of the recent convention of the NTW was the elimination of the three former officials—Weisbord, Keller, and Dawson—who, it is reported, are tainted more or less with Lovestoneism: of carrying over, one might say, the official Comintern line of 1928 into the year 1929. So far as the Lovestone clique of leaders is concerned, we have recorded our opinions fully and adequately many times, and not since yesterday. We need not repeat those opinions here except to remark that everything to be found in the party campaign against them which has political complexion and substance, is borrowed almost literally from material written by us long ago—when the present leaders of the party were united with them like a band of brothers in the war against "Trotskyism," i.e., against the fundamental teachings of Marx and Lenin.

The task of educating the communist vanguard in the ideological struggle against the petty-bourgeois theories and practices of Lovestone, Wolfe, and Company is one we have not shirked in the past and will not shirk in the future. But this educational work will be hindered and not advanced by the arbitrary removal of their adherents from the left-wing unions. Such a course will have far-reaching consequences, leading to the disruption of the unions—or their transformation into impotent sects, which amounts to the same thing; we declare emphatically against it.

The "victories" of the party caucus do not pass unnoticed either by the workers or their enemies. The masses of the textile workers who saw in Weisbord, the organizer of the great Passaic strike, the symbol of their aspiration for militant organization, will not be enthused by his removal for purely party reasons.

Labor leaders able to arouse and organize the masses are not manufactured so easily in a party caucus or a caucus-bound convention. To his faults, many and serious, we have never been blind; we had occasion to speak of them more than once when he was being artificially, and quite disgustingly, promoted and advertised like Barnum's white elephant. The elements of the careerist intellectual in him, which determined his affinity for the Lovestone faction, were as plain as a pike-staff, and these odious traits were stimulated by his factional exploitation during the Lovestone regime in the party.

But in throwing Weisbord aside without any serious or valid reason, the party manipulators are discarding a valuable and necessary force in the struggle to organize the textile workers against the mill owners and the AFL reactionaries. The harmful effects of these latest removals go deeper than the question of the individuals involved. It is another advertisement to the world that the Foster bureaucrats demand a hand-picked administration of yes-men in the unions under their control, and that no dissenting opinions will be tolerated.

A persistence in this course over a long enough period will seal the doom of the left-wing unions as mass organizations and give the game to the exploiters and their labor agents. This course is today a cancer eating the vitals of the NTW. The struggle for a correct line of policy and a drastic reformation of administrative methods is a pressing duty of communist workers, in the North as well as the South, who want to give real support to the National Textile Workers Union.

The revival of the Socialist Party

Published February 15, 1930

The following article was published in *The Militant* under the title "The Socialist Party and Radicalization of the Masses."

The ten-year period following the end of the war was marked by an integration and growth of the American Communist movement and a concurrent decline in the organization and influence of the Socialist Party. For the past year or so we have been witnessing a reversal of this process. The relation of forces between the two contending tendencies—of revolution and reform—has undergone a change. These are the important facts which merit consideration and analysis.

It profits the revolutionary wing of the labor movement nothing to evade or deny this state of affairs. On the contrary it will do harm, for the radical workers see what is going on before their eyes and are apt to draw false conclusions regarding the efficacy and future prospects of revolutionary ideas. Such indeed is the meaning of the recent noticeable shifting of allegiance of many workers, particularly in the needle trades, who had conscientiously supported the left wing and the Communist Party for several years. The Communist workers are entitled to an appraisal of the situation.

I

The advance of Communism in the struggle against the Socialist Party, and to a large extent at its expense, over a ten-year period, is undeniable. A few facts:

The left wing gained a majority in the party struggle of 1919; and the Hillquit-Berger machine was able to prevent its capture of the convention only by wholesale expulsions (aided, however, as has so often been the case, by stupidities of the left-wing leadership). Even after the split in 1919, which reduced the Socialist Party membership from 100,000 to less than 20,000, a new left wing developed within it under the pressure of communist sentiments in the ranks. This culminated in the second split—a weak one, it is true, with still weaker leadership—of the "Workers' Council" group at the end of 1921.

The Communists became organizationally stronger than the Socialists despite the terrific handicaps of the Palmer terror and the three years' period of underground organization. The CP extended its operations throughout the country while the SP influence and strength were confined to isolated localities, notably New York and Milwaukee. The superior strength and fighting ability of the Communists were graphically demonstrated in the big movements which engaged the attention of the workers: the labor party campaign, the organization of the left wing in the trade unions, the Passaic strike, the Sacco-Vanzetti movement, the needle trades struggles. The collapse of the *New York Call,* the daily paper of the SP, just preceding the establishment of the *Daily Worker,* symbolized the waning power of one party and the upward swing of the other.

Over that entire ten-year period our party continued to win recruits, individually and in groups, from its Socialist rival, with no shuffling in the other direction. The tides in those days swept out of the SP and into our ranks such eminent pillars of present-day Communism as Engdahl, Schneid, Olgin, and almost the whole *Freiheit* staff; not to speak of Kruse, who has begun to drift back by way of the Lovestone detour. Scott Nearing left the SP in 1923 and joined the CP in 1926. Weisbord, who became justly renowned as the Communist organizer of the Passaic strike in 1926, had been the secretary of the Young People's Socialist League and a campaigner for La Follette in 1924. All of these people, and many others who could be mentioned, were, in one sense of the word, weathercocks indicating the way the wind was blowing.

Now, after ten years of stagnation and decay, the Socialist Party is showing manifest signs of a revival, partly at the expense of the CP. The facts which demonstrate this trend are as incontestable as are the reasons which explain it. The greatly increased Socialist vote in the recent New York municipal election, while the Communist vote was reduced to insignificance, is one of these signs. The reestablishment of the right-wing unions in the needle trades is another. The increased recruitment of new members is a third sign. (For example, the report of the secretary at the latest meeting of the National Executive Committee claimed more members enrolled in 1929 than in the whole five preceding years.) Socialist influence in the CPLA and renewed activity in the general trade union movement are a fourth sign. The reformist Socialist Party confronts the revolutionary Communists in 1930 as a stronger foe than at any time since the split in 1919.

II

Weathercocks also reflect the new situation. The first of these was Schneid, president of a Chicago local of the Amalgamated Clothing Workers union, who came to us from the SP on the tide of Communist influence in the union in 1922. Last year, the reaction carried him back to the SP. A recent convert to reformism is Hendin, once a member of the CEC who demanded "armed insurrection"—nothing less—at the first underground convention of our party in 1920. (He overestimated the radicalization at the time.) There are many others, less prominent, traveling the same path; one in particular named Streit, who led a squad of Stalinists to break up a meeting of the Communist Opposition in Philadelphia less than a year ago.

Besides those individuals who desert Communism and pass over directly into the reformist camp of the SP—and more significant—are those who have started on an indirect route, by stages, to the same place. Speaking from the standpoint of political logic—which is decisive—and disregarding personal intentions—which are not—this is the destination of the Lovestone faction. We do not see any ground for the permanent existence of a political party halfway between Communism and reformism, which is the sum and substance of right-wing wisdom.

The example of the 2½ International and all similar national groupings excludes such a prospect. That Lovestone and Wolfe understand this as well as anyone, cannot be doubted. The *Forward*'s estimate of Lovestone's present work as the "most useful he has ever done for the working class" is, from their standpoint, a quite intelligent judgment.

It ought to be easily understood why Lovestone and Wolfe cannot proceed directly to their political destination. Conscientious worker communists, revolting against the stupidity and brutality of the Foster regime, have been caught in Lovestone's trap. Deception and maneuver are necessary to keep these workers together on a graduated reactionary course. Lovestone and Wolfe need time, but they are known for speed and they are making headway. They have already succeeded in leading their followers to Brandler and his program of "National Communism" without a centralized International. They have already translated "Socialism in one country"—the slogan under which they expelled us from the party—into "Communism in one country." This is progress enough for six months. The rest will follow.

III

A number of factors contribute to the phenomenon of a Socialist Party revival after ten years of retrogression. The most important is the beginning of a radicalization of the workers, about which so much is being written these days. The fearfully accelerated exploitation involved in the development of industrial technique, which goes by the name of *rationalization,* plus wage cuts, plus swelling unemployment and its attendant horrors, stimulates a labor discontentment which is beginning to grope for expression. It is of decisive importance to have a precise estimate of the *character* and degree of this discontent.

In this field nothing is helpful but actual facts. In the light of such facts there is no ground whatever for the assumption that this radicalization of the American workers has anything approaching immediate revolutionary implications, or that the masses are ready for Communist leadership. So far it is possible to speak of tentative movements in the worker masses as radicalization in a strictly defined and limited sense.

The traditional lack of class consciousness of the American workers, and their specific indifference to social questions, as they record it on every occasion (the elections, for example)—absolutely preclude the attempt to fit them into any European or world formula of radicalization. This term can be used intelligently only on an American scale, in comparison with the recent years of prosperity; and then only with the reservation that this radicalization is shown in its *first stages,* as symptoms of deeper movement to come.

This is the only possible conclusion which ascertainable facts will allow. Take the record of recent strikes, always a good barometer of working-class militancy. Exact figures of strike movements over a period of years are not at hand at the moment, but the general outline is well known. The textile workers' strike in the South, the sporadic strikes of auto workers, and similar outbursts certainly show an awakening mood of the workers involved. But all together they have so far involved only a few thousand workers, a number in no way comparable to the hundreds of thousands who took part in the great strike movements in coal and steel and on the railroads in 1919 and 1922.[49]

Moreover, the responsiveness of the workers generally, all over the country, to these strikes was negligible. The elections, another yardstick of proletarian class development, show a Communist debacle, a socialist gain, and a reactionary victory. The various political demonstrations organized by the Communist Party have yet to show serious working-class support. They are real Communist demonstrations in the sense that only Communists take an active part in them. It is self-deception to represent curious spectators as participants in these actions. The unemployment movement shows promise but is, as yet, only in its initial stages.

The most pronounced expressions of the symptoms of radicalization of the workers have been through reformist channels. Such is the meaning of the increased Socialist vote insofar as it came from the workers; of the general revival of SP influence among the workers; of the appearance of "progressive" movements in the trade unions under SP leadership. Such is the real explanation of the fact that thousands of workers in the needle trades are turning to the reorganized right-wing unions.

The signs of Socialist Party revival, appearing simultaneously with the beginning of working-class radicalization, is no contradiction. It appears so only to those who grossly exaggerate the extent of the radicalization process and attempt to substitute noisy and flamboyant proclamations for actual moods of the masses. They cannot reconcile these imaginary revolutionary moods with a growth of reformistic influence and they try to dispose of the latter by ignoring or denying it. The refusal to see things as they are has always been a fool's dangerous game. Nobody, least of all revolutionaries, ever yet won a war against facts. But this is precisely the whole military strategy of the Foster generals.

IV

A second reason for the recent prosperity which has overtaken the long insolvent firm of Hillquit and Company, bound up with the symptoms of labor radicalism which the capitalists see as clearly as we do and which they fear as much as we welcome, is the patronage of the liberal wing of capitalism. The more far-sighted elements of American capitalism, profiting by European postwar experience, fear a revolutionary influence on a radicalized working class and wish to prepare a buffer against it in advance.

For this purpose they are not unwilling to build up the liberalized Socialist Party, of which they have no fears whatever. The "good press" which the SP received in the New York municipal campaign, including the direct support of several papers, had far deeper implications than a mere gesture of protest against the crudities of Tammany Hall. The New York papers were helping to prepare a safety valve before the social boiler has begun to steam.

On its part, the gaining of this capitalist patronage has been facilitated by the deliberate movement of the Socialist Party to the right. It has spared no effort to establish respectability and harmlessness to the existing social order. It is more and more becoming the haven of inoffensive liberals as well as the shield of labor reactionaries, such as the Black Hundreds in the needle trades. Norman Thomas, a spokesman who makes no pretense of Marxism, is a perfect symbol of this metamorphosis of a party which once proclaimed—in words always, and sometimes in deed—the doctrine of the class struggle.

V

A third important factor which has aided the Socialists is the crisis in the Communist Party and the incompetent leadership by appointment, which is made to order for Socialist progress at Communist expense.

The party crisis, which grows deeper from day to day,

has had a profound effect on the radical workers. Without understanding the principled issues, they see only the splits and get an impression of disintegration and decay. They see a once formally united party appearing as three separate factions, each publishing its own organ. In such circumstances the official assurances of unity sound to them like a scared boy whistling in the dark. The recruiting power of the movement is paralyzed and thousands of party members fall away in discouragement and despair. Some of them have become victims of reformist illusions—a fate for which they have been prepared by the reign of opportunism in the party and in the Communist International.

The incredible weakness of the appointed leadership, which piles blunder on top of blunder in a vicious system, robs the party of its opportunity to plunge forward on the basis of the new trend in the working class, and thus facilitates the game of the reformists. The substitution of noise for thought, and vituperation for argument—the political method of Foster and Company—hurts nobody but the workers' vanguard and is grist to the SP mill. Many of the new recruits of the SP are Foster's contribution to Hillquit.

It is quite the fashion these days for the party overseers to remind the workers of the overwhelming importance of the "leadership" they are receiving like a gift, as it were, from the skies. The idea appears in the party press again and again in the most offensive and patronizing manner. Leadership undoubtedly has a great importance in the proletarian struggle. But it works both ways, and in stressing this question the bureaucrats of the day are only helping, unwittingly, to furnish an explanation of Communist defeats and Socialist victories. An ignorant and corrupt leadership, such as now afflicts the party, can deal the heaviest blows against the cause of the workers' vanguard, and is dealing them.

Looking back over the ten years' record of the party, with its ups and downs, its often sad experiences with leaders who have come and gone, one can say with complete assurance that history—insofar as it takes note of the matter—will sustain the judgment that the present leadership of the party is the worst it ever had. We say this without forgetting any past experience at any stage of the party's evolution. The Foster regime has all the stupidity of the Hourwich group without their principle, and the corruption of the Lovestone group without their intelligence.

The Communist workers, staggering under defeat after defeat in times when progress ought to be the rule, will do well to take the usurping bureaucrats at their word when they urge them to remember the decisive importance of leadership. The first conclusion they will come to after a serious consideration of this question will be the necessity of overthrowing the present leaders and organizers of defeat. They will find—since the American bureaucrats are simply the appointed agents of the Stalin ECCI—that the first steps in this direction will lead them toward participation in the great international struggle over the foundation principles of Communism, which the Bolshevik-Leninists are defending against the new revisionists. The disintegration of the American Communist movement is bound up with an international situation and cannot be isolated from it. A real fight against this disintegration can be conducted only under the banner of the International Opposition, for that is the banner of communism.

VI

The spectacle of Socialist Party advancement and Communist retrogression at a time when there are many signs of a new upward trend of working-class activity, are transient phenomena based on illusions of the workers, cleverly exploited by the reformists, and misleadership and internal crisis in the Communist movement. In the temporary fluctuation in the class struggle there is no cause for alarm, to say nothing of despair, in the revolutionary ranks. The ultimate victory belongs to communism, but there is no law that it will proceed to this victory on a straight, ascending line.

In reality there is nothing strange or inexplicable in the present developments. Reformism is a blind alley which diverts the workers from a class advancement and even from any real struggle for their immediate needs. But how are the American workers, not yet through the primer school of class education, to know that? The majority of the workers of Germany, trained for generations in the class struggle, many of whom have seen revolutionary battles, do not know it yet. If they will learn only from day to day on the basis of their own experience, as Lenin said, how will the American workers learn it overnight?

It must be remembered that the American workers have never seen Social Democratic betrayal on a big scale, for the simple reason that these agents of capitalism have not yet had such an opportunity. The American Socialists have never held any power except in such isolated and relatively unimportant sectors as the needle trades. The American worker, bound all his life to capitalist ideology, is apt to consider a vote for the Socialist Party a radical step forward. He is not fated to stop there. He is not a "fascist" when he takes that step, but a deceived worker who wants to improve the position of his class. Such a worker is, and should be regarded as, a potential Communist.

The Communist struggle for the support of the masses in America has many aspects different from those of the same struggle in the capitalistically developed countries in Europe. There, the great majority of the workers are already politically organized in the Socialist and Communist camps, and the recruiting of workers to the banner of Communism requires the breaking down of long-established traditions and habits and organizational bonds. The struggle here, in the main, is to win workers away from direct allegiance to the capitalist parties. In this the Socialist and Communist parties are and will be rivals.

Despite the primary stage of the class struggle in America, and the consequent lack of class consciousness of the workers, the prospects of the revolutionary party, even for the proximate future, are good. There is plenty of ground for the assumption that developments in America, on the basis of its inextricable involvement in world economy, once fairly started will be swift. In such a setting, Communism, given a correct policy, can bound forward and become the banner of the workers' struggles as well as of their aspirations for freedom from the capitalist yoke.

This presupposes a correct approach to the workers—the politically unorganized as well as the victims of reformist deception. The Communist International, in the fundamental documents of its first four congresses, has given a clear guide in this task. It is necessary to restore our movement to this basis and cast overboard all revisions and "improvements" which have been smuggled into the International since Lenin's death. Among other things this means to revive the united-front tactics and apply them in place of the counterfeit dogma of "social fascism." It means to strengthen and support the Opposition, which fights for communist fundamentals on an international scale.

The sooner and the more aggressively the Communist

workers turn to these basic tasks, the sooner will the present advance of reformism be transformed into a temporary incident, and the better will the awakening workers be prepared for future victories.

Lessons of the Passaic strike

Published February 22, 1930

The following article was published in *The Militant* under the title "Passaic Strike Anniversary: Some Lessons in Militant Labor Leadership for the Future."

Experience is the capital of the labor movement no less than of other human enterprises. The generalizations by which we steer toward communism are not drawn out of thin air but are the concentrated experience of the international working class. Marxism established its place as the only valid theory of the proletariat because it alone stood this test. Experience is the laboratory of the science of revolution. Those who discover and invent tactics without the aid of this laboratory and in defiance of it, substitute guesswork for science and thereby confuse and weaken the workers' movement.

This is the present-day practice. It accounts for the orgy of experimentation in all fields of activity which is running through the party like a virulent influenza. The results of this experience, though limited, are fresh and rich, and much can be learned from it to the advantage of the workers' movement. Moreover, there is no better nor easier way to teach the workers than by examples near at hand. American experience has a tenfold value for the education of the American workers, including the Communists. What we have we should treasure—and study.

The anniversary of the great Passaic strike, which has just passed by the party unnoticed, is a case in point. That was the first large-scale experience of the party in the direct organization of the workers for economic struggle; it was the biggest job and was carried through in the most workmanlike and responsible manner. Would not the manifold experience of this strike be an excellent source of study for the industrial work of the party today, especially in regard to the organization of the unorganized?

Our leaders evidently do not think so. The Passaic strike occurred before the "third period." Therefore it doesn't count. Therefore forget it; or, if it is mentioned at all, refer to it, as Browder did in an article some time ago, as a "shameful page in our history." Such a remark serves only to establish the measure of Browder. It does not in any way affect the validity of the methods employed in the Passaic strike. They stand out with conspicuous import and merit against the dubious tinkering which is being passed off by the Browders as trade union tactics.

The management of the Passaic strike was a brilliant illustration of the effectiveness of united-front tactics, which were, are, and will be the heart and core of the communist struggle for the masses. The united front, the guiding line in all phases of the direction of the Passaic strike, was vindicated in all of them on a scale which looms colossal in contrast to the sad results which have followed its rejection.

A few of the outstanding features can be mentioned:

The strike was a genuine movement of the workers. The great majority of the workers employed in the mills were drawn into the struggle and held solidly together for months. It was a strike which paralyzed the mills and never had the character of a putsch or flare-up. The masses were in it and behind it. The Communists held the unquestioned leadership although there was but a handful of Communists in the mills when the strike began. By their services and skill the Communists led the workers with a moral authority that needed no mechanical manipulation; moral authority, which, in the final analysis, is the rock on which real leadership is based. Under such conditions every step, every turn in tactics required by changes in the situation, could be and was executed with the knowledge and consent of the masses of the strikers. Compare this demonstration of real leadership with some of the recent exploits and "forced marches" of the party under the new line, such as the disgraceful exhibition in the Illinois coal field. Cannot something be learned from this comparison?

The reactionaries were isolated and nonparty forces effectively utilized in the Passaic strike. The reactionaries were busy with efforts to disrupt the Passaic strike no less than in others. But here the Communists, by their tactics, cut the ground from under their feet and robbed them of all influence. The most important weapon in this fight was the slogan of unity. This slogan has more power to move the masses than any other, and in Passaic the Communists kept it always in their hands; and with it kept the leadership, despite all the machinations of the reactionaries. The Communists appeared before the strikers, as they were in fact, the champion of a united struggle, and thereby held their allegiance.

Side by side with this isolation of sabotaging representatives of the AFL there was a skillful and successful utilization of nonparty elements in the leading bodies, both from the ranks of the strikers and from the outside. Notable among the latter was Elizabeth Gurley Flynn. This practice contributed not a little to the broadening of the base of the leadership and the strengthening of its support from below. It is a prerequisite for success in mass organizations at the present stage of development in America. The problem presents itself in every struggle that breaks out of the narrow circle of immediate party influence. The present leadership does not understand this. They cannot even find room for dissenting factions of the Communist movement in the unions they control. They knew no way to deal with the independent opinions of such an honest and influential militant as John Watt except to frame him up and throw him out. They do not know how to disarm and isolate reactionary disrupters with the slogan of unity. These are some of the reasons why they stage putsches instead of real mass struggles like the Passaic strike.

The Passaic strike mobilized nonparty mass support on a national scale. This was before the three million organized workers in America were given up as "social fascists." The conservative trade unions were deeply penetrated with the issue of Passaic. The left wing gained access to more unions on this occasion than on any other in its history with the exception of the Sacco-Vanzetti campaign. Conferences on a scale for which the present-day caricatures offer no standard of measurement were organized throughout the country. In many cases even the most conservative officials were forced into line by the sweeping appeal of the issue. Funds to the extent of hundreds of thousands of dollars for the support of the strike, which came through these conferences, were an indication of their mass support. All this work was most effectively stimulated by a vast propaganda conceived in terms of a mass movement. A weekly bulletin scattered broadcast, an illustrated pamphlet, even motion pictures were employed to dramatize the struggle before the workers.

All this work and its results did much to popularize the Communists as serious workers in the labor movement. The Passaic strike, which was made known to everybody, was a crushing answer in itself to the accusation that the "reds" are impractical theorists who are incapable of constructive organization work. Communist ideas found a readier acceptance from workers who saw the Communists competently promoting and organizing such a big movement.

It will be worthwhile for the Communist and left-wing workers to compare this mobilization with the almost total lack of it in recent struggles led by the party, and to ask the reason for the difference. The answer lies primarily in the difference in the methods and conceptions. The results of the new tactics cannot bear comparison with the results of Passaic. But are not results the best criterion by which to measure tactics?

The Passaic strike movement was conducted without any advice from the Executive Committee of the Communist International. This is mentioned not as a virtue but as a state of affairs which the crusade against "Trotskyism" had brought about in the leading organ of the world party. This was the biggest task our inexperienced party had ever undertaken in the domain of mass work, and for this there was no international advice. The Comintern building was swarming with functionaries who had nothing else in the world to do but give advice and instructions, but in this case they had none. The party had to go on its own resources. The ECCI about that time was burning up the cables with ambiguous decisions on such questions as the removal of party headquarters from Chicago to New York, but the Passaic strike was overlooked. Of course the party was not entirely without help. It had the basic Lenin teaching on the united front, which was not yet prohibited, and this was sufficient. Lately the ECCI has remedied the neglect of Passaic and has been giving the party much instruction on the trade union struggle. Unfortunately, it has all been bad.

Was the affiliation of the Passaic union to the United Textile Workers a mistake in principle? This opinion is the contribution of Lozovsky—after the event—and all the party leaders, who were hot-foot for the action at the time, are wearing it like a secondhand halo. It is a not unimportant question, and one which, in the mutations of the struggle, may rise again. Therefore an answer is in order; and, for our part, in spite of Lozovsky, or Zack, or even Browder, we say no, it was not a mistake in principle. It was not even a mistake in tactics, although, in the desire to keep alive the struggle, which was at the point of exhaustion, unnecessary concessions were made. To say that the affiliation amounted to a betrayal of the workers is childish nonsense that ignores all the facts. The strike was virtually at an end at the time. It had been prolonged for eight or ten months, and the workers were simply worn out. If the affiliation to the UTW had any effect at all it was to keep the remnants of the strike together during the negotiations until some of the mills made a sort of settlement with the organization.

The continuous proposals of the strike committee to affiliate with the UTW were the weapon which isolated Hilfers (the AFL agent of disruption), enabled the strike appeal to wedge its way into the conservative unions, and even compelled Green to withdraw his denunciation. Without a doubt it had a strong influence in holding the strikers' ranks solid month after month and in securing the funds to sustain them.

The withdrawal of Weisbord, the strike organizer, as a condition of affiliation, was a big concession, and a dangerous precedent to establish; but in the circumstances it had little effect. The Passaic union retained its local autonomy, the local leadership remained, and the influence of the party on the subsequent decisions was the same as before. The greatest error was the opportunistic manner in which the affiliation was carried out. This was particularly noticeable in the publicity of the strike committee, which began to be tainted with defeatist apologies to the labor fakers. We had occasion to make several motions in the Political Committee to correct this line, but these motions were all defeated with the help of those who now, characteristically enough, bawl loudest about "betrayal" of the strike. But the errors were incidental. It will be a disaster for the left wing if it condemns the affiliation of a left-wing union to the AFL as a mistake in principle. Lenin's teaching and international experience refute such a contention.

❖

The Foster leaders appeal to the Communist workers to bury themselves in "mass work" and let controversy alone. Not a few comrades, eager for activity in the class struggle, have been caught on the hook of this false formula, and their effectiveness as militants is thereby negated. Mass work is not simply an exercise to be gone through, like acrobatics, for its own sake. Bolshevik mass work is an art. Communists must study its underlying principles and make these principles their own.

There can be no better preparation for effective mass work than the evaluation and study of party experiences in the light of Lenin's basic teachings. The highlight of our experience in the industrial struggle was the Passaic strike. The party will gain enormously by a study of it and by a popularization of its lessons. The most important of these is the necessity of a return to the tactics of the united front as Lenin taught them. A serious investigation of the question will convince the American Communist workers of this. Then their mass work, their sacrifices, and their courage will begin to bear fruit for communism.

Karl Marx, the man

Published April 19, 1930

The following book review of *Karl Marx: Biographical Memoirs,* by Wilhelm Liebknecht (Chicago: Charles H. Kerr and Company, 1930), was published in *The Militant.*

The great figures who have helped to shape the course of history and to mold human thought are always the object of insatiable curiosity to living men. This is particularly true of those who leave a heritage of ideas on which the minds of men are fed. Light on the personalities of the great doers of the past stimulates interest in their work and aids in an understanding of it. Hence the great popularity and the great value of biography.

In this little volume devoted to memories of Karl Marx, the older Liebknecht brings the founder of the communist movement nearer to the proletariat as a man and father. Incomplete and inadequate as these sketches are, in consideration of the magnitude of the subject, they have a double merit. They come from one who lived in almost daily contact with Marx for nearly twelve years of his most fruitful activity; and one who, in a lifetime of struggle, bore the proud name of "Soldier of the Revolution." Thus he speaks with an exceptional authority.

This is not a treatise on Marx's doctrines. Liebknecht, in the book under review, confines himself to a series of reminiscences about him as he revealed himself at work and play, in the circle of his intimates, in the bosom of his family—in short, Marx the man, whom the world, seeing him from afar, did not know. He draws, if not a full portrait, at least an outline of that great figure which grows in immensity as the world moves to its remolding on his ideas. And what a man emerges from that outline!

Marx forged the incomparable weapons of the workers' emancipation struggle in a lifetime of the most assiduous and painstaking inquiry and labor. Guesswork had no part in his philosophy; ignorance, especially in one filling the role of leadership, was anathema. Politics to Marx was a study; and the business of a proletarian, to know, to understand. "How wild Marx would become when speaking of those hollow skulls who arrange matters for themselves with a few cant phrases." Reading these words of Liebknecht's one can imagine the lion rising from his grave to storm against those who transform his science into a system of catchwords devoid of reality and alien to his method.

Marx was affected not a particle by the superficial judgment of the majority at the moment. Scientific truth was his guiding line. And, rejected in his own day while scamps won the applause and favor of the world, he solaced himself with the self-confident motto of Dante: "Follow your course and let the people talk." He was concerned only to establish the wisdom and verity of that course and that, thereby, it might become the course of humanity's future.

From his evaluation of politics as a science came his contemptuous disregard of "agreements" on a false foundation, and his intransigeance in questions of principle—a quality which marked the course of Lenin when his Bolsheviks were but a handful against the world, and which now marks the leadership of Trotsky in the struggle to reform the disrupted ranks of the proletarian vanguard. It was on this point that Liebknecht himself came into conflict with his teacher—not once but twice.

The first time, in the days of his London exile, it led to an estrangement there; and the second time—some twenty years later, on a much larger scale—it led to Marx's trumpet blasts against the Gotha Program—a compromise at the expense of principle for the sake of unity. The weakness of Liebknecht on this decisive question was surely his greatest shortcoming—a shortcoming he did not recognize, for he attempts to justify it in his book about Marx. But history has already answered this question in accents which all revolutionaries must hear. In the welter of confusion which besets the Communist movement of the world, intransigeance must be their motto no less than it was the motto of Marx and Lenin.

Marx knew his value, but the legends spread by his enemies about envy, spite, conceit, and vanity—all this, says the author who worked under his direct guidance for more than a decade, is pure fantasy. He simply insisted on scientific exactitude in the doctrines of the proletariat. Marx could tolerate no blunting of their weapons, whether from ignorance or any other cause. Unworthy personal considerations were not even within his comprehension, to say nothing of their actuating him. "Marx was the most generous and just of men, when it came to acknowledging the merits of others. For envy and jealousy as well as for conceit, he was too great. Only the false greatness, the artificial fame inflated by incompetence and vulgarity, he regarded with a deadly hatred—as he did everything false and adulterated."

He was no man of mush, as Liebknecht draws him, but a doughty fighter and an irreconcilable hater of the false, the superficial, the pretentious. Windbags were an abomination to this man, whose words always stood for facts and deeds. "Woe to him who indulged in phrases. There he was inexorable. 'Phrase-monger' was in his mouth the sharpest censure—and whomever he once had recognized as a 'phrase-monger' he ignored forever. To think logically and to express your thoughts clearly—this he impressed on us 'young fellows' on every occasion and forced us to study."

In this book, Wilhelm Liebknecht paints an unforgettable picture of the group of exiles who gathered around Marx in London in the years 1850 to 1862. During that period he was almost daily in the company of the great teacher, and his reminiscences are a treasure to the present-day disciples of Marx who seek to know the man behind the doctrine. In these pages the legendary figure is brought near, made real, alive, and human. We are drawn into the march of the author's charming narrative and move in that immortal company.

The first genius of the proletariat, dead these forty-seven years, rises and walks before us. We see Marx as Liebknecht saw him through his days and nights of systematic and undeviating labor on his monumental works; we watch his furious concentration on a game of chess and his childlike exasperation when he fails to win; we see him a playmate of his children and a plaything in their hands; we walk with the group of family and friends on a holiday to Hampstead Heath, feast with them from the picnic basket, and slake our thirst with them in unforbidden British beer; we are with the lion at the graveside of his son and see him broken and humbled in the dust of grief.

The Marx that Liebknecht describes was a pure-hearted lover of children—his own and all. The sight of a helpless child in misery tore his great heart with pity. "Time and again he would suddenly tear himself away from us on wandering through districts of poverty in order to stroke the hair of some child in rags or to slip a penny or half-penny into its little hand. He mistrusted beggars. But when a beggar or beggar woman with a whimpering child accosted Marx, then he was lost without fail. . . . He could not withstand the imploring eyes of a child."

In Marx's day as now, society bestowed its honors and rewards on charlatans, cheats, and swindlers; persecution, hardship, and poverty is the coin with which it paid those who served it truly. Such was the lot of Marx. He who held up to society the picture of its future and charted the way toward it, worked with humiliating want and privation as daily companions. In his ability to endure all this, and to carry on his work and hold to his course in spite of it, he has set a stern example to all those who follow his path. For years, even when the worst of this was past, the pound sterling he received every week for his articles in the *New York Tribune* was his only certain source of income.

"On 'Capital' he was at work forty years—and he did work! Only a Marx can work so. And I am not exaggerating when I say: The worst paid laborer in Germany has received more wages in forty years than Marx did for a salary."

The economic hardships suffered by Marx and his family were "not a solitary case of want, such as anybody may meet with, especially in a foreign country where points of recourse are scarce; the misery of exile lasted for years in its most acute form for Marx and his family."

For the exiles grouped around him in London, Marx was a teacher who forced them to respect knowledge as indispensable in a revolutionist and to labor to acquire it. In such an atmosphere his first disciples were trained. While the superficial revolutionaries, like many who have come after them, were substituting wishes for knowledge and reality, intoxicating themselves with phrases about the revolution which was to start "tomorrow," Liebknecht tells of the pupils of Marx "sitting in the British Museum and trying to educate ourselves and to prepare arms and ammunition for the battles of the future."

This was Marx's way to train the leaders of the proletariat and make them fit for their occupations. "To learn! To learn! This was the categorical imperative he frequently enough loudly shouted to us, but it also was expressed by his example, yea, by the sole aspect of this forever strenuously working mind."

These are golden words for the guidance and inspiration of the young communists—and not only for the young ones—who are enlisting in the great battle for restoration of Marxism under the banner of the Opposition. Phrasemongering ignorance has had its evil day in the ranks of the workers' vanguard. Disorganization and defeat are the fruit of it. Those who aspire to reform the disrupted movement will be successful only insofar as they master the basic truths of Marxism and learn how to apply them as a guide to action.

This knowledge will not fall from heaven; it will be acquired only by those who have the mind and the will to study, as Marx required of his first disciples. Wilhelm Liebknecht's little volume of reminiscences will be an aid and stimulus in this direction. It ought to have a place on the bookshelf of every revolutionary worker.

After the founding of the International Left Opposition

Published May 10, 1930

The following article was published in *The Militant* under the title "Character and Limits of Our Faction." The preliminary conference of the International Left Opposition convened on April 6 in Paris. Delegates were present from groups in France, the U.S. (Max Shachtman), Germany, Belgium, Spain, Czechoslovakia, and Hungary.

The American movement is condemned by its position, geographically and politically, to lag behind events in the International. This has been demonstrated with an almost arithmetical precision during the entire decade of the existence of the Comintern. The developments in the Russian and West European parties have always been registered in our own—a few years later. This was the case regarding the crisis in the Russian party and the Comintern.

We were one of the latest detachments of the International Communist Opposition to take definite shape in the open, just as the Lovestone group is a somewhat belated reinforcement in the rear of the International right wing. Neither of these American factions, however, found its international connection by accident. We were "prepared by the past" for our place under the banner of the International Left Opposition. Lovestone and Company served their apprenticeship and became journeymen opportunists, qualified for union with Brandler, in the American party struggles.

The protracted period of our gestation as a faction on the line of the Bolshevik-Leninists has not been without compensating advantages. The rich experiences of the international struggle were realized for us, as it were, in advance, and we have been able to build on their foundations. This ensured for us a clearer perspective and tactical line.

On the one hand, our deductions from international experience enabled us to avoid a false attitude toward the party and an overambitious program for the creation of a new one; on the other hand, they were a shield against the capitulation panic. This sickness, which periodically attacked the Opposition movements in the other countries, was never a problem for us. Three or four weak and inconsequential people at the most, who found themselves in our ranks by mistake, denounced themselves as renegades as soon as they found that membership in the Opposition meant a hard fight.

That was all. One strives with difficulty to recall their names—so little influence did they exert on our cause.

This careful attentiveness to international development, which has served us in such good stead all along, should mark our deliberations now as we prepare to raise our struggle to a higher ground. In contradistinction to the opportunists, internationalism is the touchstone of our faction. But this does not assure for us the automatic assimilation of international experience. Continuous study of our problems in their international aspect is necessary, now as before, if we are to draw the correct inferences. Recent experiences in the international movement, particularly in Germany and France, should be the occasion for study and discussion in our ranks.[50] And from this must follow a firmer consolidation of our ideological position and a strengthening of our tactical line in the struggle for the proletarian sections of the party and left wing.

In the light of recent events in the camp of the international left, three questions present themselves with special insistence. These are: (1) the character and limits of our faction; (2) our attitude toward the party and the party bureaucrats; (3) our attitude toward the right wing. Developments in the American party since our national conference also serve to push these questions into the foreground.

We proceed from the point of view that the crisis in the Comintern arises from the reaction against the October revolution and the weakening of the position of the revolutionary movement on an international scale. This crisis has split the Comintern into three factions, and the character of each of these factions becomes clearer every day. The issues were obscured for a long time. The exceptional position of the official centrists, their monopoly of the apparatus and of unlimited material resources, gave them unprecedented opportunities for suppression, falsification, and corruption. These methods were utilized to the limit. "Six years were necessary," says Trotsky, "in order to bring the weightiest questions and differences out of the bureaucratic underworld into the world arena." But political logic is stronger than bureaucratic machinations. It has forced the ideas, and the struggle over them, into the open.

This struggle for us is a struggle for the October revolution and for the principles embodied in it and in the first four congresses of the Communist International. It is a principled fight for the foundations of Leninism. The international left wing alone defends these positions. That is the reason, and the only reason, we were expelled by the bloc of the right wing and the centrists. It is obvious that such a fight can be ended only with victory.

The question then arises: how can this fight be waged successfully?

The answer is: In the first place, by a clear and definite principled line on all questions. In the second place, by the firm organization of a faction on the basis of principle. And in the third place by an intransigeant struggle for these principles under all circumstances and through all fluctuations in the movement. Lenin taught these lessons positively—through the long struggle and final victory of the Bolsheviks by these methods; the German Leninbund has taught them negatively—through its disintegration and degeneration because of the rejection of them.

The left wing is not a party *but a faction fighting to win the party.* The Leninbund stumbled on this question. Mistaking the corrupted bureaucrats for the proletarian masses in the party ranks, it set out toward the formation of a new party. In order to get numbers quickly, it assembled heterogeneous elements. Instead of defining and sharpening its principled line, it blunted it. The Leninbund admitted people who had all kinds of "grievances" against the party but had no common basis in principle. It maintained relations with anti-Marxists and speculated on a bloc with the right wing against the party. The result: a false attitude on fundamental questions, the steady decline of a promising proletarian movement, a miserable degeneration culminating in a split.

The lesson for us in this event is the organization of

our faction on principled lines only. Our strength as a faction is our platform. Numbers will follow from that, not precede it. The right wing attacks this insistence on close principled unity as "sectarianism." That is because their aims are different from ours. Opportunism has always made allowance for all kinds of divergent tendencies—except the proletarian revolutionary tendency. Lovestone, freed by his expulsion from obligations to Communist tradition, is appealing for recruits on this basis. Anyone can join the right wing and still "have the right to think and freedom to 'express' themselves" one way or the opposite. This is the right-wing "inducement" to prospective members.

We can have nothing in common with these conceptions. We stand for party democracy because a living party can determine its united will only through democratic forms. But the democracy we advocate is a *centralized* democracy, that is to say, a form for a party of action, not a mere discussion club for the exchange of ideas. A party of action, thus governed, must have definite organizational limits. These limitations have a double application for a faction.

Lenin prescribed strict limits of principle for membership in the party, and *still narrower limits for a faction.* The sneers of *Revolutionary Age* against the "sectarianism" of Trotsky's advice to the members of the Leninbund are characteristic of opportunists.[51] Lenin, in justifying the expulsion of the *otzovists* (boycottists) from the Bolshevik faction, elucidated the question as follows:

"As a faction, i.e., as a union of those who think alike in the party, we cannot work without unity on fundamental questions. To break away from a faction is not the same as breaking away from the party. Those who have left our faction are by no means deprived of the possibility of working in the party" *(Liquidating the Liquidators).*[52]

The wisdom of this point of view is confirmed by all revolutionary experience. In order for a party to lead the proletariat to victory, it must have a clearly defined program and organizational limits. A revolutionary faction must draw still closer lines. Otherwise it will not be able to act unitedly and influence the party. It will be lost in the current of events instead of helping to shape them. We will not measure up to our historic mission if we forget the lessons.

As a group of communists convinced of our platform and confident of our future, we have no need to boast of accomplishment or to exaggerate our present influence. We know that the political line will decide and that the numerical ratio at the moment means little in the final analysis. But it is already clear that the Opposition, in spite of the heaviest obstacles, is going forward. In less than a year after our expulsion, we succeeded in uniting our forces in a national conference and adopting a platform. In less than a year since our conference, a new layer of Oppositionists is assembling in the party. Our unrelenting fight on principled lines is shaping this development. The progress in the next period and our whole future depend on our continued adherence to this intransigeant line of struggle.

Our platform is the platform of Leninism. The principled character of our faction and its definite organizational limits are the Leninist methods of organization. The slogan of intransigeance in principled questions is the slogan for Bolshevik struggle and victory. The late experiences in the camp of the international left wing, if properly assimilated, can only strengthen and reinforce our positions on this ground.

From this the question of our future attitude toward the party and party bureaucrats and to the right wing is easy to decide. These are subjects for subsequent articles.[53]

First plenum of the CLA

Published June 7, 1930

The following article was published in *The Militant.*

Another important step in the development of the Communist Opposition was marked by the full meeting of the National Committee of the Communist League of America—the first full meeting since our national conference—which has just concluded its sessions in New York City, May 24–27, 1930.

Since our committee contains representatives of most of the important districts of our organization, the committee meeting had the significance of a small conference. Such gatherings are rare with us, and not because we see a virtue in this rarity.

The great difficulties under which we conduct our fight—our numerical weakness, our poverty, and the great distances which separate us—preclude for the time being that frequency of representative gatherings toward which we aspire. This makes us value all the more those meetings which are possible under the circumstances, and imparts to them an exceptional importance in the life of our organization. We have to expect that such meetings will yield the political maximum and not be merely formal and decorative affairs.

Our national conference, held last year in Chicago, bore such a character; and the meeting of the National Committee just held in New York—a meeting, like all our activities, made possible by Spartan sacrifice—will no doubt bring fruitful results in our work for the near future.

The National Committee is a unit on all important political questions. We are at one with the leadership of the Opposition on the international field. Exhaustive discussion over a period of several days demonstrated that the fundamental unity of our conceptions on the basic principles which lie at the bottom of our fight as a regiment of the International Marxist Opposition is joined with a complete solidarity on tactical questions and perspectives. This applies to our approach to the general problems of the class struggle as well as to the narrower issues of the struggle against the centrist bureaucracy in the Communist movement. All these questions are bound together.

The platform adopted at our national conference a year ago gave a correct Marxist answer to them. All the intervening experience has served to confirm the platform, and it retains its validity today. It forms the basis of the decisions arrived at by the National Committee for the further extension of our fight.

The economic situation in the country has developed in the main along the line of our analysis and forecast a year ago. There are no important signs yet of a speedy recovery from the industrial crisis and there are many indications of tendencies which will prolong and aggravate it, driving the financial overlords of America irresistibly to seek for a solution at the expense of Europe. A still heavier pressure upon the American proletariat and a sharpening of the international rivalries and conflicts are the inescapable implications of the situation.

Even if the subjective reactions of the American workers proceed slowly—and that is so far the case—the soil is being prepared for a profound change in their attitude toward the capitalist system. There are many reasons to calculate upon an accelerated process of working-class radicalization and a vastly expanded field for the development of a proletarian communist movement. To prevent the reformist canalization of the oncoming movement and to develop its revolutionary implications is the communist task in the period that lies ahead.

The bungling, the corruption, the eclectic zigzags and leftist adventurism of the centrist bureaucracy is the greatest obstacle to the execution of this task and an objective aid to social reformism. The Lovestone right wing is an ideological bridge to social reformism which will become an increasing danger to the communist movement in a period of intensifying class struggle. The fight for Marxist methods and Marxist policies falls to the Communist Opposition and is carried on by it alone. Such, in brief, was the general estimate of our plenum which shaped its decisions regarding our future activities.

The question of perspectives in the crisis in the communist movement occupied a prominent place in the discussions of the plenum. On this point clear and definite answers were given. We will not relent in our revolutionary fight against the centrist bureaucrats for a single moment on a single issue. On the contrary, sharper, more intransigeant, more irreconcilable struggle for a Leninist party was the watchword of our plenum.

The Opposition, despite all obstacles, all perversions of

our standpoint, all suppression, all terror, all slander, is growing and will continue to grow in the proletarian ranks of the party. The internal crisis from which the Opposition is just emerging in a number of European countries has passed us by. We had no capitulators worth mentioning; no elements poisoned by Zinoviev-Maslow cynicism. We unfurled the banner of the International Opposition at the time of its lowest ebb, when there could be no perspective but that of a long and stubborn struggle as an expelled minority. Our tradition is the tradition of years of struggle for a proletarian movement against the petty-bourgeois current of Lovestone-Pepper-Wolfe and the trade union eclecticism of Foster-Johnstone-Browder. Thus we were "prepared by the past," as Trotsky said, and the intensity of the struggle does not pull us apart but binds us more firmly together.

We will continue, as before, to base ourselves primarily on the party and the left-wing workers immediately under its influence. The great bulk of the revolutionary workers are there, and this fact determines our position as a faction of the party, not as another party. We do not identify the proletarian revolutionaries in the party and the left wing with its corrupted upper stratum.

The plenum, while confirming our general policy on this question, made a just criticism of the inadequate organization of our fight within the party. Measures were adopted providing for more energetic and systematic work in this respect. The near future, thanks to these decisions, will see our unflinching criticism "from without" supplemented by a determined struggle "from within." The recruiting power of the Opposition in the party ranks is by no means exhausted. It is only beginning, as events already maturing will demonstrate. The second layer of Oppositionists will soon confront the centrist phrasemongers as an organized faction.

An especially interesting and significant phase of the National Committee meeting was a discussion of the situation in the needle trades, based on the report of a prominent comrade in the union who has recently found the way to the platform of the Opposition. This discussion laid the ground for the preparation of a comprehensive statement of policy in the needle trades crisis, similar to our statement on the miners' union, which is soon to be issued in the name of our league.[54] The trade union section of our platform is borne out by the experiences in the needle trades in all respects, and it will provide the guiding line of our concrete statement of policy. The party leadership has brought the needle trades left wing to a blind alley. The workers must be told the truth and shown the way out of this blind alley.

This means to give a Marxist analysis which ignores none of the realities, and to draw inferences based on the fundamental resolutions of the Comintern under Lenin on the trade union question. The party bureaucrats have attempted to deal with the crisis by the most shameful scandalmongering against the right-wing factional opponents of today—their factional brothers of yesterday and brothers yet under the skin. The sole beneficiaries of this monstrous example of "self-criticism" to date are the Black Hundred gang of Schlesinger, Woll, and Company, and, in the final analysis, the employers. What is needed now is an objective communist statement of policy that will show the left-wing workers how to regain their lost ground. The discussion of this question at our plenum indicated the line for such a statement.

Is it possible to continue the publication of the weekly *Militant?* This question, startling in its implications to every supporter of the Opposition who knows its incomparable

the class struggle, which is the true and proper function of the leading body of the Opposition. The progressive development of such a leading political group is unquestionably one of the great historic tasks which the Opposition must accomplish in preparation for the future.

Our struggle against the stream, under a machine-gun fire of calumny, is not without its positive sides. It is a testing and sifting process in which the capacities of revolutionaries to solve problems by their own resources and to remain steadfast in the struggle for principle are determined. Without such qualities a genuine proletarian leadership is impossible. The history of the international labor movement teaches no lesson more clearly than this one.

The ruling bureaucrats have no need to bring a Marxist objectivity and moral prerequisites to their offices. They secure appointment by an infinite capacity for obedience to those above them and they rule by arbitrary command over those below. The inevitable outcome of such a perverted system is not only a political but also a moral stultification. It would be the greatest folly to imagine that such people, on the whole, can constitute the leading force of the proletarian movement on a Leninist path. Exceptions are possible in the case of individuals, but the decisive nucleus of the future leadership will not and cannot come from that corrupted circle which is today befouling the banner of communism and undermining its influence.

Our task is to develop the leadership of the future in the struggle against them. The plenary meeting of our National Committee, by all of its work and decisions, as well as by its maturely political approach to them, was a striking demonstration that our fight has already yielded positive results along this line.

If the plenum registered a political and ideological consolidation within our organization, the mass meeting which followed its adjournment showed an expansion and an increased confidence and enthusiasm of the sympathizing forces around us. Suppression, terrorism, hooliganism—after a temporary "victory"—are bringing the unavoidable reaction. The Communist workers, more and more, want to hear our message. And when they hear it, it becomes their own. There was a warmth and friendliness in this audience, made up in large part of new people, which offered a sharp contrast to the partly hostile, partly curious, crowds we faced in the earlier days of our open struggle.

The successful mass meeting was a fitting culmination to the plenum. Both events said clearly to all who want to hear: The Opposition is on the march. Its road is forward.

'My Life' and its critics

Published June 14, 1930

The following article was published in *The Militant.*

To a revolutionary, all activity is a form of struggle and every instrument is a weapon. Cooped up in Constantinople through the amicable cooperation of Stalin and Kemal Pasha—"patiently waiting for what is to follow"—Trotsky writes his memoirs, and they become a bombshell whose explosion resounds throughout the world.

My Life is a literary sensation. The critics are amazed at the brilliance of its literary execution. In their conception, the skillful arrangement of words is an art which belongs exclusively to those who have nothing to say. The legend that wisdom expresses itself through dullness has a wide popularity, but that does not give it any real value. Why should those who devote themselves to the struggle for ideas not learn the art of presenting them effectively? Trotsky has done this to a superlative degree and has thereby added to his power and stature as a revolutionary politician. His book, besides being a literary masterpiece, is a mighty weapon in the political struggle. This, in fact, is its essence.

"In these pages," says the author, "I continue the struggle to which my whole life is devoted. Describing, I also characterize and evaluate; narrating, I also defend myself, and more often attack." And again: "This is a book of polemics. It reflects the dynamics of that social life which is built entirely on contradictions." So, in the introduction, the author sets the keynote for his work. That he has succeeded in his design is attested by the flood of comment which the book has called forth—comment which shows that his political blows have hit their mark.

The positive political qualities of Trotsky's memoirs have already been evaluated in *The Militant.* Since then a number of hostile reviews have appeared in other columns. A review of these should enable us to bring out more sharply and clearly the essential character of the autobiography, since a book, like a man, is also to be judged by the enemies it has made.

As far as the bourgeois writers are concerned, it suffices to say that not one of them, to our knowledge, has failed to understand that Trotsky's standpoint is what it has always been. The millions of words that have been written to prove that he has become a renegade to the revolution and an ally of the bourgeoisie, have all been wasted as far as these same bourgeois are concerned. For them, now as before, Trotsky is the symbol and representative of the October revolution; and, insofar as they depart from the purely literary side of his book and express opinions on the party struggle, their sympathies are invariably given to the "practical" Stalin as against the "visionary" Trotsky. This simple fact speaks volumes.

If we turn to the Social Democratic press we meet the

same phenomenon. "Trotskyism" has more than once been labeled a "Social Democratic deviation" in solemn official documents of the Comintern. But with a strange perversity, these people also fail to catch the point. The *New Leader*'s review of *My Life* is no less hostile than those of the Stalinist press, and—what is especially noteworthy—its bitter criticisms reveal such an identity of content with the Stalinist reviews that one could hardly distinguish between them if they were printed side by side in the same journal, with the names of the authors omitted.

Let us first consider the review in the *New Leader* for May 10 by S.A. DeWitt. The reviewer is somewhat of a literary man himself and the conductor of "The Chatter Box." One might think that Trotsky has suffered enough of misfortune and tribulation. But no, another cruel disappointment awaits him: "Comrade" DeWitt disapproves of Trotsky and his book, too. He says so straight out, with all the heavy solemnity of a man who knows the weight and import of his words.

Trotsky's autobiography is a masterful exposition of the historic process in which individuals are playing their parts. His own activities are related and subordinated to it with an objectivity that is unique in literature of this kind. But, even so, the book remains an autobiography, not a history. It does not merely describe the historic events but relates also the part the author played in them. And this is the first point of DeWitt's complaint.

"There is so much of Leon Trotsky in those six hundred pages of print and phrase that one receives only a hazy outline of the Russian episode." Again: "I'm terribly sorry to have allowed so much animus to creep into a review of a book. But Trotsky has left me so little of impersonal material to judge, and so much of himself, that no other procedure is possible." Well, that's too bad. But how could it be helped? As Trotsky himself remarked: "Nobody has yet succeeded in writing an autobiography without writing about himself."

A big section of the book is devoted to the party struggle that began with Lenin's fatal illness. The account is a political analysis which shows that it was not, as the philistines think, simply a struggle of persons for power. "The struggle of the epigones for power, as I shall try to prove, was not merely a struggle of personalities; it represented a new political chapter—the reaction against October, and the preparation of the Thermidor." On this thesis Trotsky bases his account of the party struggle; but it is all lost on DeWitt.

He sees, or pretends to see, only the personal side of the struggle and takes Trotsky to task for failing to play the game like a good sport. The conductor of "The Chatter Box" chides the organizer of the revolution and the Red Army: "When it came to stepping down from your pet theories, and playing along with your political comrades on a 'give and take' basis, you flopped miserably. Either they would do as you ordered, or they were betraying the revolution.

"This business of being as infallible as God is so stupid."

One might think that DeWitt would stop at this and call it a day. But the Trotsky-killer has tasted blood and presses on remorselessly. "I, for one, wouldn't swap a regiment of strutting Trotskys for one Stalin." There's another vote to make it still more "unanimous." He must have thought he was writing a party thesis. He continues: "Calling all of us names, and then spitting so viciously at Stalin, convinces us beyond further argument that your present fall from grace is the direct result of the poetic judgment . . . wherein great pride cometh before a fall."

Trotsky might receive a grace if he would be a bit 'umble under his adversities, but his stubborn pride shuts out even that. And he doesn't understand the workers either! "There is an aristocracy about your carriage," says DeWitt, "throughout the adventure which belies your oft-quoted love for the proletariat. There is so little about the workers in your narrative. All you are taken up with is your theoretical paragraphing in this radical journal and that." And so on and so forth. We must leave DeWitt here while we try to catch up with his line of argument in other columns.

The Stalinists had to take notice of the book in question in order to bury once again the doctrine that has died so many deaths at their hands. And they have done the job this time with characteristic brilliance, choosing for the medium the *New Masses*.

Why the *New Masses,* of all places and all things? The explanation is simple. Up till now the *New Masses* confined itself in the war against "Trotskyism" to the modest role of keeping quiet, suppressing all material on the question, and refusing paid advertisements for our publications. This course was predicated on the theory that it was a "political" matter; and the *New Masses* is a hothouse for the cultivation of that flower of the ages: the proletarian writer who has nothing to say about politics.

But *My Life,* it seems, is a "literary" product, and that makes it duck soup for the *New Masses,* which, as everybody knows, is literary at all costs. Consequently we have in the June number not one review but two, and both of them from eminent literati—Earl Browder and Mike Gold.

Quotations from these reviews, after DeWitt's, would weigh this article down with an unavoidable burden of repetition. The soul of DeWitt is marching on in them. The words of "The Chatter Box" leap from the pages of the *New Masses* like armed men from ambush.

Browder, like DeWitt, estimates the historic party struggle as a contest for personal position, and dismisses

Trotsky's pretensions in the same cavalier fashion. "The theme of the book is how Trotsky happened to become subordinated to Lenin; how he planned to come into his own when Lenin died; and how the degenerate leadership of the Communist movement entered into a conspiracy to despoil Trotsky of his inheritance. Around this rather trite detective story scheme the book is built up."

Needless to say, the shrewd Browder is not fooled by this dodge about "political issues" at the bottom of the contest; and, like DeWitt, he refuses to be lured into a discussion of these extraneous questions. "I, Trotsky, had power," he says. "This was taken away from me by a conspiracy of the degenerate leadership of the Party headed by Stalin." And from this follows logically his pontifical admonition: "The dictatorship of the proletariat can have no more dangerous or insidious enemy than a leader inside its apparatus who thinks in terms of personal power."

For Browder, as for his confrere of the *New Leader,* there is too much Trotsky in Trotsky's book about his life, and the two reviewers meet again in protest against his "underestimation of the working class." "As a matter of fact"—we are quoting Browder now—"it is almost impossible to find any hint of the existence of the working class in this book. It exists only to provide a dark background which throws into higher relief the brilliant exploits of Trotsky."

What is left of Trotsky after these withering blasts? Putting an upstart in his place, is what we call it. And it is to be hoped that he will stay there when he gets the following profound diagnosis of the whole trouble. Trotsky refers to Marx and tries to hinge his case on the Marxian method of social analysis. Browder declines to follow him into this field, being too smart, as they say in the West, to play another man's game.

Browder appeals to Freud, and the result is fatal—for

Marx as well as for Trotsky. Trotsky has a "complex," says the reviewer—Browder, not DeWitt. Lenin once gave him a pair of shoes which hurt his feet so badly that he recalls the incident in the book after many years. And what does that prove? It proves everything. Says Browder: "Let each amateur Freudian give his own analysis of this interesting paragraph. Our own analysis is that Trotsky's ruling idea, from the time he met Lenin, was connected in one way or another with occupying Lenin's shoes." What mud could be clearer?

After all this, it might be well to let the matter rest. But the review of Mike Gold remains, and who can ignore him? Mike has "arrived," so to speak, and success has made him bold. He thinks he can get away with anything—even plagiarism. There has to be some honor, among writers as well as among thieves, and DeWitt has a just ground to complain at the way Gold has stolen his stuff on Trotsky and has passed it off as his own.

An example: "One point that struck me in Trotsky's autobiography. What Luciferian pride in every line! . . . Trotsky is too convinced that he is a great man. . . . but there are no supermen. All men are fallible," etc. That's clever, but DeWitt said it first. Why not give him credit?

Another example: "Trotsky writes of the revolution as a chess player might, or a general." And—believe it or not—"He has no feeling for the pathos, the poetry and human beauty of the proletarian masses." This is more literary larceny against which DeWitt may rightly protest. These quotations are the core of Gold's review, and they are lifted bodily, almost literally, from "The Chatter Box."

This thing can't go on. For the good of the profession, literary ethics must be observed, and swiping the other fellow's stuff must be cut out. Even if such a ruling would debar the *New Masses* from further participation in the

Trotsky discussion, there would be nothing really lost. The *New Leader* will say it for them—and say it first.

The fundamental similarity of the three reviews mentioned, has its own meaning for those who look for the political content in literary polemics. It is quite possible that many will fail to see any significance in this united front and ask: "Are people not allowed to have the same opinions once in a while?" And to this we can answer: It is not only allowed; it is unavoidable when they approach questions from the same essential standpoint.

The common ground, on the matter at issue, of the Social Democratic philistine and the Stalinist Hessians of the pen only demonstrates how far the official Communist Party has departed from the Marxist method of analysis—the method which seeks the underlying social explanation of historic events and which sees persons, even the greatest, as representatives of social forces.

We Oppositionists who fight under the banner of Marxism in the International are often reproached with merely being adherents of Trotsky in a personal struggle. But it is precisely the Oppositionists who protest against such an interpretation of the cleavage in the party. The struggle of the Opposition against the reaction in the Soviet Union is no more a mere fight of persons for power than was the struggle of the Bolsheviks against Kerensky. In each case the philistines and reactionaries saw only the persons fighting for place, while the Marxists sought to explain the causal social factors and their potential manifestations.

Trotsky applies this scientific method to his entire book about all stages of the Russian revolution up to the present moment. The failure of DeWitt, Browder, and Gold to grasp this issue and meet it condemns their interpretations to absolute worthlessness. They miss the point entirely and throw no light on the real questions at issue. The worker who seeks an understanding of these questions must turn from the critics of Trotsky's book to the book itself. They will find it there.

Aftermath of the Needle Trades convention

Published June 21 and 28 and July 12, 1930

The following articles were published in *The Militant.*

1. Questions of a left-wing program

The convention of the Needle Trades Workers Industrial Union met at a critical period in the left-wing labor movement.[56] Great and complicated questions of the struggle for a class union, directly affecting the welfare of the sweated and oppressed workers in the industry and bearing on the course of left-wing unionism in general, pressed insistently upon this convention for an answer. They pressed in vain. A false answer was given there to the basic questions of external policy as well as to those relating to the internal life of the union.

Errors which have accumulated into a system and brought about a crisis in the organization, weakening it in the face of its great tasks and responsibilities and supplying a corresponding strength to its enemies, were formally ratified and laid down as a guiding line for the future. The Stalin faction of the Communist Party, which held the convention in the steel vise of mechanical control, gave another demonstration there of its bankruptcy on the trade union question. Repercussions from the convention decisions will be sure and swift; they will fall upon the union, and consequently upon the workers whose fate is bound up with it, like heavy blows over the head.

The convention was a field day for party factionalism. It was consecrated primarily to a pogrom against the adherents of Lovestone—a disgusting exhibition of mob spirit, full of menace for the future of a union. Howls and boos and the caucus steamroller—these were the answers to all criticisms and proposals, regardless of their merit, which did not emanate from the party steering committee. Not even blows were spared in the "ideological" struggle.

The Lovestoneites, who were the first to employ these methods in the Communist and left-wing movement, got a double dose of their own medicine at the Needle Trades Workers convention. But it was not they who will be the losers by it. The Stalinists, who imagined that their mob and hooligan tactics were contributing to the struggle against Lovestoneism, were only demonstrating how well they have acquired some of its most abominable features. The left-wing movement and the Communist Party will pay a heavy price for every "victory" gained by these means.

Factional exclusion from the leading bodies of the union did not stop at the Lovestoneites, the excluders of yesterday. Members of the party who have ventured to exercise a mild "self-criticism" against the ruling bureaucrats were also eliminated from all positions. Everything was cut and dried in advance to the last detail. The "democracy" was simply window-dressing for the gullible. Johnstone, the party representative, bossed the convention like an arrogant drill-sergeant, the veritable symbol of triumphant ignorance. The leadership of the union, which had already been whittled down to party members, was still further narrowed to members of the Stalin faction of the party. Thus the Stalinists strengthen their position in the apparatus by weakening the base of the union among the masses. On the side of internal policy the union is worse off than before.

In the most important and decisive questions of external policy the convention also gave the wrong answers. By declaring formally against the organization of a left wing in the reactionary unions in the industry, the convention chopped away the bridge to the workers in these unions, and they are the overwhelming majority of the organized workers in the industry. This decision, and the theory which motivates it—that the right-wing unions are "company unions"—are both wrong and are bound to bring catastrophic results.

There may be some who go so far as to think that this decision has sealed the doom of the new union of the left wing. But in our judgment such an opinion is not well founded. The danger that the Needle Trades Workers Industrial Union will degenerate into an impotent sect no doubt exists, and this danger has been increased by the unwise decisions of the convention, but there is yet time to correct the errors and to change the course.

It is to this task that the militants of the Left Opposition who are assembling in the union must devote themselves. The first prerequisite for success in this struggle for the salvation of the union is clarity in their own ranks on the question of a program for the union. This is the decisive question. The present relation of forces means little; it will be shattered by the impact of events, and soon enough. The correct program is the basis on which the Opposition Communists, triumphant forces of tomorrow, will secure their victory—and the victory of the left-wing workers.

Our policy must proceed from an analysis of the actual situation and the present relation of forces in the industry. Facts and not wishes are important here. The situation is approximately as follows:

In the industry as a whole there are over 500,000 workers.

The right-wing unions have between 150,000 and 200,000 members.

The left-wing union has at most 5,000 members—fewer in good standing.

Consider these figures for a moment. The right-wing unions contain about 40 percent of the workers in the entire industry; the left-wing union has about one percent. A further concretization shows that the membership of the left-wing union has the bulk of its organized strength in the dress-making shops. Its hold on the cloak makers and furriers is very weak organizationally at the present time. In the men's clothing field, the field dominated by the Amalgamated, the strongest union in the industry, it has nothing. In the millinery section it has little. These figures are very important as a point of departure, but they do not tell the whole story. There are other important factors more favorable to the left union.

The figures cited above are not a true representation of the actual strength of the rival organizations. The membership of the right-wing unions, and particularly of the International Ladies Garment Workers, is based on shop control, agreements with the bosses, and job compulsion. Thanks to the partnership of the union officials with the bosses, a partnership sealed by the capitalist state power, the workers are compelled to belong to the right-wing union in order to get work in the shops affected. Terrorism, hunger, and the demoralization of the left-wing forces were the whips with which the workers were driven into the right-wing ranks.

Sympathy for the left wing is very strong among large sections of these registered workers. All informed workers in the trade testify to this. "My heart is with you but I must make a living" is a common answer of the registered workers to the appeals of the left wing. There is no doubt that the left-wing influence has declined in the past two years, but it remains a powerful force in the masses. And the leadership of the Communist Party in the left-wing movement is indisputable. There is no other important power.

These facts are a remarkable testimony to the vitality of the left-wing movement among the needle trades workers and to their deep-seated hatred for the Socialist betrayers. Not all the compulsion and terrorism of the bosses, the reactionary labor leaders, and the police, and—what is equally noteworthy—not all the blunders of the party and left union leadership, have been able to change fundamentally the sentiments of the workers. The real strength of the left-wing union is much stronger in the sympathy of the masses than its organization, as that of the right-wing unions is weaker.

The five or six thousand members of the left-wing union are, for the most part, the battle-tried militants, the dynamic force in the industry. They constitute, and will constitute, the core of the future fighting movement which will smash the present alignment. A communist policy for the next stages of the struggle must be based on them, as in the past. There is the *reserve power* which is not shown by the membership figures of the rival unions.

The Needle Trades Workers Industrial Union is not an artificial creation. It was formed as the result of an unavoidable split forced by the traitorous leaders of the ILGWU and the furriers' union. It had masses of workers behind it. The left union has a real base *in sections of the industry* and, as such, has every claim to support. The first point in communist policy must be: to organize the unorganized and build the new union.

But this is only part of the proper program, not the whole of it as the convention proclaimed. In next week's article we will undertake to explain the necessity of organizing a broad left wing in the reactionary unions of the industry, the methods and slogans with which this task can be accomplished, and the falsity of the theory of "company unionism," which has been invented to justify a suicidal policy.

The Militant invites left-wing needle trades workers to write for its columns on the situation in the union and to give their views on the problems of their movement. Articles written in any language will be translated into English and printed. The *Daily Worker* is the closed organ of the cynical bureaucrats—*The Militant* aims to become the voice of the militant rank and file.

2. Character of the right-wing unions

One of the chief errors of the convention of the Needle Trades Workers Industrial Union—an error, like all the others, forced upon it by the party leadership—was to regard the split in the furriers' and ladies garment workers' unions, and the formation of the new industrial union, as the final settlement of accounts with the reactionary leaders within the old organizations throughout the industry, including those unions which were not affected by the split.

This estimation of the situation is profoundly false. The

issue is not yet settled even with the unions in which the split occurred, and will not be settled as long as these right-wing organizations control the majority of the organized workers in these trades. And in the field of the other unions, where there has been no split and where the new union has created no base in the shops, such an assumption is a sheer absurdity. A policy founded on this false assumption collides with facts which cannot be wished away.

The split and the formation of the new union in a section of the industry must rather be regarded as a stage in a long-drawn-out and complicated struggle. The first necessary stage was the formation of the left wing in the old unions and its consolidation in battle. Without that, the present existence of the new union would have been impossible. The left wing is still confronted with this preliminary task in the Amalgamated Clothing Workers and in the Cap and Millinery Workers Union. It has yet to complete it in the ILGWU and the furriers' union. It also has the problem of uniting this activity in a comprehensive strategy with the task of strengthening the new left union and organizing the unorganized. The goal of the left wing is to unite the masses of needle trades workers into a single organization of the class struggle.

The goal is still some distance away, as the membership figures demonstrate with merciless logic. Under what conditions can the left wing move in the direction of this goal? Only by demonstrating in practice that it is able to improve the material conditions of the workers in the shops. The most revolutionary program will not be accepted as a substitute for this. The workers want results in terms of bread and butter. If the left-wing union fails in this, it fails in everything.

The new union has the will to do this, but it is blocked by the right unions, which have the help of the bosses and the police—and, besides, have the great bulk of the organized workers in their ranks. The existence of these right-wing unions under the control of the reactionaries and traitors is not only a barrier to the new union in the organized shops; it is also a powerful force for the sabotage and disruption of any serious organizing campaign of the new union among the unorganized. The left wing must cope with this problem. That is the key to its future development.

The question of the attitude of the revolutionaries toward the right-wing unions needs clarification. The convention of the new union, under the guidance of the party leadership, put the question on the simple basis of either/or; that is, *for* the new left-wing union and *against* the old right-wing unions throughout the entire industry. The convention program states: "The I.L.G.W.U., the A.C.W., the I.F.W.U., and the other so-called right wing organizations are company unions in the real sense of the word. . . . The company unions cannot be reformed, they must be destroyed." It follows with the decision: "To abandon the maintenance of the T.U.U.L. groups within the company unions." And to "call upon every needle trade worker, regardless of craft or occupation, to join the new union."

This is a false approach to the problem as well as a false estimation of the old unions. What is needed is a two-sided policy of strengthening the new union and simultaneously working within the old unions, with a single objective: to unite the workers on a broader basis under the left-wing banner. Simple solutions—either/or—will not work out. To liquidate the new unions would mean to deprive the workers of the concentrated gains of their long struggle and paralyze their fighting power for a long time. To fail at the same time to build a strong left wing in the old unions would rob the new union of any possibilities of broad expansion and condemn it to sectarian impotence.

The Stalinist masterminds who can see only along a straight line, and that only as far as the end of their noses, will have none of this "complicated" strategy. And lacking reasons to justify their narrow and sectarian policy, they invent them. One of these inventions is the theory that the right-wing unions are company unions. Even if this were so, it would not free the revolutionaries from the necessity of working within them as long as they embrace masses of workers. Foster explained this some years ago in his writings on company unions, and Lenin explained it before him in his account of the work of the Bolsheviks in the *tsarist police-controlled unions* in *Left-wing Communism*. But, alas, we live in the "third period," and the onetime wisdom of Foster, to say nothing of the wisdom of Lenin, is a forgotten song of long ago. Stalinist education requires that we forget today everything we learned yesterday.

The "company union" argument is a theoretical fraud invented to motivate a false policy. There is no doubt, however, that many of the left-wing workers are deluded by this schematic explanation of the matter; and this delusion stands in the way of a clear comprehension of the problems and tasks of the left wing. This circumstance justifies and necessitates a discussion of the formula which is designed to save thought and avoid a complicated struggle.

The history of the American and international labor movement shows two types of trade unions: those based on the idea of the partnership of labor and capital—class-collaboration unions—and those based on the class struggle. Even between these two main types the line of demarcation is not always clear. They frequently overlap each other. More than one "revolutionary" union has proved to be conservative, even reactionary, in practice. And many a militant strike has been conducted by unions officially committed to a policy of class collaboration. These contradictions between practice and program arise from the fact that the trade unions are not static bodies. They have their existence in the class struggle and are constantly under its pressure and influence.

The trade unions, which are the basic and elementary organizations of the workers, reflect in a general way the stage of class development of the workers in their ranks.

The corrupt and reactionary bureaucracy exerts a certain influence, of course, in holding back the development of the union on the path of the class struggle; just as the communists, at the other pole, are a force for its acceleration. Between these two factors of conscious pressure for opposing ends, the general level of class consciousness in the masses asserts itself and determines the character of the unions in practice regardless of their predetermined program. A revolutionization of the labor movement presupposes a revolutionization of the masses and has no serious meaning without it. On the other hand, with a real development of working-class radicalization, all the machinations of the bureaucrats cannot prevent the trade unions from reflecting and expressing it.

The fact that this organizational expression may, and most frequently will, be realized through deep splits in the old unions and the formation of new ones—a process that has *begun* in the needle trades—does not alter the fundamental proposition. The very existence of the new needle trades industrial union, *which was first crystallized as a left wing in the old unions,* is positive proof that these unions are susceptible to the pressure of the class struggle and the agitation of the revolutionaries. It is proof that, despite the despicable fakers at their head, they are actual organizations of the workers, the natural and legitimate field for revolutionary activity.

Company unionism is a different question altogether. Company unions are organizations formed directly by the bosses and directly controlled by them. Their officers are the bosses' *employees,* foremen, stool-pigeons, etc. They have no independent life and no independent power to enforce decisions. They have no functions except those conferred on them by the bosses. History has never yet recorded a struggle of the workers conducted under the banner of a company union; although there have been a few instances where they served as the starting point for movements of revolt against the company unions, smashing through them and forming independent unions of the workers. No worker, even the most ignorant, ever mistook a company union for a real union.

Can the right-wing unions in the needle trades, with all the corruption and treachery of their leaders, properly be classified as company unions? Certainly not, if definitions mean anything. These are quite different organizations, and this fundamental difference is not abolished by the recent trend of the right-wing officials toward closer and more open partnership with the bosses.

The right-wing organizations are *class-collaboration unions* in all the accepted meaning and implication of that term. It is quite true that the right-wing officials have introduced a new efficiency and a higher technique into the business of betraying the workers under the old theory of a partnership between labor and capital. But at bottom there is nothing new in principle. The right-wing unions in practice are more or less typical examples of the doctrine of class collaboration.

What is there about the practice of the right-wing unions that distinguishes them from the standard type of reactionary American trade unions? Is it the agreement with the bosses to compel the workers in the shop to register in the right union? Almost every American trade union for years and even for decades has attempted to make such an agreement with the employers. Many of them are based on such contracts. The printing trades, building trades, and many other unions have such agreements.

The most conspicuous illustration is the United Mine Workers. For more than twenty years this organization maintained control of the organized coal fields, and froze out such rivals as the IWW and the One Big Union through the check-off system—an arrangement whereby the mine operators collected the union dues by deducting them from the miners' wages. The program of the left-wing convention cites the check-off as one of the "characteristics of company unions." This is really laughable when it is recalled that the check-off was one of the *left-wing demands* in the miners' union up till a short while ago; the surrender of the check-off by Lewis in the anthracite strike in 1926 was bitterly attacked by the Communist Party.

Is it cooperation of their officials with the bosses and the police to fight the militant workers which makes the right-wing unions company unions? This again is the established and traditional practice of reactionaries in the labor movement; it is such practices, among others, that stamp them as reactionaries and agents of the bosses. Lenin speaks of this in *Left-wing Communism.* The traitor leaders of the German trade unions were the saviors of capitalism and the butchers of the revolutionary workers. *After that,* Lenin wrote his pamphlet advising the German Communists to go into these unions in order to wrest the workers out of the control of these betrayers.

Is it, perhaps, the enforcement of "production standards" on the workers and the selling of the unions as agencies of efficiency, that "transforms" them into company unions? This again is nothing new. Such a policy is inherent in the very idea of class-collaboration unionism. The slogan of traditional trade unionism, "a fair day's wages for a fair day's work," which Marx polemicized against, is the germ of all such policies. The latter-day agents of the capitalists in the labor movement have only extended and modernized the basic ideas and practices of the conservative unionism of the past.

While in all essential and fundamental features the right-wing unions in the needle trades conform to the standard type of reactionary labor organization represented by the AFL, there is no ground for confusing them with company unions. The basic difference consists in this: The company union is a lifeless organization *created by the bosses,* in which no outside force is consulted and *no agreement* is required. The reactionary labor union, on the other hand, is based on an agreement of the bosses with an outside force—namely, the unions represented by the right-wing officialdom.

This relationship imparts to the union certain features never seen in a company union. These are: a formal independent life of the union organization and an independent apparatus not employed in the shop; a constitution and formal democratic procedure—business meetings, conventions, etc., without direct interference of the bosses; an independent treasury for the self-maintenance of the union; the settlement of disputes by *agreement* with an implied reserve weapon of compulsion on the part of the union. These are the essential features of a labor organization, a potential instrument in the class struggle and a natural field for revolutionary work.

It is quite obvious that company unions and reactionary trade unions are entirely different kinds of organizations. And this difference is not disposed of by the assertion that the right-wing unions, through their corrupt officials, also serve the bosses. This is true enough, and it must never be forgotten; but they serve the bosses *in a different way* than do the officials of the company unions, who are directly employed by the bosses and represent no independent power. This is what we have to understand before we can draw the correct inferences regarding revolutionary tactics.

To characterize the old unions in the needle trades as company unions means to play with catchwords. Those who want to think straight—and revolutionaries above all others must do this—must beware of catchwords. What we need are precise definitions of our problems and tasks. Intelligent thought requires that words have a definite meaning, although this elementary truth has not yet occurred to the phrasemongering leaders who try to answer complicated problems with careless epithets.

If we compare the old unions in the needle trades with the standard AFL unions and such conservative independent bodies as the railroad brotherhoods, we see that they all have the same characteristic features. The differences and variations between them are incidental and peculiar to the particular situation surrounding them. The important thing to see—because it is an inescapable fact—is that they are of the same basic type. Consequently, a policy of withdrawal from the reactionary unions in the needle trades, of refusing to organize a left wing within them—on the ground that they are company unions—is, in reality, a decision to give up the fight in all the reactionary unions. Make no mistake about it. That is what the newly baked theory of "company unionism" means.

Such proposals have been made before. In 1920 and 1921 we fought the issue out in bitter conflicts in the party. The rise of the left wing in the needle trades and all its great historic accomplishments would have been impossible if we had not defeated the abstentionist policy at that time and steered the communist militants into the mass organizations controlled by the reactionaries—the same Schlesingers and Hillmans. In the early days of the Comintern a historic struggle on this question took place, the results of which were summed up at the Second World Congress of the Comintern and the First World Congress of the RILU. Thanks to the decisive leadership of Lenin and Trotsky, the program of deserting the old mass unions, proposed by the German ultraleft opposition and sections of the British and American delegations, was rejected, and the Comintern directed its course toward the masses in the reactionary unions. Without this decision, the expansion of the Communist parties of Europe as great organizations of the masses could not have taken place.

3. Tactics and slogans for the left-wing struggle

It is high time to restate the fundamental tactics of Bolshevism on the trade union question and organize the struggle against their revision. The future of the left wing in the American labor movement—and the future of the Communist Party—hinges on this issue. The decision of the convention of the Needle Trades Workers Industrial Union against the formation of a left wing inside the old unions of the industry strengthens the grip of the reactionary leaders on these unions and thus strengthens the grip of the bosses on the workers. The nucleus of the Communist Opposition which is taking shape in the union, has for its first and most insistent duty the organization of a struggle to change this decision. Life itself will smash the decision, but the communist militants must hasten the process in order that the least possible harm for the left-wing movement will result.

The building of the new industrial union and the

organization of a fighting left wing in the old unions are not contradictory tasks. They are two sides of the same task and are indissolubly bound together. The slogans and methods for the conduct of this two-sided struggle require explanation and discussion. This is all the more necessary since the convention failed to give a proper lead, and the document issued by the Lovestoneites at the convention is a typical product of opportunist straddling and half measures.

The policy adopted at the convention of the industrial union deals a double blow against the left-wing movement in the needle trades. On the one hand it forcibly tears away the more advanced and revolutionary elements from organizational contact with the masses of workers in the old unions. On the other hand it brings about a split in the ranks of the left wing. In both of these consequences the policy runs counter to the basic line of Bolshevist tactics.

In the Amalgamated, which has a firm grip on the men's clothing section of the industry and where membership in the union is tied up with the question of a job, the new policy encounters insurmountable difficulties from the start; and these difficulties will accumulate if any serious effort is made to enforce the policy. It will soon be demonstrated there that the workers who are willing to sacrifice their living in order to justify the stupidity of the party are few. In the Cap and Millinery Union the new policy has already hit the rocks. The attempt to enforce the decision of the convention has split the left wing of the New York blockers' local of this union in the middle.

The developments in the blockers' local are very instructive, and they are symptomatic of what is to follow on a broader scale. In this local of 1,500 workers, constituting about 50 percent of the workers in the trade in New York, the bloc of the left-wing and progressive forces has constituted a strong minority. The instructions to join the new industrial union have met with a categoric refusal on the part of all the left-wing and progressive elements except a handful of party members. Let the Communist workers take heed of this situation in the blockers' local. It is a warning of what will happen everywhere.

Is it possible under the present conditions to organize a strong left wing in the old unions of the needle trades? Now more than ever. The program which the party leadership forced on the industrial union convention in arguing against it, cites the destruction of standards won in years of struggle and the failure of the right-wing officialdom to defend the interests of the workers at any point. The answer is: just because this is so, just because the conditions of the workers grow more and more intolerable and the treachery of the right-wing bureaucrats becomes more clearly manifest, the soil becomes more favorable for the organization and rapid development of a broad left-wing movement within the old unions.

The bureaucrats are powerless to prevent it. The only real obstacle is the policy of the party, which has been imposed on the present left-wing forces in the industry. And, so loudly do all the circumstances cry out for such an organized movement in the old unions, not even the party can hold it back for long. If not with the official party, then without it for the time being, the movement must and will be organized. The nucleus of needle trades communists now crystallizing under our banner have the duty to take the lead in this struggle and show the way, regardless of the decisions of the party bureaucrats to the contrary.

The first and most important step in this direction is the formulation of a concrete program of economic demands and a vigorous agitation for them within the *old unions.* This is the Achilles' heel of the right-wing regime; and there is nothing they can do to prevent a sympathetic response to such an agitation in the ranks of the membership. The more they join hands with the bosses against the workers, the more they collaborate with them in robbing the workers of their standards, the more do they create the conditions for a movement of revolt against them on the basis of our economic demands.

Every attempt on the part of the right-wing fakers to throttle this agitation will strengthen the position of the left wing for the advocacy of another powerful slogan—the slogan of democracy in the unions. In view of the narrow, bureaucratic, and arbitrary practices which have been smuggled into the administration of the new industrial union itself, it may be thought that this slogan is out of date. Nothing could be falser than such an assumption. Those who hold it reckon without the workers and their deep-rooted impulse for self-governing organizations, one of the truest impulses of the advanced elements of the class.

Not for nothing has been the long schooling of the needle trades workers in trade union organization; not in vain the historic struggles of the left wing for this slogan of the rank and file. The sentiment for trade union democracy, developed and strengthened in these long struggles, is not dead. Given a sensible policy and leadership, this sentiment will reassert itself and be a source of power for the new left-wing struggle in the old unions.

Does the policy of reopening the fight in the old unions imply any reconciliation with the traitorous and bribed officials of these unions, as the soft-headed experts of the "third period" say? Just the opposite. It means the elevation of the left-wing fight from phrasemongering futility into action which will animate the left-wing movement with a new vitality. We do not speak in favor of a tiptoe activity in the old unions by grace of the fakers, but an open, militant, and ruthless war to exterminate them and all their influence.

This means to expose and denounce them before the workers on the basis of every concrete act of betrayal which they commit from day to day. It means to explain, theoretically and practically, their role as agents of the bosses and to imbue the workers with a deathless hatred for them. The constitution of a new left-wing movement within the old unions, uniting its struggle with that of the militants in the new industrial union, means to enter on another stage in the fight to cleanse the needle trades movement of the reactionary lieutenants of the employing class.

The fourth important phase of left-wing strategy is the revival of the tactics of the united front and the slogan of trade union unity. The slogan of unity has power to move the masses. It corresponds to the necessities of their struggle and to their own inmost convictions, born of tragic experience in splits and defeats. The left wing must raise again the slogan of unity in the new union *and in the old ones*. It must explain to the workers over and over again that it is the right-wing reactionaries who bring division and split into the labor movement, and that it is the left wing which fights for unity.

The left wing must prove this in its daily policy because words alone are not enough; it is deeds which convince. The left wing in the needle trades took shape, grew, and became consolidated in battle under the slogan of unity. The abandonment of the slogan has been accompanied by a weakened organization and a dwindling influence. The revival of the slogan now is necessary to turn the helm and change the course toward new victories for the left wing and for the masses of the workers.

A general phrase about unity means nothing. What is

required is a precise formulation for the concrete circumstances. The party's talk about unity is good for nothing because it goes hand in hand with a policy of split. The workers are not as dumb as the bureaucrats think, and they are not so easily fooled by words which are contradicted by deeds.

The slogan put forth by the Lovestoneite faction—a typical production of opportunist generality and evasion—is no better. This shoddy crew, trying to capitalize on the sentiment for unity in the old unions and fearing to offend the sectarian patriotism of the members of the new union, has issued the slogan "Fight for one industrial union in the industry!" What does that mean? Like all the slogans of the opportunists, it means anything you like. As to how it is to be realized, how it is to be put *concretely* in the new union and in the old unions—this is left to guesswork and interpretation.

The Opposition Communists in the needle trades cannot trifle with double-meaning slogans. Their aim is to clarify the issues, not to attract the workers with catchwords. They are duty bound to act in the spirit of Lenin, who said: "Argue about tactics *but give clear slogans!"* Therefore they must formulate the slogan of unity with such precision that there can be no misunderstanding about it.

The Stalinists propose to achieve "unity" by having the 175,000 workers in the right-wing unions withdraw from them individually and join the six or seven thousand members in the new industrial union. This is absurd.

The Lovestoneites formulate the slogan so that it can be interpreted one way when they are under the attacks of the Stalinists in the new union, and the opposite way when they are under the attack of the officials in the old unions. This is misleading; this is playing with issues according to the time-honored practice of these unprincipled opportunists.

In our opinion the slogan of unity should be formulated as follows: "Unite the old unions with the new industrial union into a single organization for the entire industry!" The slogan, thus formulated, should be raised in direct connection with the other slogans mentioned above regarding the fight for economic demands, trade union democracy, and the elimination of the right-wing leaders. It should be issued by the new industrial union and by the organized left wing in the old unions in precisely the same way and would be the most important means of uniting their struggles into one, along the front of the entire industry. The two sections of the left wing, working in different fields of organization, would thereby be bound together into a single ideological force. From this, organizational coordination of the joint struggle would follow.

On this basis both sections of the left wing would bound forward in the confidence of the workers, and each section—the new union in the sphere of the unorganized and the organized left wing in the old unions—would expand its organization. There is no contradiction in such a perspective. The two lines of activity supplement and strengthen each other. The existence of the new union as a growing force would constitute a standing threat to the bureaucrats of the right-wing unions against mass expulsions. In fear of the new union they will be compelled to hesitate and temporize with a left wing in their own organization, and allow it a certain room for development.

On the other hand, a desperate fear of the movement within the right-wing unions, driving the officials to mass expulsions and splits again, would bring new forces to swell the ranks of the industrial union; not handfuls of Communists, as will be the case under the present policy, but masses of workers who would impart to the new union the character of a mass organization.

Against our proposals and perspective there remains a question of last resort for the Stalinist tacticians: "Is it possible to 'reform' the old unions and transform them into genuine organs of the class struggle?" The Stalinists have answered this question in the negative and thereby disposed of it as far as they are concerned. As for us, this schematic formulation has no meaning. We do not advise the left-wing workers to waste their time in speculation as to the possibilities of a "legal" conquest of the apparatus of the old unions. Experience in the needle trades struggle has already provided a certain answer on this point.

When we speak of a conquest of the old unions we do not think in terms of the offices, the buildings, and the banks. We think of the 175,000 workers in these unions, and we say they can and they will be won to the revolutionary banner. When we proclaim the slogan of uniting the old unions with the new industrial union in a single organization, we do not promise that this unity will be legally confirmed by the reactionary leaders with a voluntary abdication. But our slogan of unity is nevertheless a sincere one and it is put forward with confidence that it will be realized.

With a correct policy and a competent leadership, the left wing will win over the masses and unite them—if not all, then the great majority—into one union. Let the reactionaries think of the unions in terms of contracts with the bosses, offices, buildings, and banks. Let us think of the unions in terms of the workers within them. This conception will guide us toward the slogans and tactics of victory.

Deeper into the party!

Published July 26, 1930

The following article was published in *The Militant.*

In a previous article on the character and limits of our faction, reference was made to the experiences of the German Leninbund and to the flabbiness of principle which brought it to impotence and ruin. In this case, as always, confusion and looseness on principled questions were bound up with errors in tactics which contributed to and hastened the debacle. One of the greatest errors of the Leninbund in this field, as the results have shown, was its false attitude toward the party.

In common with the entire International Opposition, we have drawn the lessons of the split in the Leninbund and reacted with a firmer intransigeance in regard to principled questions. We must make use of these lessons also in determining our attitude toward the party. It is particularly necessary now because we stand on the eve of new developments in the party which will be vitally affected by our tactics.

For us this is a tactical question. We do not make a fetish of the party organization; our disregard of the bureaucrats' "discipline" is a sufficient indication that we do not put the form before the substance. What we are concerned with at the present moment is the composition of the party, its influence among the radical workers, and the present relation of forces in the struggle in the Communist ranks.

Our task is to win over the workers' vanguard to the platform of the Opposition. A tactic which gives us the best approach to them is the one we must seek and apply. A tactic which hampers our approach to them is wrong on the face of it. Such a tactic would block the path of future development for the Opposition.

Where are the American revolutionary workers today? This question we must answer first of all. Unless we close our eyes to all reality, we have to recognize that the great bulk of revolutionary workers who play an active role in the class struggle today are in the party, and *around the party.* The party has the unquestionable hegemony in the left-wing labor movement. Take the needle trades as an example. It is true that Communist influence has declined as a result of the monstrous errors of the party leadership; but the party remains the decisive leading force in the left wing. The same thing applies to other fields; for instance, the miners. There are many communist workers not in the party—thousands of them—but they are not an organized force.

It is possible, with an aggressive policy and energetic independent activity, to reach some of these revolutionary workers directly and bring them into the ranks of our organization. This we must do. But the main road of approach to them is through the party. Under the present circumstances and relation of forces, a complete break with the party—a course toward the organization of another party—would weaken, not strengthen our connection with the left-wing workers who are sympathetic to communism.

This relation is not fixed and final for all time; it simply determines the attitude for the present and the near future. In Comrade Trotsky's letter, published in *The Militant* some months ago, he expressed the opinion that the relation of forces in America justified an orientation on our part toward the formation of an independent party. We did not agree with it at the time and we thought Comrade Trotsky would change his opinion when he received more complete and detailed material on the situation in the Communist and left-wing labor movement. This proved to be the case, as attested by a second letter from him.[57]

The peculiarities of our position as a body of expelled Communists impose upon us a flexibility of tactics. Dogmatic narrowness and one-sidedness will be fatal to our future development. We are confronted with the necessity of maintaining our position as a faction of the party, despite the prohibition of the officialdom, and at the same time of developing an independent organization with its own independent activities and its own discipline. To combine these tasks, to make each supplement the other, is our problem.

The most important means of approach to the party members is the tactic of *the united front with the party.* Our participation in the demonstration for the Indian revolution was an excellent illustration of this policy, and we must follow it more energetically in the future.[58] On the same order is our offer to participate in the New York election campaign, our repeated attempts to enter into joint class-struggle action with the official party in behalf of the unemployed, the class-war prisoners, etc. By these means we are continually refuting *in action* the slanders of the party overseers against us and gaining in the sympathy of the Communist workers.

The centrist leaders are always aroused to the greatest fury by our attempts to make a united front with the party in common struggle against the class enemy. And that fact ought to be instructive for our own members. The bureaucrats fear our contact with the party workers on the firing line of the class struggle. They fear the influence of our example. They fear our arguments and our slogans. They want to tear us away from all contact with the proletarian Communists. This ambition of theirs is quite understandable. But we must not help them realize it by false tactics.

The party—that is, the party membership—is not a dead body. It is a living organism constantly under the pressure of the class struggle. It cannot be kept in a strait-jacket. The party reacts to events. It is influenced by criticism—especially so when the party members see the criticism confirmed in life. Things which have just recently happened in the party, and others which are in a course of preparation, bear out this contention.

A long time after the echoes of our expulsion had died down in the party, after it seemed on the surface that all our contact was broken—the party was startled a few weeks ago by another bombshell. This was the declaration of Hugo Oehler for the platform of the Opposition, followed the next week by a whole group of young Communists in New York. There are more to come. Just the other day we received a letter from a comrade in a city where we had no supporters up till now. The letter states that a number of comrades have been reading *The Militant* very attentively for some time and that they are about ready to make a declaration in our behalf. Hardly a week goes by without similar news.

There can no longer be any doubt that our propaganda is penetrating into the party ranks and influencing the Communist workers more and more as they see it borne out by events. What is happening now is not the adhesion of isolated individuals here and there, but the beginning of a *movement* for the Opposition. We are breaking through the wall reared against us by the centrist leadership. The *second layer* of Oppositionists is taking shape in the party.

The new movement for the Opposition shows certain distinctive features. Its main current is made up of the best types of proletarian Communists who have been attempting to carry out the policy of the party on the battlefield of the class struggle. Here they are confronted with the contradiction between the bluff and fakery of the party jacks-in-office and the realities of the situation. The more these comrades in the field try to apply the official policy the more they bump their heads against this contradiction. The result is a gradual awakening to the fact that something is amiss.

They begin to criticize and to propose modifications, and are met with accusations of "right-wing tendencies" and threats of discipline. The swivel-chair generals in the party office have no sympathy for the grievances and complaints of the fighters in the field. Slogans and "instructions" cost the Browders nothing; they don't have to carry them out. Therefore they can be as bombastic as language will allow. Not so the party workers in the field.

Deprived of the right to discuss anything really important in the official party channels, the comrades begin to discuss among themselves. The gap between them and the leadership widens. This process has been going on now for a long time. That it has not exploded before now in a faction struggle over questions of current policy is accounted for by the terror regime in the party and the lack of "prominent" leaders. This lack of leadership is not altogether a minus quality. While it retards the open manifestations of the proletarian current, it drives it deeper into itself, compels it to weigh the questions more carefully and to relate them to the fundamental issues.

The logic of the situation drives the proletarian revolt in the party toward the platform of the Opposition. Only on that basis can it develop into a real power. There are some who understand this already but who shrink from its implications. To think the conflicts through to the end means to connect the contradictions in local policy with the national, and the national with the international. This leads inevitably to a consideration of the standpoint of the Opposition. To study the platform of the Opposition objectively and honestly means, for a conscientious worker-Communist, to support it. This means "disgrace." Loss of "position." Expulsion. Slander. The severing of social relations and other trifles. Some fear this. Others go forward resolutely and tell the truth to the party. Such a type is Hugo Oehler. There will be other Oehlers.

It is our most important task at the moment to establish closer bonds with this coalescing proletarian movement in the party and help it to take shape as a genuine political force. We must help from a political standpoint. We must stimulate its organization.

Regardless of the vacillations of some of the potential leaders, this movement in the proletarian ranks of the party will develop and go forward. It will do this because it is rooted in the deepest needs of the party of the proletariat to coordinate its policy with the realities of the class struggle. And this is not a question of empirical and short-sighted shrewdness and practicality. It is a question, in the last analysis, of the Marxist fundamentals on the main issues of international import, from which, and only from which, the correct everyday tactics flow.

To make this clear to the revolting workers in the party ranks is the task of the Leninist Opposition. In order to do this we must have the closest contact with the party. We must go deeper into the party. The decisive trend of this movement in our direction, already noticeable, is a justification of our attitude toward the party. The successful development of the movement into a new fighting regiment for Leninism will confirm these tactics beyond all further dispute.

As the new developments show, the party cannot be judged by the apparatus. With most of these people, political stultification has been blended with moral corruption, and their reclamation is beyond the power of politics. Not to trust them, but to fight them; not to count on them for the regeneration of the party, but to see that they will be its first victims—that is our attitude toward them. It is different with the Communist worker who has no axe to grind. Let us not forget this distinction.

One way—and one of the very best ways—to give real support to those comrades fighting for our views inside the party is to increase the independent activity of the Communist League. The stronger we are as an independent force, the more rapid will be our progress in the party ranks. The steps we have taken since the plenum of our National Committee toward the formation of an Opposition group in the needle trades unions as an independent factor, has a special value and importance in this regard.

We cannot foretell every fluctuation of the struggle for Leninism in the Communist movement nor the forms it will always take. The main tasks and the main line, however, are clear to us. Under a shower of slander we are organizing the fundamental nucleus of the future Communist Party, and we must connect this nucleus with the larger body of worker-revolutionaries and win them for our platform. At the present stage of the struggle—which we visualize as a long one—it is above all a fight for the party. A clear understanding of this will hasten our victory.

Signs of a crisis

December 16, 1930, and January 5, 1931

The following letter was written to Vincent R. Dunne in Minneapolis.

Dear Vincent:

I have been intending to write to you all for some time. During the time this idea was germinating I also accumulated a few thoughts which I will touch on here. In political struggle the all-important question always is—what to do next. Recent developments in our movement confront us with the necessity of answering this question. If we succeed in giving the right answer we will easily surmount the difficulties and forge ahead. If we give the wrong answer we will go under.

There are some signs of the approach of an ideological crisis in our ranks. The recent affair of the Farmer-Labor Party was one of these signs, but not the only one.[59] There have been a number of others which I will mention. The problem now is to see the situation as it really is, to try to understand it and to prescribe a remedy.

All of the national sections of the Opposition in Europe have experienced ideological crises which culminated in splits. We alone succeeded in maintaining a formal unity and a considerable degree of ideological cohesion. The crisis which arose in the National Committee a year ago should not be minimized, of course; and by no means should it be forgotten. It was a serious matter and had a decidedly harmful effect on our work. But the fact that it did not lead to a split or to the disintegration of the movement into factions was a proof of a fundamental unity on the most decisive questions. The things which bound us together were more important than those which pulled us apart.

Will this remain the case? Will we succeed in overcoming the symptoms of ideological crisis in the ranks and emerge stronger and more firmly united? I feel quite confident that it will be so if we face the situation squarely and stick to the political line we have already laid down in the national conference and reaffirmed at the plenum. This is a prerequisite, in my opinion. The dangers come from tendencies, some conscious and some unconscious, to revise the platform.

I will not elaborate my opinions here at great length. Just now I am giving some lectures at our forum which attempt to deal with the questions in general, and soon they will be worked over into articles for *The Militant* as discussion material for the forthcoming plenum and conference. Here I will refer briefly to the points which I think pertain most directly to our present internal situation. These are: the role of the Opposition, its specific tasks at the moment, and its prospects for the near future.

We have already defined the role and tasks of the Opposition for the period at hand. Our fight is an intransigeant fight for principle as a faction of the party. So we decided at the conference and again at the plenum. Under the given conditions this view condemns us for the moment to the position of a comparatively small group and decrees our activity to be mainly propagandistic and critical. Along this line we must have the perspective of a long and stubborn struggle. During the early part of this struggle—perhaps for a long time, perhaps for years yet—we will occupy the position of a minority.

This perspective is a hard one and so is the fight. But we can escape from it only at the cost of principle, and this means, in the end, disintegration and defeat. *Our strength is our platform!* If we forget that, we are lost. And yet that is precisely the mistake made by those who seek a way out of the situation by a shortcut under the enticing but thoroughly false slogan of "mass work."

Our next plenum, and after that the next conference, will have to take up and analyze this slogan more precisely than has been done up till now. We have had two years of experience which ought to have an instructive value, and in each case the experience confirms the policy we have followed and refutes the revolts against it. Our first capitulator, Gerry Allard, should not be forgotten. He broke with us, and quite honestly, I believe, because he wanted to engage in the "mass work" of the party in southern Illinois. His defense of our platform placed obstacles in the way of this design. So, instead of fighting to penetrate the mass work with our ideas he renounced them, mistaking the right to rub elbows freely with a bigger crowd of people for Bolshevik work among the masses. What is the result? After a year and a half of feverish "mass work," Allard is back where he started, disillusioned and discouraged, with nothing to show but a trail of ruin among the miners.

Not long ago Toronto presented us with another capitulator in the person of Comrade Blugerman. He also broke down under the severity of the struggle as a member of the small Marxist minority and began to demand that we do mass work at all costs. It soon developed that his prescription was to capitulate to the treacherous trade union policy of the Stalinists. And for the sake of a little social "company"—that is what these shameless capitulators are really thinking of when they talk about the masses—he has given up the struggle for principle and betrayed his own convictions. And will he really do effective mass work now? Just the contrary. His first undertaking, in accord with the Stalinist policy, is to try to split the Amalgamated Clothing Workers in Toronto and bring the workers into the left-wing union. Hillman and Company will gain by this mass work and so will the clothing bosses. None others.

Now we have a little flurry in the New York branch. Some comrades—only a very few, but some, and that has significance—think we are too narrow and perhaps sectarian in refusing to admit Weisbord. Weisbord is promising them that if he is admitted to the Opposition he will pull mass movements out of his sleeve. The present leaders, according to him, are sectarian, and the smallness of our movement is due to their policy of passivity and fear of mass work and maneuvers. But what does he offer in place of our policy? Well, as his articles in *The Militant* show, he offers first of all a bloc with the Lovestone adventurers for no less a purpose than to "revive mass work" and to "save the Communist movement." In other words, instead of capitulating to the Stalinists we should compromise with the right wing. As to what would become of our principled program—and consequently of our historical right to exist—this form of capitulationism, like its Stalinist twin, has nothing to offer.

The fourth example is the recent exchange about the

Farmer-Labor Party. I don't know to what extent the comrades in Minneapolis played with this project nor how much real difference you have with our letter after thorough reflection. But O'Flaherty, who called himself an Oppositionist, sponsored this monstrosity. In a letter to a comrade several months ago O'Flaherty declared himself a supporter of Trotsky, but not of the American Trotskyites. This is the same thing that Weisbord says. Next he wrote an editorial in the Plentywood paper (I assume he wrote it) endorsing Weisbord's plan of unity with the right wing. His proposal for the Farmer-Labor mishmash was quite in line with this orientation.

The incongruous feature of this affair is the reaction to the proposal in the Minneapolis Opposition ranks. We should not gloss this over. Rather we should think very seriously as to what causes were at the bottom of it.

I had to leave off this letter in the middle to go to a meeting and have been so busy in the meantime that the letter remained unfinished. The fight with Weisbord came to a head and we had a real battle in the New York branch over him and the platform which he brought forward as a substitute for ours. We accepted his offer to collaborate with us to a certain extent in good faith and gave him a class in Marxian economics to teach. Like a true graduate of the Pepper school he then set about to utilize the contacts thus given him to organize a faction against us. He had eight or ten comrades—mostly young ones who came to us last spring from the Lovestone party faction—lined up to fight for his admission to the league and for the overthrow of the present leadership. . . . The present leadership of the league, according to him, are sectarians; and, moreover, they are all recruited from the so-called

Cannon group in the party; therefore, since they show no disposition to renounce their past, they have to be removed before the Opposition can make any real headway.

We called a special meeting of the branch to discuss the issues. One of Weisbord's arguments, which some of the comrades took seriously, was to the effect that we did not want to admit him to the league because we were afraid of his rivalry in the matter of leadership. Therefore we invited him to come to the branch meeting and debate the questions with us face to face. This is an extraordinary step to take—allowing a nonmember to participate in our discussions—and it certainly should not establish a precedent; but we wanted to clear the air and not to allow any confusion to be created by secondary questions.

It is really too bad that our entire membership throughout the country could not participate in this discussion before the New York branch. I think it was a fundamental one and that the questions most deeply concerning all of our comrades—the question of the role, the tasks, and the perspectives of our movement—were answered there. The New York branch membership thought so. When the smoke cleared away there was nothing left of the Weisbord faction, and the hero himself left the hall under a volley of questions from us which he refused to answer. All the comrades who had been caucusing with him, with the possible exception of one, changed their position in the course of the discussion, and the branch is solidly united now in support of the National Committee. The net results have been very beneficial in every way. The whole affair had a real educational value and the morale of the branch is higher, much higher, than ever.

I will not undertake to deal with the questions fully here because I must go to another meeting in a few minutes and I do not want to delay the letter longer. I intend to make a copy of the outline of my speech to the branch and send it to you. Perhaps we can also make copies for all the branches. There is no doubt that this discussion is in order now throughout our organization. It should at least begin in a preliminary way. At the forthcoming national conference we can finish it.

❖

Arne arrived here a few days ago. We have had one meeting with him already and it was decided that he should take over the position of national secretary. This will include the political and organizational direction of the branches in accord with committee decisions, and the financial administration of the organization.

At the first meeting we had a discussion of the financial affairs and prospects of the league. Tonight we are having a political discussion. You will get full reports from Arne about our financial situation and the status of the organization in respect to the functioning of the branches. Briefly, the organization throughout the country is in bad shape. It could not be otherwise under the circumstances when there has been practically no administration for months. However, I think the situation can be repaired in a reasonable time and that we will succeed in saving all, or nearly all, that we have had.

The financial report shows that our only real difficulty has been lack of a functioning organization. It is not as though we had been overstraining the organization and were confronted with the necessity for retrenchment. Just the contrary. We are just before the prospect of a real expansion, which is possible on the basis of our present forces, to say nothing of new prospects. The New York branch, to which some serious attention has been given, has made great strides since the plenum. You may remember that we spoke then of being able to *double* its activities and financial support of the center after the internal difficulties were overcome. Well, what really happened was a *quadruple* improvement! New York alone contributed nearly half of all the funds of the national office during the past four months. And the present activity can be doubled again in a few months, from all indications. We have finally got a needle trades fraction and a group of sympathizers around it in functioning order. From this there will be fruitful results. Our weekly forum now has a steady attendance of over a hundred and is growing steadily.

We now have a printing press, which we got without a cent of investment. It was installed with no down payment and with monthly installments of thirty dollars. We are going to break in one of the comrades to run it, and the saving we will make on press work, even on the basis of our present production, will more than make up the installments.

Our present difficulties come from the fact that the machinery is not used enough. An increase in production is what we need. Just consider: Our irreducible overhead is about four hundred dollars per month, even with the semimonthly *Militant*. The change to a weekly would increase it only sixty dollars! That means that if we sold only half of the extra papers (two issues of three thousand each) and got the money for them, the weekly would be no more expensive than the semimonthly.

Or look at another angle: A monthly theoretical magazine of ninety-six pages would cost us not more than eighty dollars for the production of a thousand copies. If we sold five hundred of them, to say nothing at all of subs, it would pay the cost of production and not injure our financial status. If we sold a thousand copies we would have about eighty dollars a month profit *at the very least.*

This profit would more than pay the additional cost of the weekly over the semimonthly.

If our national organization were in functioning order I would not hesitate to make a motion tomorrow to begin the issuance of the monthly organ at once and to begin the issuance of the weekly as soon as the magazine proves a profit-maker on the first number or two. The point to remember on these calculations is that they are all made on the basis of our existing forces. All that is required is an increase in activity in the disposition of the literature and the businesslike accounting for that which is sold. Since this is simply a question of organization, and since there is every reason to believe that with Arne's work in the office and the help of Rose on the business management, the organization can be put in shape in a reasonable time, I consider the issuance of the monthly magazine and the transfer to a weekly *Militant* very near—and this time it will be on a firm foundation.[60]

Besides that, you can expect a steady stream of pamphlets and books—about one a month. But that is again another question involving a plan to establish a publishing house, about which I will write separately. The type is already set on the pamphlet *The Five-Year Plan and World Unemployment*. The linotyper has started to set *Communism and Syndicalism*. The question is: Can we gear up the organization to dispose of this literature as fast as we can turn it out? Every branch ought to organize this business systematically. The simple task of selling a certain amount of each pamphlet and paying for it promptly has a decisive importance.

Fraternally,

J.

Our policy and present tasks

December 23, 1930

The following is the outline of a speech to the New York branch. Cannon was reporting for the National Committee in a debate with Albert Weisbord.

1. The duty of the leadership

a) To establish the theoretical and political foundations of the movement and lay out its perspectives.

b) To define the tasks.

c) To employ tactics suited to the moment and consonant with our principled line.

d) This means concretely to have the right answer to the question: what to do next?

Has our policy, in the main, corresponded to these requirements, or is it necessary now to make a drastic change, as Weisbord proposes, as well as a change of the leadership, as he also proposes? Let us examine the whole question and see.

2. The genesis of the Opposition

a) Formally speaking, the American section of the International Left Opposition was formed a little more than two years ago. It began its public formal existence with the declaration read to the Political Committee by Abern, Shachtman, and Cannon in October 1928.

b) But neither the ideas of the Opposition nor we who represent them fell from the sky on that date. The whole situation is an outgrowth of the evolution and development of the party and the Comintern. The founders of the American section of the Opposition were "prepared by the past" for their present stand. This is equally true of the Lovestone and the Foster factions, that is, of the right wing and the centrists of our party. Anyone who denies this has to ground his position on the theory that political groupings and political developments are accidental and arbitrary. Such methods of analysis never had any standing among Marxists.

3. The crux of the issue consists in this:

a) The World War and the Russian revolution brought the conflict between opportunism and Marxism to a head and resulted in a split in the Second International.

b) The revolutionary wing of the labor movement has been organized, over a period of more than eleven years, under the banner of the Comintern and the respective parties. This must not be forgotten for a moment. Under the banner of the Comintern *and nowhere else* the revolutionary workers have been organized.

c) The first four congresses of the Comintern represent in their theses and resolutions the revolutionary Marxist doctrines.

d) The period since the Fourth Congress has been a period of reaction, of sliding backward, in the Russian party and in the Comintern.

These are the main conditions of the crisis in the Communist movement from which all our conclusions must be drawn.

4. The fundamental basis of the three factions

a) The crisis in the Comintern has revealed three clearly defined faction groupings. The struggle between them represents, in the final analysis, the struggle of the classes.

b) In this struggle the Left Opposition represents the proletarian class in its highest historic interests.

c) "The right wing is the handle on which the enemy classes are pulling. . . . The success of this wing will be but a temporarily disguised victory of the bourgeoisie over the proletariat" (Trotsky). The right wing is the objective representative of the pressure of the bourgeoisie upon the proletariat and the party.

d) The apparatus centrists stagger between the right and left wings and carry out a petty-bourgeois policy.

e) Thus the crisis in the Russian party and throughout the Comintern is not a mere faction fight between comrades of equal merit as revolutionaries over episodic questions. Weisbord seems to think it is, and that is his fundamental error. His whole point of departure is false to the bottom and consequently his tactics cannot be right.

5. The task of the left wing

a) To base its whole activity on the principles of Marx and Lenin.

b) To make its policy become the policy of the workers' vanguard.

This main principled line is a settled question in our ranks. The entire work of our first national conference was conducted under this sign and it is reflected in our platform adopted at the conference.

As we see the issue a discussion of the validity of these

two points is in place only with outsiders. In our ranks they are settled questions—we proceed from them.

6. Abnormal features of the faction struggle in the party

a) Under normal conditions we would wage our fight within the framework of the party. Why?

b) Because we are communists and not anarchists, because we regard the principle of party organization as an inseparable part of Marxist revolutionary conceptions.

c) Because we believe the communists and none other constitute the vanguard of the proletariat.

d) Because we adhere to the Marxist principle of organization and regard the organized movement more highly than the unorganized. The dispersed and unorganized elements, just because they are dispersed and unorganized, cannot be relied on to any great extent.

e) Our expulsion only makes the situation, and consequently some of the methods of struggle, abnormal. It does not, of itself, alter the situation fundamentally. It does not change the fact that we remain in essence a faction of the party struggling to win over the proletarian majority to our standpoint. What else can we mean when we say so repeatedly: "The Opposition has a correct line. The task is to make this the line of the proletarian vanguard" (Trotsky, *Militant,* January 2, 1929).[61]

f) The question now arises: Have we followed a correct line of policy in the party struggle—have we understood the main task—or must we now reverse our position and take another course? Such is the question posed by the proposals of Weisbord.

7. The question has been discussed before

a) At this point it is proper to remark that we are not discussing this question for the first time. Our policy has been discussed quite thoroughly before, during, and even after the national conference. Decision has been made and American as well as international experience has confirmed the decision as correct.

b) We cannot make a practice of returning continually to the discussion of positions already won in struggle. Such a course would be fit only for irresponsible cafe revolutionists whose talk is endless and means nothing. Bolsheviks discuss only in order to come to a decision and to act upon it.

c) We return to the question once more only because the tested policy and experience of the Opposition on an international scale has not been fully assimilated by some comrades—new in the struggle for the greater part—whom we wish to pull along with us if we can.

8. What is the real issue here?

a) The real issue—from a political standpoint—is: a faction of the party on a Bolshevik platform, or a new party on an opportunist platform. A dissection of the various so-called new arguments in the light of our principled line will make this clear.

b) The contrasting methods of approach to the question are quite in accord with all international experience in the struggle between the Marxists and the opportunists.

c) The Marxists put the *principle* bluntly, and subordinate tactics to principle. The opportunists hide the principle and try to smuggle it in under the cloak of "tactical differences." This is what Weisbord is trying to do now with his talk about correcting our "tactics."

d) Compare, for example, the contrast between the methods employed by us in launching the organization of the Left Opposition with the methods of the right wing at the time of their break with the party. We *began* with a declaration of principle in our very first document (Declaration to the CEC, October 27, 1928, signed by Cannon, Abern, and Shachtman. See *Militant,* vol. 1, no. 1). Lovestone and Company began with a whole ream of faction material emphasizing personal and secondary matters and saying nothing about *principled differences.* The platform of Brandlerism was unfolded only afterward, after the workers in the right wing had been prepared by degrees and maneuvered into position for it.

These methods are alien to us. We will not allow Weisbord to draw us into a discussion on that basis. That is why we insist on putting the principled question as it really is: faction of the party on a Bolshevik platform—or new party on an opportunist platform. That our formulation of the issue is the correct one will be demonstrated clearly enough.

9. Who are the vanguard of the proletariat?

a) The definition of our task "to make our line the line of the proletarian vanguard" is not an abstraction. It means a definite formation within the working class stands nearest to us and is the bridge to the wider masses.

b) The party is the vanguard of the class. This formulation holds good even in America, where the organization of the workers as a class is still in the elementary stages.

c) The correctness of this formulation is easily demonstrated by putting the question in another way: If not the party, then *who* or *what* force constitutes the proletarian vanguard? Is it not an indisputable fact that there is no other leading force on a national scale at the present time? If there is such another leading force, more advanced than the party, please name it. Its existence is not known to us.

d) The party, under centrist domination, leads the mass of workers who have partly awakened to consciousness.

It leads them badly, as we have proved, it leads them to more defeats than victories, *but it leads them just the same at present.*

e) What can be the meaning of the March 6 demonstrations last year—a fairly imposing movement.[62] Compare the party's demonstrations of 20,000 workers at Madison Square Garden with our little meetings of 200 or 300 at the most. There you see a fairly accurate reflection of the relation of forces. Or, compare the party's demonstrations with those of the right wing—the disparity is about the same as with us.

f) The party has a rather formidable press—dailies in many languages, through which it influences wide circles of workers. The *Daily Worker* circulation is growing. The resolution of the last plenum says it doubled during the past year, meaning probably that it increased somewhat. There is no doubt it has made a substantial gain, especially in New York.

g) Those who want to deny that the Communist workers, organized in the party and under its direct influence in other bodies, constitute the workers' vanguard must give us another name for them. What are these people who, to the number of thousands and tens of thousands throughout the country, march in the demonstrations, resist police persecution, support strikes, sacrifice their time, their means? Are they idiots, fools, and dupes? That is stupid, reactionary talk!

h) I repeat: the proletarian vanguard is not an abstraction. If not the party, then who, or what? Is it the Socialist Party? No. Since the World War and the Russian revolution there can be no doubt on this score. In the needle trades, for example, we had a concrete illustration of the reactionary role of the SP. Is it the progressives? No. Insofar as the progressives do not support the party, that is, *follow* the party, they act as windbreaks for the reactionaries. Is it the IWW or the anarchists? No. These are both reactionary sects, reactionary through and through.

i) What elements remain? There are the scattered and demoralized workers who have left the party or been repulsed by the party. Among them there are undoubtedly many workers of potential value for the revolution. But in the mass, as a definite category, they are characterized by this fatal weakness: *they do not lead!* What else can be the meaning of the fact that they *allow themselves* to be dispersed and demoralized, that they *withdraw* from the movement and conduct no organized struggle to reform it? To seek for individual recruits in this direction is sensible enough. To expect a considerable influx of these elements into the ranks of the Opposition later on is not unreasonable, for it is the characteristic of these elements to *follow* and they will come toward us when we are stronger more than they will take up the burdens of our struggle while we are still weak. But to seek for the regeneration of the Communist movement from these discouraged and bewildered people is to leave the ground of reality altogether.

j) The talk about the party losing all its influence beyond the hope of revival—above all to say that this has already happened—is quite false. On the contrary, there is more reason to think that, in spite of the systematic errors of the leadership and the whole idiocy of the "third period" bluster, the influence of communism, and that is primarily of the party, has made gains in the past year. The German election returns tell a story about this which cannot be ignored,[63] and similar signs are to be observed in America. The doubling of the 1928 election vote, for example, is one of these signs.

The gain of party influence in the face of the blunders of the leadership is to be accounted for by the fact that the official party represents in the eyes of the workers the idea of communism and the Russian revolution. *The pressure of conditions, especially the conditions of the economic crisis, drives the workers toward communism faster than the centrist bureaucrats can drive them away.*

k) Conclusion: The communist workers organized in the party and around the party under its direct influence *are the future troops of the Opposition.* We must concentrate on the task of winning them over in the shortest possible time.

10. The position of the Opposition with relation to the class and the vanguard

a) If the party is the vanguard of the class, what is the position of the Opposition? "The Opposition is the vanguard of the vanguard" (Trotsky).

b) Our first task: "To make the line of the Opposition the line of the proletarian vanguard."

c) Our strongest weapon: our platform.

d) The nature of our principal activity: *propaganda.*

"The revolutionary Marxists are now again reduced (not for the first time and probably not for the last) to being an international propaganda society. . . . It seems that the fact that we are very few frightens you. Of course, it is unpleasant. Naturally, it would be better to have behind us organizations numbering millions. But how are we, the vanguard of the vanguard, to have such organizations the day after the world revolution has suffered catastrophic defeats brought on by the Menshevik leadership hiding under the false mask of Bolshevism? Yes, how?" (Trotsky, *Militant,* October 1, 1929).[64]

11. The relation of forces

a) We have said before and we say now that our attitude toward the official party is determined to a large extent by the relation of forces. The *present* relation of forces determines our position as a minority faction of the party, and a *small* minority faction at that. Whom will we deceive except ourselves by ignoring this fact?

b) In Comrade Trotsky's letter printed in *The Militant* for November 30, 1929, he indicated the perspective of a second party for the American Opposition. But this was wrong and it was based on incorrect information about the relation of forces. In a second letter Comrade Trotsky acknowledged this.

c) We are the nucleus of the future party. *The Opposition will become the party.* But by what dialectic process we cannot give a complete answer now and we do not have to. What we must do is to keep the goal in mind and adopt the tactics most suited to the given time and circumstances. The question whether we become the party by means of a formal reentry into the organization and the subsequent conquest of a majority by democratic vote; whether we swell our ranks through the process of further splits which unite with us; whether we gradually expand in numbers and activity and step by step supersede the official party in the class struggle; we will reach our goal by one or a combination of all these methods in the course of time. We will do this *provided* we do not derail our movement by falsely estimating the situation at the various stages of the development of the struggle. This was the cardinal error of the German Leninbund. It tried to jump over the barrier set up by the relation of forces in the beginning. (Trotsky, *Militant,* January 25, 1930.)

12. The proposal of a bloc with the right wing

a) The essence of Weisbord's policy, which he offers as a substitute for ours, is the proposal that we, the Left Opposition, should form a bloc with the right wing (the Lovestoneites). This is clearly set forth in his statement printed in *The Militant* for September 15, 1930, and again in his article on unemployment.

b) He means by this that the left and the right should form a bloc against the centrists, against the official party. In *The Militant* for September 15, for example, he says, "The Communist 'Majority' opposition group and the Communist League by working together can help to re-establish mass work and to resist the violent tactics of the party officialdom."

Further, in *The Militant* for November 1, he says—addressing what he calls "the Communist Opposition groups" (meaning the left wing and the right wing, which he puts on the same level)—"When will you join hands on this issue. . . . When will you begin the work the Party criminals cannot do?" From this, as well as from his whole conception, which denies the Thermidorian character of the right wing, which denies the existence of centrism in the Communist movement, it is quite clear that he wants a bloc of the right and left against the center.

c) This question has been raised before in the ranks of the International Left Opposition and has been decisively answered in the negative. In my very first introduction to the basic documents of the Russian Opposition, I became acquainted with this answer. In his "Appeal to the Sixth Congress of the Comintern" (a document which has not yet been published in English—I saw it in Moscow at the Sixth Congress),[65] Comrade Trotsky referred to the split in the right-center bloc and the suggestion that the left might now make a bloc with the right. He said: "Blocs between the right and the left have been made in other revolutions, and they have also ruined other revolutions." In that document, where the question was first considered, Comrade Trotsky said such a bloc was absolutely unthinkable. That has been, it is, and it will be the unalterable position of the Left Opposition.

d) Would a bloc with the right wing, that is, with the Lovestone liquidators, the faction of petty-bourgeois adventurers—would such a bloc draw us nearer to the proletarian vanguard or would it separate us more? To ask such a question is to answer it. We have taught the communist workers, and not since yesterday, to hate and distrust the rotten petty-bourgeois faction of Lovestone and Wolfe. To appear side by side with them now in a common front against the party would discredit us before the Communist workers and push them away from us.

e) The very fact that one can make such a proposal shows that he does not understand the right wing and has not really broken with it. This is what is really the matter with Weisbord. In reality he is trying to *reconcile* us with the right wing under the pretext of curing our "sectarianism." He will not succeed.

f) In *The Militant* for December 28, 1929, Comrade Trotsky warned in advance against such opportunist proposals as Weisbord makes: "I received the news of the negotiations between Bukharin and Kamenev simultaneously with the report on the ambiguous declarations of Urbahns on a bloc with Brandler. I answered with an article on the absolute inadmissibility of unprincipled blocs between the Left and Right Oppositions."[66]

g) It is a real political bloc with Lovestone that Weisbord is offering us as a means of correcting our policy. Such a bloc, he says, would enable us to "resist the violent tactics of the Party officialdom." Isn't that a brilliant idea? And who, may we ask, will help us to resist the underworld methods of the Lovestone gang? Doesn't Weisbord know that we first encountered "violent tactics" from the Lovestone faction when it was at the head of the party and that we learned to "resist" them on our own resources? Or does he think the leopard has changed its spots and that Lovestone and Company are better now, since their own weapons have been turned against them?

Weisbord goes further: By means of the bloc, he promises us, we will win "the advanced workers to a Leninist conception of Party democracy." No less. All the Oppositionists who were expelled from the party by Lovestone, who were beaten up by his gangsters, will surely believe this.

And even this is not the end of the comedy. "Only such a working-together of Communist groups [only this!] can raise those fundamental principles of Leninist organization that can reconstitute the International of Lenin." We have been under the impression, together with the entire International Left Opposition, that the International of Lenin could be reconstituted only by the defeat of the right wing, by driving out the Thermidorians and the liquidators. How can these conceptions be reconciled? How can they both exist in the same organization?

13. The subterfuge of 'united front' with the right wing on concrete questions

a) Double-facedness and subterfuge are the characteristics of all opportunists. Driven away from one position they always attempt to smuggle it in under some other pretext. This is the case in the attempt to retreat under fire from the idea of a political bloc with the right wing outlined in Weisbord's articles in *The Militant* to the proposal for a "united front" on everyday tactical questions. Can't we at least get together with them in the trade unions? they ask. No, not even in this limited sphere, *because we are not going in the same direction with them.* From the start—that is, from the day the Lovestoneites were expelled from the party—we rejected all ideas of a common front with them. And correctly so.

b) The day their expulsion was announced we did not grow softer toward them. Just the contrary, we hammered them harder than ever and we predicted they would soon come out with a Brandler platform when they were loudly denying it. (See *The Militant,* July 1, 1929.)

c) Can the Left Opposition, which fights for the regeneration of the Communist International, have anything in common with the right wing, which represents the tendency for its liquidation? Can the defenders of the October revolution have anything in common with the faction of Thermidor, "the handle upon which the enemy classes are pulling"? No. The fact that contradictory lines cross episodically must not mislead us into this fundamental error. The fact, for example, that the right-wingers want to work in the reactionary unions and that we also defend this idea—in our time also against them, as our platform, directed against them as the party leadership (*Militant,* February 15, 1929) shows—does not give any ground for a common front. We have different and irreconcilable aims in the trade unions.

d) Let the revisers of our basic policy on this question cite a single concrete situation where even a limited conception of the united front with the right wing can be formed. Is it the needle trades? No, the right wing has already made a united front with Levy—that is to say, with Sigman—in this field. Is it the marine workers? No, the right wing made a united front with the reactionary syndicalist workers there against us as well as against the party—against communism, in fact. Is it the miners? No, the right wing is trying to come to an agreement there with the fakers posing as progressives in the Fishwick union. Is it the textile workers, where Weisbord has already compromised himself with them in a "Textile Workers Unity Committee" which is in reality a committee for the liquidation of the National Textile Workers Union? No, we cannot work together with them there. Doesn't Weisbord know that Lovestone is trying to organize the workers for McMahon and that he is using Weisbord as a come-on for this perfidious work? He will not use us for it.

Take any other field of activity, and we will show that insofar as the right wing has any footing there it is forming a united front with the pseudoprogressive and reactionary elements against us and against the party—against communism. The fact that they conceal these designs under a cloud of talk about Leninism does not alter the objective logic of their course. This is necessary to "prepare" and fool the communist workers in the ranks of the right wing. It is our task to expose this camouflage and not to be deceived by it.

14. What is the international stand of the Left Opposition on the question?

a) It is worthwhile to put this question and to answer it from authoritative documents because Weisbord is trying to represent himself as a supporter of Trotsky but not of the American Trotskyites. We have heard that kind of talk before. The reformists throughout the world in their time have taken turns at declaring for communism—in Russia but not in their own countries. Purcell was for the Russian Communist Party but not for the British. Such people as Hillman, closer home, and even many of the Socialist leaders, have made similar expressions. Let us see what this pretension is worth.

b) Comrade Trotsky has written quite often and quite explicitly on the question of a bloc with the right wing, warning us in advance, as it were, against the Weisbords of various kinds. Some of these remarks have already been quoted. On the question of a united front in the trade unions, he wrote in *The Militant* for October 1, 1929:

"Do we need a platform of immediate demands? Yes. Do we need a correct tactic in the trade unions? Certainly. But we cannot speak of these questions except with those who have clearly and firmly decided for themselves *why* all this is needed. Just as I will not discuss the various tendencies in materialism with a man who makes the sign of the cross whenever he passes by a church, so I will not work out slogans with Brandler, who, in principle, calls the rear of the revolution its face (and vice versa). . . . We are now in the period of the clarification of principles for ourselves and of pitiless delimitation from the opportunists and confusionists."[67] This is an answer to Weisbord's claim that he represents the standpoint of Trotsky against the National Committee of the Communist League.

Again in *The Militant* for March 29, 1930, he wrote: "Will Treint and Paz work with Urbahns and with the Brandler blocs formed in the midst of the trade unions against the Communist Party? . . . They recognize the policy of a united front with the Social Democracy, with the reformist trade unions, with the Brandlerites, with the Alsatian nationalists—but they consider inadmissible the united-front tactic with the official Communist parties."[68]

c) The French Opposition has already accumulated a rich experience on this question of the united front in the trade unions which has an instructive value for as. Their line-up is not, as Weisbord proposes, a bloc between the right and the left oppositions. On the contrary, the Left Opposition is united with the communistic workers and is proposing a united front to the official party. The right wing, on the other hand, has made a united front with the reactionary syndicalist elements on a platform of independence of the unions from the party and the liquidation of the revolutionary unions into the reformist unions.

In this they only anticipated our stand in the marine and textile unions while the right wing anticipated the stand of Lovestone in the same unions.

d) Is it not clear that Weisbord's claim to be "for Trotsky but against the American Trotskyites" is a demagogic subterfuge that will not stand investigation? Is it not clear that the National Committee of the Communist League carries out the same policy as that of the International Left Opposition?

e) International policy and experience confirms the correctness of our policy on this question of the united front: Not a bloc with the right wing against the official party, but a united front with the party against the right wing. This is the correct line of approach to the proletarian vanguard. The fact that the party bureaucrats refuse the united front with us is not our concern. Our task is to make the Communist workers understand our policy. The rest will follow.

15. The retreat from the principle under the slogan of 'mass work'

a) In his campaign against the policy and leadership of the Communist League, Weisbord is raising a great furore about "mass work." This empty ballyhoo is offered to us as a new discovery—something we never knew till now.

b) This is not so; there is nothing new or original about this formula for quick success. In everything he advances Weisbord demonstrates his lack of originality; his chief characteristic as a political is that of the borrower. In his conflicts with us on the various main points of our platform he borrows first from the right wing and then from the centrists. In his formula of "mass work" he is only repeating the slogan under which others have deserted the banner of the Left Opposition.

c) We haven't had many capitulators in America, thanks to the firm principled foundation upon which we built the movement, but every one of them saluted us with this slogan before he departed. Every one who deserted the banner of the Opposition ran away under a cloud of dust about "mass work." This was the case with Allard, with Zalisko, and with Blugerman in Toronto. Impatience with the slow development of the Opposition in the principled struggle and the desire to get on with "mass work" on a big scale was the motivation for the great and unpardonable errors of some of the Minnesota comrades in the recent Farmer-Labor Party affair. And now Weisbord, who wants to overturn the position of the Left Opposition on nearly all its basic principles, comes forward with "mass work" as his all-embracing slogan.

d) Is this a mere coincidence? How does it happen that this demagogic slogan is always followed by capitulation to the Stalinists or by capitulation in principle to the right wing? In fact, isn't Weisbord merely repeating the time-worn arguments of the right wing in his agitation against us? Read *Revolutionary Age* and you will see there the origin of all the catchwords he uses against us. The "Trotskyites" are "sectarian," they are "passive," *they do no "mass work," etc., etc.*

16. The meaning of Bolshevist mass work

a) Mass work, in our conception, is not a form of exercise, like gymnastics, to be carried on for its own sake. It is connected with revolutionary aims and therefore it must be grounded on principle. We understand the Leninist conception of mass work. Our platform adopted two years ago shows the only road to it.

b) We will only deceive ourselves and set our movement back if we overestimate what is possible for such a small group as that of the Left Opposition, which has to work in abnormally difficult and complicated circumstances. We cannot lift ourselves by our bootstraps, no matter how much we may try. We cannot jump to the execution of a program of mass work on a wide scale over the head of the existing party. We must not forget that we have an indispensable preliminary task: to win over the proletarian vanguard and imbue it with our principles.

c) By mass work we mean prepared, planned, and developed activity to set masses of workers in motion along lines which will heighten their consciousness. We do not mean spectacular stunts which leave nothing behind; we do not mean putsches. We are not graduates of the Pepper school of politics and we do not want that spurious brand of mass work.

d) Our main task is propaganda to win over the workers' vanguard, and our main tactic is the united front with the party. This does not exclude independent work in the class struggle. In reality all our work is independent in the sense that we oppose our policy always and everywhere to that of the centrist bureaucrats. What is really involved in the dispute over mass work is the question whether we shall oppose separate mass organizations to those of the party—joining hands with the right wing for this purpose—or whether we shall penetrate the existing organizations of the party. As a rule, and in the main, we have to follow the latter course at the present time.

e) This is mainly a question of the relation of forces again. In Minneapolis, for instance, we have carried out several separate and independent actions. But to set up rival organizations and movements to those led by the party all along the line would the a fatal error. It would close the doors to the party members and sympathizers and create rallying centers for all kinds of reactionary and anticommunist elements. Our participation as an organized group in the Indian demonstration of the party last summer, in the May Day celebration, etc.—these actions should serve as a model. We organize our own independent fractions in the needle trades and in the marine workers and such other places as we have forces. These fractions are not prevented by the policy of the Opposition from carrying on an energetic activity. They are only prevented from combining with the right wing and with reactionary elements against the party. In short, we are in no way opposed to general activity in the class struggle; we only refuse to accept an opportunist formula for it; and we refuse to alter our conception of the main task of the Opposition at the moment—propaganda to win over the workers' vanguard.

17. Two kinds of criticism

a) The Left Opposition has grown up in a struggle for party democracy and against the barracks discipline of the centrist bureaucracy. The unrelenting fight against the suppression of criticism within the party, as well as the counterfeit "self-criticism" served up as a substitute, is an inseparable part of our platform.

b) This has given rise to one-sided and false conceptions in and around our movement. There are people who think the Opposition means to loosen or do away with ideas of discipline and that any kind of criticism can be tolerated interminably. That is not so. We strive toward an iron discipline, that is, a discipline grounded on uniformly conscious convictions. We are not vulgar "democrats" and our organization is not a free forum for everybody. And we make a strict distinction between what may be called legitimate criticism and criticism that is not legitimate in our organization.

c) That criticism which aims to show weakness and shortcomings in the application of our principled line is certainly in order. We stand badly in need of a thoroughgoing criticism of our lack of activity along the lines of our platform. Above all, we need—together with such a criticism—concrete proposals regarding ways and means of increasing, of multiplying, our activity. Such criticism and concrete proposals are entirely legitimate and must not be suppressed on any pretext.

d) But what we cannot allow is an attack on our principled line which masquerades as criticism and which attempts to belittle the great achievements of the Opposition, achievements which have a permanent value and which far outweigh the defects and the failures in our work. It is such "criticism" that Weisbord offers, and that we contemptuously reject.

e) According to Weisbord our two-year struggle under the banner of the Opposition means little or nothing. Nothing of importance has happened. Things will begin to happen only when we adopt his platform and turn the leadership of the movement over to him. We didn't organize a single mass movement, we didn't conduct a single grand maneuver—therefore, we are a failure. So say the opportunists and the defeatists—so say the generals of the Pepper school of strategy and the faint-hearts who want quick results.

f) Let them talk all they wish—they will not change our course. For us the past two years, with all the faults and all the flaws, are the brightest in the history of the movement. They will represent in the history of American communism the turning point, the time when a resolute handful began the conscious and open fight against the downsliding of the post-Lenin regime and organized the nucleus of the future party, giving an object lesson to the communist workers in how to fight for principle against slander and persecution, how to swim against the stream.

18. The achievements of the Opposition

a) We have laid the foundation, firmly and deeply, for the future movement. All that is done hereafter will be built upon it. Our firm insistence on the lines of principle, our stubborn intransigeance in rejecting schemes for quick results at the cost of principle, will safeguard the future movement from unnecessary internal crises and splits.

b) We raised the banner of the International Left Opposition at the darkest moment, when the leaders were expelled and scattered and exiled and the cause seemed to be on the decline everywhere—when the "wise" and practical people, the self-seekers and careerists on the make, saw nothing to gain and stood aside.

c) The American section of the Opposition, small as it was, inspired and encouraged the movement throughout the entire world and decisively helped to stimulate a revival of the international struggle. Our voices were heard in the depths of Stalin's prisons, in the farthest reaches of his exile camps, and gave the Bolshevik-Leninists new hope of international support. The formation of the American section of the Opposition was the signal of a new rise of the international struggle.

d) The American section of the Opposition managed to unite its forces on a national scale through a national conference and to adopt a platform. Up to the present time we are the only section of the Opposition outside of Russia to formulate a national platform. Comrade Trotsky has written that the platform, on the whole, is very good and that some sections, notably the trade union section, are excellent. He wrote: "Your platform is a guarantee of political success." The platform is no doubt subject to improvement, but it is a real beginning, a real foundation.

e) We had few capitulators and no splits. The basic cadre which began the fight still conducts it. While the Opposition movement throughout the world has been passing through crises and splits, we have succeeded—not without difficulties, frictions, and symptoms of crisis—in strengthening the principled unity of our organization. It is true that the factional maneuvers of Weisbord represent an attempt to break the unity of our movement, to "Austrianize" it and disintegrate it into factions. But these maneuvers will be defeated and we will finish the discussion more firmly united than before.

f) The opportunists and the defeatists—the people who echo the sentiments of the right-wingers and the centrists—want to discredit our achievements. And why? Because they want to discredit the principled line upon which these achievements have been based.

g) They are coming too late. Two years of rich experience are behind us. They have not been in vain. We will build upon them. We will overcome all the obstacles and make the line of the Opposition the line of the proletarian vanguard. We must be imbued with the conviction that we are not fighting merely for the day. Ours is a great historic mission. This thought must animate us in every detail of our work. This conviction, which makes necessary the greatest sacrifices, also makes them possible.

Financing 'Communism and Syndicalism'

January 13, 1931

The following letter was written to A.A. "Shorty" Buehler in Kansas City.

Dear Shorty:

I haven't heard from you directly for some time and have begun to wonder if anything is the matter. Didn't you get the letter I sent you? You see, I don't judge you by the same standards as I judge myself. If I neglect to write, it is nothing new and nothing to worry about, but if you fall down on correspondence I begin to fear something is wrong. I hope you will clear this up. I am anxious to know how you are getting along. . . .

Here is another little matter which I wish you would take up with the comrades in Kansas City. We are preparing to bring out a pamphlet *Communism and Syndicalism* by Trotsky for which I am writing the introduction. This will be a very timely publication and should have a big influence on the syndicalist workers. We have to print it under the "sponsor plan." That is, a number of comrades contribute to the cost of the printing and their names are printed on the flyleaf of the pamphlet. We can get it out very cheap as we have our own machinery—all we have to pay for is the labor and the paper. This will cost sixty dollars.

A group of comrades in New York are going to raise half of it. I wonder if the Kansas City militants can't raise the other half. I have a special reason for making the proposal: that is, to see the name of the Kansas City branch down as one that helped to make possible the publication of this historic work. Round up the old guard and tell them now is the time for the "spiritual men" to come forward once more and put their names down on the first page of this pamphlet as sponsors who made its publication possible. This should be considered something extra—aside from the regular contributions the comrades are making for the support of *The Militant.*

Our work is booming in New York. We took in six new members last night, and the New York branch is gaining steadily on every front. In a short time we expect to see the revival manifested on a national scale. We are at work on plans for the organization of a publishing company which will publish Marxian literature in a cheap form for workers in a systematic manner. This will have a great value for the education of the new movement and will also be a source of profit for the support of *The Militant.* Don't be surprised if you hear soon that we are going to return to the weekly basis of publication of *The Militant* and that we are also going to bring out a theoretical magazine on the order of the old *Class Struggle.* No foolin'. Just a little more effort on the part of the branches and it will be realized. Along with this program of expansion is the plan for me to return to full-time work for the movement. As soon as the ground is solidly prepared I will take the step.

My last spell of professional work for the revolution lasted over ten straight years. I will never forget the comrades in Kansas City who made that possible at the beginning. Nothing is ever lost. If the organization of the Opposition in America began with me—as it did—and if our little movement is the hope of the future for America and a force for the inspiration of the entire international movement—as Trotsky said it is—then it is just to say that the revolution owes something to the group of militants who engaged me to devote my full time to the movement in Kansas City in 1919 and pledged themselves to provide for my family in case I was put in jail. It is true that the same people are also responsible for Browder and, consequently, for a certain degree of support to Stalinism, which is a disintegrating factor for the revolution. But that can be charged up as a mistake which could not be foreseen at the time; and I am doing all I can to reduce the harmful consequences of that mistake to the minimum. In this I hope for more and more cooperation from all those responsible. An extra contribution to pay for the publication of *Communism and Syndicalism* will be one way of atoning for their sin in the matter; the labor of writing the introduction will be a part payment on my penance.

I hope to see you before another year has gone by—if not in Kansas City on a tour, then at the national conference. If we have good luck, perhaps both. Warmest regards to all the comrades.

As always,

[Jim]

American syndicalism and problems of communism

Published February 15, 1931

The following was written as the introduction to Leon Trotsky's pamphlet *Communism and Syndicalism*. It was published in *The Militant* prior to the publication of the pamphlet. Trotsky's essay is reprinted in *Trade Unions in the Epoch of Imperialist Decay* (New York: Pathfinder Press, 1990).

The arguments brought forward in this pamphlet are devoted specifically to the problems of the labor movement of France, the classic land of syndicalism. But dealing as they do with such fundamental questions as the role of the revolutionary workers' party, the state, the bureaucracy in the labor movement, and trade union tactics in general, they have universal application. This is particularly true of America.

The historical development of the revolutionary labor movement in the United States has posed the question of syndicalism in its specific American form (the IWW) with special prominence. The task of assembling the revolutionary elements in the working class into a single body has been greatly hampered by theoretical confusion on the issues which the author illuminates in these pages. Some of these losses are irretrievable, for neither movements nor their participants can stand on one spot. Degeneration is the unfailing price for failure to develop and advance. In the period since the war, we have seen not a little of this degeneration in the camp of the class-conscious workers, and precisely for this reason.

Much can yet be gained, however, by a clarification of the questions. This pamphlet, so sharp and clear in its reasoning, so fortified in every line by the tested theory of Marxism, can justly be called a timely and significant contribution to this work of clarification. For that reason we believe it deserves the particular attention of the American revolutionaries.

In the decade before the World War, the proletarian revolt against the parliamentary reformism of the Socialist Party and the sectarian sterility and legalism of the Socialist Labor Party, found two main points of crystallization. One of these was the left wing in the SP. The other was the IWW. Both of these movements had elements of a revolutionary party. The task of Communism in America was to unite them into a single revolutionary organization. To the failure to understand this task, and consequently the failure to accomplish it to any appreciable degree, we owe not a little of the weakness of the American Communist movement.

A large share of the responsibility for this belongs to the party itself. It could not see the revolutionary implications of the IWW movement and did not know how to mature and assimilate them. But this fact does not absolve the revolutionary syndicalists from responsibility. They contributed more than a generous measure of prejudice and dogmatism to the issue. If the party walked blindfolded, the IWW militants, for the greater part, put stumbling blocks in its path.

In its essence the prewar IWW was a variant of French syndicalism. Its distinctive features were its centralized form of organization and its indifference toward the syndicalist theory of the role of the "militant minority."

In its struggle against parliamentary reformism and legalism, the IWW introduced and popularized a number of ideas and practices of a decidedly progressive and revolutionary character, ideas which retain their validity today. Its emphasis on "direct action" was an anticipation, incomplete it is true, of the Bolshevik principle which puts the mass action of the workers above parliamentary activity. Its advocacy of industrial as against craft unionism prepared the way for modern organization of the workers.

Another progressive feature was the emphasis the IWW placed on the unskilled—the most deprived and exploited, the most numerous, and potentially the most revolutionary section of the working class. From its first convention onward it declared solidarity with the Negro and welcomed him into its ranks. The members of the IWW went through a number of historic class battles and displayed unexampled militancy and sacrifice. Solidarity with all struggling workers everywhere and an unceasing emphasis on the revolutionary goal of the struggle, were central features in all of its activity.

These aspects of the IWW were its strong, progressive, and revolutionary side. That it represented, as did revolutionary syndicalism in general, a step forward from parliamentary socialism, was acknowledged by the theses of the Second Congress of the Communist International. That it occupied a place in the vanguard of the American working class was attested by the fierce persecution launched against it. Particularly during the war, the attacks of the government were concentrated on the IWW.

The significance of the wartime persecution consisted in the fact that it was led by the federal government, as distinguished from the customary local persecutions arising out of purely economic strikes. This persecution had a national, political character—an acknowledgment in itself that the IWW was not an ordinary trade union but a revolutionary, and therefore a political, force.

The weak side of the IWW movement, as of the syndicalist movement on an international scale, was its theoretical incompleteness. Because of its indifference to revolutionary theory, it did not and could not pose the fundamental questions of the revolution in their full implications and find the answer to them. As a consequence the movement contained a contradiction within itself. There cannot be a really revolutionary movement without a revolutionary theory, as Lenin said long ago.

The conditions of the war sharpened the class relations to an extraordinary degree and exposed this contradiction with shattering force. The negative attitude toward the state—the ostrich policy of "ignoring" the state—disarmed the movement when this same state, the "executive committee of the capitalist class" and "its special body of armed men," was hurled against it. The proletarian reaction against parliamentary reformism, developing into opposition to "politics" and indifference to political questions in general, left the IWW without a compass before the complicated problems of war, problems which in their very essence were political to the highest degree.

The justifiable hostility to bourgeois and reformist parties grew, as a result of loose thought, into an opposition to the concept even of a proletarian revolutionary party. This was the crowning theoretical error of the movement of American syndicalism, or industrialism. It prevented the conscious organization of the proletarian vanguard into a single uniform body able to work out the program of the revolution and strive for its application with united force.

The experiences of the war and the Russian revolution disclosed the shortcomings of the IWW, as well as those of the left wing in the SP. The problems elucidated in the living experience of the Russian revolution became, as they remain to this very day, the touchstone for revolutionary organizations throughout the world. The Marxist teachings on the state and on the role of the workers' party as the vanguard of the class, without which the class cannot raise itself to power, received brilliant and irrefutable confirmation in the Bolshevik revolution. Adjustment to these lessons taught by life could not be evaded.

In the failure to make this adjustment is written the whole story of the postwar degeneration of the IWW. The record of this entire period is a record of the steady and systematic displacement of the IWW from its old position in the vanguard of the struggle; of its transformation into the antipode of its former revolutionary self. As far as the upper and official stratum of the organization is concerned, the keynote of anticapitalism sounded in the best days has been transformed into anticommunism. Out of a militant body of revolutionaries they strive to make a reactionary sect. "No politics" and "no party"—these are the formulae under which this degeneration has proceeded. And together with them has gone the slogan of "no leaders"—that slogan of demagogues who themselves aspire to leadership without qualifications.

As has been remarked before, the leadership of the Communist Party contributed to the tragic failure to build the new Communist movement in part on the foundations of the militant IWW. Intellectualism, condescension, the control and command sickness, played here, as always, an evil role. It is necessary to understand this and to say it plainly.

But an understanding and acknowledgment of this fact cannot undo the past. We must start from where we are. If we bear in mind the mistakes of the past in order to avoid them in the future, something can yet be done of positive value for the revolution. It is not too late even now to make a place for those syndicalist workers who are imbued with a hatred of capitalism and the will to struggle against it—and there are many of them—under the communist banner. It is quite true that the official party leadership is unable to do this, as it is unable to solve any of the problems of communism. All the greater, therefore, is the responsibility of the Opposition.

In the ranks of the former members and sympathizers of the IWW, and to a lesser extent within the organization, are experienced militants who have not forgotten the old tradition, whose concepts do not begin and end with the phobia against communism. Their spirit is alien to the spirit of the Gahans and Sandgrens. They are sympathetic to the Russian revolution and to communism. Only, they have no faith in the party. Their skepticism about the American Communist Party has had a certain amount of justification, as we have always known. But, granting serious defects in the party, what is to be done about it?

As we see the thing—since we proceed from the point of view that a party cannot be dispensed with—one must either struggle to reform the party or, if he thinks it is hopeless, form a new one. We, the Opposition, have taken the former course. The great mass of the radical workers who have lost faith in the dogmas of the IWW without acquiring confidence in the party, have fallen into passivity. The postwar prosperity, which depressed the entire labor movement to a low point, facilitated this passive attitude. "Nothing is happening. Let us wait and see," became a sort of platform for many during this period. People who had been concerned with the problem of making a revolution turned to the problem of making a living while awaiting further developments.

But what now? The economic crisis is smashing all this calm routine. Class relations are being sharpened and all the conditions are being created for a revival of the militant labor movement. What path will this movement take and what part will be played by those who consider themselves to be revolutionaries? This question calls for an answer. In any case, it cannot be answered with a waiting, or passive attitude. A time of storm, and that is what is before us, above all is a time when nobody can stand aside; that is, nobody who doesn't want to play the part of a reactionary. Revolutionary health requires exercise.

In such a moment as the present one—which is a time of preparation for the great days impending—it is good to shake the advanced sections of the labor movement with discussion. And it is doubly fortunate if the discussion is precipitated by an objective Marxist analysis which, at the very beginning, lifts the fundamental questions to the high level of theoretical consideration. Such a service is rendered to the American movement by Comrade Trotsky in the collection of articles which this pamphlet comprises. We have no doubt that it will make its way and be the means of strengthening the current of communism in the resurgent labor movement of America. . . .

How the miners were defeated

Published March 1, 1931

The following article was published in *The Militant.*

The article of Gerry Allard in the last number of *The Militant* paints a picture of catastrophe in the Illinois mine fields, the old-time seat of labor militancy and the stronghold of communism. His remarks on the situation have a value, but that value, unfortunately, is a purely negative one. They are an excellent example of how not to solve the problems of communism. For that reason, and that only, they deserved publication in our paper.

The left wing for years was a power in southern Illinois, based on mass support of the militant miners. The "Save the Union" movement under left-wing leadership challenged all the fakers for supremacy. The coal towns and camps were dotted with thriving locals of the Communist Party—the surest sign of a conscious movement. But, as has been told before, and as Comrade Allard's article points out again, this whole movement has slipped away. The mighty revolt of the miners has been broken for the time being. The rebels have been corralled again by the labor fakers with the help of Howat and other so-called progressives.[69]

And with it there is "the complete collapse of the Party apparatus" and "the nonfunctioning of a single local union" of the left-wing miners' union. In the recent elections the party candidate for senator "polled only 24 votes" in Franklin County, where we once had "over 400 party members"! So says Comrade Allard, and he ought to know because he is on the spot. He cites these facts as "a clear cut example of weakness." Weakness indeed! Better to say an example of catastrophic defeat. And better yet to ask what are the real causes of it. Instead of that, Comrade Allard muddles the issue further by arguments over secondary questions.

For the results in the Illinois mine fields there is a chain of causes, one linked to another. Fishwick and Farrington, the direct agents of the mine owners, were sufficiently discredited. They could not recapture the revolting miners by themselves. For this they needed Howat and other pseudoradicals. This explains the necessary prominence, as decorations, of these elements in the Fishwick union.

But Howat and the other "progressives" in turn could not harness the miners again to the chariot of the mine bosses, driven by Fishwick and Farrington, by their own efforts alone. In order to accomplish this, they needed the disruption of the workers' vanguard—the party. The policy of Foster accomplished this for them from within. The policy, concocted to fit the exigencies of the spurious "third period," was criminally false. The course of expelling and blackguarding the most reliable communist militants was absolutely reactionary. By these means Stalinism disorganized the vanguard and prepared the way for the betrayal of the "progressives" and the victory of the reactionaries and the bosses. Foster helped Howat no less than Howat helped Fishwick and the mine owners.

The communist miners will not be able to take a single step forward out of this blind alley of defeat until they understand its whole chain of causes and their connection with each other. Comrade Allard bears a direct responsibility for the present sad state of affairs. At a critical moment of the fight he deserted the banner of the Opposition and capitulated to the centrist bureaucrats, who were organizing the defeat of the vanguard from within. It is quite necessary to expose the role of Howat. The function of "progressivism" as a come-on for reaction is graphically illustrated by the Illinois experience. Even the Opposition, which suffered very little from illusions on this score, can learn something from this example. But we cannot allow a discussion of this factor in the defeat to cover up an even more decisive one—the disarming of the workers' vanguard by the bureaucrats of centrism.

An emphasis on this side of the question is doubly necessary when Comrade Allard is speaking. This is the first and most important lesson of the Illinois defeat. When Comrade Allard begins to explain this to the miners we can begin to have some confidence that he will be able to serve the interests of the party and the working class again and to make good some of the great harm he has done. As long as he avoids this question he puts a chasm between himself and the principled policy of the Opposition. We are not in the least interested in self-humiliating "confessions" according to the Stalin ritual. We only want the questions put straight and the lessons clearly drawn.

Not the least of the crimes of Lovestone and Foster was

their poisoning the movement with diplomacy. This diplomacy, this muddling, hiding, twisting, and obscuring the principled questions, is not a proletarian but a bourgeois method. Let us have none of it in the Communist League.

Trifling with the Negro question

Published March 1, 1931

The following article was published in *The Militant.*

In its struggle against the workers' movement, capitalism plays upon all the dark sentiments of ignorance, prejudice, and superstition. This is seen daily and hourly in its endeavors to divide the workers and oppressed people along national, racial, and religious lines. The very air we breathe is saturated with these prejudices, which arise from class society like foul odors from decaying matter. The revolutionary struggle for the solidarity of labor is also a struggle for knowledge and light on these questions.

These problems have a particular importance and acuteness in America, where the proletariat, enslaved by bourgeois ideology, is inflamed against the foreigner, the Jew, and the Negro. Communism cannot be other than the mortal enemy of these devastating prejudices, and the Communist Party is charged with an irreconcilable struggle against them. In no small degree, the party of the proletariat is to be judged by the vigor, and also by the wisdom, with which it conducts this struggle. And it is self-evident that the Negro question takes first place within it. Communist ideas, communist teaching and practice must break down the artificial wall which bourgeois prejudice has reared between the races; the communists must be the heralds of a genuine solidarity between the exploited workers of the white race and the doubly exploited Negroes.

This is no question to be played with. Its seriousness and its difficulty are enormous. The deep-seated prejudices of the white workers will not be extirpated by force or terror any more than the justified suspicions of the Negroes will be removed by cajolery. In this field, education takes the first place—patient, unceasing, and systematic explanation, combined with a genuine policy of equality in practice. Such a policy must be as free from discrimination on the one hand as it is free from flattery and demagogy on the other. Only along this path will real progress be recorded.

During their career as leaders of the party, Lovestone, Minor, and Company did their best to spoil this work, as they did others. For discrimination against Negroes—the instinctive attitude of all petty-bourgeois elements, but an attitude formally impossible in the name of communism—they substituted an unscrupulous demagogy, and a policy of flattery, condescension, and bribery of Negro intellectuals and careerists on the make. By this they attracted not a few outright scoundrels and adventurers while they repelled the self-reliant type of proletarian militants of the Negro race—the type which is offended, and justly so, no less by discrimination than by its twin, condescension. Thereby the Lovestoneites arrested the real work among the Negroes and transformed the whole question into a factional football.

The Foster leaders, who have set for themselves the

historic task of matching the Lovestone regime in unworthy demagogy and combining it with a stupidity all their own, are now having their fling at the Negro question—and at the Negro. They seem to labor always under a psychological fixation that their time is short and that what they do must be done quickly. The eradication of racial antagonisms, like the creation of a new trade union movement, is a small task for these high-pressure people; a task to be accomplished between plenums, by command. Prejudice against the Negro, that ugly poison which has been injected into the veins of the white workers, is to be removed at one stroke.

The *Daily Worker* of February 24 features the announcement of this major operation. Comrade Yokinen, a member of the party in Harlem, is accused of manifesting a prejudicial attitude toward Negro workers. One might think—if this is really the case and not a frame-up as we knew of in the days of the Lovestone leadership—that the incident could be made the occasion for an education of the party on the concrete case. Education, however, particularly on such a question, requires a calm atmosphere; an atmosphere free from demagogy, hypocrisy, and incitement; an atmosphere created by teachers of the proletariat, not by terrorizers.

But such methods are alien to the blustering vulgarians who feel the need to shout down their own prejudices of yesterday. They are going to summon the offending comrade to a mass trial! "This trial," they announce, "must be packed with Negro and white workers." Workers' organizations are asked to send delegations to the sport. The mass trial, they say further, "will be the forerunner of similar trials all over the country." And all this is to be done "so that the Negro workers will know that the Communist Party is in deadly earnest in its fight for the Negro masses."[70] Otherwise they would not know.

Just a moment, gentlemen! Aren't you insulting the intelligence of the Negro masses just a little? Aren't you stultifying the party with this stupid campaign of terror? If you have been educating the party properly, how does it happen that race prejudice among party members is manifested "all over the country"? For the Negro masses, racial persecution is a bitter actuality that confronts them every moment of their lives. They have learned to recognize all forms of this reactionary poison, including that form of so-called freedom from it which protests too much. Take care, triflers, lest your indecent demagogy becomes a boomerang for the party. Take care lest the Negro masses ask: If your own conscience is clear, why do you shout so loud?

For the program of expansion

Published March 1, 1931

The following article was published in *The Militant*.

Taking everything into consideration, the American section of the Opposition gave a good account of itself in the two years that have gone by since its expulsion from the party. The achievements of those two years—modest as they are when measured on the gigantic scale of the proletarian revolution—will undoubtedly have a place of honor in the history of American communism. Their significance consists in the fact that they represent a beginning. And beginnings always have a historic importance. Our militant fight during these two years has signified the appearance of a countercurrent against the stream of retrogression in the Communist movement of America; a small one, but a real one.

Those who have contributed in any way to this historic work may well take pride in it. But the satisfaction which we justly feel with the accomplishments of the first two years does not give us the right to view them as a completed task. Their importance, as has been said before, is the importance of a beginning. Their real vindication will come only if we remember that, if we build on our accomplishments and multiply them in the coming months.

The pioneer work has accumulated for the Opposition some resources in the form of supporters, sympathizers, and experiences. This capital, as it may be called, justifies a program of expansion for the coming year. We have grounds to plan for a leap forward in 1931; and if we work wisely and harmoniously, the plan will surely be realized in life. Such is the considered opinion of the National Committee, as expressed in the resolution adopted at a recent meeting and published in *The Militant* of February 15.

On the one side the resolution asks for a special fund of $2,000, of which the New York branch has already pledged to raise one-half. On the other side, with this special fund, the National Committee will undertake to guarantee the holding of our national conference; to establish a publishing concern which will expand and systematize our publishing activities; to return *The Militant* to weekly publication; to found a theoretical magazine; to strengthen the staff of the national organization and provide for a field organizer; to organize at least two national lecture tours; and to bring out the international bulletin in English regularly. These are all tasks which cannot be postponed.

To many people this argument may appear, at first glance, as an impossible bargain. But it isn't so, as we will prove when the fund is provided. Every item on the side charged to the responsibility of the National Committee will be made good. The items in the program do not stand separately. They dovetail into each other, and the realization of one will help the realization of the others.

No one should dismiss this resolution lightly as a mere

gesture made in a fit of temporary enthusiasm. We have never been inclined to leap over the barriers of circumstance and to promise the unattainable; and the experiences of the Opposition struggle have not been calculated to nurture such a tendency. The difficulties of the fight and the hard blows we took have beaten a sterner realism into our heads. The resolution of the National Committee is not a mere paper resolution. It is a realistic plan of action which can be fulfilled in every point. And, unless we sadly miscalculate the actual possibilities and the spirit of our movement, it will be realized without imposing an undue strain on the members and sympathizers of the Communist League.

For some months now, it has been evident that the Communist League has been turning the corner and overcoming the slump which took place in our activity after the first big push. For a time we suffered from a certain stagnation, which was not without internal difficulties and symptoms of crisis in the organization. The weight of objective circumstances pressed down upon us, and our movement seemed to progress at a snail's pace. In such conditions, frictions are always accentuated, and difficulties assume abnormal proportions. Isolation puts endurance to the test. Only those groups which have a firm base in principle, which are bound together by uniform conceptions, can hold out against it.

It is thanks to the vitality of our principles in the first place, and to the habit of collective work which we brought with us from the struggles of the past, that we were able to emerge from this stagnant interlude without fatal convulsions and splits. Other sections of the International Left Opposition have not been so fortunate, as we know, and for reasons inherent in the concrete conditions which surround them. Nor are we ensured against such convulsions for the future. But with all that, it is quite manifest that the elements of cohesion are uppermost now in the organization; that we are definitely on the upward grade. Our last plenum marked the beginning of this turn. The period which has intervened since that time has registered some advances, and most of all it has prepared the ground for others.

The strengthening of the forces engaged in the national direction of the league, and the improvement of its functioning generally, has already shown positive results. As was to be expected, the New York branch, which works in the most intimate contact with the National Committee, reflects the improved situation first. The activities of the New York branch have been multiplied at least fourfold in the past six months, and its communist character has been strengthened on all sides. If the fact that Weisbord's pitiful maneuvers could cause a flurry in the branch was evidence of a remnant of its earlier weakness, the vigorous and emphatic manner in which it repulsed them when the issue became fairly joined was a sign of its progress toward political stability.

The branch consists in large part of comrades who are new in the movement. They have to assimilate the ABCs of communism at the same time that they wage a fight over the complicated problems involved in the work of the Opposition. This presents difficulties, but they are not insurmountable. Ignorance is fatal only for those who are unwilling to learn.

One of the first things revolutionaries must learn, if they do not want to disgrace the name, is that speculation over the great tasks of the future is not sufficient. It is necessary to understand the task of the moment, the accomplishment of which will lead us a step nearer to the bigger ones of tomorrow, and to attack it resolutely. Not to pass a resolution on it and then forget it; but to pass a resolution and mean it, and do it. In this respect we have already seen great progress in the New York branch in the past six months. And this record gives us the confidence that the promise of the branch to raise one-half of the $2,000 fund needed for the program of expansion will be fulfilled to the letter.

From the National Committee and the New York branch, the spirit of accomplishment will spread to the other branches. The organization nationally will soon begin to gird itself for another advance. Everything argues for this confidence. The part assigned to the various branches to make this advance possible is simple, and comparatively easy. The theory that the members of the Communist League have been overloaded with responsibilities and duties is absurd. Up to now only a handful have really exerted themselves in a manner worthy of Bolshevik-Leninists, and nobody has been hurt. The program outlined in the resolution of the National Committee only calls on the membership to move one step faster. The real march is still to come.

The second national conference, already definitely scheduled for the summer, will meet—if we are not greatly mistaken—under the sign of a tightening up of the organization all along the line. "Platonic" members, who have fallen into the habit of wearing the proud badge of the Opposition without doing anything to deserve it, will be called to order. The conference should tell everybody that enrollment in the Opposition means not a release from party obligations but the assumption of double ones. The Opposition has assumed a great historic task, which cannot be trifled with. What we want and what we must have is a body of militants for whom the revolution is the most serious concern in life; for whom the demands of the movement stand first and above everything.

The Communist League is not yet such an organization and it cannot become such overnight. It will be the task of the conference to say resolutely that we are going to move in that direction. The program of expansion adopted by the National Committee is for the first step only. But it is the next step, and therefore the most important at the moment. Let us concentrate on this campaign and finish it before the conference. Bigger things will follow.

Lenin and the 'Iskra' period

Published March 15, 1931

The following book review of vol. IV of *The Collected Works of Lenin: The Iskra Period, Book 1* (New York: International Publishers, 1931) was published in *The Militant.*

Thirteen years after the Russian revolution and seven years after Lenin's death, a serious beginning is made with the publication of his collected works in English at a price workers can afford. Such unpardonable tardiness has, of course, its own significance, which need not be dealt with here. It is most important now to report that four volumes comprising six books have recently been published in the popular-priced edition. American militants thus have access now to at least a good part of this long-buried treasure. For this we must be grateful. The first book of volume IV, devoted to the early *Iskra* period, can only be a source of deep satisfaction to one who has the opportunity to read it.

What the incomparable leader wrote in this book, which covers a part of the formative period of the Bolshevik Party

(1900–1902), has the most vital import for the American Oppositionists, who follow in his path and who stand, as Lenin and his co-workers stood then, before the task of assembling and training the nucleus of the future party of proletarian struggle and victory. No duty is more pressing than the conscientious study of these volumes; no task will be more quickly and abundantly compensated. The words of Lenin himself, in contradistinction to the interpretations of those who speak in his name, reveal the indissoluble unity of the ideas of the International Opposition with the ideas of Lenin, and reinforce conviction in them.

"Our teaching," said Engels, "is no dogma but a manual of action." And no less can be said of the teaching of Lenin, who understood the doctrines of Marx and Engels in this sense and so applied them. The study of his works therefore cannot be a mere exercise in historical research. His writings are to be conceived rather as textbooks on the strategy of the proletarian revolution. They dishonor and distort Lenin who reduce his teachings to a system of lifeless formulae. The thing is to grasp their living essence, and its application to our own time and place. In other words, to study his writings not as pedants but as revolutionaries.

Iskra (The Spark), as most of our readers know, was the paper founded by Lenin in 1900. One of the most interesting documents in the volume under review is "Declaration by the Editorial Board of *Iskra*," which appeared in its first issue and outlined the ideas and aims of the editors. *Iskra* made its first appearance at a time of rise in working-class activity, when the spontaneous labor movement was running ahead of its conscious political organization. The ideas of economism—that is, of limiting the political work of the Social Democrats—were being propagated by an influential group of leaders. The Social Democratic movement of the time consisted of loosely connected circles, and was lacking in a uniform program and cohesive organization. Lenin dedicated *Iskra* to the task of uniting the political movement and overcoming the opportunist doctrines of economism.

The declaration declared war on revisionism, economism, and the "effort to push into the background the task of forming a revolutionary party to lead the struggle at the head of the whole people." Thus from the very beginning Lenin brought revolutionary theory into the foreground. "Narrow practicality," he wrote in the first draft of the declaration, "detached from the theoretical conception of the movement as a whole may destroy the contact between Socialism and the revolutionary movement in Russia on the one hand, and the spontaneous labor movement on the other." These words have a direct and immediate import today, especially for those communists immersed in trade union work who tend to lose themselves in details. The conception of the party as the highest form of proletarian organization—its unifying and directing force—was always uppermost in Lenin's thought as it is unfolded on the pages of this book.

The American Communist movement, including all of its factions, represents far less a political force than did the Social Democratic movement of Russia during the early *Iskra* period. And in view of its disintegration into factions, it cannot justly be said that it is more united. If the Social Democrats of Russia at the time constituted a disunited propaganda body, no more can be said for our present movement. How then does our party regime, with its regimentation of thought and its barracks discipline, compare with Lenin's appraisal of the situation and the tasks? In the declaration Lenin poses the question of uniting the movement. Foster, if we are not mistaken, also stands for unity—only the methods are somewhat different.

Lenin proposed a free discussion in the columns of the two journals (*Iskra* and *Zarya*). "They must reflect," he wrote, "all shades of opinion, all local peculiarities, and all the various political methods." His plan was to unite the movement through a free ideological struggle in which polemics would not be suppressed but rather encouraged.

He wrote: "Open polemics, conducted in the sight and hearing of all Russian Social Democrats and class-conscious workers, are necessary and desirable in order to explain the profoundness of the differences that exist, in order that disputed questions may be discussed from all angles, to combat the extremes into which representatives of the revolutionary movement invariably fall. *Indeed, we regard one of the drawbacks of the present-day movement to be the absence of open polemics between avowedly differing views, an effort to conceal the differences that exist over extremely fundamental questions"* (our emphasis). One has only to read these lines to comprehend the chasm which separates the real Lenin from the epigones.

And that is not to say that Lenin had in mind a discussion from which no conclusions would be drawn. His aim was to draw clearly the lines of demarcation. The publication was not to be merely a "store-house for various views. On the contrary, we shall conduct it along the lines of a strictly defined tendency. This tendency can be expressed by the word *Marxism."* Unity, said the heretic of 1900, "cannot be brought about by simply giving orders." For that idea alone he would be expelled in 1931.

Lenin was an orthodox Marxist. This fact leaps out from every page of his writings. They are profoundly wrong, therefore, who attempt to set Lenin up as a theoretician beside Marx, that is, in opposition to Marx. Lenin's own writings refute this idea. Bolshevism came into being, as he himself said in "Left Sickness," on the granite foundations of Marxian theory. A study of Lenin's works is therefore at the same time a study of Marxism.

If Engels was the greatest popularizer of Marx's doctrines in a general sense, then Lenin was undoubtedly the greatest popularizer of the same doctrines in a special and particular sense. Lenin's method was primarily the method of polemic and of concrete application. Through Lenin the word of Marx was illustrated in the deed. It was Trotsky who once remarked that the best road to Marx was through Lenin. In this book, which from first to last is a demonstration of Marxist truth in the heat of polemical battles, one can see a remarkable confirmation of this thought.

This is shown with singular clarity in the pamphlet *The Agrarian Question and the Critics of Marx,* which makes up a full third of the first of the two books devoted to the *Iskra* period. Here some of the most difficult problems of Marxism are elucidated with an ABC simplicity. Moreover, the pamphlet demonstrates the painstaking and thorough research with which the destined leader of the Russian revolution had informed himself for this conflict with the "critics." Thereby he was not only able to rout the "law of diminishing returns" on theoretical grounds alone. This "law" brought forward by the "critics" in support of the "superiority" of small-scale farming, was also demolished in Lenin's pamphlet by a detailed analysis of statistics showing the actual trend of the development of agriculture in the opposite direction.

How significant this polemic was for the Russian revolution can be estimated, for example, by citing a couple of well-known historic facts. Lenin, who defended Marxism on the agrarian question, stood, in the decisive hour, at the head of the victorious proletariat; Chernov, against whom the polemic was directed, didn't recognize the revolution when it arrived and found himself on the other side of the barricades with his Social Revolutionary Party. It is no secret that American revolutionaries have yet to undertake a serious study and application of Marxism on the agrarian question. The necessary study can very well begin with Lenin's pamphlet referred to here.

Lenin was an all-sided leader unique in all history. Nothing escaped him or was beyond his attention. The party he created, for which history has no comparable example, bears testimony to the work of a genius in whom theory and practice, in all their ramifications, were united.

Take the single question of the role of leaders, and the collective work of the group of leaders—which he truly described as an art, and an art, we may say parenthetically, which is all too little known—and see with what attentiveness he studied the problem, and solved it in advance. Lenin, the theorist and practical leader in one, knew what pedants and formalists will never know—that such a question as the personal relations between leaders can often play an enormous, even if not a finally decisive role. Did he not speak in his last testament to the party of the rudeness of Stalin and "the relations between Stalin and Trotsky" as constituting "a big half of the danger of that split" he wanted to prevent? In direct connection with this danger of split he made his proposal to remove Stalin from the post of party secretary.

And in this book there is a very illuminating article which bears the title "How the Spark Was Nearly Extinguished." Therein he shows how the newspaper enterprise with its great political aims was once on the point of disruption because of the arbitrary conduct of Plekhanov and "the spoiled *personal* relations" which ensued from it. Leaders who master the art of working together greatly enhance thereby their usefulness to the revolution.

Not the least of the qualities of Lenin's matchless genius was his unfailing ability to combine realism with farsighted vision. He knew what he wanted and how to get it. And he also *knew the next step.* That is a remarkable combination, and a rare one. Trotsky, in his autobiography, speaks of a Menshevik, Martov, who, in revolutionary situations, had thoughts for all questions "except the all-important question: What to do next?" And of Lenin he remarked that in all his preoccupations with matters great and small, the goal was never absent from his thought. But together with that, as has been said, he concentrated on the task of the moment.

He used the expression about grasping "the next link in the chain" so often that it has become a truism for the movement, repeated often enough, unfortunately, by people who could not grasp it as surely as Lenin did. If one could sum up the impression received from this first book of writings during the *Iskra* period in a word, it would be to say: Lenin gives here a series of object lessons in the art of keeping sight of the goal and knowing what to do next in the struggle toward the goal.

This is the essential quality of the notable article reprinted from the fourth number of *Iskra,* which appeared in May 1901, called "Where to Begin." There he outlined a system and plan of practical activity which would be consonant with the permanent interests of the movement and lead in the direction of its final aims. This article stirred up a great commotion throughout the ranks of the Russian Social Democrats and—in an extended form—became the basis upon which the future nucleus of the Bolshevik faction was concentrated. The scattered and disunited character of the movement, the kind of an organization needed, and the first steps toward its creation—these were the questions he put and answered in "Where to Begin."

Limits of the united front

Published April 1, 1931

The following article was published in *The Militant.*

Two years ago when the Muste movement began to take shape in the Conference for Progressive Labor Action we devoted a number of articles to the question of the "progressives" and the Communists in *The Militant.* At that time the Lovestone right wing held the leadership of the party, and—strange as it may seem in the light of later developments—they were repudiating any idea of a united front. The Opposition waged a polemical battle against the official position. We analyzed the new progressive movement from a different standpoint and drew different tactical conclusions.

In our platform and in several special articles and editorials we advocated the policy of the united front toward the new movement. In doing so, we emphasized the fact that the movement of "progressivism" had a *two-sided* character. On the one side, we said, it reflected "radicalization of the workers growing within the old unions as well as in the ranks of the unorganized masses." On the other side we defined the role of the leaders of the movement as follows: "Their role, objectively speaking, is to express this radicalization in words, to harness it in action, and to head it off from any real collision with the capitalists and the AFL machine." We said: "The new movement is a challenge to the Communists for the leadership of the coming fights" and we advocated the tactic of the united front as the weapon of the Communists. (Quotation from *The Militant,* March 1, 1929.)

The events of the past two years, and especially the more recent developments, have revived interest in this dispute and, incidentally, have confirmed the opinion we expressed in the above-mentioned article that the question would remain a live one and take on even greater importance. In our opinion the policy of the Opposition has stood up and could be restated now as the correct line for the communists. The emphasis, however, must now be shifted to another phase of the question, because the positions of the factions have radically changed.

The Foster faction is on the verge of a big swing to the right. The Lovestone faction has already made the swing. It is no longer necessary to explain to the right wing that the communists must not reject the idea of a united front under certain conditions with reformists, including the so-called progressives. They are shouting so loud now for a united front at any price that they recall the Russian proverb which Lenin quoted to people who contradicted themselves: "Don't spit in the well—you may want to drink out of it."

No, it is necessary now to discuss the problem from another angle. Two years ago the weight of argument had to be placed on the tactic of the united front against people who were opposing it in principle. Now we must emphasize *the conditions* and *the limits* of the united front. This applies to the right wing already today; and to the Fosterites—who are swinging to the right—it will be necessary tomorrow.

There is nothing in the conduct of the pseudoprogressives for the past two years to merit any more confidence than we expressed in our first analysis of their movement. On the contrary, the estimate of them should be written in harsher words of condemnation. And this applies to the entire progressive leadership *without any exceptions*. Every single one of them, from Muste to Howat, has played the contemptible role of decoy for the reactionaries. The latest and most flagrant instance is the shameful betrayal of the Illinois miners, a betrayal made possible by the so-called progressives who rallied the insurgent miners and led them back into the reactionary camp.

There is good reason to think that the present crisis is preparing a much wider field for the exploration of the progressives and thereby will magnify the problem of the Communist attitude.

The staggering burdens of the crisis are being loaded onto the shoulders of the workers. Millions have been torn away from their fancied security and hurled into the ranks of the unemployed. Millions of others are suffering drastic reductions of their income by wage cuts and part-time employment. A wholesale lowering of the workers' living standard is being effected. What result can this have on the minds of the workers?

As we see it, the main effect will be to shatter the illusions which have been the greatest barrier against the organization of a militant class movement. The discontent of the masses will increase by leaps and bounds *and will seek for radical expression*. And this will not be confined to the period of the crisis. It is perhaps more reasonable to calculate that the crisis represents primarily a period of mental preparation of the workers for the great struggles which will really get under way as the cycle turns toward economic revival.

If phrasemongering "left" demagogues have proved to be a disrupting force and a shield of reaction in the first tentative manifestations of labor's insurgency, then in the coming period they will confront the militant labor movement as the greatest menace. How to cope with this menace, how to defeat the attempt to derail the workers' revolt with the empty phrases of fake radicalism, how to strengthen the revolutionists as against the reformists—this is the crux of the problem.

One way to ensure defeat is to adopt the ostrich policy of ultraleft adventurism, which the official party has pursued over a period of two years. The complete bankruptcy of these tactics has already been demonstrated. But an even more certain guarantee of failure would be the attitude toward the progressive reformists recommended and demonstrated by the Lovestone right wing—that is, of *fusion* with Muste and Company. The crudest expression of this policy is represented by Bert Miller, who has gone over, bag and baggage, to the CPLA and is advertising it as the rallying center for the left wing.

For *joining* the Muste organization, he and his group have been expelled from the Lovestone faction, but at bottom their positions are identical. The conflict between them is more formal than real. *Revolutionary Age* advocates a *bloc* with the CPLA "for the development of a progressive, a leftward movement in the trade unions." And in doing so it *puts no conditions to the progressives,* it does not criticize and expose their actual role and warn the workers not to trust them. On the contrary it deliberately misleads the workers into the belief that the division of labor between right and left in the CPLA is a conflict in principle, and it holds out the illusion of "a union of the left forces in the CPLA with the Communists in the building up of a left-wing movement in the trade unions." (See Gitlow's article in the February 14 issue.)

Such a policy would deceive and disarm the left-wing workers. If Muste and other so-called lefts can be expected to make "a union" with the Communists, why have they organized the CPLA as a union with the reactionaries against the Communists? Why did they support Fishwick and through him Lewis against the left wing? Why did they support McMahon in the textile field against the National Textile Workers Union? Why did they expel Calhoun, the lone Communist or Communist sympathizer, from the faculty of Brookwood College? Was all of this—and much more of the same which could be mentioned—a preparation for "a union" with the Communists—an evidence of "good faith," so to speak? What is the difference between *joining* the CPLA while keeping silent about these damning facts, and *making a bloc* with it while keeping just as silent? There is no serious difference.

At the best it is the most naive conception of politics to represent, as Gitlow does in his article, that a united front between the Communists and the CPLA of itself "will hasten the schism between the reactionaries and progressives, the Left and the Right, in the C.P.L.A." Why should it? It is much more apt to hasten the "schism" between those who make such a united front and the standpoint of communism. For this inference we already have the fate of Miller and his group to show. For the other inference there is nothing to show. And there can be nothing.

The united front, as Lenin taught it, is a means of mobilizing the masses and leading them in the direction of the revolution. It is not a "partnership" with reformists, but a form of struggle against them. It does not mean to rely on them but to distrust them. Its value arises from the form in which it is proposed more than in actual agreements, and it is more *frequently* realized in that way, although agreements can and should be made at times. On this last point the "third period" strategy—which rejects all agreements with reformists—is profoundly false and reduces the whole conception of the united front to a meaningless caricature.

From this point of view we think the Communists should *attack* the "progressive" menace to the awakening labor movement with the proposal of a united front on the concrete questions of the day. This proposal should be made openly and should contain certain *stipulations* and *demands* to be complied with before the agreement and as a *condition for the agreement.* One of these conditions—since we don't take anything on credit—should be the immediate "schism" with all elements tied to the reactionary bureaucracy of the AFL and the Black Hundreds in the needle trades, the *Jewish Daily Forward,* etc.

In making such a proposal for a united front the Communists should tell the workers plainly that the progressives are not to be trusted and that a revolutionary program is the only program from which a real fighting policy in the daily struggle can flow. If the pressure of the workers for radical action is strong enough to compel the pseudo-progressive leaders, or a section of them, to meet our conditions, we will make the agreement and go with them into a common struggle.

In the course of the struggle, we, of course, will maintain our separate organization, drive them forward at every step, and criticize every vacillation and weakness they manifest. We will conceive of it all the time as a temporary agreement, which we are ready to break at any moment they betray their promises.

We know—as worldwide experience has demonstrated to the hilt—that most of them will betray. But if we have conducted ourselves properly from the start, allowed ourselves no illusions, and created no illusions among the workers, the betrayal will weaken them and strengthen the party. Some of the leaders, and the majority of the workers, who started as progressives, will be swept along with us into the stream of communism. Most of the present leaders of the Communist Party came through this door, and they should be the last to deny that others can do the same.

The Lovestone opportunists regard the united-front tactic as something that cannot be applied without an actual agreement of some kind with the reformists. That is why their principal activity consists in sniffing around the back door of some faker or other offering "blocs" which cost the fakers nothing. Witness the deal with Levy (read: Sigman) in the ILGWU. To mention little things with big ones, Weisbord also offered to "educate" us along this line.

That conception is wrong. It derives from Brandler, not from Lenin. The validity of the united-front tactic does not at all depend upon formal agreements with reformists. It depends only on such a formulation of the demands and conditions that they are comprehensible to the workers as the necessary basis of struggle for their burning demands. The question whether the reformists accept the conditions does not depend on their wishes. They are weathercocks. The decisive factor is the pressure of the masses. From this it follows that the most important aspect of the united-front tactic is not "negotiations" but widespread and intelligently conducted agitation.

Under such circumstances the refusal of the reformists

to agree to our proposals only serves to unmask them and to rob their demagogy of its power to influence the workers. On the other hand it provides the basis to extend and give point to our work among the masses for the practical program embodied in our united-front proposals. We still appear before the workers as the advocates of the united front, and the result, no less than in the case of a formal agreement, is to widen the mass movement and strengthen the influence of the Communists within it. And that is the real purpose, and the justification, of the policy of the united front.

What about Morgenstern and Goodman?

Published May 15, 1931

The following article was published in *The Militant.*

What are the officials of the party and the ILD going to do about the defense of Morgenstern and Goodman, the two members of the Communist League who are facing trial on charges of sedition in Philadelphia? Are they going to support them in the spirit of class solidarity and arouse the workers about the case, or are they going to continue to sabotage and betray these militants out of factional spite, as they have been doing up till now? We intend to have an answer to these questions, and every honest, class-conscious worker will want an answer too.

Our readers already know about the case. It is part of a general attack against the radical labor movement in Pennsylvania. The two comrades were arrested for distributing the unemployment leaflet of the Communist League, and the statement in the leaflet that "the solution of the unemployment problem can be found only in the proletarian revolution" was held to be seditious by the grand jury which brought in the indictment. A number of Communists have already been convicted under this law. Only a few weeks ago Comrade Lawrence, a party member, was convicted and sentenced. Indictments are pending against several others.

The problem is a very serious one. It involves the legality of the revolutionary labor movement in Pennsylvania and the liberty of the most active militants. A real move to arouse the workers and form a united front of class defense is needed. The ILD has the duty of organizing this fight, but it is not being done. On the contrary, the bureaucrats are playing a game of the most treacherous sabotage.

At first they refused to do anything for Morgenstern and Goodman, and the latter were compelled to get their own lawyers in the first proceedings and to raise their own bail. Up to the present date the party press has suppressed all news of the case. The ILD publicity ignores them. On top of that the united-front conference of the ILD, with Engdahl present, refused to seat the delegates of the Communist League a few days after their indictment. Retreating from this shameful position under a storm of protest from workers in the ranks of the ILD, they are now trying to cover themselves up with a promise of "legal defense" at the trial.

This is not enough! Morgenstern and Goodman are revolutionists, and they do not rely on lawyers to get them "justice" in the courts of the class enemy. We want a mass movement of working-class protest to defend them. We want a public mass meeting to inform the workers what is going on and what it means. We want a broad united-front conference of workers' organizations to launch a militant campaign against the sedition law and for the defense of all its victims. We want publicity about the case, not a conspiracy of silence worthy only of agents of the prosecution.

You are playing with fire, bureaucrats! The revolutionary workers have never yet turned their backs on class-war prisoners because of their political views. If you continue to do it, they will turn their backs on you. If the class defense of Morgenstern and Goodman cannot be organized with your help, it will be organized without you and against you!

Fighting for free speech

Published May 15, 1931

The following article was published in *The Militant*.

Minneapolis, where the Communist League branch comprises a majority of the experienced communist workers—and thereby has the possibility of applying our policy independently in the class struggle—is the present scene of a very interesting demonstration of revolutionary tactics. The city government there has been seized by a fit of red hysteria and for some time has been prohibiting and breaking up all kinds of radical meetings. The gatherings of the official party fell under this ban and several meetings of the Communist League shared the same fate, since the chief of police is an ignorant man and does not know that the real purpose of Dunne and Skoglund is to support the war against the Soviet Union.

Both wings of the communist movement were thus reduced to a virtual state of illegality, at least in regard to the right of public assemblage. Their contrasting reactions to the situation can afford a fruitful subject of discussion. The same state of affairs prevails in other places, and as the class struggle grows more acute, there will be many more.

The tactics of the Stalinists—led by the peerless Karl Reeve, who was sent to Minneapolis by his factional opponents to fight the Trotskyites and be destroyed by them—are characteristic. Imbued with the ideology of the "third period," which is only one step removed from undergroundism in principle, they have virtually accepted the situation as a proof that the capitalists are against the workers and that the city officials are tools of the capitalists. Thus they prove that there is no free speech, which they consider a point in their favor. The chief of police, at the same time, thinks it is a point in his favor. So both are satisfied—and there are no public meetings of the party.

The Left Oppositionists have a different idea. They think free speech—and democratic rights in general—have a real value for the workers' movement and should not be surrendered lightly. In view of the fact that the capitalist government professes to guarantee these rights, and that masses of workers and other citizens who are in no way connected with the communists ardently believe in them, they decided to test the issue in a fight for free speech. To that unique idea they added another: that a wide movement should be set into motion on this issue.

Their appeal to the Stalinists for joint action to initiate the fight failing, they are proceeding to the organization of a broad free speech conference which will draw the trade unions and other organizations into the fight. By this means they aim to shift the position from a fight of the city administration against the communists to a fight of the labor movement, or a large section of it—including the communists—against the illegal usurpations of the police.

For our part, we are in complete agreement with the

course adopted by the Minneapolis branch of the Communist League. It has a double importance: For the restoration of civil rights in Minneapolis and contact with a wider circle of workers in the struggle for it; and as an example—and a badly needed one—to the whole American movement of communism. The communists—a small minority—must fight to be heard. Democratic rights are of the utmost importance to the workers in their struggle for organization. We ought to inscribe them on our banner and call the workers to a joint struggle with us to defend them. The fight itself has an importance hardly less than the object, so long as it is conducted without illusions.

Stalinism has brought devastation into every phase of revolutionary ideas, methods, and practices. Not the least of this has resulted from its false approach to the question of free speech and the discredit it has brought to the idea by its own hooligan practices. It is high time to turn the helm. The Minneapolis example is a good beginning.

What is socialism?

Published June 1, 1931

The following article was published in *The Militant*.

The doctrine of socialism in one country has been the platform of a revisionist war against Marxism since its promulgation in 1924. So far is socialism in one country from the conceptions of the great teachers, that its exponents had to begin with a different definition of the word, a definition which robs socialism of the contents which the great teachers prescribed and makes fun of the revolutionary struggle to attain that goal. Stalin's well-known declaration that the Russian workers under the NEP had already attained "nine-tenths of Socialism" is a monstrous example of this perversion of ideas. And now we encounter the same brand of "socialism" in the Stalinist press of America.

The *Daily Worker* of May 16 calls for "the establishment of a socialist society under a Workers' and Farmers' Government!" Since this astounding slogan appears in the leading editorial, is it not in place to ask these people to explain what they mean by socialism? If the *Communist Manifesto* is not out of date, socialism means the abolition of classes. And that in turn—according to Marx and Engels—signifies the disappearance of the political state, which is conceivable only as a class instrument, "the organized power of one class for oppressing another." How, then, is it possible to speak of a workers' and farmers' *government* in a socialist society? Such an idea can establish kinship with reformist advocates of state socialism, but it has nothing in common with Marxism.

Perhaps it may be explained that the editorial meant to speak not of socialist society but of the transition period to it. But socialism and the dictatorship of the proletariat are entirely different social orders and cannot be used interchangeably by anyone who understands the difference between them. The workers' state is only a stage on the road to socialism; it cannot be represented as the goal of the struggle.

To make confusion worse confounded, in the characteristic manner of Stalinist revisionism, the editorial demands socialism "under a Workers' and Farmers' Government"! But socialism—again according to Marx and Engels—will abolish "the distinction between town and country." Agriculture will be conducted by cooperative social labor. The petty-bourgeois basis of agriculture will be abolished—and with it the farmers as a class (petty bourgeois)—*before* we reach the socialist society and as a *prerequisite* for it. How, then, can we have a socialist society under a workers' and *farmers'* government?

In the literature of Marxism such formulae are nowhere to be found. They belong exclusively to the school of Stalin.

The struggle against 'left' reformism

Published June 1, 1931

The following article was published in *The Militant.*

The Conference for Progressive Labor Action, which has already condemned itself forever by its bootlicking subservience to the labor reactionaries, has begun to feel the new winds blowing in the labor movement and is beginning to dress for the occasion. The May number of *Labor Age,* the official organ of the CPLA, comes out with a red cover and a startling line of radical talk. In one issue we see a demand for the defense of the Soviet Union, a denunciation of "Karl Kautsky sham Socialism," an appeal for "the building of industrial unions with a revolutionary outlook and aim," and similar words, which cost nothing and mean less as a criterion by which to judge the character and future activity of the pseudoprogressives.

Talk is cheap. He who believes in words is an idiot, said Lenin, who knew how to estimate and deal with the Russian prototypes of Muste. A section of the social reformists always plays the part of weathercocks. There is no surer sign of awakening discontent than left talk in the reformist camp. And never does reformism become more dangerous to the workers' movement than when it assumes the protective coloring of radicalism.

International experience has revealed a unique division of labor among the bourgeois agents in the labor movement. We are witnessing now an American example. The black reactionaries, who are most closely and directly bound to the capitalists and the state, held open sway in the period of reaction. The conditions of the crisis, and the suffering and disillusionment of masses of workers resulting from them, are exposing these elements to the communist attack. And in direct proportion as the outright capitalist slogans of Green and Woll lose their effectiveness, the "left" reformists come into prominence to serve the same ends through deception.

This maneuver presents a real problem to the American communists, who have yet to gain a serious influence with the workers. If the workers who are breaking away from their allegiance to the capitalist parties and the official labor reactionaries are captured by the progressives, they will only end in a blind alley. Their revolt will not mature and raise them to a higher ground of the class struggle implicit in the present situation. That this danger is a real one, only a fool can deny. When we see the fraudulent progressives replacing the communists at the head of the insurgent miners' movement—to mention only one case—it is time to wake up and examine the question and the answers offered by the three factions to it.

The best service to the Muste movement is that rendered by Lovestone. The right wing of communism paints up the "progressive" qualities of Musteism, and moderates criticism to a whisper. Thereby Lovestone deceives a section of the left-wing workers and disarms them in the struggle against it. The official centrist faction contents itself with routine denunciations and confuses the situation with the false and ridiculous formula of "social fascism." This attitude is a direct service to the "left" reformists, to which their undoubted advances testify.

The correct way to fight the "progressive" agents of reaction requires in the first place a precise explanation of their function. From this must follow an unceasing criticism, with particular emphasis on their concrete actions, combined with the revolutionary tactic of the united front. This is the policy of the Left Opposition. Its adoption by the communist workers is a pressing necessity of the struggle.

The capitalist offensive

Published July 4, 1931

The following article was published in *The Militant.*

Wage cutting began with the first manifestations of the crisis and has been proceeding ever since at a continually accelerated pace. For quite a while this practice was masked by denials and all kinds of subterfuges. The notorious conference of employers and labor leaders at the White House, at which the solemn pledge to maintain wage standards was issued, was the first big smokescreen behind which the movement began. It was followed by a campaign of reductions all along the line. But the fiction of holding up the levels was maintained, and the wage cutters resorted, primarily, to indirect methods, such as laying off and rehiring at reduced rates, in order to conceal the actual trend.

But now the process of beating down the living standards of the workers has reached a new stage. The figures on wage cuts are accumulating in such a volume that the facts can no longer be hidden or denied. And there is no point in it, for the exploiters, emboldened by the practical absence of labor resistance, have begun a real assault on the wage scales. They are coming out in the open with this policy.

This was indicated several weeks ago in the blunt declarations of the leading bankers that wages must come down still further. In these statements the keynote of capitalist policy was sounded, and the offensive against labor standards began to widen its scope. The figures of the Labor Bureau, Inc., show 185 wage reductions, averaging about 10 percent, and distributed over 175 manufacturing enterprises, for the single month ending March 15. The campaign continues in full swing. The pious sermonizing of the early months of the crisis about keeping up the wage scales is giving place to editorial apology for the lowering standards.

The *New York Times,* the most influential and authoritative organ of the capitalists, salutes the program of retrenchment at the expense of the workers and recommends it to them. "Economists and practical men," says the *Times* editorial of June 7, "are not all agreed that it has been wise . . . to insist upon the maintenance of high wages." And not only that. The *Times* does not think it "wise" to insist on other conditions and standards which interfere with the workers' efficiency as profit-makers for the bosses.

"Is it not fair to ask of them that they contribute something to the general effort to tide over the days of hardship?" it asks. They haven't contributed enough yet. So now, according to the *Times,* they should "yield something in the way of special privileges, and even arbitrary rulings, which have been established in good times, but which might be relinquished or modified." In this sugar-coated declaration of war there is the essence of the capitalist policy for the ensuing period: an unbridled offensive against the workers.

Will the workers fight back? Will they take up the defensive struggle on a wide front within the year? There are a few signs of such a development, but they are isolated and sporadic as yet. It must be admitted that a serious defensive struggle, involving masses of workers, has not yet begun. The Department of Labor figures just published show fewer strikes in the year 1930 than in any year since 1918. Six hundred fifty-three strikes and lockouts last year against 3,630 in 1919 give a comparative picture of the state of labor activity. The first three months of 1931 showed 146 strikes and lockouts, a slight decline from last year's low average.

These figures, taken by themselves, may well prove to be highly deceptive. The capitalists, proceeding full swing to a further attack on the workers, are quite likely to collide with an explosive factor hidden behind the bare figures of the strike movements for the past fifteen months. The figures alone take no account of the accumulation of grievance and discontent as yet unexpressed and therefore unspent. It is by no means assured that the new encroachments will pass unchallenged. On the contrary, they are more apt to bring matters to the combustion point.

The capitalists, bent on loading the burden of the crisis onto the backs of the workers, are preparing thereby the necessary conditions for a labor revolt. In this way they will convince the workers, as propaganda has been unable to convince them, that there is no way out but to fight. Under such conditions the prospect of a series of stormy battles, of which the American workers have many times shown themselves capable, is by no means unreasonable. In that event the communists would get a hearing the like of which has not been granted before.

The Union Square meeting

Published July 4, 1931

The following article was published in *The Militant*.

When the meeting at Union Square last Saturday was opened by the chairman with the announcement that the official Communist Party had not been invited to send a speaker for the occasion—which was ostensibly a united-front demonstration in behalf of the Centralia prisoners—the representative of the Communist League, Comrade Swabeck, took his name off the speakers' list and withdrew from the meeting.[71] In this demonstrative action there was the protest of the conscientious revolutionist against the prostitution of the interests of class-war prisoners to debased and reactionary factionalism.

Just consider! Here was proclaimed a union of all forces for the Centralia martyrs—a most commendable undertaking, in which every militant worker worthy of the name would boldly participate. Every radical and pseudoradical organization that can be thought of was represented by a speaker: yellow socialists and right communists, liberals and anarchists, Musteites and IWWs. Everybody was welcomed—everybody but the Communist Party. This, with its tens of thousands of members and supporters, was deliberately and specifically excluded. Do you call that a united front for class-war prisoners? It is a contemptible fraud, using the Centralia victims as a shield for a reactionary demonstration.

You will not get our support for such a game. Comrade Swabeck's withdrawal from the meeting was a way of saying this. He might have made the protest by taking the stand and denouncing the shameful procedure. That, however, is a secondary question and a debatable one. There is something unspeakably repugnant to an honest militant in using the platform of a labor defense meeting for polemics. The prisoners, and their burning appeal for solidarity, are apt to get lost in the shuffle.

This is what actually happened at the Union Square meeting. An anarchist windbag, taking his tip from the chairman's announcement, gives a lecture against the proletarian dictatorship in Russia. Other speakers, poisoned to the marrow by the phobia against communism, aired their prejudices. The result? The meeting degenerated into a demonstration against communism. Those who hold the Centralia men in prison have no reason to object to that.

The leaders of the IWW are directly responsible for this miserable performance, and their guilt is in no way extenuated by the fact that the Stalinists boycotted a similar meeting last year. That action of Foster and Company was a crime for which the communist workers will yet call them to account. The Union Square meeting was conducted on the same plane. By their actions its organizers said to the Stalinists: Solidarity in behalf of labor prisoners means just as little to us as it means to you; we will prove that we are just as rotten as you are.

That is what they said. That is what they proved. It is by such an attitude—in which the officials of the IWW met the officials of the Communist Party on one level—that a real movement of genuine solidarity in the fight for the Centralia victims is thwarted, and sabotaged, and made impossible.

This affair of last Saturday was rich in other instructive lessons. Despite the formidable list of organizations represented, a scant few hundred came to the meeting. Doesn't that show where the present strength of labor militancy lies? Doesn't it show that the Socialists paid only lip service to the demonstration and that they give no real support to the issue?

The IWW has come to a sad pass when, in the crusade against communism, it falls into the company of this black gang and finds itself at home there. But this is the logic of the fight against communism. Communism, despite all the worthless bureaucrats who disgrace its banner, is the only revolutionary doctrine, the only revolutionary movement of the proletariat. Whether they wish it or not, those who dedicate themselves to the war against communism come to the service of reaction. The deplorable affair at Union Square last Saturday was a striking illustration—and a warning—of this logic.

The CP, the SP, and the German situation

Published July 11, 1931

The following articles were published in *The Militant.*

The first answer of the American Stalinists to the Hoover moratorium[72] was a shocking revelation of the theoretical degeneration which has been brought into the Communist movement under the flag of "socialism in one country." The Russian Opposition attacked this theory from the very start as the cover for a fundamental revision of the Marxist doctrine of revolutionary internationalism, tending to turn the attention of the national Communist parties away from the problems of the international revolution to the pacifist office of "frontier guards," who would "defend" the Soviet Union while a complete socialist society was being constructed there. The first comment of the *Daily Worker* on the new American intervention in Europe is another demonstration of the fact that Comrade Trotsky and his Marxist fellow-thinkers did not overstate the case.

Reducing all complexities to one common formula, the *Daily Worker* had no difficulty in explaining the moratorium proposal to its readers. The issue of June 22, following the publication of Hoover's statement, devoted a leading editorial to the subject. From this statement of Hoover, says the editorial, "there can be no further doubt of the position of the United States as organizer and leader of the international anti-Soviet front." Hoover's statement, continues the editorial, "should alarm every worker as an immediate war threat against the first workers' Republic."

On this single theme the entire editorial is developed. As to the direct and immediate aim of the American proposal—to head off the proletarian revolution in Germany—and as to the connection of the proletarian revolution in Europe with the defense of the Soviet Union and the consolidation of its victory—on these questions the editorial of the *Daily Worker* had not a word to say.

And that was not a mere oversight. The theory of socialism in one country *began* by overlooking the international revolution and removing it from the agenda of practical tasks of the day; and could not do otherwise, for the two conceptions are incompatible. The American students are faithful to their Russian teachers—and paymasters.

Yesterday the oncoming proletarian revolution in Spain was viewed with uneasiness in *Pravda* because it threatened to upset the European equilibrium and endanger the Five Year Plan. Today the German revolution is overlooked in the *Daily Worker,* which sees only "defense" of the Soviet Union—as though there could be any real and permanent defense except the revolution in other countries. The whole sequence of blunders and crimes which has flowed from the Stalin leadership—in Russia and on a world scale—has proceeded from a theory that is fundamentally false.

The reactionary theory of socialism in one country is no abstraction, remote from the problems and tasks of the day, as many are apt to regard it. No, it is the thread which ties all the current revisionist policies together and unites them into a system. And for that reason, the struggle for a regeneration of the Communist International on the foundations of revolutionary internationalism is preeminently a struggle to free it from the debasing influence of this theory.

If the Hoover proposal for the suspension of war debts and reparations fails to hold back the proletarian revolution in Germany, it will not be for lack of support in the capitalist camp. In the chorus of praise which has greeted the new intervention in Europe from all the bourgeois parties and factions, there is not a note of discord to be heard. Everything is in close harmony, as though all the parts had been assigned and rehearsed in advance in readiness for the signal of the maestro. The unison is even superior to that of a practiced orchestra and more firmly based. They are all united behind the scheme by the compulsion of common interest in the existing social order, which is directly menaced by the situation in Germany. That is the real secret of the marvelous unanimity.

From this standpoint one of the applauding voices deserves a special mention. On July 1 Norman Thomas hailed the moratorium policy as a step to save Germany and Europe from "collapse." Speaking before the Union Theological Seminary, as quoted by the *Times* of the following day, he said: "The collapse of Germany under the Hitlerites or Communists threatens the collapse of all Europe, or even all of Western civilization. Although Hoover's plan does not go far enough, it is good, as far as

Even a Browder can learn

Published July 18, 1931

The following article was published in *The Militant.*

We have always maintained, in contradiction to the right wing, that centrism is not a stable and consistent political tendency, and certainly not a stubborn and incurable ultra-left policy. The long-lasting bloc of centrism and the right wing—during which the expulsion of the Left Opposition was carried out—is in itself a sufficient disproof of this contention. The adventurist plunges of the "third period" did not disclose a new face of centrism. They only rounded out and confirmed the basic thesis of the Opposition: that centrism is a policy of staggering between the classes, which yields to the pressure of the moment and is characterized by wide swings to the right and adventurist leaps to the left.

The attempts of the centrists to extricate themselves from the absurdities of the "third period" have been noted before, particularly in unemployment work and in the trade union question. Now we are witnessing an awkward somersault in the policy of the mine strike. It is needless to mention that the leading acrobat in this turn is Browder. He was the noisiest shouter of the pseudoleft season. That qualifies him, according to the ritual of Stalinism, to be the first to make a turn of 180 degrees, without, of course, saying anything about the falsity of the discarded policy.

Browder will be remembered as the impetuous revolutionist who was through forever with "progressives." He proved—to his own satisfaction—that they had become "social fascists," and from this he drew the conclusion that the tactic of united front was out of date. . . .

After more than two years of rumination over the question—and a blow in the face from the actualities of the mining situation—the same Browder comes forward with an amazing discovery: that "we cannot decline to have relations" with . . . the Musteite, Keeney. Browder could not keep such wisdom to himself. Fired with the zeal of a convert, the great man made a speech, to which—if the *Daily Worker* for July 11 does not lie—the "party leaders" had to listen. There he announced a new revelation:

"The Keeney group has the hegemony in Southern West Virginia. This requires that we have a tactic of maneuver in regard to these people. We cannot merely decline to have relations with whatever group comes out of this field, whether it is Keeney personally, or Keeney's representatives. The fact remains that one of the roads to the miners in this territory is maneuvers with this outfit."[73]

From this it can be seen that even a Browder can learn something, if he is allowed enough time. The elementary idea, explained as far back as the Third Congress of the Comintern in 1921, that "we cannot decline to have relations" with reformists has finally penetrated the thick skull of the Trotsky-killer, and that alone testifies to the power of the idea.

And along with that, Browder has assimilated another simple and obvious conception, and, as was to be expected, he also made a speech about it. Before the crisis, and after, our hero saw the "offensive of the workers" and the "revolutionary upsurge" rising high enough to drown him. But since then he has found a dry rock to sit on and collect his thoughts. The result of this cogitation is embodied in a speech to the convention of the Young Communist League, reported in the *Daily Worker* of July 14. The erstwhile fire-eater shakes the finger of caution at the assembled hotheads and warns them:

"It is therefore clear that it is absolutely wrong to speak of the 'offensive of the working class and the counter-offensive of the capitalists.' "

"The beginning of the mass actions has primarily a defensive character."

"We witness a most vicious offensive of the capitalist class against the working class."

And so on. All of which is Browder's way of conveying the impression that the present struggles of the workers are defensive. This is, of course, a correct appraisal of the situation, as *The Militant* has pointed out a hundred times. The idea itself is not new; it is Browder's sudden comprehension of it that provides the day's sensation.

These incidents demonstrate, as has been said, that centrism is able to change its mind a little; that the analysis of its policy as chronic ultraleftism is false; that even a Browder can learn. But from this we draw no optimistic conclusions, for the process takes too long, they do too much damage in the meantime, and they correct one error only in order to commit a dozen more. Centrism is not consistently leftist, but it is consistently false and consistently dangerous to the proletarian movement.

Our revolution

Published July 18, 1931

The following article was published in *The Militant*.

The more clearly the unfolding of world events demonstrates that the conception of socialism in one country—the common theoretical bond of centrism and the right wing—is a strangulating noose for the international proletarian revolution, the more evident does it become that the banner of revolutionary internationalism belongs to the Left Opposition, which has been forged in the struggle against the new revisionism. And by that, increases the greatness of its historic responsibility and the magnitude of its tasks, which brook no delay and take no heed of the weakness of our forces.

Blockaded in Russia during the Chinese revolution and the English general strike, the Opposition had to confine itself to criticism and counterproposals within a closed circle and was deprived of direct influence on the events themselves. The new rise of revolutionary development coincides with a decisive change in the internal relations of the Communist movement. The Opposition, beaten down with the defeats of the international proletariat, which flowed from the ruinous policy of the right-centrist bloc, has awakened to new life with the revolutionary revival and confronts it with a worldwide organization and with all its fundamental principles confirmed in living experience.

It is now endowed with the possibility, and the inescapable historic necessity, of bringing these principles to the fore as a direct influence on the developing revolutionary events. Every section of the International—our own among them—must put its ranks in shape for this grandiose international endeavor.

From this point of view we should greet in the warmest manner, and in deeds as well as in words, the proposals of Comrade Trotsky in regard to the Spanish revolution, which stands today in the center of the stage. To intervene directly now, and on an international scale; to study the basic questions down to the bottom; to stir the Communist ranks with discussion over the problems of the Spanish revolution and mobilize international aid in time; to expose and drive out the revolution-destroying policy of centrism and bring forward the Marxist alternative in the heat of events and directly upon them—such are the tasks envisaged for the International Left Opposition in Comrade Trotsky's letter, which we print in the current issue of *The Militant*.[74]

We have reason to hope that our detachment of the Marxian internationalists will do its part for the Spanish revolution. To a certain extent at least, we have seen the huge vista opened up by the events in Spain and understood that our weight in the scale might not be without influence in the final summing up. We have ventured to believe that, not because we deceive others or ourselves about the forces at our disposal, but because our strength is the strength of the Marxian doctrines crystallized in the international nucleus of the Opposition.

We have not seen the Chinese revolution as a subject for abstract study. The international class struggle, in its dynamic development, is posing the questions anew in Spain and raising the principled line of the Opposition against the line of centrism more insistently than ever. That is the way we see it. That is why we must strain every resource to make our mark on the situation while it is alive and fresh.

The Spanish revolution is our revolution. It is our task to make it the revolution of the American workers, and to inspire them to fight for it on the soil of America as our comrades fight for it on the soil of Spain.

Silk revolt growing

Published August 1, 1931

The following article was published in *The Militant*.

Events are developing rapidly in Paterson, center of the silk industry and scene of historical labor revolts. In the glare of the developing class struggle the various contending groups in the labor movement are being shown up in their true character, and all policies are being put to the test of life.

Last week we reported the strike called by the National Textile Workers Union and urged upon the Communists who direct this organization the adoption of a united-front policy in order to consolidate the workers and disarm the reformists. On Tuesday, the Associated and the United Textile Workers called their strike, having advanced the date from August 1 under pressure of the strike action of the NTW.[75]

The relation of forces at present appears to favor the reformists. They have an established organization, have made rather extensive preparations, and are assured of a fairly strong support among certain sections of the silk workers. The unity effected between the Associated and the United Textile Workers has had a consolidating effect in their favor.

All the developments are taking place under the compulsion of a powerful movement from below. The silk workers, oppressed to the limit of endurance, are determined to strike. No one could herd them back. The question of strike has already been settled in the minds of the workers. The only problem that could arise under the circumstances is: Who will lead the strike, and how will it be conducted?

In this dynamic situation how do the various contending elements and groups reveal themselves?

1. The Communists. The National Textile Workers Union, which is under the leadership of the Communist Party, showed the poorest preparation for the events, and was prevented from the necessary preliminary growth by incorrect tactics and leadership. They had tried to compensate for these defects and weaknesses by an arbitrary precipitation of the strike before the date set by the reformists. By a militant and aggressive campaign they quickly demonstrated that the National Textile Workers Union represents a real force in the situation, if not at present the strongest force. But their hopes to take the field away from the reformists by this coup met with failure, as could easily have been foreseen. The organization of the Associated and United Textile Workers remained intact, and the grip of the reformists upon the members was strengthened by the irresponsible, putschist tactics of the Communists.

2. The Musteites. The leadership of the combined Associated and United Textile Workers rests for the most part in the hands of adherents of the CPLA. The timidity,

vacillation, and fear of struggle which are bred in the very marrow of these come-ons for McMahon have shown themselves in the Passaic situation in full bloom. Their hesitation and delay with the strike are only an advance notice of the speed with which they will endeavor to end it and the terms they will be prepared to accept for its termination. They are jumping now because they are afraid of the Communist union. The fear of the Communists is the principal motivating factor in every step they take which gives the appearance of militancy and aggressiveness.

3. The Lovestoneites. The Paterson struggle shows these people up in their true colors more vividly than a thousand arguments. This thoroughly opportunist faction—only yesterday the official leadership of the Communist Party, supported by the Comintern—has flatly turned its back on communism at Paterson. Gitlow appears there as the cover for the Musteites in their fight against the National Textile Workers Union, as the Musteites are the cover for McMahon. The Lovestoneites took part in the negotiations to unite the two reformist organizations and are exerting all their efforts now to make it an effective unity against the National Textile Workers Union. In the real test of the class struggle at Paterson, where deeds take the place of words, the Lovestoneites have already found their place in the camp of anticommunism.

The National Textile Workers Union is undoubtedly a force in the situation. Its strength is the strength of the militant spirit of the workers, of their profound and justified hatred of the UTW officials who have sold them to the bosses more than once, and their distrust of the field men of these notorious reactionaries and betrayers—the Musteites. The weaknesses of the NTW are the incompetence and the false policy of its leadership—that is to say, the leadership of the Communist Party. They shout against the reformists, but they do not know how to fight them. They speak of a united front of the workers, but by their tactics they defeat it. This is the heart of their mistake in Paterson. And by it they are entrenching the position of the CPLA elements and through them the treacherous bureaucracy of the UTW—and through them the bosses.

In last week's *Militant* we warned the Communists at Paterson that they could not ignore the reformist organization, which has a larger membership and a better organizational base. Here we wish to repeat again the most solemn warning to the National Textile Workers Union: You must go to the workers with a genuine united-front policy. Make a direct proposal to the Associated and United Textile Workers to form a joint strike committee, to unite all the striking workers under a single directing body. Show the workers that you are willing to give them an opportunity to test the contending policies, leaders, and organizations for themselves in a united strike movement. Let the reformists refuse such a proposal at their own risk. The workers want unity, make no mistake about that. Trust the workers to understand what a real unity proposal is when they see it.

On this road the NTW will become the leading force for the consolidation and victory of the workers, and its strength will increase with the intensification of the struggle and the bankruptcy of reformist policies which will be revealed in this test of action. The present suicidal course of the NTW is leading to a certain defeat for the workers and the Communists, and consequently to a victory for the bosses and their lieutenants.

Issues of great import for the whole future of the left-wing movement are at stake in Paterson, as is the case also in the mine strikes. The trade union question, which is a life-and-death question for the American Communist movement, is being transferred from the field of abstract polemics into the field of action, and all views are being tested there. Nothing that happens will be concealed. No mistakes will go unpunished. The communist workers throughout the entire country are duty bound to watch these developing strike struggles with the greatest attentiveness. Paterson is a rehearsal of greater battles yet to come. The movement will judge everyone by his performance there.

A reply to the discussion

Published September 12, 1931

The following discussion article was published in *The Militant.*

It must be admitted that the conference discussion material has yielded very little either in the way of positive supplement to the draft thesis of the National Committee or criticism of it. The absence of any serious attacks on its main conclusions—although some of them represent a distinct and original contribution of the Left Opposition and are presented in the American movement for the first time—may be taken as an indication of the general support of the organization for the propositions of the National Committee and a forecast of the action of the conference in regard to them.

Our draft has been submitted to an international discussion, and a beneficial criticism from that source is not yet excluded. But in the ranks of our own national section the estimation of the problems and the tasks formulated by the National Committee have not yet been successfully assailed. Critics of the National Committee are not lacking, but their contributions do not go to the roots of the new issues. They attempt either to revive questions long settled in our ranks, or to obscure the main questions with superficial quibbles over minor points.

Comrades Rose and Carter are the rightful representatives of these tendencies. In their discussion articles they only recapitulate the attitude and point of view they have constantly maintained against the National Committee. Since the conflicting positions cannot be reconciled—and they cannot because they have nothing in common—nothing remains but for the national conference to pronounce a judgment on them and end the disputes. Here I wish only to make a few remarks on the critical articles of the comrades mentioned and to explain once more why we still hold to the views we have maintained against them.

Comrade Rose renews his long-standing feud with us on three very important questions: on the evaluation of the history of the party; on the present status and the perspectives of the party; and on the attitude of the Left Opposition toward the party. With us as well as with Comrade Rose, all three of these questions are intertwined, and, also in each case, the conclusions have a systematic character. They are mutually exclusive and cannot be joined together. Our first conference more than two years ago spoke very decisively on these points. In our opinion the second conference should reaffirm the judgment and put a period to contentions over them.

Comrade Rose's first fault, from which the others flow, is his grossly distorted view of the history of the party. This is not without valid reasons. During all the years of the party's formative period and its emergence as a dynamic factor in the class struggle at the head of the conscious workers' movement, he stood aside from the party and took no part in the making of its history. He learned about the party from the scandal sheets and kitchen gossip of its enemies. On that basis he serves up an account and interpretation of the party's past that bears very little relation to actual fact. And in part, by the concessions he continually makes to the standpoint of the antiparty sects who still hold him as a captive, his exposition of party history is somewhat provocative.

If it was a mistake in the first place to organize the party, if it was wrong to belong to the party since its foundation, if the circles of word-radicalism which conducted a venomous fight against the party since its inception were correct—if all this were so, Comrade Rose's approach to the question would have a certain justification. Needless to say we do not share such a view nor the conclusions deriving from it.

Take a few examples of Comrade Rose's history at random; in each instance we find them to be distorted, one-sided, and false: "The native proletarian elements . . . round the I.W.W. were at first neglected by this rising movement" (the party). But this is presented as solely the fault of the as yet groping and inexperienced party. The reactionary course of the IWW leaders in fomenting antagonism to the Communist movement—and this was the really decisive element in the situation—is left out of account. Finally, he says, there came an appeal to the IWW from the Communist International "over the heads of the American Communist leadership." Not so. It was the delegation of the party to the Comintern that drafted the appeal, and the whole party supported it.

Comrade Rose speaks of party members "sent in 'to capture or destroy the I.W.W.'" Who were they and when was such an instruction ever given out by the party? We read about it in the IWW papers in their campaign to poison

Left Opposition trifle for a moment with such an estimation? Here is a sweeping statement indeed, which forbids the party to grow regardless of external events.

The Communist Party of Germany has no better policy and no better leadership—if we allow for proportions—and yet it influences millions and continues to grow. We should not take the responsibility of prohibiting the American party to grow stronger. The facts of life will most likely veto the order and discredit us entirely. As a matter of fact the recent advances of the National Miners Union under party leadership occurred since Comrade Rose made the first draft of his document. That fact, and many others which can easily be cited, show how false and dangerous it would be to accept his view.

The theory that the party was worthless in the past and hopeless for the future brings our critic inevitably to a collision with the policy toward the party which the Left Opposition has pursued since its inception. Only one conclusion can follow from this premise—to form another party. But this idea has been so hopelessly discredited in the Left Opposition, in America as well as on an international scale, that Comrade Rose stops short of the logic of his own position and exhausts himself with negative criticism of the tactics of the National Committee, which proceed from a different premise. The content in all of his criticisms, accordingly, is indefiniteness, contradiction, and half-formed conclusions.

We cannot determine the line of the Communist League in this manner. First we must clearly define the premises upon which our work as a faction of the party is founded. Tactical conclusions follow from this. It is of course possible even then to disagree on the tactical application of the basic policy. But in that case the disputes are narrowed down; they can be put concretely and definitely. The attempt to work out a common tactic when the premise is contradictory is doomed to failure from the start. This, in our opinion, is the source of the vague and confusing proposals which Comrade Rose outlines in his articles.

Tasks of our national conference

Published September 19, 1931

The following discussion article was published in *The Militant.*

The Second National Conference of the Communist League will mark an important milestone in the development of our organization and, consequently, in the history of American communism, whose banner we bear and whose future we represent. The conference is a culminating point in three years of preparatory labor for the grueling battles yet to come. Its deliberations have been grounded by all that has gone before and its results can be anticipated, even now, with reasonable assurance.

Our ranks have been welded together on the basis of a correct political line. If the conference accepts the proposals of the National Committee it will not find it necessary to confront the organization with any new or surprising turns. Our theses and other recommendations only represent a synthesis of the policies and methods already worked out and applied in our daily work and agitation on the basis of our platform. The approval of this line by the conference will necessarily carry with it an endorsement of the course on which the National Committee has guided the movement and a repudiation of the criticisms brought against it. Any kind of indefiniteness on this point is out of the question. The conference is to draw the balance and decide.

Proceeding from this, the national conference is then obliged to declare an end to controversy over the disputed questions and to prohibit any further discussion of them. It can do this with full authority and with assurance that its command will be supported throughout the organization. Our conference preparations have been a triumph of proletarian democracy, a model illustration of its processes—the only methods yet discovered whereby a living workers' organization can assert its collective judgment.

The discussion has been thorough, free, and untrammeled by any kind of suppression. The selection of delegates proceeds in the same way. After this, it will be impossible to question the representative character of the conference or its authority to speak for the entire organization. The membership as a whole will wait for its signal to terminate the discussion and concentrate all attention on the concrete tasks worked out on the basis of the fundamental decisions.

Outstanding among the questions concerning which the National Committee will insist on a categorical decision of the conference—because it has been the one subjected to the greatest dispute—is the question of our attitude toward the party. The platform adopted at the first conference answered this question correctly. Without that, the Left Opposition would long ago have suffered shipwreck. Now, with the help of the Second National Conference, we must take another step forward on the same path we have traveled heretofore. This stands first on the list of concrete tasks which proceed logically from the general recommendation already submitted in the thesis of the National Committee.

In our judgment the practical program of the conference should run approximately as follows:

1. Settling all disputes about the role of the Left Opposition as a faction of the party, and putting a stop to all argument about it, we must intensify our work within the party ranks, organize our forces into a firm group, and work out a practical program for the direction of their work. The proletarian militants of the party and its peripheral organizations are the future troops of the Opposition: this is the idea which must guide our work and from which we must not depart. Closer to the party, deeper into the party—these are our slogans.

The Oppositionists must strive by all means to draw nearer to rank-and-file party members, approach them in a fraternal spirit, and explain the great questions again and again with the utmost patience and persistence. This work goes hand in hand with a fiery proletarian hate of the centrist bureaucracy and its corrupting influence, an unrelenting struggle against it.

2. Tighten up the organization. Make a decisive break with the habits of looseness and slackness which hamper the Bolshevist development of the league. Impose tasks on every member and hold every member to account for his activity. Establish discipline worthy of a communist organization and close the door to windbags and triflers.

3. Begin the actual formation of a cadre of professional revolutionists who put themselves entirely at the disposal of the organization. Select a group out of the younger

to higher ground and prepare it for a further ascent. That is enough. No more can reasonably be expected from the Second National Conference. There is every reason to expect that it will not yield less.

Laying the foundations

Published October 24, 1931

The following article was published in *The Militant.*

With the publication of the forthcoming book on the Chinese revolution, which Pioneer Publishers is now getting ready for the press, the American section of the Opposition will record another substantial achievement. It belongs among the fundamental and most important Marxist documents written in the heat of struggle in the Communist International since Lenin departed from its leadership.

We have regarded the publication of all these historic documents as one of our first and foremost tasks. The volume on China rounds out the great series of books and pamphlets from the pen of Comrade Trotsky in the past period which will stand for all time among the classics of our movement. It is with such weapons that the proletarian wing of the party will fight its way to victory. By its stubborn concentration on this simple and prosaic work of publication, by its refusal to be diverted from it by any kind of charlatan promises of cheap success and easy victory, the Opposition is bringing its first, and therefore its most essential, task to a successful fruition.

In this way we are laying the ideological foundations of the future movement, upon which it will stand, steadfast and sure, in the stormy days to come. There are people around the fringes of the Communist League who looked down upon this "publishing business" and ridiculed our concentration on it. The Opposition was fortunate in disregarding the pretensions of those who talk only of spectacular undertakings and overlook the essential task at hand. First things come first.

There are illustrious examples of the same point of view. The founders of scientific communism, who had a few ideas and even some great ones, were not above the simple task of assembling the technical means to publish their doctrines when that task stood first on the order of the day. In the trial number of the *Kommunistische Zeitschrift,* issued in September 1847 under the direction of Marx and Engels, one can read the modest announcement of a project not unlike the one which has engaged our efforts:

"Both intellectuals and manual workers promised their collaboration [in publishing the paper]. Yet we hesitated lest after a very short period of activity, publication should cease for lack of funds. It was finally suggested that we acquire a printing press of our own so as to give the venture a more stable foundation. A subscription list was opened . . . and in a short time the sum of 25 pounds was collected. The money permitted us to have the necessary type brought from Germany; our compositor members have set up the issue gratuitously; and here in actual fact is the first number of our paper. . . . We still lack a printing press, but as soon as we have money we intend to purchase one. Then our printing establishment will be in a position, not only to run off our newspaper, but likewise to print the pamphlets necessary for the defense of the proletariat."

That is the way we are proceeding, too. We also undertook "to print the pamphlets necessary for the defense of the proletariat." With the slenderest means, and with economies and sacrifices not unlike those described in the *Kommunistische Zeitschrift,* we have accomplished a part of the task. And we are still working along the same line.

Hail, 'Young Spartacus'!

Published October 24, 1931

The following article was published in *The Militant*.

One of the first positive results of our national conference is the decision of the National Committee, in agreement with the newly appointed National Youth Committee, to launch an independent club for young workers in New York and to begin the publication of a special youth paper. With this the Communist League will begin a momentous experiment which will call out the intense interest and warm sympathy of all who fight under our banner. So far as we know, we will be the first section of the International Left Opposition to form such an organization and to come out with a special organ appealing to the proletarian youth. We are pioneering on a new field in the worldwide struggle of the Marxian wing of the movement. But all the circumstances warrant the step, and we are confident that the results will quickly vindicate it.

The situation and the special problems confronting the

Communist youth are not the same as those of the adult movement, or at any rate they are not exactly the same; and it is from this circumstance that different tactical and organizational methods flow. The Opposition youth remain—as the conference resolution said—a faction of the Young Communist League, as our organization is a faction of the party. But the relation of forces and a number of other conditions in the youth movement are far more favorable for independent action up to a certain point.

Stalinism has wrought devastation enough in the party, but in the Young Communist League the results have been truly catastrophic. On the other hand, the Marxian educational work of the Opposition has awakened a far wider response, speaking proportionally, in the ranks of the Communist youth than in the adult organization. And this is not without valid reasons. The youth are not, and in the nature of things cannot be, weighted down with as hard and heavy a crust of bureaucratic cynicism as is the case in the party. The youth react more sensitively to revolutionary ideas. The youth are the barometer, as Trotsky said at the beginning of the struggle against bureaucratism in 1923.

All our experience in America supports this idea. We do no boasting. We have never deceived ourselves or others with exaggerated claims. But we can say with absolute confidence that the flower of the Communist youth in America are already enrolled in the ranks of the Opposition. A bold step forward is now justified and necessary.

If the youth work the Opposition is now undertaking on a wider scale has an admittedly experimental character, the same can be said with no less justice of all that has been attempted up to now in this domain by the party, and even by the Comintern. We maintain that the problem of effective work among the youth has not yet been solved in the capitalist countries, and under the regime of the epigones it has been cynically mismanaged and abused. They have been corrupting and perverting the revolutionary youth, training young bureaucrats as Fagin trained young thieves. What is wanted is the education of a cadre of frank and honest young worker-revolutionists able to organize and lead a proletarian mass movement. This task belongs to the Marxian Opposition. It will bring new methods and a new spirit to the work.

We expect that the first issue of the youth paper of the Opposition—the plans for which are already under way and which it is to be hoped will not long be delayed—will reflect this new spirit and be welcomed in the youth movement like a fresh breeze. To do this it will not have to borrow anything from the *Young Worker,* that pallid and unhealthy caricature of grown-up Stalinism at its worst. The aim which we and our young collaborators aspire to is to make a real youth paper, to interest young workers and not to command them, to convince and educate them and not to herd them like sheep for a faction that has no ideas. No pretensions, no diplomacy, no high-politics, no slavish aping of the big talk of the elders, but a young communists' paper for young workers.

In deciding to call the new paper *Young Spartacus,* the joint committee has endowed it with an inspiring historic name. The name of the great leader of the colossal slave revolts of antiquity was the banner around which Liebknecht and Luxemburg assembled the dispersed vanguard of the German proletariat. It can well become the symbol of the revolt of Communist youth against the corrupting influence of Stalinism, and their assault against the capitalist order. The name imposes obligations. We are convinced that the young militants of the Opposition will fulfill them. In their great undertaking they will have the unqualified support of every member of the Communist League.

An apologist for Stalinism

Published October 31, 1931

The following article was published in *The Militant*.

One of the surest signs of the influence of alien classes upon the course of the Stalinist bureaucracy in the Soviet Union is its rabid persecution of the left, proletarian wing of the party. It is the hounding, exiling, imprisoning, and murdering of the unwavering and incorruptible defenders of the ideas and the tradition of the October revolution which give the lie to every pretended "left" turn of the centrist regime and deprive it of the right to confidence. The defense of the proletarian dictatorship in the Soviet Union involves in the highest degree the unceasing exposure of the reactionary terror against the Bolshevik-Leninists and the most energetic defense of its victims. Every Oppositionist worthy of the name counts this among his first duties.

Weisbord, who assisted in the expulsion and terror campaign against the American Oppositionists, turned up—it will be recalled—two years later with the offer to instruct us how to interpret the principles of the Opposition in America. Now he is enlarging his territory. First he wanted to correct our misconceptions of the situation as Comrade Trotsky explained it; now it is Comrade Trotsky himself whom he takes to task.

Trotsky, who knows something about the bureaucratic degeneration of the Stalinist apparatus and its terror against the Leninist Opposition—and not by hearsay—has again illuminated this side of the question, among others, in his recently published thesis "Problems of the Development of the USSR." Therein he demonstrates once more that "the Stalinist plebiscitary regime has been converted into a main danger of the dictatorship of the proletariat." Against this reasoned and deliberate conclusion, Weisbord has intervened with a statement of his own, in which he corrects the "exaggerations."

In this statement we read the following: "Comrade Trotsky declares there is not a trace of party democracy. Local organizations are selected and automatically reorganized by secretaries. Local secretaries are appointed. Congresses are arbitrarily postponed, delegates selected from the top, every spark of those features which go to make up the nature of a revolutionist crushed; Blumkins are shot down, Bessedovskys direct the purging of the party, etc." All this is literal quotation from the thesis of Trotsky, but it is quoted with disapproval. Things are not so bad as Trotsky makes them out. Like the impartial judge who "sees both sides," he comments: "We submit (1) that this evidence is exaggerated; (2) that while some of the above is true in part, yet this is not decisive as to whether there is a party."

Exaggerated? Only "some" of it true, and that only "in part"? Where, how, and in what way, the Weisbord statement does not say, and cannot say. We know that the monstrous accusations against the Left Opposition (the "Wrangel officer" and so forth) were all exposed and refuted, but we do not know of a single instance where the Opposition was convicted of falsifying or "exaggerating." Is there a trace of party democracy? Can a worker-Bolshevik stand up and speak out for the basic ideas of the October revolution without being sent to prison or Siberia? Was not the heroic Blumkin assassinated? Was not the organizer of the October revolution and the Red Army exiled to Turkey by a dicker with Kemal Pasha and kept there by an agreement with the bourgeois governments of Europe? Did not Bessedovsky help to purge the party of "Trotskyists" before he jumped over the fence into the camp of the White Guard?

We have one more question that is of the deepest concern to every revolutionist of the entire world: Is not the sick Rakovsky, the great hero and warrior of the revolution, being slowly and deliberately done to death right now in the bitter cold of Siberian exile? Exaggerations? No! We "submit" that Comrade Trotsky has only told the indisputable truth, and that this truth must be made known to the proletarian vanguard without any mitigation or glossing over of the cruel facts. It is not Trotsky who exaggerates the bureaucracy and the terror against the Bolshevik-Leninists, but Weisbord who minimizes and thereby apologizes for them.

The Weisbord statement is, of course, no accidental error. It has an intimate connection with the whole campaign he has conducted against the American section of the Opposition with ideas and slanders borrowed from the centrists and the right wing. Our national conference unanimously rejected the proposal of Weisbord to present his "views" before it. And rightly so. We have nothing in common with such "views." It would have been a disgrace if a single delegate had expressed any doubts over this question. For our part, if we have to choose between the out-and-out Stalinist henchman who defends everything and the camouflaged apologist who blunts the edge of criticism—if we have to choose between the one who justifies the crimes and the one who "submits that they are exaggerated"—we prefer the former. It is best to have enemies out in the open. And if they conceal themselves behind the pretence of "adherence to the International Left Opposition" it is all the more necessary to drag them into the open.

Amter will get your money back?

Published November 7, 1931

The following article was published in *The Militant*.

The New York municipal election campaign of the Communist Party has not been without its funny side, even if the joke has been at the expense of communism. This was to be expected with Israel Amter as the head of the ticket. Amter is the candidate for borough president of Manhattan. If he is not elected it will not be because he did not try; not because he stopped short of extravagant promises. The revolutionary Marxists have always regarded elections as an opportunity for revolutionary propaganda. Amter has been demonstrating how they also can be utilized for the most vulgar reformist vote-catching. We are well enough acquainted with the typical American bourgeois politician, among whom the reformist Socialists can be included, who promise the voters anything and everything. It is a strange role for Communists, however, and not an edifying one.

The *Daily Worker* of October 27 reports the appearance of our candidate at a meeting of depositors of the U.S. Bank who are still whistling for their money. It was evidently an enthusiastic gathering. "A great ovation was given Amter when he was introduced," says the report. And the jubilation of his hearers did not stop there. "Several times during his speech he was loudly applauded."

If these cheers were for communism one could only be glad. But this, unfortunately, was not the case. The depositors had something far more immediate in mind when they shouted for the standard-bearer of the revolutionary party. They were simply excited at the prospect of the recovery of their lost deposits, and were hailing the man who dangled this prospect before them.

The report in the *Daily Worker* quotes Amter as saying: "The Communist Party pledges to you that if I be elected I'll use all my official power as borough president to organize all the 400,000 workers and small depositors for a militant fight to get their money back." Such are the campaign arguments of Stalinist Communism.

With all due respect to the intentions of the candidate, we do not think he could make good on this promise even if he is elected borough president. We go further and say such promises should not be made by a Communist in any case. It would be far better and certainly far more in keeping with the elementary conceptions of communism to explain to the depositors that the expropriation of small owners by bank swindles is just as much a part of the capitalist system as their ruin by competition, and that salvation lies in the revolutionary overthrow of the regime and not in the promises of a city official to halt its normal processes and restore that which existed yesterday.

Communism is the doctrine of the socialization of property, including the banks. The small proprietor, engrossed with his little store, his little farm, or his little bank deposit, is not a communist. He can become one only insofar as he comprehends the hopelessness of the contest with centralized capital and adopts the property viewpoint of the proletariat. Communist propaganda among the members of these doomed classes should emphasize this idea all the time. Such events as the bank failure create favorable opportunities for its reception. Therein lies their chief value to the revolutionists.

The Stalinists, who stand everything on its head, have not made an exception of this question. In their frenzied endeavors to mobilize the petty bourgeoisie for the election they do not stop at holding out to the small owner the illusion of security in his possessions. They even promise to restore that which has already been taken away. And this, mind you, under the existing capitalist regime, in which the progressive expropriation of the small owners and the small producer proceeds by a law of the system itself. By such methods the petty-bourgeois masses will not be won over to communism, but the party itself will be dragged into the petty-bourgeois swamp.

Where is the Mooney movement?

Published November 14, 1931

The following article was published in *The Militant.*

It is nearly three months since Tom Mooney issued his memorable appeal "To All Militant and Revolutionary Labor Organizations and Groups" for united action in his behalf. Thereby he put the fifteen-year-old case once more on the agenda of the labor movement. He aroused the enthusiasm of every conscientious militant for a new struggle for his liberation and for the cause of the working class which he symbolizes in his prison cell.

Because of the profound response which it called forth from the depths of the movement, the call of Tom Mooney sent the leaders of all the factions scurrying to prepare their answer. The class-war prisoner has a great authority and nobody dared to ignore his appeal. All the factions and groups answered. Each in his own way made a gesture of compliance. And there the matter rests at the present moment. Where is the new "Mooney movement" which the rank-and-file militants desire with all their hearts? It is not yet under way. Even the campaign to set the great movement in motion still waits the initial steps of organization.

And this is not because there is no basis for the issue. All the elements for a truly gigantic movement, one that can reach into the very depths of the most conservative labor organizations and set their members into action, are at hand. It is the method that is lacking: it is the understanding and the will of the leaders of the factions and groups to whom Mooney addressed his appeal. It must be said plainly, because it is the bitter and incontestable truth: they have all diplomatized with the appeal; they have played factional politics with it; they have sabotaged it. The problem is to break through this rotten game. And the best weapon for this is the appeal of Mooney himself. In that document the means and methods for unfolding the movement can be found.

Tom Mooney's letter of August 18 is a remarkable presentation of the question in every respect. All the sabotagers justify themselves on the ground that "Mooney is in jail and doesn't understand the situation." They are all wrong. The class-war prisoner, immured in San Quentin these fifteen years, understands the question better than they do. It is even possible that his superior wisdom can be attributed to his imprisonment. New turns and new periods percolate through the prison walls only after a certain delay. Mooney has assimilated the idea of the united front as Lenin taught it. Perhaps he has not yet learned about the new amendments. At any rate he has not been converted to them. That is his strength, and the strength of his appeal. That is why his appeal constitutes the guiding line along which alone a real mass movement for his liberation can proceed.

The open letter of Tom Mooney was and yet remains

a great opportunity for the Communist Party and the International Labor Defense. On the one hand it was a formal notice from Mooney to the trade unions, to the Socialists, and to the so-called progressives: no exclusion of the Communists from the Mooney movement. On the other hand—rightly understood—it was an intimation to the Communists: I depend on you to press the issue and lead the way, to force the reformists and the trade unions, including the most conservative ones, to fight with you in a common front. Mooney meant to say, as he said personally to the present writer three years ago: "The reds are the dynamic element; they must start the movement; they must set it into motion."

It is bad that the leaders of the party didn't understand this, and still worse that they do not understand it yet. They are people to whom the obvious is always a mystery sealed with seven seals. Anyone who has as much as a casual acquaintance with the lineup in the labor movement ought to know that the trade unions under their present leadership, and the other groups addressed in the letter, whether conservative, pseudoradical, or Socialist, will not make a genuine and militant fight for Mooney. At best they will only render lip-service in deference to the sentiments of the ranks, arrange a formal demonstration, make a mild, polite, and orderly protest—all of which means nothing, or next to nothing, in such a bitterly contested class issue as the Mooney case.

But is it not equally clear that the protests of the Communists and their close sympathizers alone—a mere handful of the American working class—scare nobody, and least of all the stiff-necked and class-conscious persecutors of Mooney? They do not care a fig for the protests of the Communists so long as these protests are not supported by wider masses of the workers. This is the crux of the question. Without the initiative and driving force of the Communists—the "dynamic element," the organizing force—there can be no militant movement on a national scale. But the agitation of the Communists cannot be effective until it penetrates the masses and sweeps them along in a joint movement. Tom Mooney understands this, as his letter shows. His letter created the most favorable ground to realize this necessary union of forces. The Stalinist leaders of the party have bungled the whole question. The next move is up to the Communist workers. It is for them to force the issue and compel a change of course.

What does this mean, concretely, now? It means for the Communist Party and the ILD to make direct, formal proposals to all the organizations and groups mentioned in Tom Mooney's letter for joint action on the single issue of the fight for Mooney. It means to give up the horseplay of a united front embracing only Communist organizations, in which the Mooney case is tacked on to a number of other issues, and in which its special appeal is lost. The other cases will not lose by this temporary segregation of the Mooney issue; they will gain a hundredfold by the sweep of the broader Mooney movement which can be created.

To change the course and correct it now while there is yet time, means in New York and such other places where separate conferences have been organized—Communist and reformist—to propose to the reformists *a merger of the conferences into one.* It goes without saying that every direct proposal to the official leadership of the reformist organizations and conferences has to be accompanied and supplemented by an intensive agitation in the ranks of these organizations to compel an acceptance of the unity proposals.

This is the way to blow the breath of life into the Mooney movement. This is the tactic of the united front as Lenin taught it, and as Mooney appealed for in his letter. The reformists are doing everything in their power to make this letter remain a scrap of paper. But we have no advice to offer them. Our suggestions are directed to the Communists as a means of forcing the reformists. The Leninist tactic of the united front is a powerful means to this end. That is not the least of its merits.

The case of Theodore Dreiser

Published November 21, 1931

The following article was published in *The Militant.*

The ideological superstructure of class society is only a reflection, and thereby a defense, of its economic basis of exploitation. This applies also to literature. Do not write against the prevailing social system, and above all do not advocate another one: this is capitalism's real standard of literary values. It is the decisive criterion which its high priests and critics bring to their judgment of literature, for all their pretenses of artistic disinterestedness and prattle about "art for art's sake." We are witnessing an illustration of this law of class society at the present moment in the beginning of the campaign to "revalue" and discredit Theodore Dreiser.

Ridicule is the first weapon with which they are attacking the great writer whom only yesterday they were hailing as the king of American novelists. Through the authoritative medium of the *New York Times* they are passing the word to make fun of Dreiser. This is the way they treated his suit to restrain the exhibition of the motion picture distortion of *An American Tragedy* as just another murder trial. In like manner the same paper has greeted his investigations of the reign of terror in the Kentucky mine fields.[77] Rest assured the critics will take the tip, as they always do when the masters of the bread speak up. A general attack against Dreiser's commanding position on the field of literature is in the cards.

Bourgeois literary opinion never welcomed Dreiser. Rather it accepted him after he had bludgeoned his way to eminence by the truly colossal achievements of his pen. He never painted the social system of his day in rosy hues. On the contrary. The author of *Sister Carrie* and *The Financier* showed it up in all its hideous ugliness and injustice down to the most sordid detail. In exposure of capitalist society as it really is—not sparing the whited sepulchre of its "morality"—he blazed the trail for other writers. Among the American writers who, following him, have taken the social milieu for their theme, he drew the truest, the most striking and revealing picture. "He stands alone," said Mencken, and in that he recorded not so much an opinion as an inescapable fact.

But it was not by virtue of these achievements alone that Dreiser won the universal acclaim that has been his in recent years. It was something in the quality, or rather, something lacking in the quality of his writings that made it possible for him to gain the "recognition" of all the literary critics, including the little word-jugglers who complained about his "style." Dreiser drew no conclusions from the tales he told. This was his saving grace in the eyes of the bourgeois censors. Over everything he wrote there hung a heavy fog of pessimism, futility, fate. Bourgeois opinion could tolerate that. Cynicism is its own creed and resignation is its prescription for the masses.

Dreiser's fall from grace is not due, of course, to any weakening of his literary powers. The shafts of ridicule that are being hurled at him now, and the heavier attack that can be expected to follow—witness his indictment in Kentucky on a "morality" charge—proceed from the profound change that has taken place in Dreiser's own attitude toward social questions. As is known, he has arrived at a positive communistic social view; and with the intellectual honesty and courage which marks him and distinguishes him from his contemporaries, he is speaking his conclusions out loud. This is his crime. For this they want to tear down and destroy the titan of American letters.

Let them try. They will not succeed. Every blow dealt at Dreiser by the literary Hessians of the slave system will only endear him all the more to the masses. Indeed, it is quite possible that the gifted writer will begin only now to find his own public and become a real tribune of the people.

That part of the proletariat which is beginning to awaken, which is not resigned to slavery, will hear him gladly. The working-class movement of the present generation has been poor and weak. It had little to offer to the intellectuals, and because of that it had but few of them to espouse its cause; and out of that few it can safely be said that 90 percent were four-flushers and pretenders. It is growing stronger now, and it will gain in strength as the exploiting system reveals increasingly the fatal weakness which proceeds from its own inner laws. With this new strength will come an accession of intellectual forces turning away from the hopeless, decaying system.

Theodore Dreiser is a herald of this development, and a most welcome one. Let us hope that his first courageous steps are motivated by a conviction that will not be shaken, and by a determination to follow the path to the end. If that proves to be the case, his loss of prestige in the bourgeois world will have abundant compensations, and will be in itself a tribute to him.

Marine workers not guilty of 'dynamite plot'

Published November 28, 1931

The following article was published in *The Militant.*

On Tuesday, November 17, the New York newspapers came out with sensational stories about an alleged plot for "the wholesale bombing of barges in New York Harbor," which, it was claimed, had been frustrated by the arrest of five members of the Independent Tidewater Boatmen's Union. From the very first we viewed the reports of the affair with the deepest suspicion, all the more so since it was being represented as a "Communist drive against capitalistically owned property and a campaign in a war of Communists against conservative labor" *(Times).* Since the opposition of the communist movement—in all of its factions and groupings—to methods of individual violence and terrorism is clearly established and well known, this attempt to pass the affair off as a communist action threw discredit on the whole story of the police. The fact that it is directed at the boatmen's union was another suspicious feature. It had the bad smell of another "plant" such as has been encountered time and time again in the experience of the labor movement in America. In common with all class-conscious workers we watched for further developments with the most intense interest.

Since we have had no association or direct acquaintance with the accused men, we did not feel that the initiative in arranging a legal defense for them belonged to us, although we were of the opinion that they were entitled to that much in any case. The fact that the revolutionary labor movement does not advocate or practice the method of individual terrorism or sabotage is no reason to fly into a panic when the police find some dynamite or plant it. Neither should we take a police accusation against a group of workers as proof of guilt. And finally we should not turn our backs on workers in the hands of the police and leave them defenseless under any circumstances. These elementary principles of labor ethics and solidarity—to say nothing of the communist class point of view—which ought to be taken for granted, are mentioned here only because they seem to have been forgotten in this case.

Therefore, when it became clear, after two days had elapsed since the arrest without anything having been done, the National Committee of the Communist League decided to come to the aid of the prisoners and make provision for their legal defense. This was promptly accomplished, thanks to the help and cooperation of Carlo Tresca, editor of *Il Martello.* Since Wednesday a competent attorney has been looking after the legal interests of the accused marine workers. The facts are now coming to light and the fog of police propaganda in the capitalist press is beginning to lift. Everything that has happened since our investigation began has tended to confirm the first suspicions about the case.

Every working-class organization, and above all the entire left wing of the movement, is duty bound to support the defense of the arrested marine workers. As we see it, this is a principled question. The accused men have entered pleas of not guilty. The letter of Soderberg, printed in another column, shows that the police claim of "confessions" is the confession of their own stool pigeon and provocateur.[78] Even bourgeois justice grants a presumption of innocence until guilt has been proven at a trial. Can revolutionary workers do less?

❖

From this point of view the strongest protest must be registered against the outrageous comments of the *Daily Worker* on November 18. There, instead of a protest against the attempt to convict the prisoners in the capitalist press before trial, we read a denunciation of them. Without lifting a finger to investigate the facts, without appealing to the workers to at least suspend judgment until the facts are known, they take the police announcements for granted and abandon the helpless prisoners to their fate, giving them a kick on the way. Of men who at that moment were being beaten and tortured by the police, they had only this to say:

"Soderberg, secretary of the Tidewater Boatmen's Union, whom the capitalist press calls a 'Red,' was expelled from the Communist Party for being a suspicious element and also from the Marine Workers' Industrial Union for disruptive and anti–working class activities. Treiger, Reily and Bunker were expelled from the Marine Workers' Industrial Union as bad elements." They do not belong to our faction—do with them what you will! Shame on such people! They are without honor, without sentiments of solidarity, without even the labor ethics of an ordinary union member.

More than that. In their panic, in their rabbit-hearted cowardice, in their fool's delusion that they can save themselves by pointing the finger at others, they approach downright provocation against the IWW and the Lovestone faction.

Consider this: "Treiger in his confession [who said he made a "confession"?] stated that he was a member of the I.W.W. and was not a Communist nor did he believe in Communist political action, but in direct individual anarchist action."

And this: "The men arrested are not members of the Communist Party, and their actions are unknown to it, with the exception of one of them, who was expelled from the Party as a suspicious character and who has been since very openly working against the Party with the renegade Lovestone group."

It is not we who harbor dynamiters—it is the IWW and the Lovestone group. You are welcome to blame it on them, but leave us alone. With such a yellow and treacherous attitude we can have nothing whatever in common. Our differences with both the IWW and the Lovestone faction are many and serious enough. We have spoken of them before and we will speak of them again. But these organizations cannot be accused, even by the remotest implication, of the advocacy or practice of individual terrorism. It is not true. And even if it were true we would not say so in such a moment. We are revolutionists, not informers.

❖

We cannot believe that the Communist workers will let the position of the *Daily Worker* prevail as the policy of the party. It is indeed a terrific revelation of the political and moral degeneration of the upper circles of the Stalinist faction. These processes of decay expose themselves with devastating swiftness in times of crisis and danger, when leaders have to act quickly; when they have no time to dissemble; when they have to show at once the contents of their minds and hearts. On the other hand the time of crisis and danger calls out the deepest class impulses of the revolutionary proletariat and impels them to assert their will in irresistible terms. An upheaval in the Communist ranks against the cowardly and treasonable attitude of the *Daily Worker* in the case of the marine workers will be the best thing that can happen for the good of the movement and the honor of the party. That will facilitate the organization of a strong working-class front against the new "dynamite plot" and similar conspiracies of the ruling powers.

The militant workers must be aroused and organized to fight. The Communist League sees no factional issue in this case, which involves the lives and liberties of the marine workers and endangers the entire left-wing labor movement. The matter necessitates the cooperation of all elements in the labor movement, regardless of the differences which divide them, who are willing to stand together on this common class point of view. The labor movement shall not be terrorized and broken up by dynamite plots. The arrested marine workers shall not be abandoned and left defenseless. They shall not be railroaded without a fight. We hope to see the labor movement, and especially its entire left-wing and militant section, united in this fight.

The hunger march

Published December 19, 1931

The following article was published in *The Militant*.

As a Communist propaganda demonstration on the issue of unemployment, the hunger march to Washington at the opening of Congress was an indubitable success. Communist initiative and organizing faculty were written all over the affair. By the demonstration the cause of the hungry millions was placed on the agenda in the most dramatic manner; the inability of the richest imperialist power to provide the necessities of life to the producers of its incredible wealth was called to the attention of the entire world. And before the world the Communists appeared as the spokesmen of the dispossessed, the hungry and shelterless workers.

All that was lacking was the participation of the masses of the unemployed. Doak, the labor-baiting secretary of labor, announced the "sensational" discovery of his secret agents that the hunger march was organized and directed by the Communist Party. This revelation needed no exceptional detective work. The facts were all too obvious. It was easy enough to point out the Communist leaders of the march. They were everywhere for all to see. If the Secret Service had been able to discover the unemployed masses following these leaders, that would have been a real exposure; and, from our point of view, a most welcome one.

But they could not do it; the masses were not there. The success of the hunger march as a propaganda manifestation of the party was on a par with its failure as a mobilization of the unemployed workers. Like nearly all of the previous actions of the party in the unemployment situation, this supreme effort was confined pretty closely—so far as direct participation is concerned—to the Communist workers and their close sympathizers. The crying disparity between the burning importance of the issue and the ability of the party to draw the masses into motion was once again demonstrated on this occasion.

This proceeds inevitably from the false policy and method of the party. You cannot whittle down a mass movement by sectarian methods from day to day and then expect to have the masses ready when the great occasion comes. This is the outstanding lesson of the hunger march. By this we do not in the least deprecate the positive sides of the undertaking. Communist propaganda demonstrations have their importance. But only a genuine movement of the masses will get results. This is yet to come. Stalinist policy and Stalinist leadership of the party are the chief factors of obstruction.

The Kentucky miners

Published December 19, 1931

The following article was published in *The Militant*.

The verdict of guilty in the case of William B. Jones, Harlan County miners' leader, with the accompanying sentence of life imprisonment, again brings this historic struggle sharply before the working class and warns against any further delay in organizing a genuine national movement in behalf of the indicted men. More than a score of workers are yet to be tried. Their lives are in danger, and with them the life of the organized labor movement in the Kentucky mine fields.

The intervention of a powerful workers' protest in the affair is one of the most important questions of the day. Here is a case of vindictive persecution not of a few individuals merely, but on a wholesale scale. The object is to wipe out unionism and terrorize all of its advocates by a fearful example of class "justice" and revenge. Can that be allowed to happen in comparative silence?

It is by no means a one-sided battle. All the strength is not on the side of Kentucky "law," which licenses thugs to maim and kill and prosecute workers who defend themselves. The acquittal of Burnett in the first trial a couple of weeks ago demonstrates that the sentiment of the masses is not without effect even on jurymen selected from another class.[79] It shows also that the position of the defendants is legally justified, even from the biased standards of capitalist law. These two factors explain the acquittal of Burnett. A relaxation of general labor interest in the second case, whether from over-confidence or neglect, turned the scale against Jones and emboldened the prosecution to go through with a conviction. The tide must be turned before it is too late. The legal defense, from all appearances, is competent enough. What is needed now is its reinforcement by the mass demands of the working masses.

The factional wrangling over the defense has been a scandal and a direct blow to the men and the cause on trial. In the welter of charges and countercharges around the cases it was hard for a time to ascertain exactly who was handling the defense. One got the impression, in this disgraceful quarrel, that the miners in the dock were regarded as bones to fight over rather than a cause to defend by common efforts. It is clear enough now that the General Defense Committee of the IWW is conducting the legal defense. But is that any reason for Communists to stand aside or—still worse—attack the defense at the moment it is under the guns of the class enemy?

No, that is factionalism in the most perverted form, a factionalism that loses all vision of the class issues, and therefore a corrupt and reactionary factionalism. Class-conscious workers are duty bound to give financial and other support to the defense in every labor case. In the present instance it means to support the General Defense

Committee without a moment's hesitation and provide it with the necessary funds to meet the heavy burdens imposed by the trials.

We do not mean by this to express any approval of the propaganda methods of the IWW in the controversy with the ILD. They create the impression that their main fight is against the Communists. This also hurts and weakens the cause at stake. The real enemy is the capitalist class and their judicial agents in Kentucky. We speak for a union of all forces of the labor movement in a common fight against this enemy.

Greetings to 'Communistes'

Published December 19, 1931

The following article was published in *The Militant*.

As this issue of *The Militant* goes to press we greet the first appearance of a fellow-fighter in the ranks of the Opposition. *Communistes* will carry to the Greek workers in America the same message which *The Militant* has carried in the English language through storm and stress for more than three years. We see in the enlistment of this ally an event of profound significance in the development of American communism. It shows to us that an important section of the communist proletariat, which has given proof in the past in labor and sacrifice of its revolutionary spirit, is finding its way, through a hailstorm of slander and misrepresentation, to the platform of the Opposition, which is the platform of Marx and Lenin.

The Greek Communists in America are not to blame if they have been disoriented and led astray on the great questions of principle which have arisen in the Comintern

The Canadian Communist trials

Published December 19, 1931

The following article was published in *The Militant.*

The helpless impotence of the party leaders on all questions which arise out of the class struggle and demand a quick answer is again illustrated in the most striking manner by their clamlike silence on the Canadian Communist trial. The conviction and sentence to five-year prison terms of the leading staff of the Canadian party is surely an event of extraordinary importance.[80] Our party cannot be unaffected by such an alarming development across the border. Moreover, it owes a duty to the party and the party leaders who have been proscribed by the Canadian government.

We have had a fairly rich experience of the same kind. Our party went through a test of fire in the Palmer raids; it lived as an illegal organization for three years; and after that, by a combination of legal and illegal methods of organization and a determined will to break out of the underground straitjacket, it reconquered the right to a legal existence as a party. All these questions are rising up before the Canadian party at the present moment. How does the leadership of the American party evaluate the trial, and what advice does it offer to the Canadian comrades in their difficult position? The *Daily Worker* answers these crucial questions with a studied neglect. It has nothing to say.

In a previous issue of *The Militant,* Comrade Spector has given a report and a political evaluation of the trial. With his comments we are in full agreement. His criticism of the showing made by the defendants was a loyal criticism that did not in any way impair the fundamental solidarity of the Opposition with the party in its hour of persecution. And it was absolutely necessary. The Canadian party will pay dearly for the attempts to dilute the revolutionary essence of its doctrines before the court. That is not the way to fight for the legality of the party as a communist party.

It is the way, rather, to discredit its leadership, to poison the ranks with an evasive legalistic retreat from principle, and to rob the party of the power to stand up under the blows of the class enemy. When the leaders of the proletariat are on trial they must not forget for a moment that they are speaking to the whole country. Then of all times they must say what they really stand for. You cannot fool the masses into communism. You will only discredit your own movement if you try.

In our opinion, Comrade Spector sounded the right note when he said the problem at the moment consists in going to every working-class organization in the country with the slogan of a common fight for the repeal of Section 98 of the Criminal Code, the section under which the prosecution was conducted. The Canadian party should under no circumstances accept the condemnation to illegality and retreat into a restricted underground existence without a further struggle.

The proscription of the Canadian party is not grounded in the present political situation and relation of class forces in the country. Social conditions for a regime of white terror, such as prevails in a number of European countries, are not matured in Canada. It is not the strength of the Canadian party which the conservative government fears, but rather its weakness—brought upon it by the cruel blows it has suffered in recent years from the Stalinist regime—that emboldens the government to experiment with a red scare. The action against the Canadian party bears a close resemblance to the assaults we experienced in the Palmer days, and has much of the same content. The Canadian party should profit by the errors, and also by the victories, which attended our struggle under somewhat similar conditions.

The party should wage a determined fight for legality. But it cannot fight successfully alone. It must make its fight the fight of the working class, in the first place of the more advanced and class-conscious workers' organizations. In order to do this it must throw overboard all the bizarre theories which have been foisted upon it in recent years, weakening and undermining it, isolating it from the labor movement, and rendering it helpless before the government attack.

What the Canadian party needs most of all is a realistic appraisal of the situation and a deliberate tactic of the united front. It needs to approach the workers of other organizations, not as "social fascists" but as brothers in a common cause. All workers' organizations have an interest in the questions of legal political rights. The party must become the champion of such rights for all. If the party approaches them in the right way and with the right policy, it can gain their support. There is every reason for confidence that a united struggle in the present situation will be victorious. The Opposition will do all it can to help the party to find this path.

The situation is becoming impossible

December 31, 1931

The following is a letter to Arne Swabeck.

Dear Arne:

I received your letters, including the note from Minneapolis with the money order of twenty-five dollars. If we have to give the Jewish paper half of the collection, I wonder where the national office is going to get anything.[81]

The situation here is becoming impossible. Not a cent comes in from the branches, so what are we going to do? I have finally become convinced that our budget has to be cut down. Otherwise we are going to have a crash. I would like to suggest that you look over the job situation in Chicago, in case the economic situation forces us to make a temporary retreat. If it should come to that, it's best not to wait until the situation becomes hopeless.

Your own health and work and personal life will suffer, and it will suddenly be discovered that you are the

Rose is taking care of all the receipts as reported by you and charging such amounts as you state to organization expenses, except that which goes direct to Inger [Swabeck].

As you know, Al is back and Max is expected in a day or two.

We have a new pamphlet from Trotsky. A wonderful analysis of the fascist problems in Germany and the whole international situation, including the position of America. We are planning to get it out as a ten-cent pamphlet, and Cudone is already started on setting; if we raise enough to pay him this week, he will continue on Monday.

About the thesis on England. There appears to be a difference of opinion about that. Why should we give space to any fool who comes along and proposes a platform for the Opposition which contradicts all our fundamental views? These people are not members of the Opposition, and from what Glotzer tells us about the English situation they cannot be considered proper material for the inaugural group.

I think we make too many concessions to the ballyhoo about democracy. It's a different thing if a member or an organization of the Opposition brings forth a thesis on some question. Then of course it has to receive a hearing even though it is wrong. But that does not mean that we open our columns to every freak who comes along and calls himself an Oppositionist. We got more criticism than praise for printing Weisbord's belchings. These are the views of P.G. Glotzer, who, as you know, has just returned from across, with all the latest dope. And I am inclined to think there is something in what the kid says.

One more paragraph and I am through. You are mistaken when you say that the sentiments I expressed in my previous letter arise as a result of the responsibilities and worry of the office in the past few weeks. I served my time at that already, and I don't think any new experience could add anything. During the weeks after my first year of work for the Opposition, I had plenty of time to reflect over everything, while Rose and I were going about from place to place trying to bum a place to sleep for the night. That was when I began to make an interesting discovery that I was the son of a bitch who was the cause of all the trouble. Well, I won't forget that, and I will not wish that experience on another. That is why I am giving you due warning.

Since you left on November 27, four weeks ago, Inger has received fifty-five dollars from the office, Marty forty-five dollars, Cudone fifteen dollars on back wages, and the bindery check for twenty-five dollars was made good. In addition to that, we have paid Cudone his regular weekly wages and brought the rent up to January 1 with a five-dollar reduction monthly, paid the paper mill their old bill. To do that, and to keep the office open at the same time with the constantly decreasing income, requires efforts of an extraordinary nature. This could not have been done without the work and sacrifices that Rose has been making. At present she has thirty-five dollars coming which she laid out, using her house rent. If she cannot draw it out by the first, and it does not look like it, she will have to make personal loans for it. If now she becomes the object of criticism and dissatisfaction because more was not done, it will not surprise me in the least. We had that experience before.

Fraternally yours,
[Jim]

P.S. Parts of this letter are of course for yourself *only*. Please treat them confidentially.

P.S. by R.K.—I took work home over the holiday, so I am not able to enclose the defense circular which Jim mentions above, as he wants me to airmail this letter, and I am not going to the office today. Taking a holiday. Get the circular from Hugo.

Notes

1. This document was signed by J.W. Johnstone, Manuel Gomez, William F. Dunne, James P. Cannon, William Z. Foster, Alexander Bittelman, and George Siskind. It predicted a deepgoing economic crisis and attacked the Lovestoneites for "following the lead of bourgeois economists in evaluating the present depression only as a 'recession.'" It included Bittelman's view that American capitalism was reaching the apex of its growth—the "apex theory" mentioned critically by Cannon later in this volume. The document was presented to the Anglo-American Secretariat of the Comintern at the Sixth World Congress in July 1928 by delegates representing the Foster and Cannon groups. Lovestone refused to publish it in the CP but it was circulated surreptitiously inside the party. After *The Militant* began publishing it in installments in November 1928 the CP published it in the *Daily Worker.*
2. The "latest decision of the secretariat of the ECCI," issued as a ten-line resolution on September 7, 1928, stated that "the charge against the majority of the Central Committee representing a Right line is unfounded."
3. Zinoviev, Kamenev, and their followers in Leningrad formed a bloc with the Bolshevik-Leninists called the United Opposition in 1926. Its platform called for industrialization and for limitations on the better-off peasants (kulaks), who were gaining strength under the Bukharin-Stalin regime. The platform is reprinted in *Challenge of the Left Opposition (1926–27)* (New York: Pathfinder Press, 1980). In 1928 a nationwide grain strike by the kulaks threatened the cities with starvation. In panic, Stalin instituted forced collectivization of the land and rapid, bureaucratic industrialization.
4. The May 1926 British general strike, called in solidarity with a bitter miners' strike (May–November 1926), brought

the country to a standstill. Its power frightened not only the capitalists but also the union bureaucrats, who called it off after nine days. Soviet trade unions continued their collaboration with the British union officials in the Anglo-Russian Trade Union Unity Committee (see glossary) until the British withdrew from that body in September 1927.

5. Trotsky's major writings on China are collected in *Leon Trotsky on China* (New York: Pathfinder Press, 1976). Zinoviev's theses were reprinted in Trotsky's *Problems of the Chinese Revolution* (Ann Arbor: University of Michigan Press, 1967). The Chinese revolution of 1925–27 began with a general strike in Shanghai; it spread with the Northern Expedition of Chiang Kai-shek's army, which conquered the proimperialist warlords of the North, unified the country, and sparked workers' uprisings and peasant land seizures on a massive scale; it was crushed when the Communist Party, after leading a successful insurrection in Shanghai in March 1927, welcomed Chiang's troops into the city, leading to a massacre of the workers. The CP, under orders of the Comintern, had joined the Kuomintang, or Nationalist Party, in 1923, and Chiang was the principal military leader of that party.

6. Trotsky's "The Draft Program of the Communist International—A Criticism of Fundamentals" was published in *The Militant* of November 15, 1928, and subsequent issues. It is reprinted in *The Third International After Lenin* (New York: Pathfinder Press, 1970).

7. This letter was from Gerry Allard (see glossary).

8. In the New York City municipal elections in 1927, Judge Jacob Panken was the SP candidate for reelection to the Second District Municipal Court of Manhattan. The CP proposed a united labor ticket, which Panken denounced. The CP then called upon its supporters to vote for Panken in the absence of a CP candidate. He lost in a close election.

9. The United Mine Workers strike began April 1, 1927, and ended in defeat in October 1928. The April 1, 1928, conference of the left wing (the "Save the Union" movement),

held in Pittsburgh, Pennsylvania, had 1,125 delegates representing 101,000 miners, according to CP reports.

10. Minor, then an anarchist, visited Russia for nine months in 1918 and published a critical interview with Lenin in the *New York World* on February 4, 1919. After he switched his position he published the article "I Change My Mind a Little" in the *Liberator,* October 1920.
11. On the nights of January 2 and 5, 1920, over 5,000 Communists and anarchists were arrested in nationwide raids organized by Democratic Attorney General A. Mitchell Palmer. As a result of this and subsequent deportations and other repression, the CP lost about four-fifths of its membership. Bertram Wolfe left the party for two years. In August 1922 the underground convention of the CP near Bridgeman, Michigan, was raided by federal and local police agents; most of the delegates escaped, but convention registration documents were seized and used in further persecution of the party. Wolfe fled to Mexico.
12. After this burglary, photostats of some letters were published in the *Daily Worker.* There was a second burglary on January 14. Cannon described the burglaries in his *History of American Trotskyism* (New York: Pathfinder Press, 1972) as follows: ". . . they had jimmied the lock on the door of my home and broken in. Everything was in disorder; all my private papers, documents, records, correspondence—anything they could lay their hands on—were strewn over the floor. Evidently we had surprised them before they could cart the plunder away. While I was on tour a few weeks later they came and finished the job. This time they took everything."
13. In 1923 a strong protest movement of the German proletariat developed, fueled by a severe economic crisis and sparked by the French occupation of the Ruhr. The Communist Party of Germany grew rapidly and won the leadership of the movement. A prerevolutionary situation developed, and a decision was made to carry out a revolution in October, beginning in Saxony, where the CP was strong and was in a united front with the Social Democrats, who controlled the state government. At the last minute,

the CP leadership cancelled the rising. As a result of this vacillation, the capitalists were able to recover. Heinrich Brandler, a German CP leader, became the scapegoat for this defeat, but the Kremlin's responsibility for it was one of the issues that led to the formation of the Russian Left Opposition. In June 1923 the Bulgarian government of the peasant leader Stambulisky was overthrown by reactionary forces. The CP remained neutral in the ensuing civil war, but the white terror against them forced the party underground. Claiming that the workers were not defeated by the civil war, which they saw as a fight between two bourgeois cliques, the CP attempted a putsch in September, which was doomed to defeat.

14. The Indonesian uprising against colonialism in 1926–27 was led by the Communist Party of Indonesia, despite disagreements within the party and lack of Comintern support. The uprising was crushed and the CP decimated. The Vienna events of 1927 began with the shooting of an old man and a child during a clash between reactionaries and armed SP defense guards. When the reactionaries were acquitted, the SP called mass demonstrations during which the Ministry of Justice was burned down and 100 were killed in street fighting with the police. The events were climaxed with a four-day general strike.
15. Litvinov, Soviet delegate to the preparatory commission for the League of Nations World Disarmament Conference, 1927–30, proposed sweeping disarmament programs.
16. In 1928 the German government, including its SP ministers, proposed to build several armored cruisers. The SP had opposed this in the previous election under the slogan "Not armored cruisers, but food for children." The CP petitioned for a referendum to stop the project, and collected over a million signatures—not enough for the referendum. The cruiser project was finally approved by the Reichstag (parliament) over the objections of its CP and SP members.
17. In 1927 Joseph Paul-Boncour (1873–1972), a French right-wing Socialist, proposed a law legitimizing rearmament,

under limits to be enforced by the French capitalist government—that the army be limited to "defense," that there be conscription of economic goods as well as manpower, and that war profits be controlled. This plan, aimed at making the French army one of the most efficient of its time, was never enacted.

18. The Dawes Plan (1924) provided for loans from U.S. investors to help Germany pay war reparations despite its economic crisis. It set yearly payments indexed to economic improvements in Germany, but set no final total on German liability. In February 1929 a Conference of Experts including two representatives of each creditor nation and two Germans, took up the question of the total and the time in which it was to be paid. Its recommendations, called the Young Plan, set the total at 121 billion Reichsmarks payable in fifty-nine yearly installments. The reparations agent in Germany was Parker Gilbert (1892–1938), a U.S. banker. In June 1927 he had criticized the German government's budget for spending too much on public works, but later he campaigned for a final agreement on reparations before the economy had a chance to either improve or go into a deeper crisis.

19. The Passaic, New Jersey, strike (1926–27) was the first big CP-led textile strike, involving 16,000 workers organized through united-front committees in the mills; it succeeded in reversing a wage cut and won the right of the workers to organize in the AFL. The miners' movement, initiated in 1925 under the slogan "Save the Union," campaigned for the UMWA to organize the unorganized miners in West Virginia, Kentucky, and the South; its slate won over 60,000 votes in a 1926 campaign against Lewis for union president. In New Bedford, Massachusetts, the CP led a strike of 26,000 cotton mill workers in 1928. The CP played a major role in the campaign to save Sacco and Vanzetti (see glossary) through the International Labor Defense, leading an international movement involving millions of workers in defense committees, conferences, and demonstrations.

20. The April 1, 1928, conference of the Save the Union movement called on miners in nonstriking fields to join the national UMW strike on April 16, but failed to organize them. During this period the CP turned away from the AFL and set out to form new unions. CPers and miners close to them founded the National Miners Union (NMU) in September 1928 after the UMW strike was settled.
21. In the needle trades there were clashes between the bureaucracy and the left wing in the mid-twenties. In 1926 an ILGWU strike was settled on terms that left 35,000 workers outside the union; in 1927 12,000 were expelled from the furriers' union. These forces formed the Needle Trades Workers Industrial Union (NTWIU) in January 1929. The new textile union, the National Textile Workers Union (NTWU) was formed in September 1928 after the CP-led strikes in Massachusetts.
22. Pepper's article in the October 1928 *Communist* said that *"Negro* Communists should emphasize in their propaganda *the establishment of a Negro Soviet Republic,"* pointing to 219 southern counties where over 3 million Blacks constituted the majority of the population. The Sixth Congress theses had included the slogan of the *right* to self-determination "in those regions of the South in which compact Negro masses are living," but did not call for a separate state. The CP raised the demand for a republic during the "third period" and at the start of the cold war; they shelved it when a class-collaborationist deal with Washington seemed near, as in the People's Front period, 1935–39; and they dropped it officially in 1959.
23. In 1927 the Stalinist secret police (GPU) accused the Russian Left Opposition of conspiring with a former officer in the White Guard army of Gen. Piotr N. Wrangel. Later they revealed that the "Wrangel officer" was their own agent.
24. The CP was reorganized following its 1925 convention to eliminate federated structures carried over from the SP, such as language branches; the new structure was based on shop nuclei (three or more members at a workplace) and

street nuclei (residential units for members not attached to shop nuclei).

25. In cities with over 200 CP members, the city organization was divided into sections, with organizational authority intermediate between that of the city organization and the basic party units, the shop and street nuclei.

26. "On the Situation in Russia," a circular letter written by Trotsky on October 21, 1928, was circulated by Left Oppositionists in the USSR; 150 were jailed or exiled for this in early 1929, according to *The Militant,* which published it on February 1, 1929. It is reprinted in *Challenge of the Left Opposition, 1928–29* (New York: Pathfinder Press, 1981), under the title "The Danger of Bonapartism and the Opposition's Role." In it Trotsky commented that while some centrists would move to the left, it would be wrong for the Left Opposition to aim toward a bloc with the center; he advocated "implacably opposing to the centrists the proletarian nucleus of the party," and said that the party could be reformed only through a "decisive intervention by the masses," which could be led only by the Left Opposition.

27. This refers to the conditions surrounding Trotsky's exile in Alma-Ata and his deportation from the USSR in January–February 1929. Trotsky and his family suffered from exposure to bitter cold while in Central Asia and also contracted malaria. In addition there was fear of an assassination attempt during the deportation.

28. The Sixth National Convention of the Workers (Communist) Party convened March 1 to 9. Its Lovestoneite majority appointed a ten-person delegation to Moscow to appeal against the Comintern's anti-Lovestone decisions. The Fosterites sent three representatives in addition. They all went before a commission that included Stalin himself. In May, after lengthy deliberations, the Comintern removed Lovestone from his posts in the CP and ordered him to remain in Moscow. In June, Lovestone disobeyed this order, returned to the U.S., and was expelled from the CP.

29. The Comintern representatives, Philipp Dengel of Germany and Harry Pollitt of Britain, also brought an open

letter containing the Comintern's political proposals for the American party.

30. The "proletarian" Lovestoneites had also cabled Stalin, appealing for him to reverse the Comintern's organizational proposals. Stalin replied that the convention could choose a CEC which would then choose the party officers, but he insisted that Lovestone, Bittelman, and Pepper come to Moscow. The result was a CEC with a Lovestoneite majority and three coequal secretaries: Gitlow as head of the executive department, Bedacht as agitation and propaganda director, and Foster as trade union secretary.
31. The books referred to here are *Permanent Revolution* and *My Life* (New York: Pathfinder Press). They were originally published in 1931 and 1930 respectively.
32. Dunne and Carl Skoglund had visited the Rubins, who were sympathetic to the Left Opposition, to ask them to donate to *The Militant*. The Rubins expressed more interest in helping to finance the publication of books by Trotsky. Cannon immediately sent estimates and the proposal that they help to establish a printshop, but their response to that was negative.
33. The Spartacus Bund, Rosa Luxemburg's revolutionary group in Germany, was formally a faction of the Independent Social Democratic Party (USPD), a much larger, centrist group that split from the right-wing German Socialist Party (SPD) in 1917; the Spartacists split from the USPD to form the Communist Party (KPD) in late 1918, but were too small and inexperienced to lead the revolution of 1919 to victory; the KPD later merged with the left wing of the USPD to form the United Communist Party in 1920. The Committee for the Third International (CTI) was a small French group founded in 1919 largely by anarchists and syndicalists, led by Alfred Rosmer and others; when the left wing of the SP, led by Louis-Olivier Frossard, split in 1920 to form the CP, the CTI got only three representatives on the leading committee of twenty-four; the CTI formally dissolved after the Third Congress of the Comintern.

34. After the Socialist Party split in 1919 there were two CPs: one called the Communist Party, which included the foreign-language groups, and the smaller Communist Labor Party, with more of the U.S.-born English speakers. Cannon was in the latter.
35. The CLP and a minority of the CP led by Ruthenberg fused in 1920 to form the United Communist Party. This then fused with the remaining majority of the CP in 1921 to form the Communist Party of America.
36. No such article was ever published, and no draft has been found in Cannon's archives.
37. At the convention of the Farmer-Labor Party in 1923, Pepper led the CP in pushing through a decision to organize a national campaign in the 1924 elections. The union leaders who had led the party until then thought the convention should just draft a platform and call a broader convention. They walked out and the CP proceeded to change the name of the party to Federated Farmer-Labor Party and to throw its support to La Follette's Progressive Party presidential campaign. When the Comintern pointed out that this was opportunist, the CP put up its own candidates. Pepper's October 1928 article "American Negro Problems" (see note 22) referred to the "mighty migration from the cotton plantations to the industrial centres" as "an *'unarmed Spartacist uprising' against slavery and oppression by a capitalist and feudal oligarchy"* (emphasis in original).
38. The CLA's position advocating a labor party was reversed at its second national conference in the fall of 1931. The political resolution adopted there criticized the former position as "reformist" and "to a certain extent an uncritical carry-over of the preceding group struggles in the party." The position was again reversed in 1938 after the formation of the Socialist Workers Party, following discussions with Trotsky on the Transitional Program—see *The Transitional Program for Socialist Revolution* (New York: Pathfinder Press, 1977).
39. The position on self-determination was discussed with Trotsky by Arne Swabeck in 1933 and by C.L.R. James

and Charles Curtiss in 1939. The Socialist Workers Party adopted two resolutions on the subject in July 1939. The discussions are published in *Malcolm X, Black Liberation, and the Road to Workers Power* (New York: Pathfinder Press, 2009) and the resolutions are published in *The Founding of the Socialist Workers Party: Minutes and Resolutions, 1938–39* (New York: Pathfinder Press, 1982).

40. The Labour Party polled 8.4 million votes (3 million more than in 1924) and won the 1929 elections; it selected James Ramsay MacDonald (1866–1937), an opponent of the 1926 general strike, as prime minister. The CP got only 50,000 votes, fewer than it got in 1924.

41. The *Daily Worker* was disrupted during the period of Lovestone's expulsion to the extent that it suspended publication for one day—June 21, 1929; otherwise the CP apparatus of Lovestone switched over to Foster once the Moscow decision on Lovestone's fate became known. The 90 percent Lovestoneite majority of the March 1929 convention melted away as an anti-Lovestone campaign was whipped up. Lovestone could muster only about forty followers at a conference in October 1929.

42. On July 10, 1929, troops of the Manchurian warlord Chang Hsueh-liang seized the Chinese Eastern Railroad and ousted the Soviet administrators; armed clashes followed in August. Soviet troops seized the railroad in November, and in December the Chinese government agreed that Chang would not contest this. The international capitalist press either condemned the Chinese seizure of the railroad or were neutral.

43. The CP-led Gastonia, North Carolina, textile strike of 1929 was one of the most spectacular and costly defeats of the "third period." The National Textile Workers Union organizers, after two months' preparation, called out 2,500 strikers in April; they were confronted with attacks by militia and vigilantes. The chief of police was killed and three deputies wounded during a June raid on the union headquarters. For this 100 workers were arrested and 7 were convicted of second-degree murder. Facing up to twenty

years in prison, the defendants jumped bail; five fled to Russia and two went underground in the U.S. One, Fred Beal, the central strike organizer, eventually served three years.

44. This article was published serially in *The Militant* from August 15 to November 30, 1929. It is reprinted in *Challenge of the Left Opposition (1928–29)* (New York: Pathfinder Press, 1981).

45. This refers to letters and articles by Joseph Angelo on the miners' movement in Illinois and the sectarian role of the CP.

46. About thirty delegates walked out of the national convention of the NMU at Belleville, Illinois, in early November 1929 in protest of the CP's campaign to oust John Watt as president of the union.

47. McMahon summed up the aims of the campaign as follows: "We aren't talking higher wages. We aren't talking shorter hours, we can't express our objective in those terms. We want to sit down with the mill owners, we want to take up their problems as our problems, we want the mill owners, ourselves, and the general public to sit down and diagnose the industry's ills and seek mutually a means to heal them."

48. The AFL's United Textile Workers led two strikes in Marion, North Carolina, in 1929. In the first, from July to September, workers went out against the advice of the union after 22 were fired for union activity; the militia were called in, and 147 were arrested for "insurrection"; 102 of the strikers were not rehired. In the second strike in October, police shot 36 workers, killing 6, and the court ruled that the police acted in self-defense.

49. In the national coal strikes of 1919 and 1922, over 400,000 miners went out. In the 1919 steel strike, up to 367,000 workers were involved. And in the 1922 railroad shop crafts strike, 400,000 participated.

50. In Germany, the Left Oppositionists had been expelled from the Leninbund; they then united with other groups to form

the United Opposition, which had a delegate in the Prussian legislature and published a biweekly newspaper. In France, the Communist League was the strongest group in the ILO, with a weekly paper, *La Verité,* and a monthly journal.

51. Trotsky's advice to members of the Leninbund, "An Open Letter to All Members of the Leninbund," dated February 6, 1930, was published in *The Militant* on March 29, 1930, and is reprinted in *Writings of Leon Trotsky (1930)* (New York: Pathfinder Press, 1975). He criticizes the Urbahns leadership's positions that the Soviet Union is capitalist and that a new party is needed, and calls for the consolidation of the International Left Opposition around the program of the Russian Bolshevik-Leninists.

52. For a different translation, see "The Liquidation of Liquidationism," *Lenin: Collected Works* (Moscow: Foreign Languages, 1963), vol. 15, p. 458. The *otzovists,* who advocated withdrawal of the Bolshevik representatives from the third tsarist Duma, were a majority in the Bolshevik faction in 1907 but soon became a minority. In 1909 they broke factional discipline by refusing to carry out trade union and other legal work or to sit in the Duma, a parliament dominated by landlords and big capitalists. The Bolshevik majority thereupon expelled the *otzovist* leader Bogdanov from the faction, declaring that *otzovism* and Bolshevism were incompatible.

53. See "Deeper Into the Party," published July 26, 1930, in *The Militant* and reprinted in this volume.

54. The CLA statement on the miners' union, "The Mining Situation and the Tasks of the Left Wing," was published in *The Militant* March 1, 1930; Trotsky submitted an "amendment" dated March 15, "Progressives in the United Mine Workers," which is reprinted in *Writings of Leon Trotsky: Supplement (1929–33)* (New York: Pathfinder Press, 1979). The statement on the needle trades, "Aftermath of the Needle Trades Convention," was published in *The Militant* June 21 and 28 and July 12, 1930, and is reprinted in this volume. The "prominent comrade in the union" was Sylvia Bleeker (see glossary).

55. The weekly *Militant,* which had started with the issue dated November 30, 1929 (which reported on the stock market crash), was forced to retreat to semimonthly publication on July 26, 1930.

56. The Needle Trades Workers Industrial Union convention met in New York City, June 7–8, 1930. There were 400 delegates from 200 shops; 307 were from New York.

57. These letters were published in *The Militant* on November 30, 1929, and March 26, 1930, respectively. In the first, dated October 19, 1929, he said: "The essential task of the American Communists consists of direct action upon the revolutionary elements of the class; the struggle for the workers who belong to the official Party or who are misled into the Right Wing not having a great importance. That means that the Communist League in America has all the necessary elements for developing into an independent party. . . ." In the second, Trotsky said: "In one of my first letters, sent upon the appearance of the weekly, I expressed the opinion that the League can arrive at the necessity to become an independent Communist Party. The relation of forces explained to me by Shachtman showed me that this 'danger' is not imminent. I wish to correct my first assumption; but without discouragement. . . ."

58. This demonstration was held June 28, 1930, and reported in *The Militant* in the July 12 issue. The New York district CP had issued an open call for a demonstration at the British Consulate; 1,500 participated; the CP attacked the CLA members and destroyed their placards, but the CLAers remained in the demonstration.

59. The Farmer-Labor Party affair was initiated by the "Farmer-Labor Party of Montana," a group around the *Producers News* of Plentywood, Montana; they proposed a conference to found a general left-wing paper in Minneapolis, to be put out by a conglomeration of factions (the CLA, the Lovestoneites, a group of Finns recently expelled from the CP, as well as former Minnesota Farmer-Labor Party activists); the paper was seen as a way to strengthen the Farmer-Labor movement in the Northwest. Some members

of the Minneapolis branch of the CLA initially supported this, but the NC issued a public statement against it in *The Militant* of November 1, 1930. This statement, drafted by Shachtman, pointed out that it was impossible to combine the views of the right and left wings in a single paper on a principled basis, and that the CLA was opposed to two-class parties like the Farmer-Labor Party.

60. *The Militant* resumed weekly publication with the July 4, 1931, issue.

61. This quotation is from the article "On the Situation in Russia," dated October 21, 1928. It actually appeared in *The Militant* of February 1, 1929. It is reprinted under the title "The Danger of Bonapartism and the Opposition's Role" in *Challenge of the Left Opposition (1928–29)* (New York: Pathfinder Press, 1981).

62. This refers to huge unemployment demonstrations called by the Trade Union Unity League on March 6, 1930, around the country. They had also called for general strikes on the same day, but the masses did not respond to this.

63. The German CP's vote in the 1930 elections was about 4.6 million, an increase of 40 percent over 1928. They saw this as proof of the correctness of their policies. However, the big winner in the 1930 elections was the Nazi Party; its vote increased from 810,000 in 1928 to 6.4 million in 1930, making it the strongest capitalist party in the country. The results really showed a deepening political polarization and the beginnings of Nazi inroads in the proletarian centers; this underscored the need for a CP-SP united front against the Nazis.

64. This is from the article "Once Again: On Brandler and Thalheimer," dated June 12, 1929. It is reprinted under a slightly different title in *Writings of Leon Trotsky (1929)* (New York: Pathfinder Press, 1975).

65. This document, dated July 12, 1928, is translated in *Challenge of the Left Opposition (1928–29)* under the title "Declaration to the Sixth Comintern Congress."

66. This is from the article "The Defense of the Soviet Union and the Opposition," dated September 7, 1929. It is reprinted in *Writings of Leon Trotsky (1929).*

67. See note 64.

68. This is from Trotsky's letter to the members of the Leninbund (see note 51).

69. Militant miners in the Illinois district had broken with the Lewis leadership in 1930, holding a convention and forming the "Reorganized United Mine Workers of America," on the pretext that the Lewis UMW constitution had lapsed since it had not held the necessary convention in 1929. Alexander Howat, a longtime militant foe of Lewis, became president of the rival UMW. The CP boycotted this movement, leaving more conservative forces a free hand. This allowed Harry Fishwick and John Walker to ease Howat out of office; they then worked out a deal with Lewis which was formalized in a March 1931 court decision upholding the legality of the Lewis union.

70. The mass trial of August Yokinen, a Finnish immigrant, was held March 1, 1931. He had attended a CP Finnish dance in Harlem at which three Blacks had been treated discourteously. After a CP investigation, all involved expressed regrets except for Yokinen, who was not accused of abusive behavior himself. At the trial, which drew an audience of 1,500 and was reported on the front page of the *New York Times,* Yokinen denounced himself but was condemned to be expelled by a "workers' jury." As a result of the publicity, he was then arrested and deported.

71. In Centralia, Washington, the Armistice Day parade in 1919 was turned into an American Legion attack on the IWW hall. The IWWs began shooting when the right-wingers broke down the door. In the fighting, three legionnaires were killed and one IWW was later lynched. Eight IWWs were convicted of second-degree murder and given twenty-five to forty year prison sentences. Five were paroled in 1934 and the last prisoner's sentence was commuted in 1939.

Glossary

Abern, Martin (1898–1949) – Came to U.S. from Romania as a child; joined Socialist movement in 1912; jailed for refusing to register for draft in World War I; founding member of CP; CEC member from 1920; first national secretary of CP youth, 1923; Chicago district organizer, 1924–26; ILD staff, 1926–28; founding leader of CLA; split from SWP in 1940 with Shachtman to form Workers Party.

Allard, Gerry – Western UMW miner expelled from CP for protesting expulsion of Left Opposition, 1928; readmitted to CP in 1929; rejoined CLA in 1931; leader of Progressive Miners of America in Illinois; left CLA in 1933 to join CPLA; after merger of CLA with Musteites in 1934, participated in entry into SP and stayed there after expulsion of Trotskyist faction.

American Federation of Labor (AFL) – Craft union federation formed in 1880s to protect jurisdictional boundaries, encourage favorable legislation, and assist in organizing skilled workers; split in 1936–37 when industrial-type unions formed CIO; merged with CIO in 1955.

Amsterdam International – Popular name for Social Democrat–dominated International Federation of Trade Unions; also called the "yellow International."

Amter, Israel (1881–1954) – Journalist and musician, joined CP in early twenties; representative to Comintern, 1923–24; CP leader in New York; arrested in 1951 after first convictions of CPers under Smith Act.

Angelo, Joseph – Left-wing miners' leader in Illinois; founding member of National Miners Union; joined CLA in 1929.

Anglo-Russian Trade Union Unity Committee – Founded in May 1925 by British and Russian trade union leaders to promote peace and progress; British members used this alliance to ward off criticism of their betrayal of 1926 general strike; they walked out of Anglo-Russian Committee in September 1927.

Apex theory – 1928 theory of Alexander Bittelman that American capitalism had reached its high point and would decline from then on.

Auto Workers Union – An independent industrial-type union; broke from AFL in 1918; declined from 45,000 in 1920 to about 1,500 in 1929, when CP captured it.

Baldwin, Stanley (1867–1947) – British Conservative prime minister, 1923, 1924–29, 1935–37.

Bedacht, Max (1883–1972) – Became Social Democrat in Germany; came to U.S. in 1908; edited German papers; a founder of CP; representative to Comintern, 1921; Lovestoneite; acting national secretary, 1929–30; headed International Workers Order (a CP-influenced fraternal organization), 1932–47; expelled in 1948 for saying CP wasn't radical enough after expulsion of Browder in 1945 and for criticizing policy of having separate old-age homes for different nationality groups; later reinstated.

Berger, Victor L. (1860–1929) – Came to U.S. from Austria-Hungary in 1878; right-wing SP leader in Milwaukee; first Socialist member of Congress, 1911–13; reelected 1918, 1919, 1922, 1924, 1926; sentenced to 20 years for sedition in World War I, reversed by Supreme Court in 1921.

Bessedovsky, Gregory – Soviet embassy official in Paris; helped purge Left Oppositionists in 1927; defected in late 1929 and wrote series of anti-Soviet articles.

Bittelman, Alexander (1890–1982) – Journalist, CP leader from early '20s; Comintern representative in India, 1929–31; then leader of party's Jewish work; jailed five years under Smith Act in 1950s; expelled in late '50s as a "revisionist."

Bleeker, Sylvia (1901–1988) – Russian immigrant; participant in Russian revolution; left-wing leader in garment industry; CP candidate for Congress in New York when she was expelled in 1930 for supporting CLA.

Blugerman, James – One of first Left Oppositionists expelled from Canadian CP in 1929; capitulated in 1930.

Blumkin, Jakob (1899–1929) – Left SR who joined Russian CP and became a GPU official; first Russian Left Opposition supporter to visit Trotsky in Turkey; shot while bringing back a letter from Trotsky; first Left Oppositionist executed by Stalinists.

Brandler, Heinrich (1881–1967) – German CP leader who was scapegoat for missed revolution of 1923; removed from leadership in 1924, expelled in 1929 for sympathy with Right Opposition in Russia; continued an independent group until World War II.

Brennan, Mart (d. 1968) – President of UMWA District 7 (anthracite region).

Brookwood Labor College – Institution for training "progressive" labor leaders founded 1921 in Katonah, N.Y., by John Fitzpatrick, John Dewey, John Brophy, and A.J. Muste; red-baited by AFL in 1928; forces around it formed CPLA in 1929.

Brophy, John A. (1883–1963) – President of UMWA District 2, 1917–28; leader of Save the Union movement; broke with CP in April 1928; expelled from UMW by Lewis in May 1928; reconciled with Lewis in 1933; CIO organizing director.

Browder, Earl R. (1891–1973) – SP left-winger; imprisoned 2 years for draft law violation in World War I; founding member of CP; CEC from 1921; Foster's assistant in trade union work; general secretary of CP, 1930–44; head of Communist Political Association, 1944–45; expelled 1946.

Budenz, Louis F. (1891–1972) – Lawyer, became labor editor, leader of streetcar and department store strikes in St. Louis in 1917; editor of *Labor Age* and a leader of CPLA; came to Workers Party in merger of CLA and Musteites in 1934, then defected to CP; edited *Daily Worker* during World War II; returned to Catholic Church and became notorious anticommunist.

Buehler, August A. ("Shorty") (1878–1934) – IWW jailed in 1913 free speech fight; member of SP left wing in Kansas City; founding member of CP and a district leader before expulsion in 1929; hunchbacked by polio as a child; ran radical bookstore.

Bukharin, Nikolai (1888–1938) – Joined Bolsheviks in 1906; editor of *Pravda*, 1918–29; head of Comintern, 1926–29; formed Right Opposition in 1928; expelled in 1929; tried and executed for "treason" in purge trials.

Carlson, Oliver – Organizer for Amalgamated Clothing Workers; NC alternate in CLA, 1929; suspended for indiscipline in Minnesota clothing workers' strike in September 1929.

Carter, Joseph – Founding member of CLA; led anti-Cannon clique in New York branch; NC alternate of Workers Party, 1934; NC at founding of SWP, 1938; left SWP with Shachtman, 1940.

Central Executive Committee (CEC) – Formal leading body of CP between national conventions.

Centrism – Trotsky's term for tendencies in the radical movement that stand or oscillate between reformism, which is the position of the labor bureaucracy and labor aristocracy, and Marxism, which represents the historic interests of the working class. Since a centrist tendency has no independent social base, it must be evaluated in terms of its origin, its internal dynamic, and the direction it is taking or being pushed in by events. Until around 1935, Trotsky saw Stalinism as a special variety—bureaucratic centrism; thereafter he felt this term was inadequate to describe what the Soviet bureaucracy was becoming.

Chamberlain, Austen (1863–1937) – British Conservative foreign secretary, 1924–29; won Nobel Prize for Locarno Pact and German entry into League of Nations; broke diplomatic relations with Soviet Union.

Chaplin, Ralph H. (1887–1961) – IWW artist and song writer; sentenced to five years under Espionage Act in World War I; joined CP in 1921; active in CIO in 1930s; converted to Catholicism in 1950s.

Chiang Kai-shek (1887–1975) – Military leader of Kuomintang during 1925–27 revolution; led 1927 massacre of Shanghai workers; headed Kuomintang from 1928; fled to Taiwan in 1949 rather than participate in coalition government with Communists.

Citrine, Walter M. (1887–1983) – General secretary of British Trades Union Congress, 1926–46; knighted in 1935 for his services to the crown.

Civic Federation – See National Civic Federation.

Comintern (Communist International) – World organization of Communist movement founded by Lenin in 1919 as revolutionary alternative to class-collaborationist Socialist International.

Committee for Progressive Labor Action (CPLA) – Formed by Muste, Salutsky, and others around Brookwood Labor College who wanted to rally labor elements who accepted neither AFL nor CP leadership; became American Workers Party in 1933; led Toledo Auto-Lite strike, 1934; fused with CLA in 1934 to form Workers Party of the U.S.

De Leon, Daniel (1852–1914) – Born in Curaçao, educated in Germany, lectured at Columbia Law School on Latin American diplomacy; active in 1886 Henry George single-tax campaign for mayor of New York; joined Socialist Labor Party in 1889 and became its main leader; founded Socialist Trades and Labor Alliance, 1895; a founder of IWW, 1905.

Devine, Patrick – Lovestoneite; a CP leader in Illinois mine field; a national leader of CP unemployed movement in 1930s.

Dreiser, Theodore (1871–1945) – Novelist; active in social causes in 1930s and '40s; applied to join CP in 1932 but not admitted until 1945; last novels, published posthumously, were mystical.

Dunne, Vincent R. (1890–1970) – Joined Western Federation of Miners in 1905; founding member of IWW; active in free speech and labor battles; joined CP in early 1920s; red-baited out of union posts; expelled from Farmer-Labor Party, 1928; a leader of Minnesota district CP; expelled November 1928; a founder and national leader of CLA; a central leader of 1934 Minneapolis Teamsters strikes; imprisoned under Smith Act in World War II.

Dunne, William F. – Older brother of Vincent; union leader and state legislator in Montana in World War I; founding member of CP; member of Cannon faction; co-editor of *Daily Worker*, 1924–27, then assistant editor; expelled in late 1940s for "left deviationism."

Eastman, Max (1883–1969) – Writer, translator, and editor sympathetic to Left Opposition in 1920s; translated several books by Trotsky; broke with Marxism, became anticommunist, editor of *Reader's Digest*.

Edwards, John – CP youth leader in 1920s, delegate to Fourth Congress of Comintern; founding member of CLA in Chicago; supported Shachtman in 1931–33 faction fight; NC alternate, 1931.

Engdahl, J. Lewis (1884–1932) – SP left-winger in 1920–21, then joined CP through Workers' Council group; co-editor of *Daily Worker*, 1924–27; representative to Comintern, 1927–28; a leader of ILD after expulsion of Left Opposition.

Engels, Frederick (1820–1895) – Co-founder with Marx of scientific socialist movement; outstanding figure in Second International until his death.

Ewert, Arthur – German CP right-winger; Comintern representative to U.S. in 1927.

Farrington, Frank (1873–1939) – President of UMW District 12 in Illinois; led opposition to Lewis, 1921–26; suspended 1926, accused of secret deal with Peabody Coal Company for a job if he ever left UMW; delegate to 1930 Reorganized UMW convention in Springfield.

Federated Farmer-Labor Party – Formed after CP captured Farmer-Labor Party convention in Chicago in 1923; main trade union forces in FLP had opposed forming a national party at the convention because it was too narrow, and walked out.

Federated Press – A labor-oriented news service controlled by the CP.

Feng Yu-hsiang (1882–1948) – North Chinese warlord who got Soviet aid; joined left wing of Kuomintang in 1926; visited Moscow; collaborated with Chiang against left Kuomintang and CP in 1927; later broke with Chiang but was defeated in 1930.

Fischer, Ruth (1895–1961) – A founding leader of German CP; expelled in 1927; helped found Leninbund in 1928 but quit after Zinoviev capitulation; was on International Secretariat of International Communist League, 1934–36; quit Fourth Internationalist movement in 1937; after World War II lived in U.S. and worked as a journalist.

Fishwick, Harry – President of UMW District 12 in Illinois; called rump UMW convention in Springfield, 1930; made deal with Lewis in 1931 and returned to UMW.

Fitzpatrick, John (1872–1946) – Immigrated from Ireland, 1882; president of Chicago Federation of Labor; leader of labor party movement from 1919; turned to right after walking out of 1923 FLP convention.

Five Year Plan – Industrialization plan adopted by Russian CP in 1929 but predated to October 1928; instead of a modest acceleration of growth, Stalin now called for the plan to be fulfilled in four years, resulting in speedup, waste, and great hardship for the workers; also included forced collectivization of agriculture.

Flynn, Elizabeth Gurley (1890–1964) – IWW defense campaign and strike leader from 1906; founding member of ACLU, 1920; a leader of ILD; writer for CP publications, joined CP in 1937; served 20 months under Smith Act, 1955–57; first woman to head CP, 1962.

Foster, William Z. (1881–1961) – Joined SP in 1901, IWW in 1910; became syndicalist; AFL official, 1915 to early 1920s; led 1919 steel strike; founded TUEL, 1920; joined CP, 1921, and led its trade union work; allied with Cannon against Lovestone and Pepper, 1923–25 and 1927–28; headed CP, 1945–57.

Freiheit – Yiddish-language Communist daily.

George, David Lloyd (1863–1945) – A British Liberal Party prime minister, 1916–22; co-author of Versailles Treaty; supported intervention in Russian civil war.

Gitlow, Benjamin (1891–1965) – Joined SP in 1907; New York state legislature, 1918; served three years under criminal syndicalist law, 1919–22; one of three national secretaries of CP, 1929; expelled with Lovestoneites and stayed with them until 1933; became anticommunist author.

Glotzer, Albert M. (1908–1999) – CP youth leader; expelled November 1928; founding NC member of CLA; split to form Workers Party, 1940; later became Social Democrat.

Gold, Mike (1894–1967) – Editor of CP literary publications *Masses* and *New Masses;* author of "proletarian literature" in 1920s and '30s; coined term *proletarian realism;* writer for CP press.

Gomez, Manuel – Member of Cannon group before expulsion of Left Opposition; CP representative to ECCI, 1928; used Gomez pseudonym but not a Latino.

Gompers, Samuel (1850–1924) – Immigrated from England, 1863; briefly supported SLP; president of AFL almost continually from 1880s until his death; staunch class collaborationist and supporter of World War I.

Goodman, Leon – A founding member of CLA after his expulsion from CP youth; served 90-day prison term under Pennsylvania antisedition law in 1931–32.

"Goose Caucus" – CP faction from 1921 to 1923 opposing end to undergroundism as a matter of principle; leaders included Amter, Gitlow, and Minor.

Gotha Program – Draft program of United Workers Party of Germany, 1875, adopted by Marxists and Lassalleans; Marx criticized his co-thinkers for making concessions on principles to Lassalleans instead of drafting a program of action.

Green, William (1872–1952) – Conservative craft union leader; secretary-treasurer of UMW, 1913–24; president of AFL, 1924–52.

Gusev, Sergei I. (1874–1933) – Old Bolshevik; secretary of Military Revolutionary Committee in Petrograd, November 1917; Comintern representative in American CP, 1925, who gave CEC majority to Ruthenberg-Lovestone-Pepper faction despite Foster-Cannon majority at convention.

Gutringer, Pauline (d. 1933) – SP left-winger before 1919 split; active in Hungarian federation of CP; founding member of CLA.

Hapgood, Powers (1899–1949) – Writer, Harvard graduate who became coal miner out of social conscience; active in Save the Union movement; beaten by goons at 1927 UMW convention; SP candidate for governor of Indiana, 1932; worked in CIO organizing drive in auto industry.

Hathaway, Clarence A. (1892–1963) – Joined CP in early '20s; IAM official, 1920–24; helped form Minnesota Farmer-Labor Federation, 1923; attended Lenin school in Moscow on Cannon's recommendation, 1926–28; editor of *Daily Worker* in 1930s.

Haymarket martyrs – Eight anarchists framed up in bombing at an 8-hour day demonstration in Chicago in 1886; four were hanged, one committed suicide before his scheduled execution, and three were pardoned in 1893.

Haywood, William D. (1869–1928) – Leader of Western Federation of Miners, 1901–07; central leader of IWW; arrested in 1917 for opposing the war; convicted in mass trial of IWW leaders in 1918; arrested under Espionage Act in 1920; went into exile in USSR in 1921.

Henderson, Arthur (1863–1935) – British Labour Party secretary, 1911–34; served in MacDonald's cabinets; president of Second International, 1923 and 1925–29.

Herberg, Will (1902–1977) – Russian immigrant, CP youth leader; left party with Lovestoneites in 1929; education director of ILGWU, 1935–48; became Zionist, author of books on religion and sociology.

Hillman, Sidney (1887–1946) – Immigrated from Lithuania, 1907; president of Amalgamated Clothing Workers, 1915–46; one of founding leaders of CIO; chief labor lieutenant of Roosevelt in World War II.

Hillquit, Morris (1869–1933) – Immigrated from Latvia, 1886; lawyer; a founder of SP; legal counsel of ILGWU.

Hoover, Herbert (1874–1964) – Headed U.S. relief effort in Europe after World War I; aided counterrevolutionary forces in Russian civil war; Republican president of U.S., 1929–33.

Hourwich, Nicholas I. – Leader of SP Russian Federation; pushed for split in SP to form CP; stressed need for propaganda for use of force as a matter of principle; advocated undergroundism, saying mass activity would corrupt Communists; went to Russia as representative to Comintern in 1920 and stayed there.

Howat, Alexander – President of UMW District 14 in early 1920s; led militant Kansas strikes; expelled by Lewis;

readmitted 1927; president of "reorganized" UMW in 1930.

Industrial Workers of the World (IWW) – Organized in 1905 as a revolutionary industrial union movement; declined after World War I.

Inprecor **(International Press Correspondence)** – Weekly news bulletin of Comintern, published in several languages in 1920s and '30s.

International Labor Defense (ILD) – Mass united-front defense organization initiated by CP in 1925; defended all working-class tendencies, not just CP; had 156 branches, 20,000 individual members, and was supported by organizations representing 75,000; became more narrow and a tool of CP after 1928; prominent in Scottsboro case in 1930s; merged into Civil Rights Congress in 1946.

Iskra **(The Spark)** – First all-Russia Marxist paper, founded by Lenin in 1900; published in exile and distributed illegally; Mensheviks controlled it after 1903 split in Russian Social Democratic Labor Party.

Johnstone, J.W. – A Chicago Federation of Labor official in early 1920s; joined CP and was a secondary leader in Foster faction.

Kamenev, Leon B. (1883–1936) – Old Bolshevik who opposed October insurrection; chairman of Moscow Soviet; high official in government and CP; allied with Stalin and Zinoviev against Left Opposition in 1923, but joined United Opposition bloc with Trotsky in 1926–27; expelled from CP in 1927 and capitulated to Stalin; expelled again in 1932, capitulated in 1933; executed after first Moscow frame-up trial.

Karsner, Rose (1890–1968) – Came to U.S. from Romania; joined SP in 1908; founding member of CP; companion and collaborator of Cannon from 1924; assistant secretary of ILD; founding member of CLA; manager of Pioneer Publishers; business manager of *The Militant;*

organized Committee for European Workers Relief to aid revolutionaries after World War II.

Kautsky, Karl (1854–1938) – Regarded as outstanding Marxist theoretician from death of Engels to World War I, when he abandoned internationalism and opposed the Russian revolution.

Kellogg Pact – 1928 agreement of 15 countries renouncing war as an instrument of national policy; eventually ratified by 63 countries, including USSR; engineered by U.S. Secretary of State Frank B. Kellogg (1856–1937).

Kemal Pasha, Mustafa (1881–1938) – Turkish dictator, leader of 1919 nationalist revolution.

Kruse, William F. – SP youth leader, came to CP through Workers' Council group; Moscow contact of Ruthenberg faction, 1926–27; Chicago district organizer in 1929; expelled for refusing to denounce Lovestone, but never active in Lovestone's organization.

Labor Age – Monthly edited by Louis F. Budenz; to all intents and purposes but not formally the organ of CPLA.

Labor Unity – Organ of TUUL.

La Follette, Robert M. (1855–1925) – Republican U.S. senator from Wisconsin, 1905–25; Progressive Party candidate for president in 1924, and got about 5 million votes.

League Against Imperialism and for National Independence – CP-dominated front headed by Willi Muenzenberg, 1927–29.

League for Industrial Democracy – Educational arm of Socialist movement; initiated by intellectuals including Upton Sinclair and Jack London before World War I; led big student movement in 1930s (Student League for Industrial Democracy) encompassing YPSL and left liberals.

League of Nations – Set up by Versailles peace conference in 1919 ostensibly to prevent future wars; excluded defeated nations for years; U.S. never joined; USSR joined in 1934; failed to stop buildup to World War II and was succeeded by United Nations during that war.

Lenin, V.I. (1870–1924) – Central leader of Bolshevik Party, Russian revolution, and Comintern; prepared fight against Soviet bureaucracy but died before he could carry it out.

Leninbund – German group including followers of Trotsky and Zinoviev, organized in 1927 by Ruth Fischer, Arkadi Maslow, and Hugo Urbahns after their expulsion from CP; close to Left Opposition until 1930 when Urbahns expelled Left Oppositionists.

Levy, Louis (1892–1951) – Leader of ILGWU Local 117, 1930–39; vice-president of union and Pacific Coast director in 1940s.

Lewis, John L. (1880–1969) – UMWA president, 1920–60; principal founder and leader of CIO, 1935–40; presided over decline of UMW during two postwar booms.

Liebknecht, Wilhelm (1826–1900) – German revolutionary, participant in 1848; emigré with Marx in London; founder of German SP in fusion with Lassalleans, 1869; Reichstag deputy, 1867–70 and 1874–1900; sentenced to two years in prison for opposing Franco-Prussian War, 1872; fought against revisionism.

Little, Frank – IWW organizer lynched by company thugs in Montana in 1917 during strike of copper miners.

Locarno Pact – Series of treaties signed by British, French, German, Italian, Belgian, Czech, and Polish governments in 1925, to "guarantee" peace and existing borders.

Lore, Ludwig (1875–1942) – Immigrated from Germany in 1903; active in IWW and left wing of SP; edited German CP paper *New Yorker Volkszeitung* from 1919; opposed Pepper and supported Russian Left Opposition, 1924; expelled, 1925; joined American Workers Party and participated in fusion with CLA; left Workers Party and became prowar journalist for *New York Post*.

Lovestone, Jay (1898–1990) – Founding member of CP; succeeded Ruthenberg as general secretary, 1927; expelled in June 1929; founded Communist Party (Opposition), later called Independent Labor League, disbanded in 1940; later became chief advisor on foreign policy for AFL-CIO as an anticommunist expert.

Lozovsky, Solomon A. (1878–1952) – Head of Red International of Labor Unions, 1921–39; arrested and shot during a Stalinist anti-Semitic campaign.

MacDonald, James Ramsay (1866–1937) – British Labour politician; opposed British entry into World War I; prime minister in 1924; opposed 1926 general strike; Labour prime minister, 1929–31; bolted from party to form "national unity" cabinet with Conservatives and Liberals, in which he was prime minister, 1931–35.

McMahon, Thomas F. (b. 1870) – Joined Knights of Labor, 1889; president of United Textile Workers, 1921–36; retired to a political job in Rhode Island.

McNary-Haugen Bill – Farm legislation vetoed by Coolidge in 1927; proposed to raise farm produce prices by setting up a government corporation to dump surplus abroad, with American Farm Bureau Federation acting as a sort of broker for its members.

Malkin, Maurice L. – CPer imprisoned for activity in furriers' strike; expelled, November 1928; made statement repudiating Left Opposition in October 1929 when ILD threatened to withdraw from his defense and stop aiding his aged parents; retracted statement in September 1930; expelled from CLA in May 1931 for making deal with bureaucrats to get back into furriers' union.

Markoff, Abraham – New York CPer and dental surgeon.

Martynov, Aleksandr S. (1865–1935) – Menshevik theoretician, 1903–23; then joined CP and became Comintern theoretician against Trotsky; authored theory of "bloc of four classes" in Chinese revolution to justify subordinating Chinese CP to "progressive" bourgeoisie.

Marx, Karl (1818–1883) – Founder with Engels of scientific socialism and leader of First International.

Mencken, H.L. (1880–1956) – Editor and satirist.

Miller, Bert – Organization secretary of CP New York district; Lovestoneite; left Lovestone group to join CPLA.

Minor, Robert (1884–1952) – Radical cartoonist, joined SP in 1907; became anarchist, 1912; joined CP in 1920; editor of *Daily Worker* from 1927; was chief lieutenant of Lovestone and then of Browder, remaining in CP after each was expelled.

Mooney, Thomas J. (1882–1942) – Leader of left bloc in California AFL; framed with Warren Billings and three others of bombing at "Preparedness" parade in San Francisco in 1916; sentenced to death but execution stayed in 1918 due to international pressure campaign; pardoned in 1939.

Morgenstern, Bernard ("Morgie") (1907–1981) – CP youth leader in Philadelphia jailed for antiwar and union activity; expelled from CP in November 1928; elected as alternate member of CLA National Committee, 1931.

Muste, Abraham J. (1885–1967) – Minister, born in Netherlands; a leader of Lawrence and Paterson textile strikes in 1919; head of Brookwood Labor College; a founding leader of CPLA and American Workers Party; became national secretary of Workers Party of the U.S. in 1934 fusion with CLA; returned to the church in 1936; established American Forum for Socialist Education in late 1950s and was a leader of antiwar movement in 1960s.

National Civic Federation – Formed in 1901 by capitalists, union bureaucrats, and "public" representatives (politicians and philanthropists) to foster class collaboration; Samuel Gompers was a vice-president; Matthew Woll was acting president from the twenties until 1935.

National Miners Union (NMU) – CP-led coal miners' union founded September 10, 1928; led unsuccessful strikes of 10,000 in southern Illinois (1929) and 40,000 in western Pennsylvania, east Ohio, and northern West Virginia (1931); attempted to organize Kentucky miners in 1931–32; dissolved in 1934.

National Textile Workers Union (NTWU) – CP-led union founded in September 1928; dissolved in 1934.

Nearing, Scott (1883–1983) – Economist, author; SP member removed from university teaching posts during World War I for his political views; SP congressional candidate, 1919; joined CP in 1926.

Needle Trades Workers Industrial Union (NTWIU) – CP-led union formed January 1, 1929; dissolved when fur workers section merged with AFL union and dress workers individually joined ILGWU around 1935.

New Masses – Monthly literary journal in U.S. under CP control.

Oehler, Hugo (1903–1983) – CP unionist in 1920s; district organizer in Kansas City; protested expulsion of Left Opposition but stayed in CP; a leader of NTWU organizing drive in North Carolina in 1929; declared for Left Opposition in June 1930; elected to CLA National Committee in 1931; expelled from Workers Party of U.S. in 1935 for indiscipline; founded Revolutionary Workers League, which survived into 1950s.

O'Flaherty, Thomas J. – CP journalist, wrote for *Daily Worker* and *Labor Defender;* removed for supporting Left Opposition; co-editor of *Producers News* of Plentywood, Montana; dropped from CLA membership in 1931.

Olgin, Moissaye J. (1874–1939) – Immigrated from Russia in 1915; a leader of Workers' Council group, joined CP in 1921; editor of *Freiheit;* sided with Lore against Pepper FFLP policy but broke with Lore in 1924, became Stalinist; led CP turn to Jewish culture in 1930s; wrote CP's main anti-Trotskyist manual, *Trotskyism: Counter-Revolution in Disguise.*

Oneal, James (1875–1962) – SP right-winger, editor of *New Leader* from 1924; leader of pro-Roosevelt split in 1936 to form Social Democratic Federation.

One Big Union – Canadian syndicalist group; sent delegates to first congress of RILU in 1921; issued a paper sympathetic with Trotsky in 1930.

Palmer, A. Mitchell (1872–1936) – Democratic attorney general, 1919–21; ordered nationwide raids against CP and other radicals in January 1920 resulting in thousands of arrests and deportations.

Paz, Maurice (1896–1985) – Early leader of Left Opposition in France; broke with Trotsky in 1929 and joined SP.

Pepper, John (1886–1938) – Hungarian Social Democrat who joined Comintern after defeat of Hungarian revolution; came to U.S. in 1922 as Comintern representative to CP and became a party leader; recalled to Moscow after FFLP affair in 1924 but returned to U.S.; supervised expulsion of Left Opposition as a leader of Lovestone-Pepper faction; ordered back to USSR in 1929 and expelled; disappeared in USSR.

Pioneers, Young – Organization of youth too young to join CP's youth group, the Young Workers League.

Political Committee (Polcom—PC) – Leading committee of CP chosen by CEC to organize party nationally on day-to-day basis; formally responsible to the CEC.

Proletarian Party – Originally the Michigan SP, expelled for left-wing views in 1919; led by Dennis E. Batt and John Keracher; briefly adhered to CP but split from it in 1920; a small propaganda sect that abstained from practical action; expelled its majority in 1932 and dissolved in late 1930s after some members became UAW officials.

Purcell, Albert A. (1872–1935) – British Labour MP in 1920s and head of organizing committee of Trades Union Congress during 1926 general strike; had been a founder of British CP.

Radek, Karl (1885–1939) – Revolutionary journalist; joined German SP in 1905 and was a founder of German CP in 1918; mainly active in Russia after 1917; on ECCI until 1924; in Left Opposition, 1923–28; expelled from Russian CP, 1927; capitulated, 1929; framed up and jailed in second Moscow trial in 1937.

Rakovsky, Christian G. (1873–1941) – Romanian SP leader before 1914; agreed with Trotsky on disputes in Second International; president of Ukrainian Soviet, 1919–23; joined Left Opposition in 1923; Soviet ambassador to Britain and France; expelled and sent to Siberia, 1927; recanted in 1934; framed up and jailed in third Moscow trial in 1938.

Red Day – Demonstrations called by Comintern for August 1, 1929, in response to repression of CP workers in Berlin on May Day that year; had ultraleft slogans; attacked by cops in several countries; in New York, 5,000 marched and call for a general strike was ignored by workers.

Red International of Labor Unions (RILU, Profintern) – CP-controlled union organization; united with Amsterdam International in 1945 to form World Federation of Trade Unions; this was split when reformists formed International Confederation of Free Trade Unions in 1949.

Reeve, Karl M. (1900–1980) – Member of editorial staff of *Daily Worker* from 1923; later active in Minnesota; son of Ella Reeve Bloor (Mother Bloor), lecturer and writer for SP (1900–1919) and then CP, and famous strike leader.

Revolutionary Age – Organ of Lovestoneites.

Rykov, Alexei I. (1881–1938) – Right-wing Bolshevik; favored coalition with Mensheviks in 1917; succeeded Lenin as head of Soviet state (1924–30); helped organize Right Opposition in 1928; recanted in 1929; purged as premier in 1930; executed after third Moscow trial.

Sacco, Nicola (1891–1927) – Italian immigrant, anarchist, shoe-factory worker, strike activist; framed on charges of payroll robbery and murder, 1920; carried out 31-day hunger strike when first imprisoned; executed after long appeals and mass defense campaign.

Salutsky, J.B. (Hardman) (1882–1968) – Russian immigrant; came to CP through Workers' Council group, 1921; editor and education director for Amalgamated Clothing Workers, 1920–24; left CP in 1923 and became anticommunist.

Sandgren, John – Swedish immigrant; IWW leader who opposed affiliation to Comintern.

Schlesinger, Benjamin (1876–1932) – Immigrant from Lithuania; joined SLP in 1895 but left it by 1899; president of ILGWU, 1914–23, 1928–32; manager of *Jewish Daily Forward* in Chicago from 1923.

Shachtman, Max (1903–1972) – Immigrated from Poland in 1904; came to CP through Workers' Council in 1921; a leader of CP youth, 1923–27; editor of *Labor Defender*, 1926–28; founding leader of CLA and its first international representative; led opposition to Cannon, 1929–33; led 1940 split of petty-bourgeois opposition to form Workers Party; this became Independent Socialist League, which dissolved into right wing of SP in 1958.

Sigman, Morris (1880–1931) – Born in Russia; came to England in 1901 and U.S. in 1903; was in STLA and IWW before coming to ILGWU in 1907; president of ILGWU, 1923–28.

Skoglund, Carl (1884–1960) – Swedish Socialist, came to U.S. in 1911; a leader of Scandinavian Federation of SP and founder of CP; expelled in 1928; on NC of CLA from its founding, and a central leader in Minnesota; president of Minneapolis Teamsters Local 544, 1938–40; member of founding IEC of Fourth International; one of 18 SWP leaders imprisoned in World War II under Smith Act; U.S. government tried to deport him in 1950s.

Smith, Alfred E. (1873–1944) – Democratic candidate for president in 1928, defeated partly by anti-Catholic propaganda.

"Social fascism" – Stalin's characterization of Social Democrats, 1924–34; he said SP and Nazis were not opposites but twins;

became part of CP line during "third period"; dropped in favor of campaign for coalition governments with capitalists and Social Democrats ("popular front") after Hitler.

Socialist Labor Party (SLP) – Formed in 1877; came under leadership of De Leon in 1890; deteriorated into a sect after founding of Socialist Party in 1901.

Socialist Party of America (SP) – Founded in 1901 by Debs, Berger, Hillquit, and others; left-wing majority split in 1919 to form CP; regained some influence in late twenties and early thirties; again weakened by loss of many workers and entire youth to Workers Party in 1936–37 entry; split in 1972 into Social Democrats USA and Democratic Socialist Organizing Committee.

Socialist Trades and Labor Alliance (STLA) – Socialist alternative to AFL and Knights of Labor founded in 1895 by Daniel De Leon; claimed 15,000 members in 1898; became an auxiliary of SLP; claimed only 500 members when it fused into IWW in 1905.

Social Revolutionary Party (SRs) – Founded in 1900 in Russia; predominant influence on peasants before 1917; right wing supported bourgeois provisional government; left SRs participated in coalition government with Bolsheviks after October revolution but soon became counterrevolutionary and were suppressed.

Spector, Maurice (1898–1968) – A founder of Canadian CP, editor of its paper, and national chairman from 1924; sympathized with Russian Left Opposition from 1923–24; expelled in 1928; on founding NC of CLA and central leader of Canadian Trotskyism; resigned from movement in 1939.

Stachel, Jacob (1900–1965) – Came to CP from SP in 1924; national organizational secretary, 1927; prominent Lovestoneite, anti-Trotskyist; broke with Lovestone after 1929 convention; headed TUUL, 1932–35; then held other leading posts; served five years under Smith Act in 1950s; was hatchetman in 1957 expulsion of Gates group.

Stalin, Joseph (1879–1953) – Old Bolshevik, favored conciliation with provisional government before April 1917 as an editor of *Pravda*; commissar of nationalities, then general secretary of CP; gradually eliminated his opponents and became virtual dictator of party and state after Lenin died.

Stimson, Henry L. (1867–1950) – U.S. secretary of state, 1929–33; secretary of war, 1940–45.

Swabeck, Arne (1890–1986) – Danish immigrant; editor of SP Scandinavian weekly before 1919 split; on CP's CEC from its foundation; Chicago district organizer, leader of left wing in Chicago Federation of Labor, and director of CP's miners' campaign; expelled, November 1928; national secretary of CLA in early 1930s and a central leader of Workers Party of the U.S.; then active in Chicago and L.A. SWP branches; became a Maoist in 1960s and was expelled for indiscipline in 1967.

Thalheimer, August (1884–1948) – Founder and leader of German CP blamed for missed revolution in 1923; removed from leadership in 1924 and expelled with right wing in 1929.

Thermidor – According to calendar adopted by French revolution, on 9 Thermidor (July 27), 1794, the radical Jacobins were overthrown by opportunists, beginning the period of reaction leading to Bonaparte's seizure of power in 1799; Trotsky made analogy with seizure of power by Soviet bureaucracy which could lead to capitalist counterrevolution; in both cases, the old property forms were not restored, but from 1929 to 1935 Trotsky used the term to refer to capitalist counterrevolution.

"Third period" – According to Comintern theory, the period of the final collapse of capitalism and triumph of socialist revolution; it followed the period of revolutionary upheavals (1917–23) and the period of capitalist stabilization, ending in 1928; they dropped the term after the rise of Hitler to power and the shift to the "popular front" line.

Thomas, Norman M. (1884–1969) – SP presidential candidate in every election from 1928 to 1948; minister, leader of League for Industrial Democracy, and associate editor of *Nation*.

Tomsky, Mikhail (1886–1936) – Right-wing leader in Russian CP; head of Soviet trade unions; helped form Right Opposition, 1928; capitulated, 1929; committed suicide during first Moscow trial.

Trachtenberg, Alexander (1885–1966) – Immigrated from Russia, 1906; active in SP, 1906–1920; led Workers' Council group into CP; founder and head of International Publishers.

Trade Union Educational League (TUEL) – Founded by Foster in 1920 to build a left wing in AFL; dominated by CP after 1921; reorganized as TUUL in 1929.

Trade Union Unity League (TUUL) – Founded in 1929 at fourth convention of TUEL; Foster was general secretary; Labor Unity was official organ; aimed to organize unorganized into industrial unions; failed due to ultraleft sectarianism; dissolved in 1935.

Treint, Albert (1889–1972) – French CP leader expelled in 1927 for supporting United Opposition; was in Left Opposition in France in 1931 before joining a syndicalist group.

Tresca, Carlo (1879–1943) – Italian anarchist, came to U.S. in 1904; close associate of Sacco and Vanzetti; editor of *Il Martello* (The Hammer); arrested many times for activity in labor struggles; served on Dewey Commission of Inquiry into Moscow Trials; assassinated in New York.

Trotsky, Leon (1879–1940) – Joined Russian revolutionary movement in 1896; collaborated with Lenin on *Iskra*, 1902; broke with Lenin over nature of party; headed St. Petersburg Soviet, 1905; wrote Zimmerwald antiwar manifesto in 1915; joined Bolsheviks in 1917; organized insurrection and served as commissar of foreign affairs and commissar of war; organized Red Army; founded Left Opposition, 1923; exiled, 1929; called for new

International after Hitler took power without CP resistance; worked to build Fourth International until his assassination by Stalinist agent in Mexico.

2 ½ International (International Association of Socialist Parties) – Formed in 1921 by centrist groups that had left Second International; they reunited with it in 1923.

United Textile Workers (UTW) – AFL textile union.

Urbahns, Hugo (1890–1947) – German SPer who joined CP in 1920 and took ultraleft positions; expelled in 1926; helped form Leninbund in 1928; expelled Left Oppositionists in 1930; authored "state capitalist" theory of class nature of USSR; emigrated to Sweden in 1933.

Vanzetti, Bartolomeo (1888–1927) – Italian immigrant worker, anarchist, framed on charges of payroll robbery and murder in 1920; executed in 1927 after long appeals and mass defense campaign.

Volkszeitung – German-language daily loosely connected to CP in 1920s, edited by Ludwig Lore; had circulation of 10,000 in 1925.

Voyzey, George – Left-wing miners' leader and CPer in Springfield, Illinois; president of NMU district; expelled in 1929 and worked with Left Opposition.

Walker, John H. – President of Illinois Federation of Labor; signed call for dissident UMW convention in Springfield in 1930.

Watt, John – Founding president of NMU; resigned from CP because he disagreed with bureaucratism; Foster supported him during fight with Lovestone, but removed him from NMU post once Lovestone was defeated; was briefly a sympathizer of Left Opposition but moved to the right.

Weinstone, William W. (1897–1985) – A founding leader of CP; national secretary, 1921–22; known for his inconsistent factional loyalties; sided with Foster and Cannon in 1927, then Lovestone, then Foster in 1928;

representative to Comintern, 1929–31; survived in CP into 1950s.

Weisbord, Albert (1900–1977) – SP youth leader, 1921–24; joined CP in 1924; secretary-treasurer of NTWU; expelled for "Lovestoneism" in 1929; maneuvered with CLA, advocating "mass work" in alliance with Lovestone rather than orientation toward CP workers; headed Communist League of Struggle, 1931–37; became AFL organizer but was fired during World War II, despite his support for the war; management consultant in 1950s witch-hunt when politically excluded from employment.

Wicks, Harry M. (1889–1957) – SP leader, turned patriotic in 1920; was denied membership in CP, 1921, but later allowed to join; representative to RILU, 1929; Comintern representative in Australia and other countries for purge of right wing; expelled from CP in 1937 on charges he had been an anticommunist agent for 18 years.

Williams, Albert Rhys (1883–1962) – Journalist who was in Russia during 1917 revolution and supported it; sympathized with Stalin in 1920s.

Winitsky, Harry M. (b. 1898) – Arrested in mass police raid on CP in New York, 1919; imprisoned 1920–22 under criminal anarchy law; manager of *Freiheit*, 1922–23; a Lovestoneite, business manager of *Labor Age*.

Wolfe, Bertram D. (1896–1981) – Fled government attacks on early CP by going to California (1919–21) and Mexico (1922–25); editor of *Communist*, 1927; expelled in 1929 with Lovestoneites; was apologist for Moscow trials until 1937; became anticommunist author.

Woll, Matthew (1880–1956) – Immigrated from Luxemburg, 1891; photoengravers' union official and lawyer; served on War Labor Board in World War I; became AFL vice-president, 1919; held leading posts in National Civic Federation until 1935.

Workers' Council group – Left-wing split from SP in 1920; united with CP in December 1921.

Young Workers League (YWL) – CP youth group, founded in 1922; later changed name to Young Communist League.

Zack, Joseph – Trade union specialist in Foster group in CP; an early advocate of "new unions"; a leader of Food Workers Industrial Union in early 1930s; left the CP in mid-1930s and was briefly in Workers Party of the U.S.

Zalisko, Mike – Young CP organizer in Illinois coal fields in late 1920s; briefly supported Left Opposition but soon capitulated.

Zarya – Scientific and political journal published by editorial board of *Iskra*, 1901–02.

Zinoviev, Gregory Y. (1883–1936) – Close collaborator with Lenin before 1917; opposed October insurrection; head of Comintern, 1919–26; allied with Stalin against Trotsky, 1923–26, then joined United Opposition; expelled from CP in 1927; capitulated in 1928 and readmitted into CP; expelled again in 1932 and recanted; jailed, 1935; framed up and executed in first Moscow trial.

Index

ALSO BY JAMES P. CANNON

The History of American Trotskyism 1928–38

Report of a Participant

"Trotskyism is not a new movement, a new doctrine," Cannon says, "but the restoration, the revival of genuine Marxism as it was expounded and practiced in the Russian Revolution and in the early days of the Communist International." Talks by a founding leader of American communism on building a proletarian party in the United States. $17. Also in Spanish and French.

The Struggle for a Proletarian Party

"The workers of America have power enough to topple the structure of capitalism at home and to lift the whole world with them when they rise," Cannon asserts. At the start of World War II, a founder of the communist movement in the US and a leader of the Communist International in Lenin's time defends the program and party-building norms of Bolshevism. $20. Also in Spanish and Farsi.

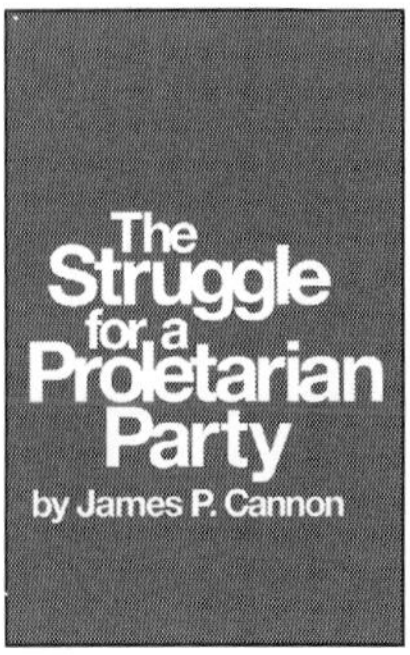

Letters from Prison

A Revolutionary Party Prepares for Post–WWII Labor Battles

The prison letters of a communist leader, jailed for his party's opposition to the US imperialist war effort in World War II. Cannon discusses organizing a revolutionary party in wartime and preparing its postwar political course. $20

The Socialist Workers Party in World War II, 1940–43

Preparing the communist workers movement in the United States to campaign against wartime censorship, repression, and anti-union assaults. $23

PATHFINDERPRESS.COM

THE RUSSIAN REVOLUTION

Lenin's Final Fight

Speeches and Writings, 1922–23

V.I. LENIN

In 1922 and 1923, V.I. Lenin, central leader of the world's first socialist revolution, waged what was to be his last political battle—one that was lost after his death. At stake was whether that revolutionary government and the world communist movement it led would remain on the revolutionary proletarian course that brought workers and peasants to power in Russia in 1917. $17. Also in Spanish, Farsi, Greek.

My Life

An Attempt at an Autobiography

LEON TROTSKY

A leader of the Russian Revolution, Red Army, and the fight to maintain Lenin's continuity recounts lessons from battles he took part in from the early 1900s to his forced exile in 1929 from the Soviet Union by Stalin's counterrevolutionary regime. $27

Women and the Family

LEON TROTSKY

How the October 1917 Russian Revolution, the first victorious socialist revolution, opened the door to an all-out fight for women's emancipation. Trotsky explains the Bolshevik government's steps to wipe out illiteracy, establish equality in economic and political life, set up childcare centers and public kitchens, guarantee the right to abortion and divorce, and more. $10

The History of the Russian Revolution

LEON TROTSKY

How, under Lenin's leadership, the Bolshevik Party led millions of workers and farmers to overthrow the state power of the landlords and capitalists in 1917 and bring to power a government that advanced their class interests at home and worldwide. Unabridged, 3 vols. in one. Written by one of the central leaders of that socialist revolution. $30. Also in French and Russian.

To See the Dawn

Baku, 1920—First Congress of the Peoples of the East

How can peasants and workers in the colonial world achieve freedom from imperialist exploitation? By what means can working people overcome divisions incited by their national ruling classes and act together for their common class interests? These questions were addressed by 2,000 delegates to the 1920 Congress of the Peoples of the East. $17

The Revolution Betrayed

What Is the Soviet Union and Where Is It Going?

LEON TROTSKY

In 1917 workers and peasants of Russia were the motor force of one of the deepest revolutions in history. Yet within ten years a political counterrevolution by a privileged social layer, whose chief spokesperson was Joseph Stalin, was being consolidated. The classic study of the Soviet workers state and its degeneration. $17. Also in Spanish, Farsi, Greek.

IMPERIALISM'S MARCH TOWARD FASCISM AND WAR

Opening Guns of World War III: Washington's Assault on Iraq

JACK BARNES

The murderous assault on Iraq in 1990–91 heralded increasingly sharp conflicts among imperialist powers, growing instability of capitalism, and more wars. Also includes:

1945: When US Troops Said 'No!'
by Mary-Alice Waters
Lessons from the Iran-Iraq War
by Samad Sharif

In *New International* no. 7. $14. Also in Spanish, French, Farsi.

The Fight Against Jew-Hatred and Pogroms in the Imperialist Epoch

Stakes for the International Working Class

V.I. LENIN, LEON TROTSKY
FARRELL DOBBS, JAMES P. CANNON
JACK BARNES, DAVE PRINCE

Jew-hatred and pogroms—such as Hamas carried out on October 7, 2023—are part of the social convulsions and wars of the imperialist epoch. The authors explain why fighting Jew-hatred is decisive to the working class and oppressed nations of the world—and *what is to be done to end it.* $10. Also in Spanish, French, Greek.

What Is American Fascism?

JAMES P. CANNON, JOSEPH HANSEN

Analyzes 20th century fascist currents in the US. "A fascist movement, if it is to be successful, must have a scapegoat on whom the petty-bourgeois masses can vent their rage in place of the capitalists who deserve it," wrote Hansen about Father Charles Coughlin's anti-Semitic "Social Justice" movement in the late 1930s. "Coughlin like Hitler and Mussolini has selected the Jew." $5

U.S. Imperialism Has Lost the Cold War

JACK BARNES

The collapse of regimes across Eastern Europe and the USSR claiming to be communist did not mean workers and farmers there had been crushed. In today's sharpening class conflicts and wars, these toilers are joining working people the world over in the class struggle against capitalist exploitation. In *New International* no. 11. $14. Also in Spanish, French, Farsi, Greek.

Imperialism's March Toward Fascism and War

JACK BARNES

"There will be new Hitlers, new Mussolinis. That is inevitable. What is not inevitable is that they will triumph. The working-class vanguard will organize our class to fight back against the devastating toll we are made to pay for the capitalist crisis. The future of humanity will be decided in the contest between these contending class forces." In *New International* no. 10. $14. Also in Spanish, French, Farsi, Greek.

The Founding of the Socialist Workers Party

Minutes and Resolutions, 1938–39

JAMES P. CANNON

At founding gatherings of the Socialist Workers Party in 1938–39, revolutionists in the US codified two decades of experience in building a communist party. They charted a working-class course in resisting the coming imperialist war, fighting fascism and Jew-hatred, the struggle for Black rights, forging an alliance with exploited farmers, and the battle to transform the unions into revolutionary instruments of struggle by working people. $23

CUBA'S SOCIALIST REVOLUTION

New!

Revolution and the Road to Peace in Colombia

The Example of the Cuban Revolution

FIDEL CASTRO

"No crime can be committed in the name of revolution," Fidel Castro declares, drawing from the example set by working people of Cuba as they took state power out of the hands of its capitalist rulers. In 2008, as part of efforts to end six decades of armed conflict in Colombia, he shared the exemplary record of Cuba's revolutionary struggle with the Revolutionary Armed Forces of Colombia (FARC) and the world. $10. Also in Spanish, French, Greek.

Cuba and the Coming American Revolution

JACK BARNES

This is a book about the example set by the Cuban people that socialist revolution is not only necessary—it can be made. A book about the struggles of workers and other exploited producers in the imperialist heartland, and the youth attracted to them. About the class struggle in the US, where the revolutionary capacities of working people are as utterly discounted by the ruling powers as were those of the Cuban toilers. $10. Also in Spanish, French, Farsi.

The First and Second Declarations of Havana

Nowhere are the questions of revolutionary strategy that today confront men and women on the front lines of struggles in the Americas addressed with greater truthfulness and clarity than in these uncompromising indictments of imperialist plunder and "the exploitation of man by man." Adopted by million-strong assemblies of the Cuban people in 1960 and 1962. $10. Also in Spanish, French, Farsi, Greek, Arabic.

New!

Cuba and the Independence War in Guinea-Bissau and Cape Verde

The Fall of the Last Colonial Empire in Africa

VÍCTOR DREKE

In 1974–75 the people of two West African countries, Guinea-Bissau and Cape Verde, put an end to 500 years of Portuguese colonial exploitation. Led by a popular movement forged by Amílcar Cabral, their struggle triggered the collapse of Portugal's entire colonial empire and brought down the 40-year fascist dictatorship in Portugal itself. Víctor Dreke's firsthand account brings to life this decisive victory. $12. Also in Spanish and French.

Women in Cuba: The Making of a Revolution Within the Revolution

VILMA ESPÍN, ASELA DE LOS SANTOS
YOLANDA FERRER

The integration of women in the ranks and leadership of the Cuban Revolution was intertwined with the proletarian course led by Fidel Castro from the start. This is the story of that revolution and how it transformed the women and men who made it. $17. Also in Spanish, Farsi, Greek.

Playa Girón/Bay of Pigs

Washington's First Military Defeat in the Americas

FIDEL CASTRO, JOSÉ RAMÓN FERNÁNDEZ

In less than 72 hours of combat in April 1961, Cuba's revolutionary armed forces defeated a US-organized invasion by 1,500 mercenaries. The Cuban people set an example for workers, farmers, and youth the world over that with political consciousness, class solidarity, courage, and revolutionary leadership, we can stand up to seemingly insurmountable odds—*and win*. $17. Also in Spanish.

WOMEN'S EMANCIPATION AND THE WORKING CLASS

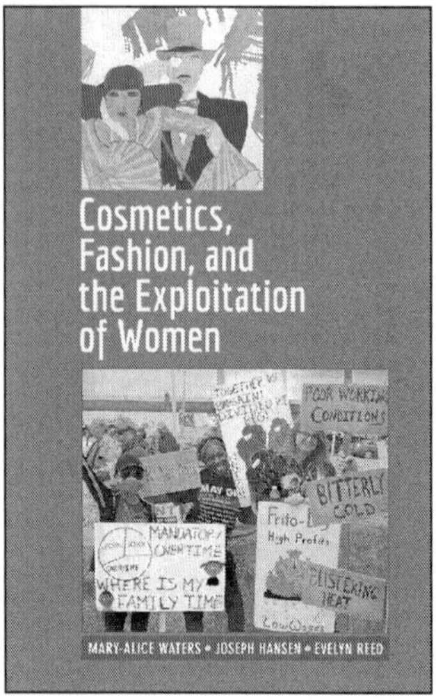

Cosmetics, Fashion and the Exploitation of Women

MARY-ALICE WATERS
JOSEPH HANSEN, EVELYN REED

"Norms of beauty and fashion are inseparable from the class struggle." That's the title of the opening chapter of this new expanded edition of a lively 1950s debate in the *Militant*, a socialist newsweekly. How cosmetics and fashion monopolies rake in profits from social insecurities of women and adolescents. Why women's integration into the workforce and unions is a major advance in the fight for emancipation. A Marxist classic on the origins of women's oppression and the working-class road forward. $15. Also in Spanish, French, Farsi, Greek.

The Origin of the Family Private Property, and the State

FREDERICK ENGELS

The emergence of class-divided society gave rise to repressive state bodies and the oppression of women to enable the ruling classes to pass along wealth and privilege. Engels discusses the consequences for working people of these class institutions—from their ancient forms to their modern versions. $15. Also in Spanish and Farsi.

Women's Liberation and the African Freedom Struggle

THOMAS SANKARA

"There is no true social revolution without the liberation of women," explains the leader of the 1983–87 revolution in the West African country of Burkina Faso. $5. Also in Spanish, French, Farsi, Arabic.

REVOLUTIONARY LEADERS IN THEIR OWN WORDS

To Speak the Truth

Why Washington's 'Cold War' Against Cuba Doesn't End

FIDEL CASTRO, CHE GUEVARA

In historic speeches before the United Nations and UN bodies, Guevara and Castro address the peoples of the world, explaining why the US government so fears the example set by the socialist revolution in Cuba. $15. Also in Greek.

Rosa Luxemburg Speaks

EDITED BY MARY-ALICE WATERS

Rosa Luxemburg's place of honor among the great revolutionary Marxist leaders of the twentieth century has often been denied her. Here she speaks for herself, with clarity and wit, taking on political battles that continue to divide revolutionaries from reformists in the workers movement even a century after her murder in Berlin in 1919 by counterrevolutionary militias. $25

Maurice Bishop Speaks

The Grenada Revolution and Its Overthrow, 1979–83

The triumph of the 1979 revolution in the Caribbean island of Grenada under the leadership of Maurice Bishop gave hope to millions throughout the Americas. Invaluable lessons from the workers and farmers government destroyed by a Stalinist-led counterrevolution in 1983. $20

Problems of Everyday Life

Creating the Foundations
for a New Society
in Revolutionary Russia

LEON TROTSKY

Articles from the early Soviet press on social and cultural issues in the struggle to forge new social relations. The advance of culture, Trotsky notes, requires an increasing level of scientific, technological, and industrial development to "free humanity from a dependence upon nature that is degrading"—a goal that can only be completed when social relationships are "free from mystery and do not oppress people." $20

Is Socialist Revolution in the US Possible?

A Necessary Debate Among Working People

MARY-ALICE WATERS

Fighting for a society only working people can create, it is our own capacities we will discover. And we will answer the question posed here with a resounding "Yes." Revolution is possible but not inevitable. That depends on us. $7. Also in Spanish, French, Farsi.

Pathfinder Press **accessible e-books**
for the blind, those with low vision,
or other challenges reading print books

For a list of current accessible titles, go to: pathfinderpress.com/collections/books-for-the-blind.

Visit bookshare.org for information on how to sign up.

PATHFINDER AROUND THE WORLD

UNITED STATES

(and Caribbean, Latin America, and East Asia)

Pathfinder Books, 306 W. 37th St., 13th Floor
New York, NY 10018
orders@pathfinderpress.com

CANADA

Pathfinder Books, 7107 St. Denis, Suite 204
Montreal, QC H2S 2S5
books@pathfinderbooks.ca

UNITED KINGDOM

(and Europe, Africa, Middle East, and South Asia)

Pathfinder Books, 5 Norman Rd.
Seven Sisters, London N15 4ND
orders@pathfinderbooks.co.uk

AUSTRALIA

(and New Zealand, Southeast Asia, and the Pacific)

Pathfinder Books, Suite 2, First floor, 275 George St.
Liverpool, Sydney, NSW 2170
Postal address: P.O. Box 73, Campsie, NSW 2194
pathfinderaustralia@outlook.com

BUILD YOUR LIBRARY!
JOIN THE PATHFINDER READERS CLUB

$10 / YEAR
25% DISCOUNT ON ALL PATHFINDER TITLES
30% OFF BOOKS OF THE MONTH

Valid at pathfinderpress.com and local Pathfinder book centers
Go to: **pathfinderpress.com/products/pathfinder-readers-club**

Pathfinder
pathfinderpress.com